The
Concise Dictionary
of
TWENTY-SIX
LANGUAGES
IN
SIMULTANEOUS
TRANSLATIONS

The
Concise Dictionary
of
TWENTY-SIX
LANGUAGES

IN
SIMULTANEOUS
TRANSLATIONS

Compiled by
Peter M. Bergman

AVENEL BOOKS
NEW YORK

English
French
Spanish
Italian
Portuguese
Rumanian
German
Dutch
Swedish
Danish
Norwegian
Polish
Czech
Serbo-Croatian
Hungarian
Finnish
Turkish
Indonesian
Swahili
Esperanto

Transliterated to
Roman spelling:

Russian
Greek
Arabic
Hebrew
Yiddish
Japanese

This edition is published by Avenel Books,
distributed by Crown Publishers, Inc.,
by arrangement with Lyle Stuart, Inc.
h g f e d c b
AVENEL 1981 EDITION

Manufactured in the United States of America

Library of Congress Cataloging in Publication Data

Bergman, Peter M.
    The concise dictionary of twenty-six languages in
simultaneous translations.

    Reprint. Originally published: New York : Polyglot
Library, 1968.
    Includes index.
    1. Dictionaries, Polyglot.   2. English language—
Dictionaries—Polyglot.   I: Title.
P361.B4   1981   413   81-3446
ISBN 0-517-34720-2   AACR2

CONTENTS

PUBLISHER'S NOTE

The purpose of this dictionary is to simplify as much as possible and not to burden the reader with rules and exceptions of grammar, syntax, different word meanings and pronunciation. However, a remark about the transliteration is necessary: Generally the continental pronunciation of Roman spelling was used in order to convey the sounds of words belonging to languages with non-Latin Alphabets. Only for Russian the sound of the letter X which is gutteral, like *ch* in the name of the composer Bach, kh was adopted as commonly used. Stress always the accented letter in Russian and the apostrophized syllable in Greek.

The
Concise Dictionary
of

TWENTY-SIX
LANGUAGES

IN
SIMULTANEOUS
TRANSLATIONS

1 able

French	capable
Spanish	capaz
Italian	abile
Portuguese	capaz
Rumanian	capabil
German	fähig
Dutch	bekwaam
Swedish	duktig
Danish	dygtig
Norwegian	dyktig
Polish	zdolny
Czech	schopný
Serbo-Croat.	sposoban
Hungarian	képes
Finnish	kykenevä
Turkish	muktedir
Indonesian	sanggup
Esperanto	kapabla
Russian	spasóbni
Greek	ikanos'
Arabic	qadir
Hebrew	muchshar
Yiddish	fehig
Japanese	dekiru
Swahili	-enye akili

2 abroad

French	à l'étranger
Spanish	en el extranjero
Italian	all'estero
Portuguese	ao estrangeiro
Rumanian	în sträinätäte
German	Ausland
Dutch	buitenland
Swedish	utlandet
Danish	udland
Norwegian	utenlands
Polish	zagranicą
Czech	cizina
Serbo-Croat.	inostranstvo
Hungarian	külföld
Finnish	ulkomailla
Turkish	ecnebi memlekette
Indonesian	luar negeri
Esperanto	ali'lande
Russian	za granítse
Greek	exoterikon'
Arabic	ilcharig
Hebrew	chuts laarets
Yiddish	oisland
Japanese	kaigwai ni
Swahili	ugenini

3 absent

French	absent
Spanish	ausente
Italian	assente
Portuguese	ausente
Rumanian	absent
German	,abwesend
Dutch	afwezig
Swedish	frånvarande
Danish	fraværende
Norwegian	fraværende
Polish	nieobecny
Czech	nepřítomný
Serbo-Croat.	otsutan
Hungarian	távollevő
Finnish	poissaoleva
Turkish	namevcut
Indonesian	tidak hadir
Esperanto	for'esta
Russian	atsútstvuyushchi
Greek	apon'
Arabic	ghaib
Hebrew	nedar
Yiddish	obvesend
Japanese	kessekisuru
Swahili	hako

4 accept

French	accepter
Spanish	aceptar
Italian	accettare
Portuguese	aceitar
Rumanian	accepta
German	annehmen
Dutch	aannemen
Swedish	antaga
Danish	modtage
Norwegian	godta
Polish	przyjmować
Czech	přijmouti
Serbo-Croat.	prihvatiti
Hungarian	elfogad
Finnish	vastaanottaa
Turkish	kabul etmek
Indonesian	terima
Esperanto	akcepti
Russian	prinimát
Greek	de'chome
Arabic	yaqbal
Hebrew	kibel
Yiddish	onnemmen
Japanese	ukeireru
Swahili	pokea

5 accident

French	accident
Spanish	accidente
Italian	accidente
Portuguese	acidente
Rumanian	accident
German	Unfall
Dutch	ongeluk
Swedish	olycks-händelse
Danish	ulykke
Norwegian	ulykke
Polish	wypadek
Czech	úraz
Serbo-Croat.	nezgoda
Hungarian	baleset
Finnish	tapaturma
Turkish	kaza
Indonesian	tjelaka
Esperanto	akcidento
Russian	neschástni slúchai
Greek	disti'chima
Arabic	haditsa
Hebrew	teunah
Yiddish	umglik
Japanese	jiko
Swahili	tukio baya

6 accompany

French	accompagner
Spanish	acompañar
Italian	accompagnare
Portuguese	acompanhar
Rumanian	însoţi
German	begleiten
Dutch	begeleiden
Swedish	beledsaga
Danish	ledsage
Norwegian	ledsage
Polish	towarzyszyć
Czech	doproviditi
Serbo-Croat.	pratiti
Hungarian	kisér
Finnish	saattaa
Turkish	refakat etmek
Indonesian	kawani
Esperanto	akompani
Russian	sapravazhdát
Greek	sinode'vo
Arabic	yas-hab
Hebrew	livah
Yiddish	begleiten
Japanese	doohan suru
Swahili	enda na

7 accordion

French	accordéon
Spanish	acordeón
Italian	fisarmonica
Portuguese	acordeon
Rumanian	armonică
German	Ziehharmonika
Dutch	harmonika
Swedish	dragspel
Danish	trækharmonika
Norwegian	trekkspill
Polish	harmonijka
Czech	harmonika
Serbo-Croat.	harmonika
Hungarian	harmonika
Finnish	hanuri
Turkish	akordeon
Indonesian	harmonika
Esperanto	akordiono
Russian	garmónika
Greek	accordeon'
Arabic	okordion
Hebrew	mapuchon
Yiddish	tsieharmonike
Japanese	akoodeon
Swahili	kinanda cha mkono

8 account

French	compte
Spanish	cuenta
Italian	conto
Portuguese	conta
Rumanian	cont
German	Konto
Dutch	rekening
Swedish	konto
Danish	konto
Norwegian	konto
Polish	konto
Czech	účet
Serbo-Croat.	račun
Hungarian	számla
Finnish	tili
Turkish	hesap
Indonesian	perhitungan
Esperanto	konto
Russian	schyót
Greek	logariasmos'
Arabic	hisab
Hebrew	cheschbon
Yiddish	konto
Japanese	keisan
Swahili	hesabu

9 across

French	à travers
Spanish	a través de
Italian	attraverso
Portuguese	através de
Rumanian	curmezişul
German	quer
Dutch	over
Swedish	över
Danish	tværs
Norwegian	tvers
Polish	poprzez
Czech	přes
Serbo-Croat.	preko
Hungarian	keresztül
Finnish	poikki
Turkish	çaprazvari
Indonesian	lintang
Esperanto	trans
Russian	paperyók
Greek	dia' me'sou
Arabic	abr
Hebrew	lever
Yiddish	ariber
Japanese	yokogitte
Swahili	katikati

10 actor

French	acteur
Spanish	actor
Italian	attore
Portuguese	ator
Rumanian	actor
German	Schauspieler
Dutch	acteur
Swedish	skådespelare
Danish	skuespiller
Norwegian	skuespiller
Polish	aktor
Czech	herec
Serbo-Croat.	glumac
Hungarian	szinész
Finnish	näyttelijä
Turkish	aktör
Indonesian	peran
Esperanto	aktoro
Russian	aktyór
Greek	ithopios'
Arabic	mumatsil
Hebrew	sachakon
Yiddish	komediant
Japanese	haiyuu
Swahili	mcheza

11 address

French	adresse
Spanish	dirección
Italian	indirizzo
Portuguese	enderêço
Rumanian	adresă
German	Adresse
Dutch	adres
Swedish	adress
Danish	adresse
Norwegian	adresse
Polish	adres
Czech	adresa
Serbo-Croat.	adresa
Hungarian	cím
Finnish	osoite
Turkish	adres
Indonesian	alamat
Esperanto	adreso
Russian	ádres
Greek	dief'thinsis
Arabic	ounwan
Hebrew	ktovet
Yiddish	adress
Japanese	juusho
Swahili	anwani

12 advertisement

French	annonce
Spanish	anuncio
Italian	annuncio
Portuguese	anúncio
Rumanian	anunţ
German	Anzeige
Dutch	advertentie
Swedish	annons
Danish	annonce
Norwegian	annonse
Polish	ogłoszenie
Czech	inzerát
Serbo-Croat.	oglas
Hungarian	hirdetés
Finnish	ilmoitus
Turkish	ilân
Indonesian	iklan
Esperanto	anonco
Russian	abyavlyéniye
Greek	diafi'misis
Arabic	ilan
Hebrew	modaah
Yiddish	bekanntmachung
Japanese	kookoku
Swahili	tangazo

13 advice

French	conseil
Spanish	consejo
Italian	consiglio
Portuguese	conselho
Rumanian	sfat
German	Ratschlag
Dutch	raad
Swedish	råd
Danish	råd
Norwegian	råd
Polish	radzić
Czech	rada
Serbo-Croat.	savet
Hungarian	tanács
Finnish	neuvoa
Turkish	nashihat
Indonesian	nasihat
Esperanto	konsilo
Russian	sovyét
Greek	simvouli'
Arabic	nasiha
Hebrew	etsah
Yiddish	etse
Japanese	chuukoku
Swahili	shauri

14 affair

French	affaire
Spanish	asunto
Italian	affare
Portuguese	assunto
Rumanian	afacere
German	Angelegenheit
Dutch	zaak
Swedish	angelägenhet
Danish	anliggende
Norwegian	anliggende
Polish	sprawa
Czech	záležitost
Serbo-Croat.	stvar
Hungarian	ügy
Finnish	asia
Turkish	iş
Indonesian	perkara
Esperanto	afero
Russian	dyélo
Greek	ipo'thesis
Arabic	amr, shan
Hebrew	inyan
Yiddish	inyen
Japanese	jiken
Swahili	jambo

15 after

French	après
Spanish	después
Italian	dopo
Portuguese	depois
Rumanian	după
German	nach
Dutch	na
Swedish	efter
Danish	efter
Norwegian	etter
Polish	potem
Czech	po
Serbo-Croat.	posle
Hungarian	után
Finnish	jälkeen
Turkish	sonra
Indonesian	sesudah
Esperanto	posta
Russian	pósle
Greek	meta'
Arabic	baad
Hebrew	achar
Yiddish	nuch
Japanese	ato ni
Swahili	baada

16 afternoon

French	après-midi
Spanish	tarde
Italian	pomeriggio
Portuguese	tarde
Rumanian	dupăamiază
German	Nachmittag
Dutch	namiddag
Swedish	eftermiddag
Danish	eftermiddag
Norwegian	ettermiddag
Polish	popołudnie
Czech	odpoledne
Serbo-Croat.	popodne
Hungarian	délután
Finnish	iltapäivä
Turkish	öğleden sonra
Indonesian	petang
Esperanto	post'ag'mezo
Russian	papalúdni
Greek	apo'yevma
Arabic	baad al-zuhr
Hebrew	achar hatsaharaim
Yiddish	nochmitog
Japanese	gogo
Swahili	alasiri

17 again

French	encore
Spanish	otra vez
Italian	ancora
Portuguese	outra vez
Rumanian	iar
German	wieder
Dutch	weer
Swedish	igen
Danish	igen
Norwegian	igjen
Polish	znowu
Czech	opět
Serbo-Croat.	opet
Hungarian	újra
Finnish	jälleen
Turkish	tekrar
Indonesian	pula
Esperanto	de'nove
Russian	apyát
Greek	pa'lin
Arabic	a-id
Hebrew	schuv
Yiddish	vidder
Japanese	futatabi
Swahili	tena

18 against

French	contre
Spanish	contra
Italian	contro
Portuguese	contra
Rumanian	contra
German	gegen
Dutch	tegen
Swedish	emot
Danish	imod
Norwegian	mot
Polish	przeciw
Czech	proti
Serbo-Croat.	protiv
Hungarian	ellen
Finnish	vastaan
Turkish	karşı
Indonesian	lawan
Esperanto	kontraŭ
Russian	prótif
Greek	enanti'on
Arabic	did
Hebrew	neged
Yiddish	kegn
Japanese	ni taishite
Swahili	juu ya

19 age

French	âge
Spanish	edad
Italian	età
Portuguese	idade
Rumanian	vîrstă
German	Alter
Dutch	leeftijd
Swedish	ålder
Danish	alder
Norwegian	alder
Polish	wiek
Czech	věk
Serbo-Croat.	doba
Hungarian	kor
Finnish	ikä
Turkish	yaş
Indonesian	umur
Esperanto	aĝo
Russian	vózrast
Greek	iliki'a
Arabic	oumr
Hebrew	gil
Yiddish	alter
Japanese	toshi
Swahili	umri

20 agree

French	consentir
Spanish	acordar
Italian	concordare
Portuguese	concordar
Rumanian	acord
German	zustimmen
Dutch	toestemmen
Swedish	ense
Danish	enig
Norwegian	enig
Polish	zgadzać się
Czech	souhlasiti
Serbo-Croat.	saglasiti se
Hungarian	egyezik
Finnish	suostua
Turkish	muvafakat etmek
Indonesian	sepakat
Esperanto	konsenti
Russian	saglashátsa
Greek	simfono'
Arabic	youwafiq
Hebrew	hiskim
Yiddish	maskimsein
Japanese	dooi suru
Swahili	kubali

21 aim

French	but
Spanish	objeto
Italian	scopo
Portuguese	alvo
Rumanian	scop
German	Ziel
Dutch	doel
Swedish	mål
Danish	mål
Norwegian	mål
Polish	cel
Czech	cíl
Serbo-Croat.	cilj
Hungarian	cél
Finnish	maali
Turkish	hedef
Indonesian	maksud
Esperanto	celo
Russian	tsel
Greek	skopos'
Arabic	hadaf
Hebrew	matarah
Yiddish	schtreben
Japanese	mokuteki
Swahili	kusudi

22 air

French	air
Spanish	aire
Italian	aria
Portuguese	ar
Rumanian	aer
German	Luft
Dutch	lucht
Swedish	luft
Danish	luft
Norwegian	luft
Polish	powietrze
Czech	vzduch
Serbo-Croat.	vazduh
Hungarian	levegő
Finnish	ilma
Turkish	hava
Indonesian	uolara
Esperanto	aero
Russian	vózdukh
Greek	ae'ras
Arabic	hawaa
Hebrew	avir
Yiddish	luft
Japanese	kuuki
Swahili	hewa

23 airplane

French	avion
Spanish	aeroplano
Italian	aeroplano
Portuguese	avião
Rumanian	aeroplan
German	Flugzeug
Dutch	vliegtuig
Swedish	flygplan
Danish	flyvemaskine
Norwegian	fly
Polish	samolot
Czech	letadlo
Serbo-Croat.	aeroplan
Hungarian	repülőgép
Finnish	lentokone
Turkish	tayyare
Indonesian	pesawat terbang
Esperanto	aeroplano
Russian	samalyót
Greek	a-eropla'non
Arabic	taira
Hebrew	aviron
Yiddish	avion
Japanese	hikooki
Swahili	ndege

24 airport

French	aéroport
Spanish	aeropuerto
Italian	aeroporto
Portuguese	aeroporto
Rumanian	aeroport
German	Flugplatz
Dutch	vliegveld
Swedish	flykhamn
Danish	lufthavn
Norwegian	lufthavn
Polish	lotnisko
Czech	letiště
Serbo-Croat.	aerodrom
Hungarian	repülőtér
Finnish	lentokenttä
Turkish	tayyare maydanı
Indonesian	lapangan terbang
Esperanto	aerohaveno
Russian	aerodróm
Greek	a-erodro'mion
Arabic	mataar
Hebrew	nemal teufah
Yiddish	flugplats
Japanese	hikoojoo
Swahili	kiwanja cha eropleni

25 all

French	tout
Spanish	todo
Italian	tutto
Portuguese	tudo
Rumanian	tot
German	alles
Dutch	geheel
Swedish	allt
Danish	all
Norwegian	all
Polish	wszystko
Czech	všechno
Serbo-Croat.	sve
Hungarian	minden
Finnish	kaikki
Turkish	bütün
Indonesian	semua
Esperanto	ĉio
Russian	fsyó
Greek	o'los
Arabic	koul
Hebrew	kol
Yiddish	alts
Japanese	zenbu
Swahili	-ote

26 alone

French	seul
Spanish	solo
Italian	solo
Portuguese	só
Rumanian	singur
German	allein
Dutch	alleen
Swedish	ensam
Danish	alene
Norwegian	alene
Polish	sam
Czech	sám
Serbo-Croat.	sam
Hungarian	egyedül
Finnish	yksin
Turkish	yalnız
Indonesian	sendiri
Esperanto	sola
Russian	adín
Greek	mo'nos
Arabic	bimoufradih
Hebrew	levad
Yiddish	alein
Japanese	hitoride
Swahili	pekee

27 also

French	aussi
Spanish	también
Italian	anche
Portuguese	também
Rumanian	deasemenea
German	auch
Dutch	ook
Swedish	också
Danish	også
Norwegian	også
Polish	także
Czech	také
Serbo-Croat.	takode
Hungarian	is
Finnish	myös
Turkish	da
Indonesian	oljuga
Esperanto	ankaǔ
Russian	tózhe
Greek	epi'sis
Arabic	aydan
Hebrew	gam
Yiddish	oich
Japanese	mata
Swahili	vilevile

28 altitude

French	altitude
Spanish	altitud
Italian	altitudine
Portuguese	altitude
Rumanian	înălțime
German	Höhe
Dutch	hoogte
Swedish	höjd
Danish	højde
Norwegian	høyde
Polish	wysokość
Czech	výška
Serbo-Croat.	visina
Hungarian	magasság
Finnish	korkeus
Turkish	irtifa
Indonesian	tingginja
Esperanto	alto
Russian	visatá
Greek	i'psos
Arabic	irtifaa
Hebrew	gova
Yiddish	heich
Japanese	koodo
Swahili	urefu

29 aluminum

French	aluminium
Spanish	aluminio
Italian	alluminio
Portuguese	alumínio
Rumanian	aluminiu
German	Aluminium
Dutch	aluminium
Swedish	aluminium
Danish	aluminium
Norwegian	aluminium
Polish	aluminjum
Czech	aluminium
Serbo-Croat.	aluminij
Hungarian	aluminium
Finnish	alumiini
Turkish	alüminyom
Indonesian	aluminium
Esperanto	aluminio
Russian	alyumíni
Greek	aloumi'nion
Arabic	alaminyoum
Hebrew	chamron
Yiddish	alominyum
Japanese	aruminyuumu
Swahili	madini nyepesi

30 ambassador

French	ambassadeur
Spanish	embajador
Italian	ambasciatore
Portuguese	embaixador
Rumanian	ambasador
German	Gesandter
Dutch	ambassadeur
Swedish	sändebud
Danish	gesandt
Norwegian	ambassador
Polish	ambasador
Czech	vyslanec
Serbo-Croat.	ambasador
Hungarian	nagykövet
Finnish	suurlähettiläs
Turkish	sefir
Indonesian	duta besar
Esperanto	ambasadoro
Russian	pasól
Greek	presveftis'
Arabic	safeer
Hebrew	schagrir
Yiddish	gesanter
Japanese	taishi
Swahili	mjumbe

31 amount

French	somme
Spanish	suma
Italian	somma
Portuguese	soma
Rumanian	cantitate
German	Betrag
Dutch	bedrag
Swedish	belopp
Danish	beløb
Norwegian	beløp
Polish	suma
Czech	částka
Serbo-Croat.	iznos
Hungarian	összeg
Finnish	määrä
Turkish	meblâğ
Indonesian	djumlah
Esperanto	kvanto
Russian	súmma
Greek	poson'
Arabic	mablagh
Hebrew	s'chum
Yiddish	ssach hakkel
Japanese	gookei
Swahili	jumla

32 and

French	et
Spanish	y
Italian	e
Portuguese	e
Rumanian	şi
German	und
Dutch	en
Swedish	och
Danish	og
Norwegian	og
Polish	i
Czech	a
Serbo-Croat.	i
Hungarian	és
Finnish	ja
Turkish	ve
Indonesian	dan
Esperanto	kaj
Russian	i
Greek	ke'
Arabic	wa
Hebrew	ve
Yiddish	un
Japanese	to
Swahili	na

33 angry

French	fâché
Spanish	enojado
Italian	adirato
Portuguese	irado
Rumanian	supărat
German	böse
Dutch	kwaad
Swedish	vred
Danish	vred
Norwegian	sint
Polish	rozgniewany
Czech	rozzlobený
Serbo-Croat.	srdit
Hungarian	haragos
Finnish	vihainen
Turkish	öfkeli
Indonesian	marah
Esperanto	furioza
Russian	zlóy
Greek	thimome'nos
Arabic	ghadib
Hebrew	koes
Yiddish	beis
Japanese	okotta
Swahili	-enye hasira

34 animal

French	animal
Spanish	animal
Italian	animale
Portuguese	animal
Rumanian	animal
German	Tier
Dutch	dier
Swedish	djur
Danish	dyr
Norwegian	dyr
Polish	zwierzę
Czech	zvíře
Serbo-Croat.	životinja
Hungarian	állat
Finnish	eläin
Turkish	hayvan
Indonesian	binatang
Esperanto	animalo
Russian	zhivótnaye
Greek	zo'on
Arabic	hayawan
Hebrew	chayah
Yiddish	chaye
Japanese	doobutsu
Swahili	mnyama

35 ankle

French	cheville
Spanish	tobillo
Italian	caviglia
Portuguese	tornozelo
Rumanian	glezna
German	Fussknöchel
Dutch	enkel
Swedish	fotknöl
Danish	ankel
Norwegian	ankel
Polish	kostka
Czech	kotnik
Serbo-Croat.	članak
Hungarian	boka
Finnish	nilkka
Turkish	topuk
Indonesian	mata kaki
Esperanto	maleolo
Russian	ladíshka
Greek	astra'galos
Arabic	choulchal al-rigl
Hebrew	karsol
Yiddish	fusknechel
Japanese	kurubushi
Swahili	kifundo cha mguu

36 another

French	autre
Spanish	otro
Italian	altro
Portuguese	outro
Rumanian	alta
German	andere
Dutch	nog een
Swedish	en annan
Danish	en anden
Norwegian	en annen
Polish	inny
Czech	druhý
Serbo-Croat.	drugi
Hungarian	másik
Finnish	toinen
Turkish	öbür
Indonesian	satu lagi
Esperanto	alia
Russian	drugóy
Greek	a'llos
Arabic	aachar
Hebrew	acheir
Yiddish	ananderer
Japanese	betsu no
Swahili	-ingine

37 answer

French	répondre
Spanish	contestar
Italian	rispondere
Portuguese	responder
Rumanian	răspunde
German	antworten
Dutch	antwoorden
Swedish	svara
Danish	svare
Norwegian	svare
Polish	odpowiadać
Czech	odpověderi
Serbo-Croat.	odgovoriti
Hungarian	felel, válaszol
Finnish	vastata
Turkish	cevap
Indonesian	djawaban
Esperanto	respondi
Russian	atvechát
Greek	apanto'
Arabic	gawab
Hebrew	laanot
Yiddish	enferen
Japanese	kotaeru
Swahili	jibu

38 ant

French	fourmi
Spanish	hormiga
Italian	formiga
Portuguese	formiga
Rumanian	furnică
German	Ameise
Dutch	mier
Swedish	myra
Danish	myre
Norwegian	maur
Polish	mrówka
Czech	mravenec
Serbo-Croat.	mrav
Hungarian	hangya
Finnish	muurahainen
Turkish	karınca
Indonesian	semut
Esperanto	formiko
Russian	muravyé
Greek	mirmin'gi
Arabic	namla
Hebrew	nemala
Yiddish	muraschke
Japanese	ari
Swahili	sisimizi

39 apartment

French	appartement
Spanish	piso
Italian	appartamento
Portuguese	apartamento
Rumanian	locuinţa
German	Wohnung
Dutch	flat
Swedish	våning
Danish	bolig
Norwegian	leilighet
Polish	mieszkanie
Czech	byt
Serbo-Croat.	stan
Hungarian	lakás
Finnish	huoneisto
Turkish	apartıman dairesi
Indonesian	bilik
Esperanto	ĉambro
Russian	kvartíra
Greek	diame'risma
Arabic	shaqa
Hebrew	dirah
Yiddish	mjeschkane
Japanese	apaato
Swahili	chumba

40 appetite

French	appétit
Spanish	apetito
Italian	appetito
Portuguese	apetite
Rumanian	poftă
German	Appetit
Dutch	eetlust
Swedish	aptit
Danish	appetit
Norwegian	matlyst
Polish	apetyt
Czech	chut'
Serbo-Croat.	apetit
Hungarian	étvágy
Finnish	ruokahalu
Turkish	ıştah
Indonesian	seléra
Esperanto	apetito
Russian	apetít
Greek	o'rexis
Arabic	shahiya
Hebrew	teavon
Yiddish	apetit
Japanese	shokuyoku
Swahili	njaa

41 apple

French	pomme
Spanish	manzana
Italian	mela
Portuguese	maçã
Rumanian	măr
German	Apfel
Dutch	appel
Swedish	äpple
Danish	æble
Norwegian	eple
Polish	jabłko
Czech	jablko
Serbo-Croat.	jabuka
Hungarian	alma
Finnish	omena
Turkish	elma
Indonesian	apel
Esperanto	pomo
Russian	yábloko
Greek	mi'lon
Arabic	tufaha
Hebrew	tapuach
Yiddish	eppel
Japanese	ringo
Swahili	tofaa

42 appointment

French	rendez-vous
Spanish	cita
Italian	appuntamento
Portuguese	prazo-dado
Rumanian	întîlnire
German	Verabredung
Dutch	afspraak
Swedish	möte
Danish	aftale
Norwegian	avtale
Polish	spotkanie
Czech	ujednáni
Serbo-Croat.	sastanak
Hungarian	találka
Finnish	sopimus
Turkish	randevu
Indonesian	tempat pertemuan
Esperanto	rendevuo
Russian	zvidániye
Greek	randevou'
Arabic	miad
Hebrew	minuie
Yiddish	farupredung
Japanese	yakusoku
Swahili	miadi

43 apricot

French	abricot
Spanish	albaricoque
Italian	albicocca
Portuguese	damasco
Rumanian	caisă
German	Aprikose
Dutch	abrikoos
Swedish	aprikos
Danish	abrikos
Norwegian	aprikos
Polish	morela
Czech	meruňka
Serbo-Croat.	kajsija
Hungarian	sárgabarack
Finnish	aprikoosi
Turkish	kaysı
Indonesian	abrikos
Esperanto	abrikoto
Russian	abrikós
Greek	very'kokkon
Arabic	mishmish
Hebrew	mischmeisch
Yiddish	meriln
Japanese	anzu
Swahili	tunda kama embe dodo

44 April

French	avril
Spanish	abril
Italian	aprile
Portuguese	abril
Rumanian	aprilie
German	April
Dutch	April
Swedish	april
Danish	april
Norwegian	april
Polish	kwiecień
Czech	duben
Serbo-Croat.	travanj
Hungarian	április
Finnish	huhtikuu
Turkish	nisan
Indonesian	April
Esperanto	Aprilo
Russian	apryél
Greek	Apri'lios
Arabic	abril
Hebrew	april
Yiddish	april
Japanese	shigwatsu
Swahili	Aprili

45 architect

French	architecte
Spanish	arquitecto
Italian	architetto
Portuguese	arquiteto
Rumanian	arhitect
German	Architekt
Dutch	architect
Swedish	arkitekt
Danish	arkitekt
Norwegian	arkitekt
Polish	architekt
Czech	architekt
Serbo-Croat.	arhitekt
Hungarian	épitész
Finnish	arkkitehti
Turkish	mimar
Indonesian	arsiték
Esperanto	arkitekto
Russian	arkhitéktor
Greek	architek'ton
Arabic	muhandis mimari
Hebrew	adrichal
Yiddish	arkhitekt
Japanese	kenchiku-gishi
Swahili	mwandishi za majengo

46 arm

French	bras
Spanish	brazo
Italian	braccio
Portuguese	braço
Rumanian	braţ
German	Arm
Dutch	arm
Swedish	arm
Danish	arm
Norwegian	arm
Polish	ramię
Czech	paže
Serbo-Croat.	ruka
Hungarian	kar
Finnish	käsivarsi
Turkish	kol
Indonesian	lengan
Esperanto	brako
Russian	ruká
Greek	vrachi'on
Arabic	tziraa
Hebrew	seroa
Yiddish	orm
Japanese	ude
Swahili	mkono

47 army

French	armée
Spanish	ejército
Italian	esercito
Portuguese	exército
Rumanian	armată
German	Armee
Dutch	leger
Swedish	här
Danish	hær
Norwegian	hær
Polish	armja
Czech	armáda
Serbo-Croat.	armija
Hungarian	hadsereg
Finnish	sotajoukko
Turkish	ordu
Indonesian	tentera
Esperanto	armeo
Russian	ármiya
Greek	stratos'
Arabic	gaysh
Hebrew	tsava
Yiddish	soldaten
Japanese	rikugun
Swahili	jeshi la askari

48 arrival

French	arrivée
Spanish	llegada
Italian	arrivo
Portuguese	chegada
Rumanian	sosire
German	Ankunft
Dutch	aankomst
Swedish	ankomst
Danish	ankomst
Norwegian	ankomst
Polish	przyjazd
Czech	příchod
Serbo-Croat.	dolazak
Hungarian	érkezés
Finnish	tulo
Turkish	muvasalat
Indonesian	kedatangan
Esperanto	al'veno
Russian	priyést
Greek	a'fixis
Arabic	wousoul
Hebrew	biah
Yiddish	onkumen
Japanese	toochaku
Swahili	mfiko

49 art

French	art
Spanish	arte
Italian	arte
Portuguese	arte
Rumanian	artă
German	Kunst
Dutch	kunst
Swedish	konst
Danish	kunst
Norwegian	kunst
Polish	sztuka
Czech	uměni
Serbo-Croat.	umetnost
Hungarian	művészet
Finnish	taide
Turkish	sanat
Indonesian	kesenian
Esperanto	arto
Russian	iskústvo
Greek	te'chni
Arabic	fann
Hebrew	amanut
Yiddish	kunst
Japanese	geijutsu
Swahili	sanaa

50 artificial

French	artificiel
Spanish	artificial
Italian	artificiale
Portuguese	artificial
Rumanian	artificial
German	künstlich
Dutch	kunstmatig
Swedish	konstgjord
Danish	kunstig
Norwegian	kunstig
Polish	sztuczny
Czech	umělý
Serbo-Croat.	veštački
Hungarian	mesterséges
Finnish	keinotekoinen
Turkish	suni
Indonesian	palsu, buatan
Esperanto	arte'far'ita
Russian	iskústvyenni
Greek	technitos'
Arabic	sinai
Hebrew	biltitivie
Yiddish	kinstlich
Japanese	jinkootekina
Swahili	-liofanywa na watu

51 ask

French	demander
Spanish	preguntar
Italian	domandare
Portuguese	perguntar
Rumanian	întreba
German	fragen
Dutch	vragen
Swedish	fråga
Danish	spørge
Norwegian	spørre
Polish	pytać
Czech	ptáti
Serbo-Croat.	pitati
Hungarian	kérdez
Finnish	kysyä
Turkish	sual etmek
Indonesian	minta, bertanja
Esperanto	demandi
Russian	spráshivat
Greek	eroto'
Arabic	yasal
Hebrew	schaal
Yiddish	fregen
Japanese	tazuneru
Swahili	uliza

52 asparagus

French	asperges
Spanish	espárrago
Italian	asparago
Portuguese	espargo
Rumanian	sparanghel
German	Spargel
Dutch	asperge
Swedish	sparris
Danish	asparges
Norwegian	asparges
Polish	szparag
Czech	chřest
Serbo-Croat.	špargla
Hungarian	spárga
Finnish	parsa
Turkish	kuşkonmaz
Indonesian	aspérsé
Esperanto	asparago
Russian	spárzha
Greek	sparan'gi
Arabic	asperge
Hebrew	heljon
Yiddish	schborgel
Japanese	asuparagasu
Swahili	namna ya mboga

53 attic

French	mansarde
Spanish	desván
Italian	attico
Portuguese	sótão
Rumanian	mansardă
German	Dachstube
Dutch	zolderkamer
Swedish	vindskupa
Danish	kvist
Norwegian	kvist
Polish	mansarda
Czech	podkrovní
Serbo-Croat.	mansarda
Hungarian	padlásszoba
Finnish	ullakko
Turkish	çati arasi
Indonesian	loténg
Esperanto	mansardo
Russian	cherdák
Greek	sofi'ta
Arabic	sandarah
Hebrew	alieah
Yiddish	dachschtiebel
Japanese	yaneurabeya
Swahili	orofa ya juu kabisa

54 August

French	août
Spanish	agosto
Italian	agosto
Portuguese	agosto
Rumanian	august
German	August
Dutch	Augustus
Swedish	augusti
Danish	august
Norwegian	august
Polish	sierpień
Czech	srpen
Serbo-Croat.	kolovoz
Hungarian	augusztus
Finnish	elokuu
Turkish	ağustos
Indonesian	Augustus
Esperanto	Aŭgusto
Russian	ávgust
Greek	Av'goustos
Arabic	aghoustouss
Hebrew	avgust
Yiddish	oigust
Japanese	hachigwatsu
Swahili	Agosti

55 aunt

French	tante
Spanish	tía
Italian	zia
Portuguese	tia
Rumanian	mătuşă
German	Tante
Dutch	tante
Swedish	tant
Danish	tante
Norwegian	tante
Polish	ciotka
Czech	teta
Serbo-Croat.	tetka
Hungarian	nagynéni
Finnish	täti
Turkish	hala, teyze
Indonesian	bibi
Esperanto	onkl'ino
Russian	tyótya
Greek	thi'a
Arabic	chala
Hebrew	dodah
Yiddish	mume
Japanese	oba
Swahili	shangazi

56 author

French	auteur
Spanish	autor
Italian	autore
Portuguese	autor
Rumanian	autor
German	Verfasser
Dutch	auteur
Swedish	författare
Danish	forfatter
Norwegian	forfatter
Polish	autor
Czech	spisovatel
Serbo-Croat.	pisac
Hungarian	szerző
Finnish	kirjailija
Turkish	müellif
Indonesian	pengarang
Esperanto	aŭtoro
Russian	áftor
Greek	singrafefs'
Arabic	moualif
Hebrew	mechabeir
Yiddish	mechaber
Japanese	chosha
Swahili	mbuni vitabu

57 authority

French	autorité
Spanish	autoridad
Italian	autorità
Portuguese	autoridade
Rumanian	autoritate
German	Behörde
Dutch	gezag
Swedish	myndighet
Danish	øvrighed
Norwegian	myndighet
Polish	władza
Czech	moc
Serbo-Croat.	vlast
Hungarian	hatóság
Finnish	viranomaiset
Turkish	otorite
Indonesian	pembesar
Esperanto	aŭtoritato
Russian	nachálstvo
Greek	exousi'a
Arabic	sulta
Hebrew	samchut
Yiddish	beherde
Japanese	ken'i
Swahili	amri

58 automatic

French	automatique
Spanish	automático
Italian	automatico
Portuguese	automático
Rumanian	automat
German	automatisch
Dutch	automatisch
Swedish	automatisk
Danish	automatisk
Norwegian	automatisk
Polish	automatyczny
Czech	automatický
Serbo-Croat.	automatski
Hungarian	önműködő
Finnish	itsetoimiva
Turkish	otomatik
Indonesian	otomatis
Esperanto	aŭtomata
Russian	aftamatícheski
Greek	afto'matos
Arabic	automatiki
Hebrew	meniaazmo
Yiddish	avtomatik
Japanese	jidootekina
Swahili	-a kujiendea

59 automobile

French	automobile
Spanish	automóvil
Italian	automobile
Portuguese	automóvel
Rumanian	automobil
German	Automobil
Dutch	automobiel
Swedish	automobil
Danish	automobil
Norwegian	bil 59
Polish	samochód
Czech	automobil
Serbo-Croat.	automobil
Hungarian	gépkocsi
Finnish	auto
Turkish	otomobil
Indonesian	mobil
Esperanto	aŭtomobilo
Russian	aftamabíl
Greek	aftoki'niton
Arabic	sayyara
Hebrew	mechonit
Yiddish	avtomobil
Japanese	jidoosha
Swahili	motakaa

60 autumn

French	automne
Spanish	otoño
Italian	autunno
Portuguese	outono
Rumanian	toamnă
German	Herbst
Dutch	herfst
Swedish	höst
Danish	høst
Norwegian	høst
Polish	jesień
Czech	podzim
Serbo-Croat.	jesen
Hungarian	ősz
Finnish	syksy
Turkish	sonbahar
Indonesian	musim runtuh
Esperanto	aŭtuno
Russian	ósen
Greek	fthino'poron
Arabic	charif
Hebrew	stav
Yiddish	herpst
Japanese	aki
Swahili	wakati wa masika

61 available

French	disponible
Spanish	disponible
Italian	disponibile
Portuguese	disponível
Rumanian	disponibil
German	verfügbar
Dutch	verkrijgbaar
Swedish	tillgäglig
Danish	disponibel
Norwegian	disponibel
Polish	dostępny
Czech	dostupný
Serbo-Croat.	raspoloživ
Hungarian	rendelkezésre álló
Finnish	saatavissa
Turkish	mevcut
Indonesian	sedia
Esperanto	hav'ebla
Russian	zapásni
Greek	diathe'simos
Arabic	mawgoud
Hebrew	nimtsa
Yiddish	gretig
Japanese	yakudatsu
Swahili	patikana

62 baby

French	bébé
Spanish	nene
Italian	bambino
Portuguese	bebé
Rumanian	prunc
German	Säugling
Dutch	baby
Swedish	dibarn
Danish	spædbarn
Norwegian	spebarn
Polish	niemowlę
Czech	nemluvně
Serbo-Croat.	beba
Hungarian	csecsemő
Finnish	vauva
Turkish	bebek
Indonesian	baji
Esperanto	bebo
Russian	rebyónak
Greek	moro'
Arabic	walid
Hebrew	tinok
Yiddish	seigling
Japanese	akanboo
Swahili	kitoto

63 back

French	dos
Spanish	espalda
Italian	schiena
Portuguese	costas
Rumanian	spate
German	Rücken
Dutch	rug
Swedish	rygg
Danish	ryg
Norwegian	rygg
Polish	plecy
Czech	záda
Serbo-Croat.	ledja
Hungarian	hát
Finnish	selkä
Turkish	arka
Indonesian	belakang
Esperanto	dorso
Russian	spiná
Greek	pla'ti
Arabic	zahr
Hebrew	gav
Yiddish	pletse
Japanese	senaka
Swahili	mgongo

64 backward

French	arrière
Spanish	atrás
Italian	indietro
Portuguese	para trás
Rumanian	înapoi
German	rückwärts
Dutch	achterwaarts
Swedish	bakåt
Danish	bagefter
Norwegian	tilbake
Polish	wtył
Czech	opozděný
Serbo-Croat.	natrag
Hungarian	hátrafelé
Finnish	takaperin
Turkish	gerı
Indonesian	mundur
Esperanto	mal'antaŭen
Russian	nazát
Greek	pi'so
Arabic	bilmouachira
Hebrew	achoranit
Yiddish	rikvertig
Japanese	koohooeno
Swahili	-a nyuma

65 bacon

French	lard
Spanish	tocino
Italian	pancetta
Portuguese	toucinho
Rumanian	slănină
German	Speck
Dutch	spek
Swedish	späck
Danish	flæsk
Norwegian	flesk
Polish	slonina
Czech	slanina
Serbo-Croat.	slanina
Hungarian	szalonna
Finnish	silava
Turkish	beykin
Indonesian	daging babi asap
Esperanto	lardo
Russian	békon, sálo
Greek	chirinon' paston'
Arabic	chanzir
Hebrew	kotel chasir
Yiddish	gerechter chaser
Japanese	beekon
Swahili	nyama ya nguruwe

66 bad

French	mauvais
Spanish	malo
Italian	cattivo
Portuguese	máu
Rumanian	rău
German	schlecht
Dutch	slecht
Swedish	dålig
Danish	slet
Norwegian	dårlig
Polish	zły
Czech	spatný
Serbo-Croat.	loš
Hungarian	rossz
Finnish	huono
Turkish	fena
Indonesian	buruk
Esperanto	mal'bona
Russian	plakhóy
Greek	kakos'
Arabic	sayyi
Hebrew	ra
Yiddish	schlecht
Japanese	warui
Swahili	-baya

67 bag

French	sac
Spanish	saco
Italian	sacco
Portuguese	saco
Rumanian	pungă
German	Tüte
Dutch	zak
Swedish	påse
Danish	taske
Norwegian	sekk
Polish	torebka
Czech	kabelka
Serbo-Croat.	torba
Hungarian	zsák
Finnish	käsilaukku
Turkish	kese
Indonesian	tas
Esperanto	sako
Russian	meshók
Greek	sak'kos
Arabic	hafiza
Hebrew	sak
Yiddish	sak
Japanese	fukuro
Swahili	mfuko

68 bake

French	cuire
Spanish	hornear
Italian	cuocere al forno
Portuguese	cozer no forno
Rumanian	coace
German	backen
Dutch	bakken
Swedish	baka
Danish	bage
Norwegian	bake
Polish	piec
Czech	péci
Serbo-Croat.	peći
Hungarian	süt
Finnish	leipoa
Turkish	pişirmek
Indonesian	bakar
Esperanto	baki
Russian	pyéch
Greek	psi'no
Arabic	yachbiz
Hebrew	affah
Yiddish	baken
Japanese	yaku
Swahili	oka

69 baker

French	boulanger
Spanish	panadero
Italian	fornaio
Portuguese	padeiro
Rumanian	brutar
German	Bäcker
Dutch	bakker
Swedish	bagare
Danish	bager
Norwegian	baker
Polish	piekarz
Czech	pekař
Serbo-Croat.	pekar
Hungarian	pék
Finnish	leipuri
Turkish	ekmekçi
Indonesian	tukang roti
Esperanto	bak'isto
Russian	pyékar
Greek	psomas'
Arabic	chabbaz
Hebrew	ofeh
Yiddish	beker
Japanese	pan'ya
Swahili	mwokaji mikate

70 balance

French	équilibre
Spanish	balance
Italian	bilancia
Portuguese	balança
Rumanian	balanţă
German	Gleichgewicht
Dutch	weegschaal
Swedish	jämvikt
Danish	ligevægt
Norwegian	likevekt
Polish	równowaga
Czech	rovnováha
Serbo-Croat.	ravnoteža
Hungarian	egyensúly
Finnish	tasapaino
Turkish	muvazene
Indonesian	imbang
Esperanto	ekvilibro
Russian	ravnovyésiye
Greek	isoropi'a
Arabic	tawazoun
Hebrew	schuvvi mischkal
Yiddish	glechgewicht
Japanese	tsuriai
Swahili	usawa wa uzito

71 balcony

French	balcon
Spanish	balcón
Italian	balcone
Portuguese	balcão
Rumanian	balcon
German	Balkon
Dutch	balkon
Swedish	balkong
Danish	balkon
Norwegian	altan
Polish	balkon
Czech	balkón
Serbo-Croat.	balkon
Hungarian	erkély
Finnish	parveke
Turkish	balkon
Indonesian	beranda
Esperanto	balkono
Russian	balkón
Greek	balko'ni
Arabic	shurfa
Hebrew	yatsia
Yiddish	ganek
Japanese	barukonii
Swahili	roshani

72 ball

French	balle
Spanish	pelota
Italian	palla
Portuguese	bola
Rumanian	minge
German	Ball
Dutch	bal
Swedish	boll
Danish	bold
Norwegian	ball
Polish	piłka
Czech	mič
Serbo-Croat.	lopta
Hungarian	labda
Finnish	pallo
Turkish	top
Indonesian	bóla
Esperanto	pilko
Russian	myách
Greek	ba'lla
Arabic	koura
Hebrew	kadur
Yiddish	bal
Japanese	booru
Swahili	mpira

73 banana

French	banane
Spanish	plátano
Italian	banana
Portuguese	banana
Rumanian	banană
German	Banane
Dutch	banaan
Swedish	banan
Danish	banan
Norwegian	banan
Polish	banan
Czech	banán
Serbo-Croat.	banana
Hungarian	banán
Finnish	banaani
Turkish	muz
Indonesian	pisang
Esperanto	banano
Russian	banán
Greek	bana'na
Arabic	mouz
Hebrew	bananah
Yiddish	banane
Japanese	banana
Swahili	ndizi

75 bank

French	banque
Spanish	banco
Italian	banca
Portuguese	banco
Rumanian	bancă
German	Bank
Dutch	bank
Swedish	bank
Danish	bank
Norwegian	bank
Polish	bank
Czech	banka
Serbo-Croat.	banka
Hungarian	bank
Finnish	pankki
Turkish	banka
Indonesian	bank
Esperanto	banko
Russian	bank
Greek	tra'peza
Arabic	bank
Hebrew	bank
Yiddish	bank
Japanese	ginkoo
Swahili	banki

74 bandage

French	bandage
Spanish	venda
Italian	bendaggio
Portuguese	venda
Rumanian	bandaj
German	Binde
Dutch	verband
Swedish	bandage
Danish	forbinding
Norwegian	bind
Polish	bandaż
Czech	obvaz
Serbo-Croat.	zavoj
Hungarian	kötszer
Finnish	side
Turkish	sargı
Indonesian	balut
Esperanto	bandaĝo
Russian	bandásh
Greek	epi'desmos
Arabic	ribat
Hebrew	eged
Yiddish	ferband
Japanese	hootai
Swahili	utambaa

76 barley

French	orge
Spanish	cebada
Italian	orzo
Portuguese	cevada
Rumanian	orz
German	Gerste
Dutch	gort
Swedish	korn
Danish	byg
Norwegian	bygg
Polish	jęczmień
Czech	ječmen
Serbo-Croat.	ječam
Hungarian	árpa
Finnish	ohra
Turkish	arpa
Indonesian	djelai
Esperanto	hordeo
Russian	yachmyén
Greek	kritha'ri
Arabic	shair
Hebrew	seorah
Yiddish	gerschten
Japanese	oomugi
Swahili	shayiri

77 barn

French	grenier
Spanish	establo
Italian	granario
Portuguese	celeiro
Rumanian	hambar
German	Scheune
Dutch	schuur
Swedish	lada
Danish	lade
Norwegian	låve
Polish	stodoła
Czech	stodola
Serbo-Croat.	štala
Hungarian	csűr
Finnish	lato
Turkish	ambar
Indonesian	bangsal
Esperanto	ten'ejo
Russian	saráy
Greek	apothi'ki yeorgou'
Arabic	gourn
Hebrew	refet
Yiddish	stodole
Japanese	naya
Swahili	ghala ya nafaka

78 barrel

French	tonneau
Spanish	barril
Italian	botte
Portuguese	barril
Rumanian	butoi
German	Fass
Dutch	vat
Swedish	tunna
Danish	tønde
Norwegian	tønne
Polish	beczka
Czech	sud
Serbo-Croat.	bure
Hungarian	hordó
Finnish	tynnyri
Turkish	fiçi
Indonesian	tong
Esperanto	barelo
Russian	bóchka
Greek	vare'li
Arabic	barmil
Hebrew	chavit
Yiddish	fass
Japanese	taru
Swahili	pipa

79 bashful

French	timide
Spanish	tímido
Italian	timido
Portuguese	tímido
Rumanian	ruşinos
German	schüchtern
Dutch	verlegen
Swedish	blyg
Danish	genert
Norwegian	sjenert
Polish	nieśmiały
Czech	ostýchavý
Serbo-Croat.	sramežljiv
Hungarian	szégyenlős
Finnish	ujo
Turkish	utangaç
Indonesian	malu
Esperanto	tim'ema
Russian	róbki, nesmyéli
Greek	dropalos'
Arabic	chagoul
Hebrew	bayeschan
Yiddish	schemedik
Japanese	uchiki no
Swahili	-enye haya

80 basket

French	panier
Spanish	cesto
Italian	paniere
Portuguese	canastra
Rumanian	coş
German	Korb
Dutch	mand
Swedish	korg
Danish	kurv
Norwegian	kurv
Polish	kosz
Czech	koš
Serbo-Croat.	korpa
Hungarian	kosár
Finnish	kori
Turkish	sepet
Indonesian	bakul
Esperanto	korbọ
Russian	karzína
Greek	kala'thi
Arabic	salla
Hebrew	sal
Yiddish	koschik
Japanese	kago
Swahili	kikapu

81 bath

French	bain
Spanish	baño
Italian	bagno
Portuguese	banho
Rumanian	baie
German	Bad
Dutch	bad
Swedish	bad
Danish	bad
Norwegian	bad
Polish	kąpiel
Czech	koupel
Serbo-Croat.	kupanje
Hungarian	fürdő
Finnish	kylpy
Turkish	banyo
Indonesian	mandi
Esperanto	bano
Russian	kupánye
Greek	ba'nio
Arabic	hammam
Hebrew	ambat
Yiddish	bod
Japanese	nyuuyoku
Swahili	maji ya kuoga

82 bathrobe

French	peignoir
Spanish	albornoz
Italian	accappatoio
Portuguese	roupão
Rumanian	halat de baie
German	Bademantel
Dutch	badjas
Swedish	badkappa
Danish	badekåbe
Norwegian	badekåpe
Polish	płaszcz kąpielowy
Czech	koupací plášť
Serbo-Croat.	orgrtač za kupanje
Hungarian	fürdőköpeny
Finnish	kylpyviitta
Turkish	burnuz
Indonesian	pakaian mandi
Esperanto	banrobo
Russian	kupálni khalát
Greek	ro'ba
Arabic	bournous
Hebrew	hilbish ambati
Yiddish	bodmantel
Japanese	keshoogi
Swahili	koti ya kuoga

83 bathtub

French	baignoire
Spanish	bañera
Italian	vasca da bagno
Portuguese	banheira
Rumanian	cadă
German	Badewanne
Dutch	badkuip
Swedish	badkar
Danish	badekar
Norwegian	badekar
Polish	wanna
Czech	vana
Serbo-Croat.	kada
Hungarian	fürdőkád
Finnish	kylpyamme
Turkish	banyo teknesi
Indonesian	tong mandi
Esperanto	banujo
Russian	vánna
Greek	banie'ra
Arabic	houd istihmam
Hebrew	ambat
Yiddish	van
Japanese	furo'oke
Swahili	birika cha kuogea

84 battery

French	batterie
Spanish	pila
Italian	batteria
Portuguese	pilha
Rumanian	baterie
German	Batterie
Dutch	batterij
Swedish	batteri
Danish	batteri
Norwegian	batteri
Polish	baterja
Czech	baterka
Serbo-Croat.	baterija
Hungarian	elem
Finnish	paristo
Turkish	pil
Indonesian	baterai
Esperanto	baterio
Russian	bateryéya
Greek	batari'a
Arabic	battariya
Hebrew	matsber
Yiddish	baterke
Japanese	denchi
Swahili	bateri

85 be

French	être
Spanish	estar
Italian	essere
Portuguese	ser
Rumanian	fi
German	sein
Dutch	zijn
Swedish	vara
Danish	være
Norwegian	være
Polish	być
Czech	býti
Serbo-Croat.	biti
Hungarian	van
Finnish	olla
Turkish	olmak
Indonesian	ada
Esperanto	esti
Russian	bit
Greek	i'me
Arabic	yakoun
Hebrew	haya
Yiddish	sein
Japanese	aru
Swahili	-wa

86 beach

French	plage
Spanish	playa
Italian	spiaggia
Portuguese	praia
Rumanian	plajă
German	Strand
Dutch	strand
Swedish	strand
Danish	strand
Norwegian	strand
Polish	plaża
Czech	pláž
Serbo-Croat.	obala
Hungarian	tengerpart
Finnish	ranta
Turkish	plâj
Indonesian	pantai
Esperanto	plaĝo
Russian	plyash
Greek	akti'
Arabic	shati
Hebrew	chof
Yiddish	schtrand
Japanese	hamabe
Swahili	pwani

87 bean

French	haricot
Spanish	judia
Italian	fagiuolo
Portuguese	feijão
Rumanian	fasole
German	Bohne
Dutch	boon
Swedish	böna
Danish	bønne
Norwegian	bønne
Polish	fasola
Czech	bob
Serbo-Croat.	pasulj
Hungarian	bab
Finnish	papu
Turkish	fasulye
Indonesian	katjang
Esperanto	fabo
Russian	bop
Greek	faso'li
Arabic	fasoulia
Hebrew	pol
Yiddish	fassolije
Japanese	mame
Swahili	haragwe

88 bear

French	ours
Spanish	oso
Italian	orso
Portuguese	urso
Rumanian	urs
German	Bär
Dutch	beer
Swedish	björn
Danish	bjørn
Norwegian	bjørn
Polish	niedźwiedź
Czech	medvěd
Serbo-Croat.	medved
Hungarian	medve
Finnish	karhu
Turkish	ayı
Indonesian	beruang
Esperanto	urso
Russian	medvyéd
Greek	arkou'da
Arabic	doub
Hebrew	dov
Yiddish	ber
Japanese	kuma
Swahili	dubu

89 beard

French	barbe
Spanish	barba
Italian	barba
Portuguese	barba
Rumanian	barbă
German	Bart
Dutch	baard
Swedish	skägg
Danish	skæg
Norwegian	skjegg
Polish	broda
Czech	vousy
Serbo-Croat.	brada
Hungarian	szakáll
Finnish	parta
Turkish	sakal
Indonesian	djanggut
Esperanto	barbo
Russian	baradá
Greek	ye'nion
Arabic	lihya
Hebrew	sakan
Yiddish	bord
Japanese	hige
Swahili	ndevu

90 beautiful

French	beau
Spanish	hermoso
Italian	bello
Portuguese	belo
Rumanian	frumos
German	schön
Dutch	mooi
Swedish	vacker
Danish	skøn
Norwegian	skjønn, vakker
Polish	piękny
Czech	krásný
Serbo-Croat.	lep
Hungarian	szép
Finnish	kaunis
Turkish	güzel
Indonesian	bagus
Esperanto	bela
Russian	krasívi
Greek	ore'os
Arabic	gamil
Hebrew	yafeh
Yiddish	schehn
Japanese	utsukushii
Swahili	-zuri

91 because

French	parce que
Spanish	porqué
Italian	perché
Portuguese	porque
Rumanian	fiindcă
German	weil
Dutch	omdat
Swedish	emedan
Danish	fordi
Norwegian	fordi
Polish	ponieważ
Czech	protože
Serbo-Croat.	jer
Hungarian	mert
Finnish	koska
Turkish	çünkü
Indonesian	sebab
Esperanto	ĉar
Russian	patamú shto
Greek	dio'ti
Arabic	li-an
Hebrew	kie
Yiddish	veil
Japanese	nazenaraba
Swahili	kwa sababu

92 bed

French	lit
Spanish	cama
Italian	letto
Portuguese	cama
Rumanian	pat
German	Bett
Dutch	bed
Swedish	säng
Danish	seng
Norwegian	seng
Polish	łóżko
Czech	postel
Serbo-Croat.	krevet
Hungarian	ágy
Finnish	vuode
Turkish	yatak
Indonesian	tempat tidur
Esperanto	lito
Russian	kravát
Greek	krevva'ti
Arabic	sarir
Hebrew	mitah
Yiddish	bet
Japanese	betto
Swahili	kitanda

93 bedroom

French	chambre à coucher
Spanish	dormitorio
Italian	camera da letto
Portuguese	quarto de dormir
Rumanian	dormitor
German	Schlafzimmer
Dutch	slaapkamer
Swedish	sovrum
Danish	soveværelse
Norwegian	soverom
Polish	sypialnia
Czech	ložnice
Serbo-Croat.	spavaća soba
Hungarian	hálószoba
Finnish	makuuhuone
Turkish	yatakodası
Indonesian	kamar tidur
Esperanto	dorm'ĉambro
Russian	spálnya
Greek	krevvatoka'mara
Arabic	hougrat al-noum
Hebrew	chadar mitod
Yiddish	spalniye
Japanese	shinshitsu
Swahili	chumba cha kulala

94 bee

French	abeille
Spanish	abeja
Italian	ape
Portuguese	abelha
Rumanian	albină
German	Biene
Dutch	bij
Swedish	bi
Danish	bi
Norwegian	bie
Polish	pszczoła
Czech	včela
Serbo-Croat.	pčela
Hungarian	·méh
Finnish	mehiläinen
Turkish	arı
Indonesian	lebah
Esperanto	abelo
Russian	pchelá
Greek	me'lissa
Arabic	nahla
Hebrew	dvorah
Yiddish	bien
Japanese	mitsubachi
Swahili	nyuki

95 beef

French	bœuf
Spanish	carne de vaca
Italian	manzo
Portuguese	carne de vaca
Rumanian	carne de vacă
German	Rindfleisch
Dutch	rundvlees
Swedish	oxkött
Danish	oksekød
Norwegian	oksekjøtt
Polish	wołowina
Czech	hovĕzi maso
Serbo-Croat.	govedjina
Hungarian	marhahús
Finnish	naudanliha
Turkish	siğır eti
Indonesian	daging sapi
Esperanto	bov'viando
Russian	gavyádina
Greek	vodino'
Arabic	lahm baqari
Hebrew	besar bakar
Yiddish	rindfleisch
Japanese	gyuuniku
Swahili	nyama ya ng'ombe

96 beefsteak

French	biftek
Spanish	biftec
Italian	bistecca
Portuguese	bife
Rumanian	biftec
German	Beefsteak
Dutch	runderlapje
Swedish	stek
Danish	bøf
Norwegian	biff
Polish	befsztyk
Czech	řízek
Serbo-Croat.	biftek
Hungarian	marhasült
Finnish	pihvi
Turkish	biftek
Indonesian	bistik
Esperanto	bifsteko
Russian	bifshtyéks
Greek	brizo'la
Arabic	biftek
Hebrew	umtsah
Yiddish	bifstek
Japanese	bifuteki
Swahili	kipande cha nyama ya ng'ombe

97 beer

French	bière
Spanish	cerveza
Italian	birra
Portuguese	cerveja
Rumanian	bere
German	Bier
Dutch	bier
Swedish	öl
Danish	øl
Norwegian	øl
Polish	piwo
Czech	pivo
Serbo-Croat.	pivo
Hungarian	sör
Finnish	olut
Turkish	bira
Indonesian	bir
Esperanto	biero
Russian	pívo
Greek	bi'ra
Arabic	bira
Hebrew	birah
Yiddish	bier
Japanese	biiru
Swahili	pombe

98 beet-root

French	betterave
Spanish	remolacha
Italian	barbabietola
Portuguese	beterraba
Rumanian	sfeclă
German	Rote Rübe
Dutch	biet
Swedish	rödbeta
Danish	rødbede
Norwegian	bete
Polish	burak
Czech	řepa
Serbo-Croat.	repa
Hungarian	cékla
Finnish	punajuuri
Turkish	pancar
Indonesian	ubi
Esperanto	beto
Russian	svyókla
Greek	pantza'ri
Arabic	bangar
Hebrew	lefet
Yiddish	borke
Japanese	tensai
Swahili	mboga

99 begin

French	commencer
Spanish	comenzar
Italian	cominciare
Portuguese	começar
Rumanian	începe
German	beginnen
Dutch	begin
Swedish	börja
Danish	begynde
Norwegian	begynne
Polish	zacząć
Czech	počiti
Serbo-Croat.	početi
Hungarian	kezd
Finnish	alkaa
Turkish	başlamak
Indonesian	mulai
Esperanto	komenci
Russian	nachát
Greek	archi'zo
Arabic	yabda
Hebrew	hitchil
Yiddish	onhoiben
Japanese	hajimeru
Swahili	anza

100 behavior

French	conduite
Spanish	comportamiento
Italian	condotta
Portuguese	comportamento
Rumanian	purtare
German	Benehmen
Dutch	gedrag
Swedish	uppförande
Danish	opførsel
Norwegian	oppførsel
Polish	zachowanie
Czech	chováni
Serbo-Croat.	ponašanje
Hungarian	magaviselet
Finnish	käytös
Turkish	davranış
Indonesian	kelakuan
Esperanto	konduto
Russian	pavedyéniye
Greek	simperifora'
Arabic	tasarouf
Hebrew	nimus
Yiddish	offierung
Japanese	furumai
Swahili	mwenendo

101 behind

French	derrière
Spanish	detrás
Italian	dietro
Portuguese	atrás de
Rumanian	îndărăt
German	hinten
Dutch	achter
Swedish	bakom
Danish	bagved
Norwegian	bak
Polish	ztyłu
Czech	vzadu
Serbo-Croat.	iza
Hungarian	hátra
Finnish	takana
Turkish	arkada
Indonesian	diba akang
Esperanto	poste
Russian	pozadí
Greek	o'pisthen
Arabic	chalf
Hebrew	achor
Yiddish	hinter
Japanese	ushiro ni
Swahili	nyuma

102 belief

French	croyance
Spanish	creencia
Italian	credenza
Portuguese	crença
Rumanian	credință
German	Glaube
Dutch	geloof
Swedish	tro
Danish	tro
Norwegian	tro
Polish	wiara
Czech	víra
Serbo-Croat.	vjera
Hungarian	hit
Finnish	usko
Turkish	iman
Indonesian	iman
Esperanto	kredo
Russian	vyéra
Greek	pis'tis
Arabic	itiqad
Hebrew	emunah
Yiddish	gloiben
Japanese	shin'nen
Swahili	imani

103 bell

French	cloche
Spanish	campana
Italian	campana
Portuguese	sino
Rumanian	clopot
German	Glocke
Dutch	klok
Swedish	klocka
Danish	klokke
Norwegian	klokke
Polish	dzwon
Czech	zvon
Serbo-Croat.	zvono
Hungarian	csengő
Finnish	soittokello
Turkish	zil
Indonesian	lontjéng
Esperanto	sonor'ilo
Russian	zvanók
Greek	koudou'ni
Arabic	naqous
Hebrew	paamon
Yiddish	glok
Japanese	beru
Swahili	kengele

104 belly

French	ventre
Spanish	vientre
Italian	ventre
Portuguese	barriga
Rumanian	pîntec
German	Bauch
Dutch	buik
Swedish	buk
Danish	bug
Norwegian	buk
Polish	brzuch
Czech	břícho
Serbo-Croat.	trbuh
Hungarian	has
Finnish	vatsa
Turkish	karın
Indonesian	perut
Esperanto	ventro
Russian	zhivót
Greek	kilia'
Arabic	batn
Hebrew	beten
Yiddish	boiech
Japanese	hara
Swahili	tumbo

105 below

French	dessous
Spanish	debajo
Italian	sotto
Portuguese	abaixo
Rumanian	dedesubt
German	unten
Dutch	beneden
Swedish	nere
Danish	nede
Norwegian	nede
Polish	poniżej
Czech	dole
Serbo-Croat.	niže
Hungarian	alul
Finnish	alla
Turkish	aşağı
Indonesian	bawah
Esperanto	sub
Russian	vnizú
Greek	ipoka'to
Arabic	asfal
Hebrew	matah
Yiddish	unter
Japanese	shita ni
Swahili	chini

106 belt

French	ceinture
Spanish	cinturón
Italian	cintura
Portuguese	cinto
Rumanian	curea
German	Gürtel
Dutch	riem
Swedish	bälte
Danish	bælte
Norwegian	belte
Polish	pas
Czech	opasek
Serbo-Croat.	pojas
Hungarian	öv
Finnish	vyö
Turkish	kemer
Indonesian	ikat pinggang
Esperanto	zono
Russian	póyas
Greek	zo'ni
Arabic	hizam
Hebrew	chagorah
Yiddish	passik
Japanese	beruto
Swahili	mshipi

107 benefit

French	bénéfice
Spanish	ventaja
Italian	beneficio
Portuguese	vantagem
Rumanian	beneficiu
German	Nutzen
Dutch	voordeel
Swedish	fördel
Danish	nytte
Norwegian	gagn
Polish	korzyść
Czech	užitek
Serbo-Croat.	korist
Hungarian	haszon
Finnish	hyöty
Turkish	fayda, menfaat
Indonesian	guna
Esperanto	profito
Russian	pólza
Greek	ofe'lia
Arabic	faida
Hebrew	gmul
Yiddish	nutsen
Japanese	rieki
Swahili	faida

108 bet

French	parier
Spanish	apostar
Italian	scommettere
Portuguese	apostar
Rumanian	prinsoare
German	wetten
Dutch	wedden
Swedish	slå vad om
Danish	vædde
Norwegian	vedde
Polish	zakładać
Czech	sázet
Serbo-Croat.	kladiti
Hungarian	fogad
Finnish	lyödä vetoa
Turkish	bahis
Indonesian	bertaruh
Esperanto	veti
Russian	derzhát parí
Greek	stichimati'zo
Arabic	rihan
Hebrew	hitarev
Yiddish	vetten
Japanese	kakeru
Swahili	weka sharti

109 betray

French	trahir
Spanish	traicionar
Italian	tradire
Portuguese	trair
Rumanian	trăda
German	verraten
Dutch	verraden
Swedish	förråda
Danish	forråde
Norwegian	forråde
Polish	zdradzić
Czech	zraditi
Serbo-Croat.	izdati
Hungarian	elárul
Finnish	kavaltaa
Turkish	hıyanet etmek
Indonesian	chianat
Esperanto	perfidi
Russian	predavát
Greek	prodi'do
Arabic	yachoun
Hebrew	bagad
Yiddish	massern
Japanese	uragiru
Swahili	haini

110 between

French	entre
Spanish	entre
Italian	fra
Portuguese	entre
Rumanian	între
German	zwischen
Dutch	tussen
Swedish	mellan
Danish	mellem
Norwegian	imellom
Polish	między
Czech	mezi
Serbo-Croat.	izmedju
Hungarian	között
Finnish	välillä
Turkish	arasında
Indonesian	antara
Esperanto	inter
Russian	myézhdu
Greek	metaxi'
Arabic	bayn
Hebrew	baemtsa
Yiddish	tsvischen
Japanese	no aida ni
Swahili	kati (ya)

111 bicycle

French	bicyclette
Spanish	bicicleta
Italian	bicicletta
Portuguese	bicicleta
Rumanian	bicicletă
German	Fahrrad
Dutch	fiets
Swedish	cykel
Danish	cykel
Norwegian	sykkel
Polish	rower
Czech	kolo
Serbo-Croat.	bicikl
Hungarian	kerékpár
Finnish	polkupyörä
Turkish	bisiklet
Indonesian	sepéda
Esperanto	biciklo
Russian	velasipyéd
Greek	podi'laton
Arabic	darraga
Hebrew	ofanaim
Yiddish	fohrredel
Japanese	jitensha
Swahili	baisikeli

112 bill

French	facture
Spanish	cuenta
Italian	fattura
Portuguese	conta
Rumanian	factură
German	Rechnung
Dutch	rekening
Swedish	räkning
Danish	regning
Norwegian	regning
Polish	rachunek
Czech	účet
Serbo-Croat.	račun
Hungarian	számla
Finnish	lasku
Turkish	fatura
Indonesian	rekening
Esperanto	bilo
Russian	schyot
Greek	logariasmos'
Arabic	faturah
Hebrew	cheschbon
Yiddish	rechnug
Japanese	kanjoogaki
Swahili	hesabu

113 billiard

French	billard
Spanish	billar
Italian	bigliardo
Portuguese	bilhar
Rumanian	biliard
German	Billard
Dutch	biljart
Swedish	biljard
Danish	billard
Norwegian	biljard
Polish	bilard
Czech	kulečnik
Serbo-Croat.	bilijar
Hungarian	biliárd
Finnish	biljardipeli
Turkish	bilârdo
Indonesian	permainam bola diatas
Esperanto	bilardo
Russian	bilyárd
Greek	billiar'do
Arabic	biliardo
Hebrew	biljard
Yiddish	biljard
Japanese	tamatsuki
Swahili	namna ya mcheza

114 bird

French	oiseau
Spanish	ave
Italian	uccello
Portuguese	pássaro
Rumanian	pasăre
German	Vogel
Dutch	vogel
Swedish	fågel
Danish	fugl
Norwegian	fugl
Polish	ptak
Czech	pták
Serbo-Croat.	ptica
Hungarian	madár
Finnish	lintu
Turkish	kuş
Indonesian	burung
Esperanto	birdo
Russian	ptítsa
Greek	pouli'
Arabic	asfour
Hebrew	tsipor
Yiddish	foigel
Japanese	tori
Swahili	ndege

115 birth

French	naissance
Spanish	nacimiento
Italian	nascita
Portuguese	nascimento
Rumanian	naştere
German	Geburt
Dutch	geboorte
Swedish	födelse
Danish	fødsel
Norwegian	fødsel
Polish	urodzenie
Czech	narození
Serbo-Croat.	rodjenje
Hungarian	születés
Finnish	synty
Turkish	doğum
Indonesian	kelahiran
Esperanto	nask'iĝo
Russian	razhdyéniye
Greek	ye'nisis
Arabic	milad
Hebrew	ledah
Yiddish	geburt
Japanese	tanjoo
Swahili	uzazi

116 birthday

French	anniversaire
Spanish	cumpleaños
Italian	compleanno
Portuguese	dia de anos
Rumanian	zi de naştere
German	Geburtstag
Dutch	verjaardag
Swedish	födelsedag
Danish	fødselsdag
Norwegian	fødselsdag
Polish	urodziny
Czech	narozeniny
Serbo-Croat.	rodjendan
Hungarian	születésnap
Finnish	syntymäpäivä
Turkish	doğum günü
Indonesian	hari lahir
Esperanto	nask'tago
Russian	dyen razhdyéniya
Greek	yene'thlia
Arabic	id milad
Hebrew	jomhuledet
Yiddish	geburtstog
Japanese	tanjoobi
Swahili	maulidi

117 bitter

French	amer
Spanish	amargo
Italian	amaro
Portuguese	amargo
Rumanian	amar
German	bitter
Dutch	bitter
Swedish	bitter
Danish	bitter
Norwegian	bitter
Polish	gorzki
Czech	hořký
Serbo-Croat.	gorak
Hungarian	keserű
Finnish	katkera
Turkish	acı
Indonesian	pahit
Esperanto	amara
Russian	górki
Greek	pikros'
Arabic	mour
Hebrew	mar
Yiddish	biter
Japanese	nigai
Swahili	-chungu

118 black

French	noir
Spanish	negro
Italian	nero
Portuguese	prêto
Rumanian	negru
German	schwarz
Dutch	zwart
Swedish	svart
Danish	sort
Norwegian	svart
Polish	czarny
Czech	černý
Serbo-Croat.	crn
Hungarian	fekete
Finnish	musta
Turkish	kara
Indonesian	hitam
Esperanto	nigro
Russian	chórni
Greek	ma'vros
Arabic	aswad
Hebrew	schachor
Yiddish	schvarts
Japanese	kuroi
Swahili	-eusi

119 bladder

French	vessie
Spanish	vejiga
Italian	vescica
Portuguese	bexiga
Rumanian	băşică
German	Blase
Dutch	blaas
Swedish	blåsa
Danish	blære
Norwegian	blære
Polish	pęcherz
Czech	měchýř
Serbo-Croat.	mehur
Hungarian	hólyag
Finnish	rakko
Turkish	mesane
Indonesian	gelembung
Esperanto	veziko
Russian	puzír
Greek	ky'stis
Arabic	matsana
Hebrew	schalpuchit
Yiddish	pencher
Japanese	bookoo
Swahili	kibofu

120 blame

French	blâmer
Spanish	culpar
Italian	biasimare
Portuguese	culpar
Rumanian	învinui
German	tadeln
Dutch	berispen
Swedish	klandra
Danish	dadle
Norwegian	dadle
Polish	ganić
Czech	hanět
Serbo-Croat.	kriviti
Hungarian	hibáztat
Finnish	moittia
Turkish	tekdir
Indonesian	tjela
Esperanto	mallaŭdi
Russian	paritsát
Greek	katigoro'
Arabic	yaloum
Hebrew	aschmah
Yiddish	todel
Japanese	hinan suru
Swahili	karipia

121 blanket

French	couverture
Spanish	manta
Italian	coperta
Portuguese	cobertor
Rumanian	cuvertură de lînă
German	Decke
Dutch	deken
Swedish	filt
Danish	uldtæppe
Norwegian	ullteppe
Polish	koc
Czech	pokrývka
Serbo-Croat.	prekrivač
Hungarian	takaró
Finnish	peite
Turkish	battaniye
Indonesian	selimut
Esperanto	lankovr'ilo
Russian	adeálo
Greek	kouver'ta
Arabic	battaniya
Hebrew	maateh
Yiddish	koldre
Japanese	moofu
Swahili	blanketi

122 bleach

French	blanchir
Spanish	blanquear
Italian	imbiancare
Portuguese	branquear
Rumanian	înălbi
German	bleichen
Dutch	bleken
Swedish	bleka
Danish	blege
Norwegian	bleike
Polish	bielić
Czech	bíliti
Serbo-Croat.	pobjeliti
Hungarian	fehérít
Finnish	valkaista
Turkish	beyazlatmak
Indonesian	kelantang
Esperanto	blank'igi
Russian	belít
Greek	lefke'no
Arabic	yubayyid
Hebrew	liben
Yiddish	veissen
Japanese	sarasu
Swahili	fanya rangi -eupe

123 blind

French	aveugle
Spanish	ciego
Italian	cieco
Portuguese	cego
Rumanian	orb
German	blind
Dutch	blind
Swedish	blind
Danish	blind
Norwegian	blind
Polish	ślepy
Czech	slepý
Serbo-Croat.	slep
Hungarian	vak
Finnish	sokea
Turkish	kör
Indonesian	buta
Esperanto	blinda
Russian	slepóy
Greek	tiflos'
Arabic	aama
Hebrew	iver
Yiddish	blind
Japanese	moomoku no
Swahili	-pofu

124 blonde

French	blond
Spanish	rubio
Italian	biondo
Portuguese	louro
Rumanian	blondă
German	blond
Dutch	blond
Swedish	blond
Danish	blond
Norwegian	blond
Polish	blond
Czech	plavý
Serbo-Croat.	plav
Hungarian	szőke
Finnish	vaaleaverinen
Turkish	sarışın
Indonesian	putih kuning
Esperanto	blonda
Russian	byelokúri
Greek	xanthos'
Arabic	ashqar
Hebrew	tsahov
Yiddish	blond
Japanese	kinpatsu
Swahili	rangi ya shaba

125 blood

French	sang
Spanish	sangre
Italian	sangue
Portuguese	sangue
Rumanian	sînge
German	Blut
Dutch	bloed
Swedish	blod
Danish	blod
Norwegian	blod
Polish	krew
Czech	krev
Serbo-Croat.	krv
Hungarian	vér
Finnish	veri
Turkish	kan
Indonesian	darah
Esperanto	sango
Russian	krof
Greek	e'ma
Arabic	dam
Hebrew	dam
Yiddish	blut
Japanese	chi
Swahili	damu

126 blouse

French	blouse
Spanish	blusa
Italian	blusa
Portuguese	blusa
Rumanian	bluză
German	Bluse
Dutch	blouse
Swedish	blus
Danish	bluse
Norwegian	bluse
Polish	bluza
Czech	blůza
Serbo-Croat.	bluza
Hungarian	blúz
Finnish	pusero
Turkish	bluz
Indonesian	blus
Esperanto	korsaĵ'eto
Russian	blúza
Greek	blou'za
Arabic	blouza
Hebrew	chalikah
Yiddish	bluse
Japanese	burausu
Swahili	vazi la kike

127 blue

French	bleu
Spanish	azul
Italian	azzuro
Portuguese	azul
Rumanian	albastru
German	blau
Dutch	blauw
Swedish	blå
Danish	blå
Norwegian	blå
Polish	błękitny
Czech	modrý
Serbo-Croat.	plav
Hungarian	kék
Finnish	sininen
Turkish	mavi
Indonesian	biru
Esperanto	bluo
Russian	síni
Greek	ble'
Arabic	azraq
Hebrew	kachol
Yiddish	bluh
Japanese	aoi
Swahili	rangi ya samawati

128 blueberry

French	myrtille
Spanish	mora
Italian	mirtillo
Portuguese	airela
Rumanian	afină
German	Blaubeere
Dutch	bosbes
Swedish	blåbär
Danish	blåbær
Norwegian	blåbær
Polish	borówka
Czech	borůvka
Serbo-Croat.	vrsta jagoda
Hungarian	áfonya
Finnish	mustikka
Turkish	yaban mersine
Indonesian	biru buah ketjil
Esperanto	mirtelo
Russian	cherníka
Greek	vato'mouron
Arabic	oullaiq
Hebrew	uchmaniah
Yiddish	borovkes
Japanese	kokemomo
Swahili	namna ya tunda

129 boat

French	bateau
Spanish	barco
Italian	battello
Portuguese	barco
Rumanian	barcă
German	Boot
Dutch	boot
Swedish	båt
Danish	båd
Norwegian	båt
Polish	łodż
Czech	lod'ka
Serbo-Croat.	čamac
Hungarian	csónak
Finnish	vene
Turkish	kayık
Indonesian	kapal
Esperanto	boato
Russian	lótka
Greek	kara'vi
Arabic	bachira
Hebrew	sirah
Yiddish	lodke
Japanese	booto
Swahili	mashua

130 body

French	corps
Spanish	cuerpo
Italian	corpo
Portuguese	corpo
Rumanian	corp
German	Körper
Dutch	lichaam
Swedish	kropp
Danish	legeme
Norwegian	legeme
Polish	ciało
Czech	tělo
Serbo-Croat.	telo
Hungarian	test
Finnish	ruumis
Turkish	vücut
Indonesian	badan
Esperanto	korpo
Russian	tyélo
Greek	so'ma
Arabic	gism
Hebrew	guf
Yiddish	kerper
Japanese	karada
Swahili	mwili

131 boil

French	bouillir
Spanish	cocer
Italian	bollire
Portuguese	ferver
Rumanian	fierbe
German	kochen
Dutch	koken
Swedish	koka
Danish	koge
Norwegian	koke
Polish	gotować
Czech	vařiti
Serbo-Croat.	kuvati
Hungarian	főz
Finnish	keittää
Turkish	kaynatmak
Indonesian	merebus
Esperanto	boli
Russian	kipyét
Greek	vra'zo
Arabic	yaghli
Hebrew	ratach
Yiddish	kochen
Japanese	wakasu
Swahili	chemsha

132 boiler

French	chaudière
Spanish	caldera
Italian	caldaia
Portuguese	caldeira
Rumanian	căldare
German	Kessel
Dutch	stoomketel
Swedish	ångpanna
Danish	kedel
Norwegian	kjele
Polish	kocioł
Czech	kotel
Serbo-Croat.	kotao
Hungarian	üst
Finnish	höyrykattila
Turkish	kazan
Indonesian	kétél kukus
Esperanto	kaldrono
Russian	katyól
Greek	vrasti'ras
Arabic	ghallayah
Hebrew	dud
Yiddish	kocher
Japanese	boiraa
Swahili	sufuria

133 bomb

French	bombe
Spanish	bomba
Italian	bomba
Portuguese	bomba
Rumanian	bombă
German	Bombe
Dutch	bom
Swedish	bomb
Danish	bombe
Norwegian	bombe
Polish	bomba
Czech	bomba
Serbo-Croat.	bomba
Hungarian	bomba
Finnish	pommi
Turkish	bomba
Indonesian	bomb
Esperanto	bombo
Russian	bómba
Greek	vom'va
Arabic	qounboula
Hebrew	petsatsah
Yiddish	bombe
Japanese	bakudan
Swahili	kombora

134 bone

French	os
Spanish	hueso
Italian	osso
Portuguese	osso
Rumanian	os
German	Knochen
Dutch	bot
Swedish	ben
Danish	ben
Norwegian	ben
Polish	kość
Czech	kost
Serbo-Croat.	kost
Hungarian	csont
Finnish	luu
Turkish	kemik
Indonesian	tulang
Esperanto	osto
Russian	kost
Greek	ko'kkalon
Arabic	azma
Hebrew	etsem
Yiddish	bein
Japanese	hone
Swahili	mfupa

135 book

French	livre
Spanish	libro
Italian	libro
Portuguese	livro
Rumanian	carte
German	Buch
Dutch	boek
Swedish	bok
Danish	bog
Norwegian	bok
Polish	książka
Czech	kniha
Serbo-Croat.	knjiga
Hungarian	könyv
Finnish	kirja
Turkish	kitap
Indonesian	buku, kitab
Esperanto	libro
Russian	kníga
Greek	vivli'on
Arabic	kitab
Hebrew	sefer
Yiddish	buch
Japanese	hon
Swahili	kitabu

136 border

French	frontière
Spanish	frontera
Italian	frontiera
Portuguese	fronteira
Rumanian	graniţă
German	Grenze
Dutch	grens
Swedish	gräns
Danish	grænse
Norwegian	grense
Polish	granica
Czech	hranice
Serbo-Croat.	granica
Hungarian	határ
Finnish	raja
Turkish	hudut
Indonesian	batas, watas
Esperanto	land'limo
Russian	granítsa
Greek	si'noron
Arabic	houdoud
Hebrew	gvul
Yiddish	grenets
Japanese	sakai
Swahili	mpaka

137 bottle

French	bouteille
Spanish	botella
Italian	bottiglia
Portuguese	garrafa
Rumanian	sticlă
German	Flasche
Dutch	fles
Swedish	flaska
Danish	flaske
Norwegian	flaske
Polish	butelka
Czech	láhev
Serbo-Croat.	flaša
Hungarian	palack
Finnish	pullo
Turkish	şişe
Indonesian	botol
Esperanto	botelo
Russian	butílka
Greek	boti'lia
Arabic	zougaga
Hebrew	bakbuk
Yiddish	flasch
Japanese	bin
Swahili	chupa

138 bowl

French	bol
Spanish	cuenco
Italian	scodella
Portuguese	tijela
Rumanian	strachină
German	Schüssel
Dutch	schaal
Swedish	skål
Danish	skål
Norwegian	skål
Polish	miska
Czech	mísa
Serbo-Croat.	zdela
Hungarian	tál
Finnish	vati
Turkish	kâse
Indonesian	batil
Esperanto	pelvo
Russian	blyúdo
Greek	bo'oul
Arabic	soultaniya
Hebrew	misrak
Yiddish	schissel
Japanese	hachi
Swahili	bakuli

139 boy

French	garçon
Spanish	muchacho
Italian	ragazzo
Portuguese	menino
Rumanian	băiat
German	Knabe
Dutch	jongen
Swedish	pojke
Danish	dreng
Norwegian	gutt
Polish	chłopiec
Czech	chlapec
Serbo-Croat.	dječak
Hungarian	fiú
Finnish	poika
Turkish	oğlan
Indonesian	anak iclaki
Esperanto	knabo
Russian	málchik
Greek	ago'ri
Arabic	walad
Hebrew	naar
Yiddish	jungel
Japanese	otoko no ko
Swahili	kivulana

140 bracelet

French	bracelet
Spanish	pulsera
Italian	braccialetto
Portuguese	bracelete
Rumanian	brăţară
German	Armband
Dutch	armband
Swedish	armband
Danish	armbånd
Norwegian	armbånd
Polish	bransoletka
Czech	brazleta
Serbo-Croat.	narukvica
Hungarian	karkötő
Finnish	rannerengas
Turkish	bilezik
Indonesian	gelang
Esperanto	braceleto
Russian	braslyét
Greek	vrachio'li
Arabic	siwar
Hebrew	etsadah
Yiddish	branzlet
Japanese	udewa
Swahili	kikuku

141 brain

French	cerveau
Spanish	seso
Italian	cervello
Portuguese	cérebro
Rumanian	creier
German	Gehirn
Dutch	hersens
Swedish	hjärna
Danish	hjerne
Norwegian	hjerne
Polish	mózg
Czech	mozek
Serbo-Croat.	mozak
Hungarian	agy
Finnish	aivot
Turkish	beyin
Indonesian	otak
Esperanto	cerbo
Russian	mosk
Greek	mialo'
Arabic	mouch
Hebrew	moach
Yiddish	moyech
Japanese	noo
Swahili	ubongo

142 brake

French	frein
Spanish	freno
Italian	freno
Portuguese	freio
Rumanian	frînă
German	Bremse
Dutch	rem
Swedish	broms
Danish	bremse
Norwegian	bremse
Polish	hamulec
Czech	brzda
Serbo-Croat.	kočnica
Hungarian	fék
Finnish	jarru
Turkish	fren
Indonesian	rém
Esperanto	bremso
Russian	tórmas
Greek	fre'no
Arabic	farmala
Hebrew	maatser
Yiddish	brems
Japanese	bureeki
Swahili	breki

143 brass

French	laiton
Spanish	latón
Italian	ottone
Portuguese	latão
Rumanian	alamă
German	Messing
Dutch	geel koper
Swedish	mässing
Danish	messing
Norwegian	messing
Polish	mosiądz
Czech	mosaz
Serbo-Croat.	bronza
Hungarian	sárgaréz
Finnish	messinki
Turkish	pirinç
Indonesian	kuningan, tembaga
Esperanto	latuno
Russian	latún
Greek	ori'chalkos
Arabic	nihas
Hebrew	nechschet kalal
Yiddish	mesch
Japanese	shinchuu
Swahili	shaba

144 bread

French	pain
Spanish	pan
Italian	pane
Portuguese	pão
Rumanian	pîine
German	Brot
Dutch	brood
Swedish	bröd
Danish	brød
Norwegian	brød
Polish	chleb
Czech	chléb
Serbo-Croat.	hleb
Hungarian	kenyér
Finnish	leipä
Turkish	ekmek
Indonesian	roti
Esperanto	pano
Russian	khlep
Greek	psomi'
Arabic	aish
Hebrew	lechem
Yiddish	broit
Japanese	pan
Swahili	mkate

145 breakfast

French	déjeuner
Spanish	desayuno
Italian	colazione
Portuguese	café da manhã
Rumanian	micul dejun
German	Frühstück
Dutch	ontbijt
Swedish	frukost
Danish	morgenmad
Norwegian	frokost
Polish	śniadanie
Czech	snídaně
Serbo-Croat.	doručak
Hungarian	reggeli
Finnish	aamiainen
Turkish	kavaltı
Indonesian	makanan pagi, sarapan
Esperanto	maten'manĝo
Russian	záftrak
Greek	pro'gevma
Arabic	iftar
Hebrew	aruchat boker
Yiddish	frischtik
Japanese	chooshoku
Swahili	chakula cha asubuhi

146 breast

French	sein
Spanish	seno
Italian	seno
Portuguese	seio
Rumanian	sîn
German	Busen
Dutch	borst
Swedish	barm
Danish	barm
Norwegian	barm
Polish	łono
Czech	prsa
Serbo-Croat.	prsa
Hungarian	kebel
Finnish	povi
Turkish	göğüs
Indonesian	téték
Esperanto	brusto
Russian	grut
Greek	sti'thos
Arabic	tsadye
Hebrew	chaseh
Yiddish	brust
Japanese	mune
Swahili	kifua

147 breath

French	haleine
Spanish	respiro
Italian	respiro
Portuguese	fôlego
Rumanian	suflare
German	Atem
Dutch	adem
Swedish	anda
Danish	ånde
Norwegian	ånde
Polish	oddech
Czech	dech
Serbo-Croat.	dah
Hungarian	lélegzet
Finnish	henki
Turkish	nefes
Indonesian	napas
Esperanto	spiro
Russian	dikhániye
Greek	anapnoe'
Arabic	nafas
Hebrew	neschimah
Yiddish	otim
Japanese	iki
Swahili	pumzi

148 brick

French	brique
Spanish	ladrillo
Italian	mattone
Portuguese	tijolo
Rumanian	cǎramidǎ
German	Ziegelstein
Dutch	baksteen
Swedish	tegelsten
Danish	tegl
Norwegian	murstein
Polish	cegła
Czech	cihla
Serbo-Croat.	opeka
Hungarian	tégla
Finnish	tiili
Turkish	tuğla
Indonesian	bata
Esperanto	briko
Russian	kirpích
Greek	tou'vlo
Arabic	toub
Hebrew	levenah
Yiddish	tsiegel
Japanese	rengwa
Swahili	tofali

149 bride

French	mariée
Spanish	novia
Italian	fidanzata
Portuguese	noiva
Rumanian	mireasă
German	Braut
Dutch	bruid
Swedish	brud
Danish	brud
Norwegian	brud
Polish	narzeczona
Czech	nevěsta
Serbo-Croat.	nevjesta
Hungarian	menyasszony
Finnish	morsian
Turkish	gelin
Indonesian	pengantin
Esperanto	fianĉ'ino
Russian	nevyésta
Greek	ni'fi
Arabic	arous
Hebrew	kalah
Yiddish	kalle
Japanese	hanayome
Swahili	bibi arusi

150 bridge

French	pont
Spanish	puente
Italian	ponte
Portuguese	ponte
Rumanian	pod
German	Brücke
Dutch	brug
Swedish	bro
Danish	bro
Norwegian	bru
Polish	most
Czech	most
Serbo-Croat.	most
Hungarian	híd
Finnish	silta
Turkish	köprü
Indonesian	djambatan
Esperanto	ponto
Russian	most
Greek	ye'fira
Arabic	koubri
Hebrew	gescher
Yiddish	brik
Japanese	hashi
Swahili	tingetinge

151 bring

French	apporter
Spanish	traer
Italian	portare
Portuguese	trazer
Rumanian	aduce
German	bringen
Dutch	brengen
Swedish	bringa
Danish	bringe
Norwegian	bringe
Polish	przynieść
Czech	přinésti
Serbo-Croat.	doneti
Hungarian	hoz
Finnish	tuoda
Turkish	getirmek
Indonesian	bawa
Esperanto	porti
Russian	prinasít
Greek	fer'no
Arabic	youhdir
Hebrew	hevie
Yiddish	brengen
Japanese	motte kuru
Swahili	leta

152 brooch

French	broche
Spanish	broche
Italian	spillo
Portuguese	broche
Rumanian	broşă
German	Brosche
Dutch	broche
Swedish	brosch
Danish	broche
Norwegian	brosje
Polish	broszka
Czech	brož
Serbo-Croat.	broš
Hungarian	melltű
Finnish	rintaneula
Turkish	broş
Indonesian	bros
Esperanto	broĉo
Russian	brosh
Greek	karfi'tsa
Arabic	mashbak
Hebrew	siekah
Yiddish	tsiering
Japanese	buroochi
Swahili	bizimu

153 broom

French	balai
Spanish	escoba
Italian	scopa
Portuguese	vassoura
Rumanian	mătură
German	Besen
Dutch	bezem
Swedish	kvast
Danish	fegekost
Norwegian	kost
Polish	miotła
Czech	koště
Serbo-Croat.	metla
Hungarian	seprű
Finnish	luuta
Turkish	süpürge
Indonesian	sapu
Esperanto	bala'ilo
Russian	metlá
Greek	skou'pa
Arabic	miqasha
Hebrew	matateh
Yiddish	besim
Japanese	hooki
Swahili	ufagio

154 brother

French	frère
Spanish	hermano
Italian	fratello
Portuguese	irmão
Rumanian	frate
German	Bruder
Dutch	broer
Swedish	broder
Danish	broder
Norwegian	bror
Polish	brat
Czech	bratr
Serbo-Croat.	brat
Hungarian	fivér
Finnish	veli
Turkish	erkek kardeş
Indonesian	saudara laki-laki
Esperanto	frato
Russian	brat
Greek	adelfos'
Arabic	ach
Hebrew	ach
Yiddish	bruder
Japanese	kyoodai
Swahili	ndugu

155 brown

French	brun
Spanish	moreno
Italian	bruno
Portuguese	marrom
Rumanian	brun
German	braun
Dutch	bruin
Swedish	brun
Danish	brun
Norwegian	brun
Polish	brunatny
Czech	hnědý
Serbo-Croat.	mrk
Hungarian	barna
Finnish	ruskea
Turkish	kahverengi
Indonesian	mérah tua
Esperanto	bruna
Russian	karíchnevi
Greek	kastanos'
Arabic	bounni
Hebrew	schachom
Yiddish	broin
Japanese	kasshoku no
Swahili	nye kundu nyeusi

156 brush

French	brosse
Spanish	cepillo
Italian	spazzola
Portuguese	escôva
Rumanian	perie
German	Bürste
Dutch	borstel
Swedish	borste
Danish	børste
Norwegian	børste
Polish	szczotka
Czech	kartáč
Serbo-Croat.	četka
Hungarian	kefe
Finnish	harja
Turkish	fırça
Indonesian	sikat
Esperanto	broso
Russian	shchótka
Greek	vour'tsa
Arabic	foursha
Hebrew	mivreschet
Yiddish	berschtel
Japanese	burashi
Swahili	burashi

157 building

French	bâtiment
Spanish	edificio
Italian	edificio
Portuguese	edifício
Rumanian	clădire
German	Gebäude
Dutch	gebouw
Swedish	byggnad
Danish	bygning
Norwegian	bygning
Polish	budynek
Czech	budova
Serbo-Croat.	zgrada
Hungarian	épület
Finnish	rakennus
Turkish	bina
Indonesian	gedung
Esperanto	konstruo
Russian	zdániye
Greek	kti'rion
Arabic	binaa
Hebrew	binian
Yiddish	gebeide
Japanese	tatemono
Swahili	nyumba

158 bullet

French	balle
Spanish	bala
Italian	pallottola
Portuguese	bala
Rumanian	glonţ
German	Kugel
Dutch	kogel
Swedish	kula
Danish	kugle
Norwegian	kule
Polish	kula
Czech	kulka
Serbo-Croat.	metak
Hungarian	golyó
Finnish	luoti
Turkish	kurşun
Indonesian	peluru
Esperanto	kuglo
Russian	púlya
Greek	sfe'ra
Arabic	rousasa
Hebrew	kaliah
Yiddish	kugel
Japanese	juudan
Swahili	risasi ya bunduki

159 burn

French	brûler
Spanish	quemar
Italian	bruciare
Portuguese	queimar
Rumanian	arde
German	brennen
Dutch	branden
Swedish	bränna
Danish	brænde
Norwegian	brenne
Polish	palić
Czech	hořeti
Serbo-Croat.	goreti
Hungarian	éget
Finnish	palaa
Turkish	yanmak
Indonesian	bakar
Esperanto	bruli
Russian	zhech, garyét
Greek	ke'o
Arabic	yahtariq
Hebrew	saraf
Yiddish	brenen
Japanese	yaku
Swahili	choma

160 business

French	commerce
Spanish	negocio
Italian	commercio
Portuguese	negócio
Rumanian	afacere
German	Geschäft
Dutch	zaak
Swedish	affär
Danish	forretning
Norwegian	forretning
Polish	interes
Czech	obchod
Serbo-Croat.	posao
Hungarian	üzlet
Finnish	liikeasia
Turkish	ticaret
Indonesian	dagang
Esperanto	komerco
Russian	targóvlya
Greek	epichi'risis
Arabic	schugil
Hebrew	essek
Yiddish	essek
Japanese	shoobai
Swahili	biashara

161 butcher

French	boucher
Spanish	carnicero
Italian	macellaio
Portuguese	carniceiro
Rumanian	măcelar
German	Fleischer
Dutch	slager
Swedish	slaktare
Danish	slagter
Norwegian	slakter
Polish	rzeźnik
Czech	řezník
Serbo-Croat.	mesar
Hungarian	mészáros
Finnish	teurastaja
Turkish	kasap
Indonesian	djagal
Esperanto	viand'isto
Russian	myesník
Greek	chasa'pis
Arabic	gazzar
Hebrew	katsaf
Yiddish	katsof
Japanese	nikuya
Swahili	mchinjaji

162 butter

French	beurre
Spanish	mantequilla
Italian	burro
Portuguese	manteiga
Rumanian	unt
German	Butter
Dutch	boter
Swedish	smör
Danish	smør
Norwegian	smør
Polish	masło
Czech	máslo
Serbo-Croat.	buter
Hungarian	vaj
Finnish	voi
Turkish	tereyaği
Indonesian	mentéga
Esperanto	butero
Russian	máslo
Greek	vou'tiro
Arabic	zoubd
Hebrew	chemah
Yiddish	putter
Japanese	bataa
Swahili	siagi

163 butterfly

French	papillon
Spanish	mariposa
Italian	farfalla
Portuguese	borboleta
Rumanian	fluture
German	Schmetterling
Dutch	vlinder
Swedish	fjäril
Danish	sommerfugl
Norwegian	sommerfugl
Polish	motyl
Czech	motýl
Serbo-Croat.	leptir
Hungarian	lepke
Finnish	perhonen
Turkish	kelebek
Indonesian	kupu-kupu
Esperanto	papilio
Russian	bábochka
Greek	petalou'da
Arabic	farasha
Hebrew	parpar
Yiddish	schmetterling
Japanese	choo
Swahili	kipepeo

164 button

French	bouton
Spanish	botón
Italian	bottone
Portuguese	botão
Rumanian	buton
German	Knopf
Dutch	knoop
Swedish	knapp
Danish	knap
Norwegian	knapp
Polish	guzik
Czech	knoflík
Serbo-Croat.	dugme
Hungarian	gomb
Finnish	nappi
Turkish	düğme
Indonesian	kantjing
Esperanto	butono
Russian	púgavitsa, knópka
Greek	koumbi'
Arabic	zir
Hebrew	kaftor
Yiddish	knepel
Japanese	botan
Swahili	kifungo

165 buy

French	acheter
Spanish	comprar
Italian	comprare
Portuguese	comprar
Rumanian	cumpăra
German	kaufen
Dutch	kopen
Swedish	köpa
Danish	købe
Norwegian	kjøpe
Polish	kupować
Czech	koupiti
Serbo-Croat.	kupiti
Hungarian	vásárol
Finnish	ostaa
Turkish	satın almak
Indonesian	beli
Esperanto	aĉeti
Russian	kupít
Greek	agora'zo
Arabic	yashtari
Hebrew	kanah
Yiddish	koifen
Japanese	kau
Swahili	nunua

166 cabaret

French	cabaret
Spanish	cabaret
Italian	cabaret
Portuguese	cabaré
Rumanian	cabaret
German	Kabarett
Dutch	cabaret
Swedish	kabarett
Danish	kabaret
Norwegian	kabaret
Polish	kabaret
Czech	kabaret
Serbo-Croat.	kabaret
Hungarian	kabaré
Finnish	kabarett
Turkish	kabare
Indonesian	kabaret
Esperanto	kabaredo
Russian	kabaryé
Greek	kabare'
Arabic	kabarai
Hebrew	moadon laila
Yiddish	kabaret
Japanese	kyaboree
Swahili	mkahawa

167 cabbage

French	chou
Spanish	col
Italian	cavolo
Portuguese	couve
Rumanian	varză
German	Weisskohl
Dutch	kool
Swedish	kål
Danish	kål
Norwegian	kål
Polish	kapusta
Czech	kapusta
Serbo-Croat.	kupus
Hungarian	káposzta
Finnish	kaali
Turkish	lâhana
Indonesian	kubis
Esperanto	brasiko
Russian	kapústa
Greek	la'chana
Arabic	kouroumb
Hebrew	kruv
Yiddish	kroit
Japanese	kyabetsu
Swahili	kabichi

168 cabin

French	cabine
Spanish	cabina
Italian	cabina
Portuguese	cabina
Rumanian	cabină
German	Kabine
Dutch	hut
Swedish	kajuta
Danish	kahyt
Norwegian	kahytt
Polish	kabina
Czech	kajuta
Serbo-Croat.	kabina
Hungarian	fülke
Finnish	hytti
Turkish	kamara
Indonesian	kabin
Esperanto	kajuto
Russian	kabína
Greek	kabi'na
Arabic	qamara, kouch ta
Hebrew	
Yiddish	kayute
Japanese	senshitsu
Swahili	kijumba

169 café

French	café
Spanish	café
Italian	caffè
Portuguese	café
Rumanian	cafenea
German	Café
Dutch	café
Swedish	kafé
Danish	kafé
Norwegian	kafé
Polish	kawiarnia
Czech	kavárna
Serbo-Croat.	kafana
Hungarian	kávéház
Finnish	kahvila
Turkish	kahvehane
Indonesian	kedai copi
Esperanto	kaf'ejo
Russian	kafyé
Greek	kafeni'on
Arabic	qahwa
Hebrew	bait kahva
Yiddish	kavehois
Japanese	kafee
Swahili	mkaawa

170 cake

French	gâteau
Spanish	pastel
Italian	pasta
Portuguese	bôlo
Rumanian	cozonac
German	Kuchen
Dutch	cake
Swedish	kaka
Danish	kage
Norwegian	kake
Polish	ciastko
Czech	koláč
Serbo-Croat.	kolač
Hungarian	kalács
Finnish	kaakku
Turkish	pasta
Indonesian	kuéh
Esperanto	kuko
Russian	pirózhnaye
Greek	ke'ik
Arabic	halwa
Hebrew	tufin
Yiddish	lekach
Japanese	kwashi
Swahili	mkate mtamu

171 calf

French	veau
Spanish	ternero
Italian	vitello
Portuguese	vitela
Rumanian	viţel
German	Kalb
Dutch	kalf
Swedish	kalv
Danish	kalv
Norwegian	kalv
Polish	cielę
Czech	tele
Serbo-Croat.	tele
Hungarian	borjú
Finnish	vasikka
Turkish	dana
Indonesian	anak sapi
Esperanto	bov'ido
Russian	telyónok
Greek	moscha'ri
Arabic	igl radi
Hebrew	egel
Yiddish	kalb
Japanese	koushi
Swahili	ndama

172 call

French	appeler
Spanish	llamar
Italian	chiamare
Portuguese	chamar
Rumanian	chema
German	rufen
Dutch	opbellen
Swedish	ropa
Danish	kalde
Norwegian	kalle
Polish	wołać
Czech	volati
Serbo-Croat.	pozvati
Hungarian	hív
Finnish	huutaa
Turkish	çağirmak
Indonesian	panggilan
Esperanto	voki
Russian	zvat
Greek	kalo'
Arabic	younadi
Hebrew	kara
Yiddish	rufen
Japanese	yobu
Swahili	ita

173 camel

French	chameau
Spanish	camello
Italian	cammello
Portuguese	camelo
Rumanian	cămilă
German	Kamel
Dutch	kameel
Swedish	kamel
Danish	kamel
Norwegian	kamel
Polish	wielbłąd
Czech	velbloud
Serbo-Croat.	kamila
Hungarian	teve
Finnish	kameli
Turkish	deve
Indonesian	unta
Esperanto	kamelo
Russian	verblyút
Greek	kami'la
Arabic	gamal
Hebrew	gamal
Yiddish	kemel
Japanese	rakuda
Swahili	ngamia

174 camera

French	appareil photographique
Spanish	cámara fotográfica
Italian	macchina fotografica
Portuguese	máquina fotográfica
Rumanian	cameră fotografica
German	Photoapparat
Dutch	fototoestel
Swedish	kamera
Danish	kamera
Norwegian	kamera
Polish	aparat fotograficzny
Czech	fotografický aparát
Serbo-Croat.	kamera
Hungarian	fényképezőgép
Finnish	valokuvauskone
Turkish	fotoğraf makinası
Indonesian	kamera
Esperanto	kamer'eto
Russian	foto apparát
Greek	fotografiki' michani'
Arabic	aalat taswir
Hebrew	matslemah
Yiddish	fotografiraparat
Japanese	kamera
Swahili	chombo kupigia picha

175 camp

French	camp
Spanish	campamento
Italian	campo
Portuguese	campo
Rumanian	lagăr
German	Lager
Dutch	legerplaats
Swedish	läger
Danish	lejr
Norwegian	leir
Polish	obóz
Czech	tábor
Serbo-Croat.	logor
Hungarian	tábor
Finnish	leiri
Turkish	kamp
Indonesian	perkémahan
Esperanto	tend'ejo
Russian	láger
Greek	kataski'nosis
Arabic	mouaskar
Hebrew	machaneh
Yiddish	geleger
Japanese	kyanpu
Swahili	kambi

176 canal

French	canal
Spanish	canal
Italian	canale
Portuguese	canal
Rumanian	canal
German	Kanal
Dutch	gracht
Swedish	kanal
Danish	kanal
Norwegian	kanal
Polish	kanał
Czech	kanál
Serbo-Croat.	kanal
Hungarian	csatorna
Finnish	kanava
Turkish	kanal
Indonesian	terusan
Esperanto	kanalo
Russian	kanál
Greek	kana'li
Arabic	qanat
Hebrew	tealah
Yiddish	kanal
Japanese	unga
Swahili	njia ya maji

177 candle

French	bougie
Spanish	vela
Italian	candela
Portuguese	vela
Rumanian	lumînare
German	Kerze
Dutch	kaars
Swedish	ljus
Danish	kerte
Norwegian	lys
Polish	świeca
Czech	svíčka
Serbo-Croat.	sveća
Hungarian	gyerta
Finnish	kynttilä
Turkish	mum
Indonesian	dian, kandil
Esperanto	kandelo
Russian	svechá
Greek	keri'
Arabic	shamaa
Hebrew	ner
Yiddish	licht
Japanese	roosoku
Swahili	mshumaa

178 cane

French	canne
Spanish	bastón
Italian	bastone
Portuguese	bengala
Rumanian	baston
German	Spazierstock
Dutch	wandelstok
Swedish	käpp
Danish	spadserestok
Norwegian	stokk
Polish	laska
Czech	hůl
Serbo-Croat.	štap
Hungarian	pálca
Finnish	keppi
Turkish	baston
Indonesian	tongkat
Esperanto	bastono
Russian	pálka
Greek	kala'mi
Arabic	asa
Hebrew	makel
Yiddish	schpatsierschteken
Japanese	tsue
Swahili	henzerani

179 capital

French	capitale
Spanish	capital
Italian	capitale
Portuguese	capital
Rumanian	capitală
German	Hauptstadt
Dutch	hoofdstad
Swedish	huvudstad
Danish	hovedstad
Norwegian	hovedstad
Polish	stolica
Czech	hlavní město
Serbo-Croat.	glavni grad
Hungarian	főváros
Finnish	pääkaupunki
Turkish	baş şehir
Indonesian	ibu kota
Esperanto	ĉef'urbo
Russian	stalítsa
Greek	prote'vousa
Arabic	aasima
Hebrew	birah
Yiddish	hoiptschtot
Japanese	shufu
Swahili	mji mkuu wa nchi

180 capsize

French	chavirer
Spanish	volcar
Italian	capovolgere
Portuguese	capotar
Rumanian	răsturna
German	kentern
Dutch	kapseizen
Swedish	kantra
Danish	kæntre
Norwegian	kantre
Polish	wywracać
Czech	převrhnouti
Serbo-Croat.	prevrnuti
Hungarian	felborul
Finnish	mennä kumoon
Turkish	devrilmek
Indonesian	terbalik
Esperanto	renversi
Russian	aprakídivat
Greek	anatre'po
Arabic	yanqalib
Hebrew	hafach
Yiddish	iberkehren
Japanese	hikkuri kaesu
Swahili	pindua

181 captain

French	capitaine
Spanish	capitán
Italian	capitano
Portuguese	capitão
Rumanian	căpitan
German	Kapitän
Dutch	kapitein
Swedish	kapten
Danish	kaptajn
Norwegian	kaptein
Polish	kapitan
Czech	kapitán
Serbo-Croat.	kapetan
Hungarian	kapitány
Finnish	kapteeni
Turkish	kaptan
Indonesian	nachoda
Esperanto	kapitano
Russian	kapitán
Greek	kapeta'nios
Arabic	qabtaan
Hebrew	kabarnit
Yiddish	kapitan
Japanese	senchoo
Swahili	kapiteni

182 capture

French	capturer
Spanish	capturar
Italian	catturare
Portuguese	capturar
Rumanian	captură
German	festnehmen
Dutch	buit maken
Swedish	gripa
Danish	gribe
Norwegian	gripe
Polish	zdobyć
Czech	odejiti
Serbo-Croat.	uhvatiti
Hungarian	elfog
Finnish	vallata
Turkish	zaptetmek
Indonesian	penangkapan
Esperanto	kapti
Russian	zakhvatít
Greek	kirie'vo
Arabic	yaqboud
Hebrew	lechidah
Yiddish	fangen
Japanese	tsukamaeru
Swahili	kamata

183 car

French	voiture
Spanish	coche
Italian	vagone
Portuguese	carro
Rumanian	vagon
German	Wagen
Dutch	wagen
Swedish	vagn
Danish	vogn
Norwegian	vogn
Polish	wóz
Czech	vůz
Serbo-Croat.	kola
Hungarian	kocsi
Finnish	vaunu
Turkish	araba
Indonesian	kendaraan
Esperanto	vagono
Russian	pavóska
Greek	aftoki'niton
Arabic	araba
Hebrew	mechonit
Yiddish	vogen
Japanese	kuruma
Swahili	gari

184 cardboard

French	carton
Spanish	cartón
Italian	cartone
Portuguese	papelão
Rumanian	carton
German	Karton
Dutch	karton
Swedish	kartong
Danish	karton
Norwegian	kartong
Polish	karton
Czech	lepenka
Serbo-Croat.	karton
Hungarian	karton
Finnish	pahvi
Turkish	karton
Indonesian	karton
Esperanto	kartono
Russian	kartón
Greek	charto'ni
Arabic	kartoun
Hebrew	karton
Yiddish	papendekel
Japanese	boorugami
Swahili	karatasi nene

185 careful

French	soigneux
Spanish	cuidadoso
Italian	cauto
Portuguese	cuidadoso
Rumanian	prudent
German	vorsichtig
Dutch	voorzichtig
Swedish	aktsam
Danish	forsigtig
Norwegian	forsiktig
Polish	ostrożnie
Czech	opatrný
Serbo-Croat.	pažljiv
Hungarian	óvatos
Finnish	varovainen
Turkish	dikkatli
Indonesian	awas
Esperanto	zorga
Russian	astarózhni
Greek	prosektikos'
Arabic	haris
Hebrew	sahir
Yiddish	forsichtig
Japanese	chuui bukai
Swahili	-angalifu

186 cargo

French	cargaison
Spanish	carga
Italian	carico
Portuguese	carga
Rumanian	încărcatură
German	Fracht
Dutch	lading
Swedish	last
Danish	fragt
Norwegian	last
Polish	ładunek
Czech	náklad
Serbo-Croat.	tovar
Hungarian	rakomány
Finnish	lasti
Turkish	yük
Indonesian	muatan
Esperanto	kargo
Russian	grus
Greek	forti'o
Arabic	shouhna
Hebrew	mitan
Yiddish	lodung
Japanese	funani
Swahili	shehena

187 carnation

French	oeillet
Spanish	clavel
Italian	garofano
Portuguese	cravo
Rumanian	garoafă roşie
German	Nelke
Dutch	anjer
Swedish	nejlika
Danish	nellike
Norwegian	nellik
Polish	gwoździk
Czech	karafiát
Serbo-Croat.	karanfil
Hungarian	szegfű
Finnish	neilikka
Turkish	karanfil
Indonesian	anjelir
Esperanto	dianto
Russian	gvazdíka
Greek	gari'fallon
Arabic	zahr al-qourounfoul
Hebrew	tsiporen
Yiddish	gwodsigblimel
Japanese	kaaneeshon
Swahili	namma ya ua

188 carpenter

French	charpentier
Spanish	carpintero
Italian	carpentiere
Portuguese	carpinteiro
Rumanian	dulgher
German	Schreiner
Dutch	timmerman
Swedish	snickare
Danish	snedker
Norwegian	snekker
Polish	stolarz
Czech	truhlář
Serbo-Croat.	stolar
Hungarian	asztalos
Finnish	kirvesmies
Turkish	marangoz
Indonesian	tukang kaju
Esperanto	ĉarpent'isto
Russian	stalyár
Greek	marangos'
Arabic	naggar
Hebrew	nagar
Yiddish	stoller
Japanese	daiku
Swahili	seremala

189 carpet

French	tapis
Spanish	alfombra
Italian	tappeto
Portuguese	tapête
Rumanian	covor
German	Teppich
Dutch	vloerkleed
Swedish	matta
Danish	gulvtæppe
Norwegian	teppe
Polish	dywan
Czech	koberec
Serbo-Croat.	ćilim
Hungarian	szőnyeg
Finnish	matto
Turkish	halı
Indonesian	permadani
Esperanto	tapiŝo
Russian	kavyór
Greek	chali'
Arabic	siggada
Hebrew	schatiach
Yiddish	divan
Japanese	juutan
Swahili	zulia

190 carrot

French	carotte
Spanish	zanahoria
Italian	carota
Portuguese	cenoura
Rumanian	morcov
German	Mohrrübe
Dutch	wortel
Swedish	morot
Danish	gulerod
Norwegian	gulrot
Polish	marchew
Czech	mrkev
Serbo-Croat.	mrkva
Hungarian	sárgarépa
Finnish	porkkana
Turkish	havuç
Indonesian	bortol
Esperanto	karoto
Russian	markóf
Greek	karo'to
Arabic	gazar
Hebrew	geser
Yiddish	meren
Japanese	ninjin
Swahili	karoti

191 carry

French	porter
Spanish	llevar
Italian	portare
Portuguese	levar
Rumanian	purta
German	tragen
Dutch	dragen
Swedish	bära
Danish	bære
Norwegian	bære
Polish	nosić
Czech	nositi
Serbo-Croat.	nositi
Hungarian	visz
Finnish	kantaa
Turkish	taşımak
Indonesian	angkut
Esperanto	porti
Russian	nasít
Greek	fe'ro
Arabic	yahmul
Hebrew	nassa
Yiddish	trogen
Japanese	hakobu
Swahili	chukua

192 cash

French	argent comptant
Spanish	dinero contante
Italian	contante
Portuguese	dinheiro de contado
Rumanian	bani gata
German	Bargeld
Dutch	kas
Swedish	kontanter
Danish	rede penge
Norwegian	kontanter
Polish	gotówka
Czech	hotově peníze
Serbo-Croat.	gotovina
Hungarian	készpénz
Finnish	käteinen
Turkish	peşin para
Indonesian	kontan
Esperanto	kontanto
Russian	nalíchniye
Greek	metrita'
Arabic	naqd
Hebrew	mesumanim
Yiddish	bargeld
Japanese	genkin
Swahili	sarafu

193 cat

French	chat
Spanish	gato
Italian	gatto
Portuguese	gato
Rumanian	pisică
German	Katze
Dutch	kat
Swedish	katt
Danish	kat
Norwegian	katt
Polish	kot
Czech	kočka
Serbo-Croat.	mačka
Hungarian	macska
Finnish	kissa
Turkish	kedi
Indonesian	kutjing
Esperanto	kato
Russian	kóshka
Greek	ga'ta
Arabic	qit
Hebrew	chatul
Yiddish	kats
Japanese	neko
Swahili	paka

194 catch

French	attraper
Spanish	coger
Italian	acchiappare
Portuguese	apanhar
Rumanian	prinde
German	fangen
Dutch	vangen
Swedish	fånga
Danish	fange
Norwegian	fange
Polish	złapać
Czech	chytiti
Serbo-Croat.	hvatati
Hungarian	megfog
Finnish	pyydystää
Turkish	yakalamak
Indonesian	tangkap
Esperanto	kapti
Russian	lavít
Greek	pia'no
Arabic	qabada aia
Hebrew	tafas
Yiddish	chapn
Japanese	toraeru
Swahili	kamata

195 cathedral

French	cathédrale
Spanish	catedral
Italian	duomo
Portuguese	catedral
Rumanian	catedrală
German	Kathedrale
Dutch	kathedraal
Swedish	domkyrka
Danish	domkirke
Norwegian	domkirke
Polish	katedra
Czech	katedrála
Serbo-Croat.	katedrala
Hungarian	székesegyház
Finnish	tuomiokirkko
Turkish	katedral
Indonesian	geredja jang besar
Esperanto	katedralo
Russian	sabór
Greek	mitro'polis
Arabic	abrashia
Hebrew	kenesiyah
Yiddish	hoipttume
Japanese	daigaran
Swahili	kanisa kuu

196 cattle

French	bétail
Spanish	ganado
Italian	bestiame
Portuguese	gado
Rumanian	vite
German	Rindvieh
Dutch	vee
Swedish	boskap
Danish	kvæg
Norwegian	buskap
Polish	bydło
Czech	dobytek
Serbo-Croat.	stoka
Hungarian	marha
Finnish	nautakarja
Turkish	sığır
Indonesian	ternak
Esperanto	bovoj
Russian	skot
Greek	kopa'di agela'don
Arabic	mashiya
Hebrew	bakar
Yiddish	beheimeh
Japanese	kachiku
Swahili	mifugo

197 cauliflower

French	chou-fleur
Spanish	coliflor
Italian	cavolfiore
Portuguese	couve-flor
Rumanian	conopidă
German	Blumenkohl
Dutch	bloemkool
Swedish	blomkål
Danish	blomkål
Norwegian	blomkål
Polish	kalafjor
Czech	květák
Serbo-Croat.	karfiiol
Hungarian	karfiol
Finnish	kukkakaali
Turkish	karnabahar
Indonesian	kol kembang
Esperanto	flor'brasiko
Russian	tsvetnáya kapústa
Greek	kounoupi'di
Arabic	qarnabit
Hebrew	kruvit
Yiddish	karfiol
Japanese	hanakyabetsu
Swahili	namna ya mboga

198 caution

French	caution
Spanish	cautela
Italian	cautela
Portuguese	cautela
Rumanian	precauţiune
German	Vorsicht
Dutch	vorsichtigheid
Swedish	försiktighet
Danish	forsigtighed
Norwegian	forsiktighet
Polish	ostrożność
Czech	pozor
Serbo-Croat.	opomena
Hungarian	vigyázat
Finnish	varovaisuus
Turkish	ihtiyat
Indonesian	hati-hati
Esperanto	sin'gardo
Russian	astarózhnost
Greek	prosochi'
Arabic	ihtiras
Hebrew	hatraha
Yiddish	hazuru
Japanese	yoojin
Swahili	uangalifu

199 cellar

French	cave
Spanish	bodega
Italian	cantina
Portuguese	adega
Rumanian	pivniţă
German	Keller
Dutch	kelder
Swedish	källare
Danish	kælder
Norwegian	kjeller
Polish	piwnica
Czech	sklep
Serbo-Croat.	podrum
Hungarian	pince
Finnish	kellari
Turkish	bodrum
Indonesian	ruangan tanah
Esperanto	kelo
Russian	pógreb
Greek	ipo'yion
Arabic	qabwe
Hebrew	martef
Yiddish	keler
Japanese	chikashitsu
Swahili	ghala ya chini ya nyumba

200 cemetery

French	cimetière
Spanish	cementerio
Italian	cimitero
Portuguese	cemitério
Rumanian	cimitir
German	Friedhof
Dutch	begraafplaats
Swedish	kyrkogård
Danish	kirkegård
Norwegian	kirkegård
Polish	cmentarz
Czech	hřbitov
Serbo-Croat.	groblje
Hungarian	temető
Finnish	hautausmaa
Turkish	mezarlık
Indonesian	pekuburan
Esperanto	tomb'ejo
Russian	kládbishche
Greek	nekrotafi'on
Arabic	gabbana
Hebrew	beth-kevuroth
Yiddish	beis hakvuros
Japanese	bochi
Swahili	makaburini

201 century

French	siècle
Spanish	siglo
Italian	secolo
Portuguese	século
Rumanian	secol
German	Jahrhundert
Dutch	eeuw
Swedish	århundrade
Danish	århundrede
Norwegian	århundre
Polish	stulecie
Czech	stoleti
Serbo-Croat.	vek
Hungarian	évszázad
Finnish	vuosisata
Turkish	asır
Indonesian	abad
Esperanto	cent'jaro
Russian	stalyétiye
Greek	eon'
Arabic	qarn
Hebrew	meah
Yiddish	johrhundert
Japanese	isseiki
Swahili	karne

202 chain

French	chaîne
Spanish	cadena
Italian	catena
Portuguese	cadeia
Rumanian	lanţ
German	Kette
Dutch	ketting
Swedish	kedja
Danish	kæde
Norwegian	kjede
Polish	łańcuch
Czech	řetĕz
Serbo-Croat.	lanac
Hungarian	lánc
Finnish	ketju
Turkish	zincir
Indonesian	rantai
Esperanto	ĉeno
Russian	tsep
Greek	alisi'da
Arabic	silsila
Hebrew	kevel
Yiddish	keit
Japanese	kusari
Swahili	mnyororo

203 chair

French	chaise
Spanish	silla
Italian	sedia
Portuguese	cadeira
Rumanian	scaun
German	Stuhl
Dutch	stoel
Swedish	stol
Danish	stol
Norwegian	stol
Polish	krzesło
Czech	židle
Serbo-Croat.	stolica
Hungarian	szék
Finnish	tuoli
Turkish	sandalye
Indonesian	kursi
Esperanto	seĝo
Russian	stul
Greek	karek'la
Arabic	maqaad
Hebrew	kissai
Yiddish	benkel
Japanese	isu
Swahili	kiti

204 chambermaid

French	femme de chambre
Spanish	camarera
Italian	cameriera
Portuguese	criada de quarto
Rumanian	fată în casă
German	Zimmermädchen
Dutch	kamermeisje
Swedish	städerska
Danish	stuepige
Norwegian	stuepike
Polish	pokojówka
Czech	pokojská
Serbo-Croat.	sobarica
Hungarian	szobálany
Finnish	siivooja
Turkish	oda hizmetçisi
Indonesian	babu kamar
Esperanto	ĉambr'ist'ino
Russian	górnichnaya
Greek	kamari-e'ra
Arabic	kamarira
Hebrew	oseret-bajit
Yiddish	dienst
Japanese	okujochuu
Swahili	mtumishi wa kike

205 change

French	changer
Spanish	cambiar
Italian	cambiare
Portuguese	mudar
Rumanian	schimba
German	ändern
Dutch	veranderen
Swedish	ändring
Danish	forandre
Norwegian	forandre
Polish	zmienić
Czech	měniti
Serbo-Croat.	menjati
Hungarian	változtat
Finnish	vaihtaa
Turkish	değiştirmek
Indonesian	berubah
Esperanto	ŝanĝi
Russian	peremenít
Greek	alla'zo
Arabic	fidda faka
Hebrew	schina
Yiddish	enderen
Japanese	kawaru
Swahili	badili

206 cheap

French	bon marché
Spanish	barato
Italian	economico
Portuguese	barato
Rumanian	ieftin
German	billig
Dutch	goedkoop
Swedish	billig
Danish	billig
Norwegian	billig
Polish	tani
Czech	levný
Serbo-Croat.	jevtin
Hungarian	olcsó
Finnish	halpa
Turkish	ucuz
Indonesian	murah
Esperanto	mal'kara
Russian	dishóvi
Greek	fthinos'
Arabic	rachis
Hebrew	sol
Yiddish	volvl
Japanese	yasui
Swahili	rahisi

207 cheek

French	joue
Spanish	mejilla
Italian	guancia
Portuguese	bochecha
Rumanian	obraz
German	Wange
Dutch	wang
Swedish	kind
Danish	kind
Norwegian	kinn
Polish	policzek
Czech	tvář
Serbo-Croat.	obraz
Hungarian	orca
Finnish	poski
Turkish	yanak
Indonesian	pipi
Esperanto	vango
Russian	shcheká
Greek	ma'goulo
Arabic	chad
Hebrew	lechi
Yiddish	bak
Japanese	hoho
Swahili	shavu la uso

208 cheese

French	fromage
Spanish	queso
Italian	formaggio
Portuguese	queijo
Rumanian	brînză
German	Käse
Dutch	kaas
Swedish	ost
Danish	ost
Norwegian	ost
Polish	ser
Czech	sýr
Serbo-Croat.	sir
Hungarian	sajt
Finnish	juusto
Turkish	peynir
Indonesian	kédju
Esperanto	fromaĝo
Russian	sir
Greek	tiri'
Arabic	goubn
Hebrew	gevinah
Yiddish	kes
Japanese	chiizu
Swahili	jibini

209 chemistry

French	chimie
Spanish	química
Italian	chimica
Portuguese	química
Rumanian	chimie
German	Chemie
Dutch	chemie
Swedish	kemi
Danish	kemi
Norwegian	kjemi
Polish	chemia
Czech	chemie
Serbo-Croat.	hemija
Hungarian	vegytan
Finnish	kemia
Turkish	kimya
Indonesian	kimia
Esperanto	kemio
Russian	khímiya
Greek	chimi'a
Arabic	kimyaa
Hebrew	kimjah
Yiddish	kemje
Japanese	kwagaku
Swahili	kemistri

210 cherry

French	cerise
Spanish	cereza
Italian	ciliegia
Portuguese	cereja
Rumanian	cireaşă
German	Kirsche
Dutch	kers
Swedish	körsbär
Danish	kirsebær
Norwegian	kirsebær
Polish	wiśnia
Czech	třešně
Serbo-Croat.	trešnja
Hungarian	cseresznye
Finnish	kirsikka
Turkish	kiraz
Indonesian	kérsen
Esperanto	ĉerizo
Russian	víshnya
Greek	kera'si
Arabic	karaz
Hebrew	divdevan
Yiddish	karsch
Japanese	sakuranboo
Swahili	namna ya tunda dogo

211 chess

French	échecs
Spanish	ajedrez
Italian	scacchi
Portuguese	jôgo de xadrez
Rumanian	şah
German	Schach
Dutch	schaak
Swedish	schack
Danish	skakspil
Norwegian	sjakk
Polish	szachy
Czech	šachy
Serbo-Croat.	šah
Hungarian	sakk
Finnish	šakki
Turkish	şatranç
Indonesian	tjatur
Esperanto	ŝakoj
Russian	shákhmati
Greek	ska'ki
Arabic	shatarang
Hebrew	ischkukah
Yiddish	schach
Japanese	shoogo
Swahili	sataranji

212 chest

French	poitrine
Spanish	pecho
Italian	petto
Portuguese	tórax
Rumanian	piept
German	Brust
Dutch	borst
Swedish	bröst
Danish	bryst
Norwegian	bryst
Polish	pierś
Czech	hrud'
Serbo-Croat.	grudi
Hungarian	mell
Finnish	rinta
Turkish	göğüs
Indonesian	dada
Esperanto	brusto
Russian	grudnáya klyétka
Greek	sti'thos
Arabic	sadr
Hebrew	chaseh
Yiddish	brust
Japanese	mune
Swahili	kifua

213 chicken

French	poulet
Spanish	pollo
Italian	pollo
Portuguese	frango
Rumanian	pui
German	Huhn
Dutch	kip
Swedish	kyckling
Danish	høne
Norwegian	kylling
Polish	kura
Czech	kuře
Serbo-Croat.	pile
Hungarian	csirke
Finnish	kana
Turkish	tavuk
Indonesian	ajam
Esperanto	kok'ido
Russian	kúritsa
Greek	koto'poulo
Arabic	farcha
Hebrew	tarnegol
Yiddish	hindel
Japanese	niwatori
Swahili	kuku

214 child

French	enfant
Spanish	niño
Italian	bambino
Portuguese	criança
Rumanian	copil
German	Kind
Dutch	kind
Swedish	barn
Danish	barn
Norwegian	barn
Polish	dziecko
Czech	dítě
Serbo-Croat.	djete
Hungarian	gyermek
Finnish	lapsi
Turkish	çocuk
Indonesian	anak
Esperanto	infano
Russian	dityá
Greek	pedi'
Arabic	tifl
Hebrew	yeled
Yiddish	kind
Japanese	kodomo
Swahili	mtoto

215 chin

French	menton
Spanish	barbilla
Italian	mento
Portuguese	queixo
Rumanian	bărbie
German	Kinn
Dutch	kin
Swedish	haka
Danish	hage
Norwegian	hake
Polish	podbródek
Czech	brada
Serbo-Croat.	brada
Hungarian	áll
Finnish	leuka
Turkish	çene
Indonesian	dagu
Esperanto	mentono
Russian	padbaródok
Greek	pigou'ni
Arabic	tzaqn
Hebrew	santer
Yiddish	morde
Japanese	ago
Swahili	kidevu

216 chive

French	ciboulette
Spanish	ceboletta
Italian	foglie di cipolline
Portuguese	cebolinha
Rumanian	praz
German	Schnittlauch
Dutch	bieslook
Swedish	gräslök
Danish	purløg
Norwegian	gressløk
Polish	szczypiorek
Czech	pažitka
Serbo-Croat.	drobnjak
Hungarian	metélöhagyma
Finnish	ruoholaukka
Turkish	yeşil soğan
Indonesian	aris
Esperanto	ŝenoprazo
Russian	myélki luk
Greek	pra'son
Arabic	soughar
Hebrew	kreschah
Yiddish	schnitloch
Japanese	ezonegi
Swahili	kitunguu kidogo

217 chocolate

French	chocolat
Spanish	chocolate
Italian	cioccolata
Portuguese	chocolate
Rumanian	ciocolată
German	Schokolade
Dutch	chocolade
Swedish	choklad
Danish	chokolade
Norwegian	sjokolade
Polish	czekolada
Czech	čokoláda
Serbo-Croat.	čokolada
Hungarian	csokoládé
Finnish	suklaa
Turkish	çikolata
Indonesian	tjoklat
Esperanto	ĉokolado
Russian	shokalát
Greek	sokola'ta
Arabic	shoukoulata
Hebrew	schokolad
Yiddish	schokolade
Japanese	chokoreeto
Swahili	chokolati

218 Christmas

French	Noël
Spanish	Navidad
Italian	Natale
Portuguese	natal
Rumanian	Grăciun
German	Weihnachten
Dutch	Kerstmis
Swedish	jul
Danish	jul
Norwegian	jul
Polish	Boże Narodzenie
Czech	vánoce
Serbo-Croat.	Božić
Hungarian	karácsony
Finnish	joulu
Turkish	Noel
Indonesian	Hari Natal
Esperanto	Krist'nasko
Russian	razhdestvó
Greek	Christou'yenna
Arabic	id al-milad
Hebrew	chagamolad hanotsri
Yiddish	nitel
Japanese	kurisumasu
Swahili	krismasi

219 church

French	église
Spanish	iglesia
Italian	chiesa
Portuguese	igreja
Rumanian	biserică
German	Kirche
Dutch	kerk
Swedish	kyrka
Danish	kirke
Norwegian	kirke
Polish	kościół
Czech	kostel
Serbo-Croat.	crkva
Hungarian	templom
Finnish	kirkko
Turkish	kilise
Indonesian	gerédja
Esperanto	preĝ'ejo
Russian	tsérkof
Greek	eklisi'a
Arabic	kanisa
Hebrew	knesiyah
Yiddish	time
Japanese	kyookwai
Swahili	kanisa

220 cigar

French	cigare
Spanish	puro
Italian	sigaro
Portuguese	charuto
Rumanian	ţigară de foi
German	Zigarre
Dutch	sigaar
Swedish	cigarr
Danish	cigar
Norwegian	sigar
Polish	cygaro
Czech	doutník
Serbo-Croat.	cigara
Hungarian	szivar
Finnish	sikaari
Turkish	sigar
Indonesian	tjerutu
Esperanto	cigaro
Russian	sigára
Greek	pou'ron
Arabic	sigar
Hebrew	sigara
Yiddish	tsigar
Japanese	hamaki
Swahili	sigara

221 cigarette

French	cigarette
Spanish	cigarrillo
Italian	sigaretta
Portuguese	cigarro
Rumanian	ţigară
German	Zigarette
Dutch	sigaret
Swedish	cigarrett
Danish	cigaret
Norwegian	sigarett
Polish	papieros
Czech	cigareta
Serbo-Croat.	cigareta
Hungarian	cigaretta
Finnish	savuke
Turkish	sigara
Indonesian	sigaret, rokok
Esperanto	cigaredo
Russian	papirósa
Greek	sigaret'ton
Arabic	sigara
Hebrew	sigriyah
Yiddish	papiros
Japanese	tabako
Swahili	sigareti

222 circle

French	cercle
Spanish	círculo
Italian	circolo
Portuguese	círculo
Rumanian	cerc
German	Kreis
Dutch	cirkel
Swedish	krets
Danish	kreds
Norwegian	sirkel
Polish	koło
Czech	kruh
Serbo-Croat.	krug
Hungarian	kör
Finnish	ympyrä
Turkish	daire
Indonesian	lingkaran
Esperanto	cirklo
Russian	kruk
Greek	ki'klos
Arabic	daira
Hebrew	igul
Yiddish	keikel
Japanese	en
Swahili	duara

223 citizen

French	citoyen
Spanish	ciudadano
Italian	cittadino
Portuguese	cidadão
Rumanian	cetăţean
German	Bürger
Dutch	burger
Swedish	borgare
Danish	borger
Norwegian	borger
Polish	obywatel
Czech	občan
Serbo-Croat.	gradjanin
Hungarian	polgár
Finnish	kansalainen
Turkish	şehirli
Indonesian	penduduk kota
Esperanto	civit'ano
Russian	grazhdanín
Greek	poli'tis
Arabic	mouwatin
Hebrew	ezrach
Yiddish	birger
Japanese	shimin
Swahili	mwenyeji

224 clean

French	propre
Spanish	limpio
Italian	puro
Portuguese	limpo
Rumanian	curat
German	rein
Dutch	schoon
Swedish	ren
Danish	ren
Norwegian	ren
Polish	czysty
Czech	čistý
Serbo-Croat.	čist
Hungarian	tiszta
Finnish	puhdas
Turkish	temiz
Indonesian	bersih
Esperanto	pura
Russian	chísti
Greek	katharos'
Arabic	nazif
Hebrew	naki
Yiddish	rein
Japanese	kirei na
Swahili	safi

225 clear

French	clair
Spanish	claro
Italian	chiaro
Portuguese	claro
Rumanian	clar
German	klar
Dutch	helder
Swedish	klar
Danish	klar
Norwegian	klar
Polish	jasny
Czech	jasný
Serbo-Croat.	jasan
Hungarian	világos
Finnish	kirkas
Turkish	açık
Indonesian	terang, djernih
Esperanto	klara
Russian	yásni, svyétli
Greek	diavgis'
Arabic	safi
Hebrew	tsach
Yiddish	klor
Japanese	meiryoo
Swahili	dhahiri

226 clergy

French	clergé
Spanish	clero
Italian	clero
Portuguese	clero
Rumanian	cler
German	Geistlichkeit
Dutch	geestelijkheid
Swedish	prästerskap
Danish	gejstlighed
Norwegian	geistlighet
Polish	duchowieństwo
Czech	duchovenstvo
Serbo-Croat.	sveštenstvo
Hungarian	papság
Finnish	papisto
Turkish	rahipler sınıfı
Indonesian	paderi
Esperanto	pastr'aro
Russian	dukhavyénstvo
Greek	kli'ros
Arabic	rigal al-din
Hebrew	kehunah
Yiddish	ksinorz
Japanese	bokushi
Swahili	mapadre

227 climb

French	grimper
Spanish	subir
Italian	arrampicarsi
Portuguese	trepar
Rumanian	urca
German	klettern
Dutch	klimmen
Swedish	klättra
Danish	klatre
Norwegian	klatre
Polish	wspinać
Czech	šplhati
Serbo-Croat.	penjati
Hungarian	mászik
Finnish	kiivetä
Turkish	tırmanmak
Indonesian	naiki
Esperanto	grimpo
Russian	lyést
Greek	anaricho'me
Arabic	yatasalaq
Hebrew	tipes
Yiddish	drapevan
Japanese	yoji-noboru
Swahili	panda

228 clock

French	horloge
Spanish	reloj
Italian	orologio
Portuguese	relógio
Rumanian	ceasornic
German	Uhr
Dutch	klok
Swedish	klocka
Danish	ur
Norwegian	ur
Polish	zegar
Czech	hodiny
Serbo-Croat.	sat
Hungarian	óra
Finnish	kello
Turkish	saat
Indonesian	djam
Esperanto	horloĝo
Russian	chasí
Greek	rolo'i
Arabic	saat hait
Hebrew	schaon
Yiddish	zeiger
Japanese	tokei
Swahili	saa

229 close

French	fermer
Spanish	cerrar
Italian	chiudere
Portuguese	fechar
Rumanian	închide
German	schliessen
Dutch	gesloten
Swedish	stänga
Danish	lukke
Norwegian	lukket
Polish	zamykać
Czech	zavřený
Serbo-Croat.	zatvoriti
Hungarian	elzár
Finnish	sulkea
Turkish	kapamak
Indonesian	tutup
Esperanto	fermi
Russian	zakrít
Greek	klistos'
Arabic	mouqfal
Hebrew	sagur
Yiddish	farmachen
Japanese	shimeru
Swahili	funga

230 clothing

French	vêtements
Spanish	ropa
Italian	vestiario
Portuguese	vestuário
Rumanian	îmbrăcăminte
German	Kleidung
Dutch	kleding
Swedish	kläder
Danish	klædning
Norwegian	kledning
Polish	ubiór
Czech	oděv
Serbo-Croat.	odjelo
Hungarian	ruházat
Finnish	vaatetus
Turkish	elbise, melbusat
Indonesian	pakaian
Esperanto	vestoj
Russian	adyézhda
Greek	rou'cha
Arabic	malabis
Hebrew	malbusch
Yiddish	malbisch
Japanese	irui
Swahili	nguo

231 cloud

French	nuage
Spanish	nube
Italian	nuvola
Portuguese	nuvem
Rumanian	nor
German	Wolke
Dutch	wolk
Swedish	moln
Danish	sky
Norwegian	sky
Polish	chmura
Czech	mrak
Serbo-Croat.	oblak
Hungarian	felhő
Finnish	pilvi
Turkish	bulut
Indonesian	awan
Esperanto	nubo
Russian	óblako
Greek	sin'efon
Arabic	sihab
Hebrew	anan
Yiddish	volken
Japanese	kumo
Swahili	wingu

232 clove

French	clou de girofle
Spanish	clavo
Italian	chiodo di garofano
Portuguese	cravo da India
Rumanian	cuişor
German	Gewürznelke
Dutch	kruidnagel
Swedish	kryddnejlika
Danish	kryddernellike
Norwegian	kryddernellik
Polish	goździk korzenny
Czech	kořeni
Serbo-Croat.	karanfilič
Hungarian	szegfűszeg
Finnish	mausteneilikka
Turkish	bahar karanfil
Indonesian	tjengkih
Esperanto	kariofilo
Russian	gvazdíka
Greek	moschokar'fi
Arabic	zir qorounfoul
Hebrew	karpol
Yiddish	gozdiki
Japanese	chooji
Swahili	karafuu

233 clover

French	trèfle
Spanish	trébol
Italian	trifoglio
Portuguese	trevo
Rumanian	trifoi
German	Klee
Dutch	klaver
Swedish	klöver
Danish	kløver
Norwegian	kløver
Polish	koniczyna
Czech	jetel
Serbo-Croat.	detelina
Hungarian	lóhere
Finnish	apila
Turkish	yonca
Indonesian	rumput
Esperanto	trifolio
Russian	klyéver
Greek	trifil'li
Arabic	nfala
Hebrew	schilaschon
Yiddish	konishine
Japanese	oranda-renge
Swahili	namna ya maua

234 coal

French	charbon
Spanish	carbón
Italian	carbone
Portuguese	carvão
Rumanian	cărbune
German	Kohle
Dutch	steenkool
Swedish	kol
Danish	kul
Norwegian	kull
Polish	węgiel
Czech	uhlí
Serbo-Croat.	ugalj
Hungarian	szén
Finnish	hiili
Turkish	kömür
Indonesian	arang batu
Esperanto	karbo
Russian	úgol
Greek	kar'vouno
Arabic	fahm
Hebrew	pecham
Yiddish	keulen
Japanese	sekitan
Swahili	makaa ya mawe

235 coat

French	manteau
Spanish	chaqueta
Italian	giacca
Portuguese	casaco
Rumanian	palton
German	Mantel
Dutch	jas
Swedish	rock
Danish	frakke
Norwegian	frakk
Polish	płaszcz
Czech	kabát
Serbo-Croat.	kaput
Hungarian	kabát
Finnish	takki
Turkish	palto
Indonesian	djas, mantel
Esperanto	palto
Russian	paltó
Greek	palto'
Arabic	mitaf
Hebrew	meiel
Yiddish	rok
Japanese	kooto
Swahili	koti

236 cockroach

French	cafard
Spanish	cucaracha
Italian	scarafaggio
Portuguese	barata
Rumanian	şvab
German	Schabe
Dutch	kakkerlak
Swedish	kackerlacka
Danish	kakerlak
Norwegian	kakerlakk
Polish	karaluch
Czech	šváb
Serbo-Croat.	buba švaba
Hungarian	swabbogar
Finnish	torakka
Turkish	hamamböceği
Indonesian	lipas
Esperanto	blato
Russian	tarakán
Greek	katsari'da
Arabic	sirsir
Hebrew	chipuchit abayit
Yiddish	preiss
Japanese	aburamushi
Swahili	mende

237 cocoa

French	cacao
Spanish	cacao
Italian	cacao
Portuguese	cacau
Rumanian	cacao
German	Kakao
Dutch	cacao
Swedish	kakao
Danish	kakao
Norwegian	kakao
Polish	kakao
Czech	kakao
Serbo-Croat.	kakao
Hungarian	kakaó
Finnish	kaakao
Turkish	kakao
Indonesian	tjoklat bubuk
Esperanto	kakao
Russian	kakáo
Greek	kaka'o
Arabic	kakawe
Hebrew	kako
Yiddish	kako
Japanese	kokoa
Swahili	mbegu za mti cacao

238 codfish

French	morue
Spanish	bacalao
Italian	merluzzo
Portuguese	bacalhau
Rumanian	moruă
German	Kabeljau
Dutch	kabeljauw
Swedish	torsk
Danish	torsk
Norwegian	torsk
Polish	dorsz
Czech	treska
Serbo-Croat.	bakalar
Hungarian	tőkehal
Finnish	turska
Turkish	morina balıgı
Indonesian	ikan laut
Esperanto	moruo
Russian	treská
Greek	bakalia'ros
Arabic	hout
Hebrew	iltit
Yiddish	schtokfisch
Japanese	tara
Swahili	namna ya samaki

239 coffee

French	café
Spanish	café
Italian	caffè
Portuguese	café
Rumanian	cafea
German	Kaffee
Dutch	koffie
Swedish	kaffe
Danish	kaffe
Norwegian	kaffe
Polish	kawa
Czech	káva
Serbo-Croat.	kafa
Hungarian	kávé
Finnish	kahvi
Turkish	kahve
Indonesian	kopi
Esperanto	kafo
Russian	kófe
Greek	kafes'
Arabic	qahwa
Hebrew	kavah
Yiddish	kave
Japanese	koohii
Swahili	kahawa

240 cold

French	froid
Spanish	frío
Italian	freddo
Portuguese	frio
Rumanian	rece
German	kalt
Dutch	koud
Swedish	kall
Danish	kold
Norwegian	kald
Polish	zimno
Czech	studený
Serbo-Croat.	hladan
Hungarian	hideg
Finnish	kylmä
Turkish	soğuk
Indonesian	dingin
Esperanto	mal'varma
Russian	khalódni
Greek	kri'o
Arabic	barid
Hebrew	kar
Yiddish	kalt
Japanese	samui
Swahili	baridi

241 collar

French	col
Spanish	cuello
Italian	colletto
Portuguese	colarinho
Rumanian	guler
German	Kragen
Dutch	boord
Swedish	krage
Danish	flip
Norwegian	krage
Polish	kołnierz
Czech	límec
Serbo-Croat.	ovratnik
Hungarian	gallér
Finnish	kaulus
Turkish	yaka
Indonesian	kerah
Esperanto	kol'umo
Russian	varatník
Greek	kolla'ro
Arabic	yaqa
Hebrew	tsavaron
Yiddish	kolner
Japanese	eri
Swahili	ukosi

242 color

French	couleur
Spanish	color
Italian	colore
Portuguese	côr
Rumanian	culoare
German	Farbe
Dutch	kleur
Swedish	färg
Danish	farve
Norwegian	farge
Polish	kolor
Czech	barva
Serbo-Croat.	boja
Hungarian	szín
Finnish	väri
Turkish	renk
Indonesian	warna
Esperanto	farbo
Russian	tsvyet
Greek	chro'ma
Arabic	lawn
Hebrew	tzeva
Yiddish	farb
Japanese	iro
Swahili	rangi

243 comb

French	peigne
Spanish	peine
Italian	pettine
Portuguese	pente
Rumanian	pieptene
German	Kamm
Dutch	kam
Swedish	kam
Danish	kam
Norwegian	kam
Polish	grzebień
Czech	hřeben
Serbo-Croat.	česalj
Hungarian	fésü
Finnish	kampa
Turkish	tarak
Indonesian	sisir
Esperanto	komb'ilo
Russian	gryében
Greek	kte'na
Arabic	misht
Hebrew	masrek
Yiddish	kam
Japanese	kushi
Swahili	kitana

244 come

French	venir
Spanish	venir
Italian	venire
Portuguese	vir
Rumanian	veni
German	kommen
Dutch	kom
Swedish	komma
Danish	komme
Norwegian	komme
Polish	przyjść
Czech	přijíti
Serbo-Croat.	doći
Hungarian	jön
Finnish	tulla
Turkish	gelmek
Indonesian	datang
Esperanto	veni
Russian	prikhadít
Greek	er'chome
Arabic	yahdir, yati
Hebrew	ba
Yiddish	kumen
Japanese	kuru
Swahili	ja

245 comfort

French	confort
Spanish	confort
Italian	conforto
Portuguese	comfôrto
Rumanian	confort
German	Bequemlichkeit
Dutch	gemak
Swedish	bekvämlighet
Danish	bekvemmelighed
Norwegian	bekvemmelighet
Polish	wygoda
Czech	pohodlí
Serbo-Croat.	udobnost
Hungarian	kényelem
Finnish	mukavuus
Turkish	rahat
Indonesian	kenikmatan
Esperanto	komforto
Russian	udóbstvo
Greek	a'nesis
Arabic	muwasa
Hebrew	nochiyut
Yiddish	vigodne
Japanese	nagusame
Swahili	raha

246 compartment

French	compartiment
Spanish	compartimiento
Italian	compartimento
Portuguese	compartimento
Rumanian	compartiment
German	Abteil
Dutch	afdeling
Swedish	kupé
Danish	kupé
Norwegian	avdeling
Polish	przedział
Czech	odděleni
Serbo-Croat.	odeljenje
Hungarian	szakasz
Finnish	osasto
Turkish	bölme
Indonesian	pangsa, bagian
Esperanto	fako
Russian	atdelyéniye
Greek	diame'risma
Arabic	divan
Hebrew	machalakah
Yiddish	ubteil
Japanese	kyakushitsu
Swahili	kijumba

247 competition

French	concurrence
Spanish	competencia
Italian	competizione
Portuguese	competição
Rumanian	concurenţă
German	Konkurrenz
Dutch	concurrentie
Swedish	konkurrens
Danish	konkurrence
Norwegian	konkurranse
Polish	konkurencja
Czech	soutěž
Serbo-Croat.	takmičenje
Hungarian	verseny
Finnish	kilpailu
Turkish	müsabaka
Indonesian	saingan
Esperanto	konkuro
Russian	kankuryéntsiya
Greek	sinagonismos'
Arabic	mousabaqa
Hebrew	tacharut
Yiddish	konkurents
Japanese	kyoosoo
Swahili	shindano

248 concert

French	concert
Spanish	concierto
Italian	concerto
Portuguese	concêrto
Rumanian	concert
German	Konzert
Dutch	concert
Swedish	konsert
Danish	koncert
Norwegian	konsert
Polish	koncert
Czech	koncert
Serbo-Croat.	koncert
Hungarian	hangverseny
Finnish	konsertti
Turkish	konser
Indonesian	konsér
Esperanto	koncerto
Russian	kantsért
Greek	synavli'a
Arabic	firqa mousiqiya
Hebrew	neschef
Yiddish	kontsert
Japanese	konsaato
Swahili	ngoma

249 condition

French	condition
Spanish	condición
Italian	condizione
Portuguese	condição
Rumanian	condiţie
German	Bedingung
Dutch	staat
Swedish	betinga
Danish	betingelse
Norwegian	vilkår
Polish	warunek
Czech	podmínka
Serbo-Croat.	uslov
Hungarian	feltétel
Finnish	ehto
Turkish	şart
Indonesian	sjarat
Esperanto	kondiĉo
Russian	uslóviye
Greek	o'ros
Arabic	shart
Hebrew	tnai
Yiddish	tnay
Japanese	jooken
Swahili	sharti

250 connection

French	connexion
Spanish	conexión
Italian	connessione
Portuguese	conexão
Rumanian	legătură
German	Verbindung
Dutch	verbinding
Swedish	förbindelse
Danish	forbindelse
Norwegian	forbindelse
Polish	związek
Czech	spojení
Serbo-Croat.	veza
Hungarian	összeköttetés
Finnish	yhdistys
Turkish	bağlantı
Indonesian	hubungan, koneksi
Esperanto	kun'ig'ilo
Russian	svyas
Greek	sche'sis
Arabic	sila
Hebrew	chibur
Yiddish	farbindung
Japanese	kwankei
Swahili	kiungo

251 consulate

French	consulat
Spanish	consulado
Italian	consolato
Portuguese	consulado
Rumanian	consulat
German	Konsulat
Dutch	consulaat
Swedish	konsulat
Danish	konsulat
Norwegian	konsulat
Polish	konsulat
Czech	konzulát
Serbo-Croat.	konzulat
Hungarian	konzulátus
Finnish	konsulaatti
Turkish	konsolosluk
Indonesian	konsolat
Esperanto	konsul'ejo
Russian	kónsulstvo
Greek	proxeni'on
Arabic	qounsoliya
Hebrew	konsul
Yiddish	konsulat
Japanese	ryoojikwan
Swahili	cheo cha balozi

252 control

French	contrôle
Spanish	control
Italian	controllo
Portuguese	revisão
Rumanian	control
German	Kontrolle
Dutch	controle
Swedish	kontroll
Danish	kontrol
Norwegian	kontroll
Polish	kontrola
Czech	kontrola
Serbo-Croat.	nadzor
Hungarian	ellenőrzés
Finnish	tarkastus
Turkish	kontrol
Indonesian	pengawasan
Esperanto	reg'ado
Russian	kontról
Greek	e'lenchos
Arabic	mouragaa, mouraqaba
Hebrew	bakarah
Yiddish	kontrol
Japanese	choosetsu
Swahili	usimamizi

253 conversation

French	conversation
Spanish	conversación
Italian	conversazione
Portuguese	conversa
Rumanian	conversaţie
German	Gespräch
Dutch	conversatie
Swedish	samtal
Danish	konversation
Norwegian	samtale
Polish	rozmowa
Czech	rozmluva
Serbo-Croat.	razgovor
Hungarian	beszelgetés
Finnish	keskustelu
Turkish	konuşma
Indonesian	pertijakapan
Esperanto	konversacio
Russian	razgavór
Greek	kouven'ta
Arabic	mouhadatsa
Hebrew	sichah
Yiddish	geschprech
Japanese	kwaiwa
Swahili	mazungumzo

254 cook

French	cuisinier
Spanish	cocinero
Italian	cuoco
Portuguese	cozinheiro
Rumanian	bucătar
German	Koch
Dutch	kok
Swedish	kock
Danish	kok
Norwegian	kokk
Polish	kucharz
Czech	kuchař
Serbo-Croat.	kuvar
Hungarian	szakács
Finnish	keittäjä
Turkish	aşçıbaşı
Indonesian	koki
Esperanto	kuiristo
Russian	póvar
Greek	ma'yiros
Arabic	tabbach
Hebrew	tabach
Yiddish	kocher
Japanese	ryoorichoo
Swahili	mpishi

255 copper

French	cuivre
Spanish	cobre
Italian	rame
Portuguese	cobre
Rumanian	aramă
German	Kupfer
Dutch	rood koper
Swedish	koppar
Danish	kobber
Norwegian	kopper
Polish	miedź
Czech	měd'
Serbo-Croat.	bakar
Hungarian	réz
Finnish	kupari
Turkish	bakır
Indonesian	tembaga
Esperanto	kupro
Russian	myet
Greek	chalkos'
Arabic	nihas
Hebrew	nechoschet
Yiddish	kuper
Japanese	doo
Swahili	shaba nyekundu

256 copy

French	copie
Spanish	copia
Italian	copia
Portuguese	cópia
Rumanian	copie
German	Abschrift
Dutch	afschrift
Swedish	kopia
Danish	afskrift
Norwegian	avskrift
Polish	odpis
Czech	opis
Serbo-Croat.	kopija
Hungarian	másolat
Finnish	jäljennös
Turkish	kopya, nüsha
Indonesian	salinan
Esperanto	kopio
Russian	kópiya
Greek	anti'grafon
Arabic	nouscha
Hebrew	hetek
Yiddish	kopje
Japanese	utsushi
Swahili	nakili

257 corkscrew

French	tire-bouchon
Spanish	sacacorchos
Italian	cavaturaccioli
Portuguese	saca-rôlhas
Rumanian	tirbuşon
German	Korkzieher
Dutch	kurketrekker
Swedish	korkskruv
Danish	proptrækker
Norwegian	korketrekker
Polish	korkociag
Czech	vývrtka
Serbo-Croat.	vadičep
Hungarian	dugóhúzó
Finnish	korkkiruuvi
Turkish	tirbuşon
Indonesian	kotrék
Esperanto	kork'tir'ilo
Russian	shtópor
Greek	anichti'ri
Arabic	barrima
Hebrew	machlets
Yiddish	korkentsieher
Japanese	sen'nuki
Swahili	kizibuo

258 corn (maize)

French	maïs
Spanish	maíz
Italian	granturco
Portuguese	milho
Rumanian	porumb
German	Mais
Dutch	maïs
Swedish	majs
Danish	majs
Norwegian	mais
Polish	kukurydza
Czech	kukuřice
Serbo-Croat.	kukuruz
Hungarian	kukorica
Finnish	maissi
Turkish	mısır
Indonesian	djagung
Esperanto	maizo
Russian	kukurúza
Greek	araposi'ti
Arabic	tzura
Hebrew	tiras
Yiddish	kugeruts
Japanese	toomorokoshi
Swahili	mahindi

259 correct

French	exact
Spanish	correcto
Italian	corretto
Portuguese	correto
Rumanian	corect
German	richtig
Dutch	correct
Swedish	riktig
Danish	korrekt
Norwegian	riktig
Polish	poprawny
Czech	správný
Serbo-Croat.	tačan
Hungarian	helyes
Finnish	oikea
Turkish	doğru
Indonesian	benar, betul
Esperanto	korekta
Russian	právilni
Greek	sostos'
Arabic	madbout
Hebrew	nachon
Yiddish	richtik
Japanese	tadashii
Swahili	sahihi

260 cost

French	coût
Spanish	coste
Italian	costo
Portuguese	custo
Rumanian	pret
German	Kosten
Dutch	kosten
Swedish	kostnad
Danish	amkostning
Norwegian	pris
Polish	koszt
Czech	cena
Serbo-Croat.	koštati
Hungarian	költség
Finnish	hinta
Turkish	fiyat
Indonesian	belandja, harga
Esperanto	kosto
Russian	raskhódi
Greek	kos'tos
Arabic	tsaman
Hebrew	hotsaha
Yiddish	kosten
Japanese	hiyoo
Swahili	bei

261 costly

French	coûteux
Spanish	costoso
Italian	costoso
Portuguese	dispendioso
Rumanian	scump
German	kostspielig
Dutch	kostbaar
Swedish	kostbar
Danish	kostbar
Norwegian	kostbar
Polish	kosztowny
Czech	nákladny
Serbo-Croat.	skup
Hungarian	költséges
Finnish	kallis
Turkish	pahalı
Indonesian	harganja, mahal
Esperanto	kosta
Russian	daragóy
Greek	akrivon'
Arabic	ghali
Hebrew	yakar
Yiddish	teier
Japanese	kooka na
Swahili	ghali

262 cotton

French	coton
Spanish	algodón
Italian	cotone
Portuguese	algodão
Rumanian	bumbac
German	Baumwolle
Dutch	katoen
Swedish	bomull
Danish	bomuld
Norwegian	bomull
Polish	bawełna
Czech	bavlna
Serbo-Croat.	pamuk
Hungarian	pamut
Finnish	puuvilla
Turkish	pamuk
Indonesian	kapan
Esperanto	kotono
Russian	khlópok
Greek	vamva'ki
Arabic	qoutn
Hebrew	tsemer gefen
Yiddish	bavel
Japanese	momen
Swahili	pamba

263 couch

French	couche
Spanish	diván
Italian	divano
Portuguese	sofá
Rumanian	canapea
German	Chaiselongue
Dutch	bank
Swedish	schäslong
Danish	chaiselongue
Norwegian	sjeselong
Polish	kanapa
Czech	pohovka
Serbo-Croat.	divan
Hungarian	kerevet
Finnish	makuusija
Turkish	kanepe
Indonesian	randjang
Esperanto	kanapo
Russian	kushétka
Greek	sofas'
Arabic	arika
Hebrew	sapah
Yiddish	kanape
Japanese	nagaisu
Swahili	kitanda

264 cough

French	tousser
Spanish	toser
Italian	tossire
Portuguese	tossir
Rumanian	tuşi
German	husten
Dutch	hoesten
Swedish	hosta
Danish	hoste
Norwegian	hoste
Polish	kaszleć
Czech	kašlati
Serbo-Croat.	kašljati
Hungarian	köhög
Finnish	yskiä
Turkish	öksürmek
Indonesian	batuk
Esperanto	tusi
Russian	káshlyat
Greek	vi'cho
Arabic	yasoul
Hebrew	hischtael
Yiddish	hiessen
Japanese	seki wo suru
Swahili	kohoa

265 count

French	compter
Spanish	contar
Italian	contare
Portuguese	contar
Rumanian	socoti
German	zählen
Dutch	tellen
Swedish	räkna
Danish	regne
Norwegian	regne
Polish	liczyć
Czech	počitati
Serbo-Croat.	računati
Hungarian	számol
Finnish	laskea
Turkish	saymak
Indonesian	hitung
Esperanto	kalkuli
Russian	schitát
Greek	metro'
Arabic	yahsib
Hebrew	mana
Yiddish	tsehlen
Japanese	kazoeru
Swahili	hesabu

266 country

French	pays
Spanish	país
Italian	paese
Portuguese	país
Rumanian	ţară
German	Land
Dutch	land
Swedish	land
Danish	land
Norwegian	land
Polish	kraj
Czech	země
Serbo-Croat.	zemlja
Hungarian	vidék
Finnish	maa
Turkish	memleket
Indonesian	negeri
Esperanto	lando
Russian	straná
Greek	patri'da
Arabic	balad
Hebrew	erets
Yiddish	medineh
Japanese	kuni
Swahili	nchi

267 courage

French	courage
Spanish	coraje
Italian	coraggio
Portuguese	coragem
Rumanian	curaj
German	Mut
Dutch	moed
Swedish	mod
Danish	mod
Norwegian	mot
Polish	odwaga
Czech	odvaha
Serbo-Croat.	hrabrost
Hungarian	bátorság
Finnish	rohkeus
Turkish	cesaret
Indonesian	keberanian
Esperanto	kuraĝo
Russian	múzhestvo
Greek	tha'ros
Arabic	shagaa
Hebrew	omets
Yiddish	mut
Japanese	yuuki
Swahili	ushujaa

268 cousin

French	cousin
Spanish	primo
Italian	cugino
Portuguese	primo
Rumanian	văr
German	Vetter
Dutch	neef, nicht
Swedish	kusin
Danish	fætter
Norwegian	fetter
Polish	kuzyn
Czech	bratránek
Serbo-Croat.	sestrić
Hungarian	unokafivér
Finnish	serkku
Turkish	kuzen
Indonesian	saudara sepupu
Esperanto	kuzo
Russian	dvayúrni brat
Greek	exa'delfos
Arabic	ibn am
Hebrew	dodan
Yiddish	schvesterkind
Japanese	itoko
Swahili	binamu

269 cow

French	vache
Spanish	vaca
Italian	vacca
Portuguese	vaca
Rumanian	vacă
German	Kuh
Dutch	koe
Swedish	ko
Danish	ko
Norwegian	ku
Polish	krowa
Czech	kráva
Serbo-Croat.	krava
Hungarian	tehén
Finnish	lehmä
Turkish	inek
Indonesian	sapi, lembu
Esperanto	bov'ino
Russian	karóva
Greek	ayela'da
Arabic	baqara
Hebrew	parah
Yiddish	kuh
Japanese	meushi
Swahili	ng'ombe jike

270 cracker

French	bisquit
Spanish	galleta
Italian	biscotto
Portuguese	biscoito
Rumanian	biscuit
German	Keks
Dutch	biscuitje
Swedish	käx
Danish	kiks
Norwegian	kjeks
Polish	sucharek
Czech	keks
Serbo-Croat.	dvopek
Hungarian	keksz
Finnish	keksi
Turkish	bisküit
Indonesian	biskuit
Esperanto	biskvito
Russian	sukhár
Greek	bisko'to
Arabic	baskawit
Hebrew	rakik
Yiddish	kucharki
Japanese	kurakkaa
Swahili	biskuti

271 cranberry

French	airelle
Spanish	arándano
Italian	bacco di mortella
Portuguese	arando
Rumanian	merişoara
German	Preiselbeere
Dutch	veenbes
Swedish	tranbär
Danish	tranebær
Norwegian	tranebær
Polish	borówka czerwona
Czech	brusinka
Serbo-Croat.	brusnica
Hungarian	vörös áfonya
Finnish	karpalo
Turkish	kızılcik
Indonesian	kranbai
Esperanto	oksikoko
Russian	klyúkva
Greek	kou'maron
Arabic	tout barri
Hebrew	kruchit
Yiddish	dzuravine
Japanese	tsurukoke-momo
Swahili	namna ya tunda

272 crane

French	grue
Spanish	grúa
Italian	gru
Portuguese	guindaste
Rumanian	macara
German	Kran
Dutch	kraan
Swedish	lyftkran
Danish	kran
Norwegian	heisekran
Polish	kran
Czech	jeřáb
Serbo-Croat.	dizalica
Hungarian	daru
Finnish	nosturi
Turkish	vinç
Indonesian	mesin dérék-dérék
Esperanto	lev'maŝino
Russian	kran
Greek	yeranos'
Arabic	yashtahi
Hebrew	manof
Yiddish	oifheiber
Japanese	kijuuki
Swahili	winchi

273 cream

French	crème
Spanish	crema
Italian	crema
Portuguese	creme
Rumanian	smîntînă
German	Sahne
Dutch	room
Swedish	grädde
Danish	fløde
Norwegian	fløte
Polish	śmietana
Czech	smetana
Serbo-Croat.	kajmak
Hungarian	tejszín
Finnish	kerma
Turkish	kaymak
Indonesian	kepala susu
Esperanto	kremo
Russian	slífki
Greek	kre'ma
Arabic	qishda
Hebrew	schammenet
Yiddish	smetene
Japanese	kuriimu
Swahili	maziwa ya mtindi

274 crib

French	crèche
Spanish	camita de niño
Italian	culla
Portuguese	berço
Rumanian	pat de copil
German	Krippe, Wiege
Dutch	krib
Swedish	krubba
Danish	krybbe
Norwegian	krybbe
Polish	kołyska
Czech	jesle
Serbo-Croat.	jasle
Hungarian	jászol
Finnish	seimi
Turkish	yemlik
Indonesian	lawak-lawak
Esperanto	lit'eto
Russian	kalibyél
Greek	krevva'ti pedion'
Arabic	mahd
Hebrew	eres
Yiddish	vieg
Japanese	wakutsuki shindai
Swahili	kitanda kidogo

275 crime

French	crime
Spanish	crimen
Italian	delitto
Portuguese	crime
Rumanian	crimă
German	Verbrechen
Dutch	misdaad
Swedish	brott
Danish	forbrydelse
Norwegian	forbrytelse
Polish	zbrodnia
Czech	zločin
Serbo-Croat.	zločin
Hungarian	bűntény
Finnish	rikos
Turkish	cinayet
Indonesian	kedjahatan
Esperanto	krimo
Russian	prestuplyéniye
Greek	en'glima
Arabic	garjma
Hebrew	pescha
Yiddish	ferbrechen
Japanese	hanzai
Swahili	taksiri

276 cry

French	crier
Spanish	gritar
Italian	gridare
Portuguese	gritar
Rumanian	striga
German	schreien
Dutch	schreeuwen
Swedish	skrika
Danish	skrige
Norwegian	skrike
Polish	krzyczeć
Czech	křičeti
Serbo-Croat.	vikati
Hungarian	kiált
Finnish	huutaa
Turkish	bağırmak
Indonesian	seru, teriak
Esperanto	krii
Russian	krichát
Greek	kle'o
Arabic	yousih
Hebrew	tsaak
Yiddish	schreien
Japanese	naku
Swahili	lia

277 cucumber

French	concombre
Spanish	pepino
Italian	cetriolo
Portuguese	pepino
Rumanian	castravete
German	Gurke
Dutch	komkommer
Swedish	gurka
Danish	agurk
Norwegian	agurk
Polish	ogórek
Czech	okurka
Serbo-Croat.	krastavac
Hungarian	uborka
Finnish	kurkku
Turkish	hıyar
Indonesian	entimum
Esperanto	kukumo
Russian	aguryéts
Greek	angou'ri
Arabic	chiar
Hebrew	kischu
Yiddish	ugerke
Japanese	kyuuri
Swahili	tango

278 cup

French	tasse
Spanish	taza
Italian	tazza
Portuguese	xicara
Rumanian	ceaşcă
German	Tasse
Dutch	kopje
Swedish	kopp
Danish	kop
Norwegian	kopp
Polish	filiźanka
Czech	šálek
Serbo-Croat.	šalica
Hungarian	csésze
Finnish	kuppi
Turkish	fincan
Indonesian	mangkok
Esperanto	taso
Russian	cháshka
Greek	flitza'ni
Arabic	fingan
Hebrew	sefel
Yiddish	teppalle
Japanese	koppu
Swahili	kikombe

279 curtain

French	rideau
Spanish	cortina
Italian	tendina
Portuguese	cortina
Rumanian	cortină
German	Vorhang
Dutch	gordijn
Swedish	gardin
Danish	gardin
Norwegian	gardin
Polish	firanka
Czech	záclona
Serbo-Croat.	zavjesa
Hungarian	függöny
Finnish	verho
Turkish	perde
Indonesian	tirai, tabir
Esperanto	kurteno
Russian	sánavyes
Greek	kourti'na
Arabic	sayyara
Hebrew	parochet
Yiddish	forhang
Japanese	kaaten
Swahili	pazia

280 custom house

French	douane
Spanish	aduana
Italian	dogana
Portuguese	alfândega
Rumanian	vamal
German	Zollhaus
Dutch	douane
Swedish	tullhus
Danish	tolbod
Norwegian	tollbod
Polish	celny
Czech	celnice
Serbo-Croat.	carinarnica
Hungarian	vámház
Finnish	tullikamari
Turkish	gümrük
Indonesian	pebéan
Esperanto	dogano
Russian	tamózhnya
Greek	teloni'on
Arabic	goumrouk
Hebrew	meches
Yiddish	tsollhois
Japanese	zeikwan
Swahili	forodha

281 cut

French	couper
Spanish	cortar
Italian	tagliare
Portuguese	cortar
Rumanian	tăia
German	schneiden
Dutch	snijden
Swedish	skära
Danish	skære
Norwegian	skjære
Polish	ciąć
Czech	řezati
Serbo-Croat.	rezati
Hungarian	vág
Finnish	leikata
Turkish	kesmek
Indonesian	potong
Esperanto	tranĉi
Russian	ryésat
Greek	ko'vo
Arabic	yaqtaa
Hebrew	karas
Yiddish	schneiden
Japanese	kiru
Swahili	kata

282 damage

French	dommage
Spanish	daño
Italian	danno
Portuguese	dano
Rumanian	pagubă
German	Schaden
Dutch	schade
Swedish	skada
Danish	skade
Norwegian	skade
Polish	szkoda
Czech	škoda
Serbo-Croat.	šteta
Hungarian	kár
Finnish	vahinko
Turkish	zarar
Indonesian	rugi
Esperanto	difekto
Russian	vryét
Greek	zimi'a
Arabic	talaf
Hebrew	nesek
Yiddish	schoden
Japanese	songai
Swahili	hasara

283 dance

French	danse
Spanish	baile
Italian	danza
Portuguese	dança
Rumanian	dansa
German	Tanz
Dutch	dans
Swedish	dans
Danish	dans
Norwegian	dans
Polish	taniec
Czech	tanec
Serbo-Croat.	ples
Hungarian	tánc
Finnish	tanssi
Turkish	dans
Indonesian	tari, dangsa
Esperanto	danco
Russian	tánets
Greek	choros'
Arabic	raqs
Hebrew	rikud
Yiddish	tants
Japanese	dansu
Swahili	ngoma

284 danger

French	danger
Spanish	peligro
Italian	pericolo
Portuguese	perigo
Rumanian	primejdie
German	Gefahr
Dutch	gevaar
Swedish	fara
Danish	fare
Norwegian	fare
Polish	niebezpieczeństwo
Czech	nebezpečí
Serbo-Croat.	opasnost
Hungarian	veszély
Finnish	vaara
Turkish	tehlike
Indonesian	bahaja
Esperanto	danĝero
Russian	apásnost
Greek	kin'dinos
Arabic	chatar
Hebrew	sakanah
Yiddish	ssekune
Japanese	kiken
Swahili	hatari

285 dark

French	obscur
Spanish	obscuro
Italian	oscuro
Portuguese	escuro
Rumanian	întunecat
German	dunkel
Dutch	donker
Swedish	mörk
Danish	mørk
Norwegian	mørk
Polish	ciemno
Czech	tmavý
Serbo-Croat.	taman
Hungarian	sötét
Finnish	tumma, pimeä
Turkish	karanlık
Indonesian	gelap
Esperanto	mal'luma
Russian	tyómni
Greek	skotinos'
Arabic	muzlim
Hebrew	choschech
Yiddish	tunkel
Japanese	kurai
Swahili	-a giza

286 date

French	datte
Spanish	dátil
Italian	dattero
Portuguese	tâmara
Rumanian	dată
German	Dattel
Dutch	dadel
Swedish	dadel
Danish	daddel
Norwegian	daddel
Polish	daktyl
Czech	datle
Serbo-Croat.	datulja
Hungarian	datolya
Finnish	taateli
Turkish	hurma
Indonesian	kurma
Esperanto	daktilo
Russian	fínik
Greek	imeromini'a
Arabic	tarich
Hebrew	tamar
Yiddish	teitel
Japanese	hizuke
Swahili	tende

287 daughter

French	fille
Spanish	hija
Italian	figlia
Portuguese	filha
Rumanian	fiică
German	Tochter
Dutch	dochter
Swedish	dotter
Danish	datter
Norwegian	datter
Polish	córka
Czech	dcera
Serbo-Croat.	kći
Hungarian	leány
Finnish	tytär
Turkish	kiz
Indonesian	puteri
Esperanto	fil'ino
Russian	doch
Greek	ko'ri
Arabic	ibna
Hebrew	bat
Yiddish	tochter
Japanese	musume
Swahili	binti

288 day

French	jour
Spanish	día
Italian	giorno
Portuguese	dia
Rumanian	zi
German	Tag
Dutch	dag
Swedish	dag
Danish	dag
Norwegian	dag
Polish	dzień
Czech	den
Serbo-Croat.	dan
Hungarian	nap
Finnish	päivä
Turkish	gün
Indonesian	hari
Esperanto	tago
Russian	dyen
Greek	ime'ra
Arabic	youm
Hebrew	yom
Yiddish	tog
Japanese	hi
Swahili	siku

289 deaf

French	sourd
Spanish	sordo
Italian	sordo
Portuguese	surdo
Rumanian	surd
German	taub
Dutch	doof
Swedish	döv
Danish	døv
Norwegian	døv
Polish	głuchy
Czech	hluchý
Serbo-Croat.	gluv
Hungarian	süket
Finnish	kuuro
Turkish	sağır
Indonesian	tuli
Esperanto	surda
Russian	glukhóy
Greek	koufos'
Arabic	assam
Hebrew	cheresch
Yiddish	toib
Japanese	tsunbo no
Swahili	-ziwi

290 death

French	mort
Spanish	muerte
Italian	morte
Portuguese	morte
Rumanian	moarte
German	Tod
Dutch	dood
Swedish	död
Danish	død
Norwegian	død
Polish	śmierć
Czech	smrt
Serbo-Croat.	smrt
Hungarian	halál
Finnish	kuolema
Turkish	ölüm
Indonesian	mati
Esperanto	morto
Russian	smyert
Greek	tha'natos
Arabic	mawt
Hebrew	mavet
Yiddish	toit
Japanese	shi
Swahili	kifo

291 debt

French	dette
Spanish	deuda
Italian	debito
Portuguese	dívida
Rumanian	datorie
German	Schulden
Dutch	schuld
Swedish	skuld
Danish	skylda
Norwegian	gjeld
Polish	dług
Czech	dluh
Serbo-Croat.	dug
Hungarian	adósság
Finnish	velka
Turkish	borç
Indonesian	utang
Esperanto	ŝuldo
Russian	dolk
Greek	chre'os
Arabic	dayn
Hebrew	chovah
Yiddish	choif
Japanese	shakkin
Swahili	deni

292 December

French	décembre
Spanish	diciembre
Italian	dicembre
Portuguese	dezembro
Rumanian	decembrie
German	Dezember
Dutch	December
Swedish	december
Danish	december
Norwegian	desember
Polish	grudzień
Czech	prosinec
Serbo-Croat.	prosinac
Hungarian	december
Finnish	joulukuu
Turkish	aralık
Indonesian	Desémber
Esperanto	Decembro
Russian	dekábr
Greek	Dekem'vrios
Arabic	disembar
Hebrew	detsember
Yiddish	detsember
Japanese	juunigwatsu
Swahili	Desemba

293 deep

French	profond
Spanish	hondo
Italian	profondo
Portuguese	fundo
Rumanian	adînc
German	tief
Dutch	diep
Swedish	djup
Danish	dyb
Norwegian	dyp
Polish	głęboki
Czech	hluboký
Serbo-Croat.	dubok
Hungarian	mély
Finnish	syvä
Turkish	derin
Indonesian	dalam
Esperanto	profunda
Russian	glubóki
Greek	vathis'
Arabic	amiq
Hebrew	amok
Yiddish	tief
Japanese	fukai
Swahili	-refu

294 defective

French	défectueux
Spanish	defectuoso
Italian	difettoso
Portuguese	defectivo
Rumanian	defectuos
German	mangelhaft
Dutch	gebrekkig
Swedish	bristfällig
Danish	mangelfuld
Norwegian	mangelfull
Polish	wadliwy
Czech	vadný
Serbo-Croat.	nepotpun
Hungarian	hiányos
Finnish	puutteellinen
Turkish	kusurlu
Indonesian	tjatjat
Esperanto	ne'perfekta
Russian	nedastátochni
Greek	elatomatikos'
Arabic	souab
Hebrew	pagum
Yiddish	felerdig
Japanese	fukwanzen na
Swahili	punguani

295 degree

French	degré
Spanish	grado
Italian	grado
Portuguese	grau
Rumanian	grad
German	Grad
Dutch	rang
Swedish	grad
Danish	grad
Norwegian	grad
Polish	stopień
Czech	stupeň
Serbo-Croat.	stepen
Hungarian	fok
Finnish	aste
Turkish	derece
Indonesian	pangkat
Esperanto	grado
Russian	gráduss
Greek	vathmos'
Arabic	daraga
Hebrew	dargah
Yiddish	grad
Japanese	teido
Swahili	kadiri

296 deliver

French	livrer
Spanish	entregar
Italian	consegnare
Portuguese	entregar
Rumanian	livra
German	liefern
Dutch	leveren
Swedish	överlämna
Danish	levere
Norwegian	levere
Polish	dostawić
Czech	dodávati
Serbo-Croat.	predati
Hungarian	szállít
Finnish	toimittaa
Turkish	teslim etmek
Indonesian	bawa
Esperanto	liveri
Russian	dastávit
Greek	paradi'do
Arabic	yusalim
Hebrew	pada
Yiddish	ibergeben
Japanese	haitatsu suru
Swahili	kabidhi

297 dentist

French	dentiste
Spanish	dentista
Italian	dentista
Portuguese	dentista
Rumanian	dentist
German	Zahnarzt
Dutch	tandarts
Swedish	tandläkare
Danish	tandlæge
Norwegian	tannlæge
Polish	dentysta
Czech	zubní lékař
Serbo-Croat.	zubar
Hungarian	fogorvos
Finnish	hammaslääkäri
Turkish	dişci
Indonesian	doktor gigi
Esperanto	dent'isto
Russian	zubnóy vrach
Greek	ondontoyiatros'
Arabic	tabib asnan
Hebrew	schinan
Yiddish	tsundokter
Japanese	haisha
Swahili	daktari wa meno

298 departure

French	départ
Spanish	salida
Italian	partenza
Portuguese	partida
Rumanian	plecare
German	Abfahrt
Dutch	vertrek
Swedish	avresa
Danish	afrejse
Norwegian	avreise
Polish	odjazd
Czech	odjezd
Serbo-Croat.	polazak
Hungarian	indulás
Finnish	lähtö
Turkish	hareket
Indonesian	berangkat
Esperanto	for'iro
Russian	atyést
Greek	anacho'risis
Arabic	rahil
Hebrew	yetsiah
Yiddish	ubfohren
Japanese	shuppatsu
Swahili	kuondoka

299 desert

French	désert
Spanish	desierto
Italian	deserto
Portuguese	deserto
Rumanian	pustiu
German	Wüste
Dutch	woestijn
Swedish	öken
Danish	ørken
Norwegian	ørken
Polish	pustynia
Czech	poušt'
Serbo-Croat.	pustinja
Hungarian	sivatag
Finnish	autiomaa
Turkish	çöl
Indonesian	pandang pasir
Esperanto	dezerto
Russian	pustínya
Greek	e'rimos
Arabic	sahara
Hebrew	midbar
Yiddish	midber
Japanese	sabaku
Swahili	jangwa

300 dessert

French	dessert
Spanish	postre
Italian	postpasto
Portuguese	sobremesa
Rumanian	desert
German	Nachspeise
Dutch	dessert
Swedish	dessert
Danish	efterret
Norwegian	dessert
Polish	deser
Czech	zákusek
Serbo-Croat.	desert
Hungarian	deszert
Finnish	jälkiruoka
Turkish	yemek sonu
Indonesian	tambul
Esperanto	deserto
Russian	desért
Greek	epidor'pion
Arabic	houlwe
Hebrew	kinuach seudah
Yiddish	tsimes
Japanese	dezaato
Swahili	chakula cha mwisho wa kula

301 diarrhea

French	diarrhée
Spanish	diarrea
Italian	diarrea
Portuguese	diarréia
Rumanian	diaree
German	Durchfall
Dutch	diarrhee
Swedish	diarré
Danish	diarré
Norwegian	diaré
Polish	biegunka
Czech	průjem
Serbo-Croat.	proliv
Hungarian	hasmenés
Finnish	ripuli
Turkish	ıshal
Indonesian	tjiriti
Esperanto	diareo
Russian	panós
Greek	dia'ria
Arabic	ishal
Hebrew	schilschul
Yiddish	durchfal
Japanese	geri
Swahili	tumbo la kuhara

302 dictionary

French	dictionnaire
Spanish	diccionario
Italian	dizionario
Portuguese	dicionário
Rumanian	dictionar
German	Wörterbuch
Dutch	woordenboek
Swedish	ordbok
Danish	ordbog
Norwegian	ordbok
Polish	słownik
Czech	slovník
Serbo-Croat.	rečnik
Hungarian	szótár
Finnish	sanakirja
Turkish	lûgat
Indonesian	kamus
Esperanto	vor'taro
Russian	slavár
Greek	lexikon'
Arabic	qamous
Hebrew	milon
Yiddish	verterbuch
Japanese	jiten
Swahili	kamusi

303 different

French	différent
Spanish	diferente
Italian	differente
Portuguese	diferente
Rumanian	diferit
German	verschieden
Dutch	verschillend
Swedish	olika
Danish	forskellig
Norwegian	forskjellig, ulik
Polish	różny
Czech	různý
Serbo-Croat.	različit
Hungarian	különböző
Finnish	erilainen
Turkish	muhtelif
Indonesian	lain
Esperanto	diversaj
Russian	rázni
Greek	diaforetiko's
Arabic	mouchtalif
Hebrew	nivdal
Yiddish	ferschieden
Japanese	kotonatta
Swahili	mbalimbali

304 digestion

French	digestion
Spanish	digestión
Italian	digestione
Portuguese	digestão
Rumanian	digestie
German	Verdauung
Dutch	spijsvertering
Swedish	matsmältning
Danish	fordøjelse
Norwegian	fordøyelse
Polish	trawienie
Czech	trávení
Serbo-Croat.	probava
Hungarian	emésztés
Finnish	ruoansulatus
Turkish	hazım
Indonesian	pentjernaan
Esperanto	digesto
Russian	pishchevaryéniye
Greek	cho'nefsis
Arabic	hadm
Hebrew	ikul
Yiddish	ferdeien
Japanese	shookwa
Swahili	kazi ya tumbo

305 dining room

French	salle à manger
Spanish	comedor
Italian	sala da pranzo
Portuguese	sala de jantar
Rumanian	sufragerie
German	Speisezimmer
Dutch	eetkamer
Swedish	matsal
Danish	spisestue
Norwegian	spisestue
Polish	jadalnia
Czech	jídelna
Serbo-Croat.	trpezarija
Hungarian	ebédlő
Finnish	ruokasali
Turkish	yemek odası
Indonesian	kamar marken
Esperanto	manĝo'ĉambro
Russian	stalóvaya
Greek	trapezari'a
Arabic	hougrat al. taam
Hebrew	chadar haochel
Yiddish	esstsimer
Japanese	shokudoo
Swahili	chumba cha kulia

306 dinner

French	dîner
Spanish	comida
Italian	pranzo
Portuguese	jantar
Rumanian	masă
German	Mittagessen
Dutch	middagmaal
Swedish	middag
Danish	middagsmad
Norwegian	middag
Polish	obiad
Czech	oběd
Serbo-Croat.	ručak
Hungarian	ebéd
Finnish	päivällinen
Turkish	öğle yemegi
Indonesian	markan malam
Esperanto	manĝo
Russian	abyét
Greek	yev'ma
Arabic	ghatza
Hebrew	aruchah
Yiddish	mittogessen
Japanese	seisan
Swahili	chakula cha jioni

307 direction

French	direction
Spanish	dirección
Italian	direzione
Portuguese	direçao
Rumanian	direcţie
German	Richtung
Dutch	leiding
Swedish	riktning
Danish	retning
Norwegian	retning
Polish	kierunek
Czech	směr
Serbo-Croat.	pravac
Hungarian	irány
Finnish	suunta
Turkish	istikamet
Indonesian	arah
Esperanto	direkto
Russian	napravlyéniye
Greek	katef'thinsis
Arabic	ittigah
Hebrew	hadrachah
Yiddish	richtung
Japanese	hookoo
Swahili	upande

308 dirty

French	sale
Spanish	sucio
Italian	sporco
Portuguese	sujo
Rumanian	murdar
German	schmutzig
Dutch	vies
Swedish	smutsig
Danish	smudsig
Norwegian	siktten
Polish	brudny
Czech	špinavý
Serbo-Croat.	prljav
Hungarian	piszkos
Finnish	likainen
Turkish	kirli
Indonesian	tjemar, kotor
Esperanto	mal'pura
Russian	gryázni
Greek	aka'thartos
Arabic	qatzir
Hebrew	meluchlach
Yiddish	brudne
Japanese	yogoreta
Swahili	-chafu

309 disease

French	maladie
Spanish	enfermedad
Italian	malattia
Portuguese	doença
Rumanian	boală
German	Krankheit
Dutch	ziekte
Swedish	sjukdom
Danish	sygdom
Norwegian	sykdom
Polish	choroba
Czech	nemoc
Serbo-Croat.	bolest
Hungarian	betegség
Finnish	tauti
Turkish	hastalık
Indonesian	penjakit
Esperanto	mal'sano
Russian	balyézn
Greek	aros'tia
Arabic	marad
Hebrew	machalah
Yiddish	krenk
Japanese	byooki
Swahili	ugonjwa

310 dish

French	plat
Spanish	plato
Italian	piatto
Portuguese	prato
Rumanian	farfurie
German	Teller
Dutch	schotel
Swedish	tallrik
Danish	tallerken
Norwegian	tallerken, fat
Polish	talerz
Czech	talíř
Serbo-Croat.	činija
Hungarian	tányér
Finnish	lautanen
Turkish	tabak
Indonesian	pinggan
Esperanto	plado
Russian	taryélka
Greek	pia'to
Arabic	tabaq
Hebrew	tsealachat
Yiddish	schissel
Japanese	sara
Swahili	sahani

311 distance

French	distance
Spanish	distancia
Italian	distanza
Portuguese	distância
Rumanian	distanţă
German	Entfernung
Dutch	afstand
Swedish	avstånd
Danish	afstand
Norwegian	avstand
Polish	odległość
Czech	vzdálenost
Serbo-Croat.	udaljenost
Hungarian	távolság
Finnish	välimatka
Turkish	mesafe
Indonesian	djauh
Esperanto	distanco
Russian	rastayániye
Greek	apo'stasis
Arabic	masafa
Hebrew	merchak
Yiddish	veitkeit
Japanese	kyori
Swahili	urefu

312 document

French	document
Spanish	documento
Italian	documento
Portuguese	documento
Rumanian	document
German	Urkunde
Dutch	document
Swedish	dokument
Danish	dokument
Norwegian	dokument
Polish	dokument
Czech	listina
Serbo-Croat.	dokument
Hungarian	okmány
Finnish	asiakirja
Turkish	vesika
Indonesian	dokumen
Esperanto	dokumento
Russian	dakumyént
Greek	e'ngrafon
Arabic	watsiqa
Hebrew	teudah
Yiddish	dokument
Japanese	shorui
Swahili	hati

313 dog

French	chien
Spanish	perro
Italian	cane
Portuguese	cão
Rumanian	cîine
German	Hund
Dutch	hond
Swedish	hund
Danish	hund
Norwegian	hund
Polish	pies
Czech	pes
Serbo-Croat.	pas
Hungarian	kutya
Finnish	koira
Turkish	köpek
Indonesian	andjing
Esperanto	hundo
Russian	sabáka
Greek	ski'los
Arabic	kalb
Hebrew	kelev
Yiddish	hunt
Japanese	inu
Swahili	mbwa

314 donkey

French	âne
Spanish	burro
Italian	asino
Portuguese	burro
Rumanian	măgar
German	Esel
Dutch	ezel
Swedish	åsna
Danish	æsel
Norwegian	esel
Polish	osioł
Czech	osel
Serbo-Croat.	magarac
Hungarian	szamár
Finnish	aasi
Turkish	eşek
Indonesian	keledai
Esperanto	azeno
Russian	asyól
Greek	gai'daros
Arabic	himar
Hebrew	chamor
Yiddish	chamer
Japanese	roba
Swahili	punda

315 door

French	porte
Spanish	puerta
Italian	porta
Portuguese	porta
Rumanian	uşă
German	Tür
Dutch	deur
Swedish	dörr
Danish	dør
Norwegian	dør
Polish	drzwi
Czech	dveře
Serbo-Croat.	vrata
Hungarian	ajtó
Finnish	ovi
Turkish	kapı
Indonesian	pintu
Esperanto	pordo
Russian	dver
Greek	por'ta
Arabic	bab
Hebrew	delet
Yiddish	tier
Japanese	to
Swahili	mlango

316 down

French	en bas
Spanish	abajo
Italian	giù
Portuguese	debaixo
Rumanian	jos
German	nieder
Dutch	naar beneden
Swedish	nedåt
Danish	ned
Norwegian	ned
Polish	na dół
Czech	dolů
Serbo-Croat.	dole
Hungarian	le
Finnish	alas
Turkish	aşağı
Indonesian	kebawah
Esperanto	mal'supre
Russian	vnis
Greek	ka'to
Arabic	asfal
Hebrew	matah
Yiddish	arop
Japanese	shita e
Swahili	chini

317 drawing

French	dessin
Spanish	dibujo
Italian	disegno
Portuguese	desenho
Rumanian	desen
German	Zeichnung
Dutch	tekening
Swedish	teckning
Danish	tegning
Norwegian	tegning
Polish	rysunek
Czech	kresba
Serbo-Croat.	crtanje
Hungarian	rajz
Finnish	piirustus
Turkish	resim
Indonesian	gambar
Esperanto	desegn'ado
Russian	risúnok
Greek	s-che'dion
Arabic	rasm
Hebrew	tsiyur
Yiddish	tseichenen
Japanese	e
Swahili	picha

318 dream

French	rêve
Spanish	sueño
Italian	sogno
Portuguese	sonho
Rumanian	vis
German	Traum
Dutch	droom
Swedish	dröm
Danish	drøm
Norwegian	drøm
Polish	sen
Czech	sen
Serbo-Croat.	san
Hungarian	álom
Finnish	uni
Turkish	rüya
Indonesian	mimpi
Esperanto	sonĝo
Russian	son
Greek	on'iron
Arabic	haulm
Hebrew	chalom
Yiddish	cholem
Japanese	yume
Swahili	ndoto

319 dress

French	robe
Spanish	vestido
Italian	abito
Portuguese	vestido
Rumanian	rochie
German	Kleid
Dutch	jurk
Swedish	klänning
Danish	kjole
Norwegian	kjole
Polish	suknia
Czech	šaty
Serbo-Croat.	haljina
Hungarian	ruha
Finnish	puku
Turkish	elbise
Indonesian	pakaian
Esperanto	robo
Russian	plátye
Greek	fo'rema
Arabic	tsawb
Hebrew	simlah
Yiddish	kleid
Japanese	i fuku
Swahili	kanga

320 drink

French	boire
Spanish	beber
Italian	bere
Portuguese	beber
Rumanian	bea
German	trinken
Dutch	drinken
Swedish	dricka
Danish	drikke
Norwegian	drikke
Polish	pić
Czech	píti
Serbo-Croat.	piti
Hungarian	iszik
Finnish	juoda
Turkish	içmek
Indonesian	minum
Esperanto	trinki
Russian	pít
Greek	pi'no
Arabic	yashrab
Hebrew	schatah
Yiddish	trinken
Japanese	nomu
Swahili	-nywa

321 drive

French	conduire
Spanish	conducir
Italian	andare
Portuguese	conduzir
Rumanian	merge
German	fahren
Dutch	rijden
Swedish	köra
Danish	køre
Norwegian	kjøre
Polish	jechać
Czech	jeti
Serbo-Croat.	voziti
Hungarian	hajt
Finnish	ajaa
Turkish	kullanmak
Indonesian	djalanakan
Esperanto	veturi
Russian	yékhat
Greek	odigo'
Arabic	yasouq
Hebrew	nahag
Yiddish	fohren
Japanese	unten suru
Swahili	endesha

322 driver

French	chauffeur
Spanish	chófer
Italian	guidatore
Portuguese	motorista
Rumanian	şofer
German	Chauffeur
Dutch	chauffeur
Swedish	chaufför
Danish	chauffør
Norwegian	sjåfør
Polish	szofer
Czech	šofér
Serbo-Croat.	vozač
Hungarian	sofőr
Finnish	ajaja
Turkish	şöfor
Indonesian	sopir
Esperanto	vetur'ig'isto
Russian	shofyór
Greek	odigos'
Arabic	saiq
Hebrew	nehag
Yiddish	baalhaguleh
Japanese	untenshu
Swahili	mwendeshi

323 drop

French	tomber
Spanish	dejar caer
Italian	cadere
Portuguese	deixar cair
Rumanian	picura
German	fallen lassen
Dutch	laten vallen
Swedish	tappa
Danish	lade falde
Norwegian	slippe
Polish	spuszczać
Czech	upustiti
Serbo-Croat.	padati
Hungarian	leejt, elejt
Finnish	pudota
Turkish	düşmek
Indonesian	tetes
Esperanto	fali
Russian	uranít
Greek	rich'no
Arabic	nouqta
Hebrew	hipil
Yiddish	falenlozen
Japanese	otosu
Swahili	acha

324 drown

French	(se) noyer
Spanish	ahogarse
Italian	affogarsi
Portuguese	afogarse
Rumanian	îneca
German	ertrinken
Dutch	verdrinken
Swedish	dränka
Danish	drunkne
Norwegian	drunke
Polish	utonąć
Czech	utopitti, utonouti
Serbo-Croat.	utopiti
Hungarian	fullad, vizbe
Finnish	hukkua
Turkish	boğulmak
Indonesian	tenggelamkan
Esperanto	droni
Russian	tanút
Greek	pni'go
Arabic	yaghriq
Hebrew	hitbia
Yiddish	dertrinken
Japanese	oboreru
Swahili	tosa majini

325 drug

French	drogue
Spanish	droga
Italian	droga
Portuguese	medicamento
Rumanian	drog
German	Arznei
Dutch	geneesmiddel
Swedish	drog
Danish	medicinalvare
Norwegian	droge
Polish	lekarstwo
Czech	lék, droga
Serbo-Croat.	lek
Hungarian	gyógyszer
Finnish	rohdos
Turkish	ecza
Indonesian	obat
Esperanto	drogo
Russian	lekárstvo
Greek	far'makon
Arabic	dawaa
Hebrew	refuah
Yiddish	medikament
Japanese	yakuhin
Swahili	dawa

326 drum

French	tambour
Spanish	tambor
Italian	tamburo
Portuguese	tambor
Rumanian	tobă
German	Trommel
Dutch	trommel
Swedish	trumma
Danish	tromme
Norwegian	tromme
Polish	bęben
Czech	buben
Serbo-Croat.	bubanj
Hungarian	dob
Finnish	rumpu
Turkish	davul
Indonesian	tambur
Esperanto	tamburo
Russian	barabán
Greek	tim'panon
Arabic	tabl
Hebrew	tof
Yiddish	poik
Japanese	taiko
Swahili	ngoma

327 dry

French	sec
Spanish	seco
Italian	secco
Portuguese	sêco
Rumanian	uscat
German	trocken
Dutch	droog
Swedish	torr
Danish	tør
Norwegian	tørr
Polish	suchy
Czech	suchý
Serbo-Croat.	suh
Hungarian	száraz
Finnish	kuiva
Turkish	kuru
Indonesian	kering
Esperanto	seka
Russian	sukhóy
Greek	xeros'
Arabic	gaaf
Hebrew	yavesch
Yiddish	truken
Japanese	kawaita
Swahili	-kavu

328 duck

French	canard
Spanish	pato
Italian	anitra
Portuguese	pato
Rumanian	rață
German	Ente
Dutch	eend
Swedish	anka
Danish	and
Norwegian	and
Polish	kaczka
Czech	kachna
Serbo-Croat.	patka
Hungarian	kacsa
Finnish	ankka
Turkish	ördek
Indonesian	bébék, itik
Esperanto	anaso
Russian	útka
Greek	pa'pia
Arabic	batta
Hebrew	barvaz
Yiddish	katschke
Japanese	ahiru
Swahili	bata

329 dust

French	poussière
Spanish	polvo
Italian	polvere
Portuguese	pó
Rumanian	praf
German	Staub
Dutch	stof
Swedish	damm
Danish	støv
Norwegian	støv
Polish	kurz
Czech	prach
Serbo-Croat.	prašina
Hungarian	por
Finnish	tomu
Turkish	toz
Indonesian	abu, debu
Esperanto	polvo
Russian	pil
Greek	sko'ni
Arabic	ghoubar
Hebrew	avak
Yiddish	schtoib
Japanese	hokori
Swahili	vumbi

330 duty

French	droits de douane
Spanish	arancel
Italian	tassa
Portuguese	direitos alfandegários
Rumanian	vamă
German	Zoll
Dutch	invoerrecht
Swedish	tull
Danish	told
Norwegian	toll
Polish	cło
Czech	clo, celni
Serbo-Croat.	carina
Hungarian	vám
Finnish	tulli
Turkish	gümrük
Indonesian	bea
Esperanto	imposto
Russian	póshlina
Greek	kathi'kon
Arabic	wagib
Hebrew	meches
Yiddish	tsol
Japanese	gimu
Swahili	kodi

331 eagle

French	aigle
Spanish	águila
Italian	aquila
Portuguese	águia
Rumanian	vultur
German	Adler
Dutch	adelaar
Swedish	örn
Danish	ørn
Norwegian	ørn
Polish	orzeł
Czech	orel
Serbo-Croat.	orao
Hungarian	sas
Finnish	kotka
Turkish	kartal
Indonesian	burung radjawali
Esperanto	aglo
Russian	aryól
Greek	a-etos'
Arabic	nisr
Hebrew	nescher
Yiddish	odler
Japanese	washi
Swahili	tai

332 ear

French	oreille
Spanish	oreja
Italian	orecchio
Portuguese	orelha
Rumanian	ureche
German	Ohr
Dutch	oor
Swedish	öra
Danish	øre
Norwegian	øre
Polish	ucho
Czech	ucho
Serbo-Croat.	uho
Hungarian	fül
Finnish	korva
Turkish	kulak
Indonesian	telinga, kuping
Esperanto	orelo
Russian	úkho
Greek	afti'
Arabic	outzoun
Hebrew	osen
Yiddish	oier
Japanese	mimi
Swahili	sikio

333 earring

French	boucle d'oreille
Spanish	pendiente
Italian	orecchino
Portuguese	brinco
Rumanian	cercel
German	Ohrring
Dutch	oorring
Swedish	örring
Danish	ørenring
Norwegian	dobb
Polish	kolczyk
Czech	naušnice
Serbo-Croat.	minduša
Hungarian	fülbevaló
Finnish	korvarengas
Turkish	küpe
Indonesian	antin-anting
Esperanto	orel'ringo
Russian	sergá
Greek	skoulari'ki
Arabic	qourt
Hebrew	agil
Yiddish	oierringel
Japanese	mimiwa
Swahili	bali

334 east

French	est
Spanish	este
Italian	est
Portuguese	este
Rumanian	est
German	Osten
Dutch	oost
Swedish	öster
Danish	østen
Norwegian	øst
Polish	wschód
Czech	východ
Serbo-Croat.	istok
Hungarian	kelet
Finnish	itä
Turkish	şark
Indonesian	timur
Esperanto	oriento
Russian	vastók
Greek	anatoli'
Arabic	sharq
Hebrew	misrach
Yiddish	misrechseit
Japanese	higashi
Swahili	mashariki

335 eat

French	manger
Spanish	comer
Italian	mangiare
Portuguese	comer
Rumanian	mînca
German	essen
Dutch	eten
Swedish	äta
Danish	spise
Norwegian	spise
Polish	jeść
Czech	jísti
Serbo-Croat.	jesti
Hungarian	eszik
Finnish	syödä
Turkish	yemek
Indonesian	makan
Esperanto	manĝi
Russian	yést, kúshat
Greek	tro'go
Arabic	yaakoul
Hebrew	achal
Yiddish	essen
Japanese	kuu
Swahili	-la

336 eel

French	anguille
Spanish	anguila
Italian	anguilla
Portuguese	enguia
Rumanian	ţipar
German	Aal
Dutch	paling
Swedish	ål
Danish	ål
Norwegian	ål
Polish	węgorz
Czech	úhoř
Serbo-Croat.	jegulja
Hungarian	angolna
Finnish	ankerias
Turkish	yılan balığı
Indonesian	ikan belut
Esperanto	angilo
Russian	úgor
Greek	che'li
Arabic	hanash
Hebrew	tselofah
Yiddish	aalfisch
Japanese	unagi
Swahili	mkunga

337 egg

French	oeuf
Spanish	huevo
Italian	uovo
Portuguese	ôvo
Rumanian	ou
German	Ei
Dutch	ei
Swedish	ägg
Danish	æg
Norwegian	egg
Polish	jajko
Czech	vejce
Serbo-Croat.	jaje
Hungarian	tojás
Finnish	muna
Turkish	yumurta
Indonesian	telur
Esperanto	ovo
Russian	yitsó
Greek	avgo'
Arabic	bayda
Hebrew	beytsah
Yiddish	ay
Japanese	tamago
Swahili	yai

338 eight

French	huit
Spanish	ocho
Italian	otto
Portuguese	oito
Rumanian	opt
German	acht
Dutch	acht
Swedish	atta
Danish	otte
Norwegian	åtte
Polish	osiem
Czech	osm
Serbo-Croat.	osam
Hungarian	nyolc
Finnish	kahdeksan
Turkish	sekiz
Indonesian	delapan
Esperanto	ok
Russian	vósem
Greek	okto'
Arabic	tsamaniya
Hebrew	schmonah
Yiddish	acht
Japanese	hachi
Swahili	nane

339 eighteen

French	dix-huit
Spanish	dieciocho
Italian	diciotto
Portuguese	dezoito
Rumanian	optsprezece
German	achtzehn
Dutch	achttien
Swedish	aderton
Danish	atten
Norwegian	atten
Polish	osiemnaście
Czech	osmnáct
Serbo-Croat.	osamnaest
Hungarian	tizennyolc
Finnish	kahdeksantoista
Turkish	onsekiz
Indonesian	delapan belas
Esperanto	dek ok
Russian	vasemnátset
Greek	deka-okto'
Arabic	tsamaniyat ashar
Hebrew	schmonah-assar
Yiddish	achtsen
Japanese	juuhachi
Swahili	kumi na nane

340 eighty

French	quatre-vingt
Spanish	ochenta
Italian	ottanta
Portuguese	oitenta
Rumanian	optzeci
German	achtzig
Dutch	tachtig
Swedish	åttio
Danish	firs
Norwegian	åtti
Polish	osiemdziesiąt
Czech	osemdesát
Serbo-Croat.	osamdeset
Hungarian	nyolcvan
Finnish	kahdeksankymmentä
Turkish	seksen
Indonesian	delapan puluh
Esperanto	ok'dek
Russian	vósemdesyat
Greek	ogdon'ta
Arabic	tsamanoun
Hebrew	schmonim
Yiddish	achtsig
Japanese	hachijuu
Swahili	themanini

341 elbow

French	coude
Spanish	codo
Italian	gomito
Portuguese	cotovêlo
Rumanian	cot
German	Ellenbogen
Dutch	elleboog
Swedish	armbåge
Danish	albue
Norwegian	albue
Polish	łokieć
Czech	loket
Serbo-Croat.	lakat
Hungarian	könyök
Finnish	kynärpää
Turkish	dirsek
Indonesian	siku
Esperanto	kubuto
Russian	lókat
Greek	ango'nas
Arabic	mirfaq
Hebrew	marpek
Yiddish	elenboigen
Japanese	hiji
Swahili	kivi

342 electric light bulb

French	ampoule électrique
Spanish	bombilla
Italian	lampadina
Portuguese	lâmpada eléctrica
Rumanian	bec
German	Glühbirne
Dutch	gloeilamp
Swedish	glödlampa
Danish	glødelampe
Norwegian	elektrisk pære
Polish	żarówka
Czech	zárovka
Serbo-Croat.	sijalica
Hungarian	villanykörte
Finnish	hehkulamppu
Turkish	ampul
Indonesian	lampu pidjar
Esperanto	inkandeska
Russian	lámpochka
Greek	lampti'ras
Arabic	lamba
Hebrew	nurah
Yiddish	elektrik lempel
Japanese	denkyuu
Swahili	kioo cha taa ya umeme

343 elevator

French	ascenseur
Spanish	ascensor
Italian	ascensore
Portuguese	elevador
Rumanian	ascensor
German	Fahrstuhl
Dutch	lift
Swedish	hiss
Danish	elevator
Norwegian	heis
Polish	winda
Czech	zdviž
Serbo-Croat.	lift
Hungarian	felvonó
Finnish	hissi
Turkish	asansör
Indonesian	lift
Esperanto	lifto
Russian	lift
Greek	asanser'
Arabic	misaad
Hebrew	maalit
Yiddish	oiftsug
Japanese	erebeetaa
Swahili	mashine kiinuacho

344 eleven

French	onze
Spanish	once
Italian	undici
Portuguese	onze
Rumanian	unsprezece
German	elf
Dutch	elf
Swedish	elva
Danish	elleve
Norwegian	elleve
Polish	jedenaście
Czech	jedenáct
Serbo-Croat.	jedanaest
Hungarian	tizenegy
Finnish	yksitoista
Turkish	on bir
Indonesian	sebelas
Esperanto	dek unu
Russian	adínnatsit
Greek	en'deka
Arabic	ihda ashar
Hebrew	achadassar
Yiddish	elf
Japanese	juuichi
Swahili	kumi na moja

345 empty

French	vide
Spanish	vacío
Italian	vuoto
Portuguese	vazio
Rumanian	gol
German	leer
Dutch	leeg
Swedish	tom
Danish	tom
Norwegian	tom
Polish	pusty
Czech	prásdný
Serbo-Croat.	prazan
Hungarian	üres
Finnish	tyhjä
Turkish	boş
Indonesian	kosong
Esperanto	mal'plena
Russian	pustóy
Greek	a'dios
Arabic	farigh
Hebrew	reik
Yiddish	pusst
Japanese	kara no
Swahili	-tupu

346 enemy

French	ennemi
Spanish	enemigo
Italian	nemico
Portuguese	inimigo
Rumanian	duşman
German	Feind
Dutch	vijand
Swedish	fiende
Danish	fjende
Norwegian	fiende
Polish	nieprzyjaciel
Czech	nepřítel
Serbo-Croat.	neprijatelj
Hungarian	ellenség
Finnish	vihollinen
Turkish	düşman
Indonesian	musuh, seteru
Esperanto	mal'amiko
Russian	vrak
Greek	echthros'
Arabic	adouwe
Hebrew	oyev
Yiddish	ssoine
Japanese	teki
Swahili	adui

347 energy

French	energie
Spanish	energía
Italian	energia
Portuguese	energia
Rumanian	energie
German	Energie
Dutch	energie
Swedish	energi
Danish	energi
Norwegian	kraft
Polish	energia
Czech	energie, síla
Serbo-Croat.	energija
Hungarian	energia
Finnish	tarmo
Turkish	enerji
Indonesian	tenaga
Esperanto	energio
Russian	enyérgiya
Greek	ener'yia
Arabic	taqa
Hebrew	merets
Yiddish	energye
Japanese	chikara
Swahili	bidii

348 engineer

French	ingénieur
Spanish	ingeniero
Italian	ingegnere
Portuguese	engenheiro
Rumanian	inginer
German	Ingenieur
Dutch	ingenieur
Swedish	ingenjör
Danish	ingeniør
Norwegian	ingeniør
Polish	inżynier
Czech	inženýr
Serbo-Croat.	inženjer
Hungarian	mérnök
Finnish	insinööri
Turkish	mühendis
Indonesian	injinjur
Esperanto	inĝeniero
Russian	inzhenyér
Greek	michanikos'
Arabic	mouhandis
Hebrew	mehandess
Yiddish	indsinir
Japanese	gishi
Swahili	fundi wa mashine

349 entrance

French	entrée
Spanish	entrada
Italian	entrata
Portuguese	entrada
Rumanian	intrare
German	Eingang
Dutch	ingang
Swedish	ingång
Danish	indgang
Norwegian	inngang
Polish	wejście.
Czech	vchod
Serbo-Croat.	ulaz
Hungarian	bejárat
Finnish	sisäänkäytävä
Turkish	giriş
Indonesian	djalan masuk
Esperanto	en'ir'ejo
Russian	fkhot
Greek	i'sodos
Arabic	madchal
Hebrew	kenissah
Yiddish	areingang
Japanese	iriguchi
Swahili	mwingilio

350 envelope

French	enveloppe
Spanish	sobre
Italian	busta
Portuguese	envelope
Rumanian	plic
German	Briefumschlag
Dutch	envelop
Swedish	kuvert
Danish	kuvert
Norwegian	konvolutt
Polish	koperta
Czech	obálka
Serbo-Croat.	koverta
Hungarian	boríték
Finnish	kirjekuori
Turkish	zarf
Indonesian	amplop
Esperanto	koverto
Russian	kanvyért
Greek	fa'kelos
Arabic	mazrouf
Hebrew	maatafah
Yiddish	kovert
Japanese	fuutoo
Swahili	bahasha

351 evening

French	soir
Spanish	tarde
Italian	sera
Portuguese	tardinha
Rumanian	seară
German	Abend
Dutch	avond
Swedish	afton
Danish	aften
Norwegian	kveld
Polish	wieczór
Czech	večer
Serbo-Croat.	veče
Hungarian	este
Finnish	ilta
Turkish	akşam
Indonesian	malam
Esperanto	vespero
Russian	vyécher
Greek	vra'thi
Arabic	masaa
Hebrew	erev
Yiddish	ovend
Japanese	yuugata
Swahili	jioni

352 exchange office

French	bureau de change
Spanish	oficina de cambio
Italian	ufficio di cambio
Portuguese	casa de câmbio
Rumanian	schimbare
German	Wechselstube
Dutch	wisselkantoor
Swedish	växelkontor
Danish	vekselkontor
Norwegian	veksle kontor
Polish	kantor wymiany
Czech	směnárna
Serbo-Croat.	menjačnica
Hungarian	váltóüzlet
Finnish	vaihtokonttori
Turkish	kambiyo
Indonesian	kantor penukaran
Esperanto	makler'ejo
Russian	menyálnaya kantóra
Greek	grafi'on sinalag'matos
Arabic	maktab al-sarraf
Hebrew	chiluf
Yiddish	vekselbank
ǝsǝuɐdɐ∫	torihikijo
Swahili	afisi ya kuvunja feda

353 excuse

French	excuse
Spanish	escusa
Italian	scusa
Portuguese	desculpa
Rumanian	scuză
German	Entschuldigung
Dutch	verontschuldiging
Swedish	ursäkt
Danish	undskyldning
Norwegian	unnskylde
Polish	usprawiedliwienie
Czech	omulva
Serbo-Croat.	izvinjenje
Hungarian	bocsánat
Finnish	anteeksipyyntö
Turkish	özür
Indonesian	máaf, ampun
Esperanto	sen'kulp'igo
Russian	izvinyéniye
Greek	signo'min
Arabic	outzr
Hebrew	mechilah
Yiddish	antshuldigung
Japanese	iiwake
Swahili	udhuru

354 exit

French	sortie
Spanish	salida
Italian	uscita
Portuguese	saída
Rumanian	ieşire
German	Ausgang
Dutch	uitgang
Swedish	utgång
Danish	udgang
Norwegian	utgang
Polish	wyjście
Czech	východ
Serbo-Croat.	izlaz
Hungarian	kijárat
Finnish	uloskäytävä
Turkish	çıkış
Indonesian	tempat keluar
Esperanto	el'ir'ejo
Russian	víkhot
Greek	ex'odos
Arabic	chouroug
Hebrew	motsa
Yiddish	heroisgang
Japanese	deguchi
Swahili	njia ya kutokea

355 expense

French	frais
Spanish	gasto
Italian	spesa
Portuguese	despesa
Rumanian	cheltuialâ
German	Spesen
Dutch	onkosten
Swedish	omkostnad
Danish	udgift
Norwegian	omkostning
Polish	wydatek
Czech	útraty
Serbo-Croat.	trošak
Hungarian	költség
Finnish	kulut
Turkish	masraf
Indonesian	ongkos
Esperanto	el'spezo
Russian	izdyérshki
Greek	e'xodon
Arabic	masroufat
Hebrew	hotsuah
Yiddish	hoitsues
Japanese	shuppi
Swahili	gharama

356 expensive

French	cher
Spanish	caro
Italian	dispendioso
Portuguese	caro
Rumanian	costisitor
German	teuer
Dutch	duur
Swedish	dyr
Danish	dyr
Norwegian	dyr
Polish	drogi
Czech	drahý
Serbo-Croat.	skup
Hungarian	drága
Finnish	kallis
Turkish	pahalı
Indonesian	mahal
Esperanto	kara
Russian	daragóy
Greek	akrivos'
Arabic	ghali
Hebrew	yakar
Yiddish	teier
Japanese	kooka na
Swahili	ghali

357 expire

French	expirer
Spanish	expirar
Italian	scadere
Portuguese	expirar
Rumanian	expira
German	ablaufen
Dutch	aflopen
Swedish	utlöpa
Danish	ophøre
Norwegian	utlope
Polish	upłynąć
Czech	uplynouti
Serbo-Croat.	isteći
Hungarian	lejár
Finnish	loppua
Turkish	sona ermek
Indonesian	liwat waktu
Esperanto	fin'iĝi
Russian	kanchát
Greek	li'go
Arabic	yantahi
Hebrew	hessif
Yiddish	obloifen
Japanese	manki ni naru
Swahili	koma

358 export

French	exportation
Spanish	exportación
Italian	esportazione
Portuguese	exportação
Rumanian	export
German	Ausfuhr
Dutch	uitvoer
Swedish	export
Danish	eksport
Norwegian	eksport
Polish	wywóz
Czech	vývoz
Serbo-Croat.	izvoz
Hungarian	kivitel
Finnish	vienti
Turkish	ihraç
Indonesian	ékspor
Esperanto	eksporto
Russian	vívos
Greek	exagoge'
Arabic	yousadir
Hebrew	yitsu
Yiddish	oisfuhr
Japanese	yushutsu
Swahili	bidhaa zinozotoka

359 exposition

French	exposition
Spanish	exposición
Italian	esposizione
Portuguese	exposição
Rumanian	expoziţie
German	Ausstellung
Dutch	tentoonstelling
Swedish	utställning
Danish	udstilling
Norwegian	utstilling
Polish	wystawa
Czech	výstava
Serbo-Croat.	izložba
Hungarian	kiállítás
Finnish	näyttely
Turkish	sergi
Indonesian	pertunjukan
Esperanto	ekspozicio
Russian	vístafka
Greek	ek'thesis
Arabic	ard
Hebrew	taarucha
Yiddish	oisstellung
Japanese	hakurankwai
Swahili	onyesho

360 extreme

French	extrême
Spanish	extremo
Italian	estremo
Portuguese	extremo
Rumanian	extrem
German	äusserst
Dutch	uiterst
Swedish	ytterst
Danish	yderst
Norwegian	ytterst
Polish	nazwyczajny
Czech	krajní
Serbo-Croat.	krajnji
Hungarian	fölöttébb
Finnish	äärimmäinen
Turkish	son derece
Indonesian	terlalu
Esperanto	ekstrema
Russian	kráinye
Greek	a'kros
Arabic	moutatarif
Hebrew	kitsonie
Yiddish	oisserst
Japanese	kyokutan na
Swahili	-a mwisho

361 eye

French	oeil
Spanish	ojo
Italian	occhio
Portuguese	ôlho
Rumanian	ochi
German	Auge
Dutch	oog
Swedish	öga
Danish	øje
Norwegian	øye
Polish	oko
Czech	oko
Serbo-Croat.	oko
Hungarian	szem
Finnish	silmä
Turkish	göz
Indonesian	mata
Esperanto	okulo
Russian	glas
Greek	ma'ti
Arabic	ayn
Hebrew	ayin
Yiddish	oig
Japanese	me
Swahili	jicho

362 eyeglasses

French	lunettes
Spanish	lentes
Italian	occhiali
Portuguese	óculos
Rumanian	ochelari
German	Brille
Dutch	bril
Swedish	glasögon
Danish	briller
Norwegian	briller
Polish	okulary
Czech	brýle
Serbo-Croat.	naočare
Hungarian	szemüveg
Finnish	silmälasit
Turkish	gözlük
Indonesian	katja mat
Esperanto	okul'vitroj
Russian	achkí
Greek	yialia'
Arabic	nazzarat
Hebrew	mischkafayim
Yiddish	brilen
Japanese	megane
Swahili	miwani

363 face

French	visage
Spanish	cara
Italian	faccia
Portuguese	rosto
Rumanian	faţă
German	Gesicht
Dutch	gezicht
Swedish	ansikte
Danish	ansigt
Norwegian	ansikt
Polish	twarz
Czech	obličej
Serbo-Croat.	lice
Hungarian	arc
Finnish	kasvot
Turkish	yüz
Indonesian	muka
Esperanto	fronto
Russian	litsó
Greek	pro'sopon
Arabic	waghe
Hebrew	panim
Yiddish	punim
Japanese	kao
Swahili	uso

364 factory

French	usine
Spanish	fábrica
Italian	fabbrica
Portuguese	fábrica
Rumanian	fabrică
German	Fabrik
Dutch	fabriek
Swedish	fabrik
Danish	fabrik
Norwegian	fabrikk
Polish	fabryka
Czech	továrna
Serbo-Croat.	tvornica
Hungarian	gyár
Finnish	tehdas
Turkish	fabrika
Indonesian	paberik
Esperanto	fabrik'ejo
Russian	zavód
Greek	ergosta'sion
Arabic	masnaa
Hebrew	bet-charoschet
Yiddish	fabrik
Japanese	koojoo
Swahili	kiwanda

365 far

French	loin
Spanish	lejos
Italian	lontano
Portuguese	longe
Rumanian	departe
German	weit
Dutch	ver
Swedish	fjärran
Danish	fjernt
Norwegian	fjern
Polish	daleko
Czech	daleko
Serbo-Croat.	dalek
Hungarian	messze
Finnish	kaukana
Turkish	uzak
Indonesian	djauh
Esperanto	mal'proksima
Russian	dalekó
Greek	makria'
Arabic	baid
Hebrew	rachok
Yiddish	veit
Japanese	kanata ni
Swahili	mbali

366 farm

French	ferme
Spanish	granja
Italian	fattoria
Portuguese	fazenda
Rumanian	gospodărie
German	Bauernhof
Dutch	boerderij
Swedish	bondgård
Danish	bondegård
Norwegian	gård
Polish	zagroda
Czech	selský dvůr
Serbo-Croat.	salaš
Hungarian	tanya
Finnish	maatalo
Turkish	çiftlik
Indonesian	ketanian, kebun
Esperanto	farmo
Russian	fyérma
Greek	kti'ma
Arabic	mazraa
Hebrew	chavah
Yiddish	giet
Japanese	noojoo
Swahili	shamba

367 fast

French	vite
Spanish	de prisa
Italian	rapido
Portuguese	rápido
Rumanian	iute
German	schnell
Dutch	snel
Swedish	snabb
Danish	faste
Norwegian	hurtig
Polish	szybko
Czech	rychlý
Serbo-Croat.	brz
Hungarian	gyors
Finnish	nopea
Turkish	hızlı
Indonesian	ladju, tepjat
Esperanto	rapida
Russian	skóro
Greek	gri'gora
Arabic	sari
Hebrew	bimhirut
Yiddish	giech
Japanese	hayaku
Swahili	upesi

368 fat

French	graisse
Spanish	grasa
Italian	grasso
Portuguese	gordura
Rumanian	grăsime
German	Fett
Dutch	vet
Swedish	fett
Danish	fedt
Norwegian	fett
Polish	tłuszcz
Czech	tuk, sádlo
Serbo-Croat.	mast
Hungarian	zsír
Finnish	rasva
Turkish	yağ
Indonesian	lemak, gemuk
Esperanto	graso
Russian	zhir
Greek	pa'chos
Arabic	shahm
Hebrew	chelev
Yiddish	fet
Japanese	shiboo
Swahili	mafuta

369 father

French	père
Spanish	padre
Italian	padre
Portuguese	pai
Rumanian	tată
German	Vater
Dutch	vader
Swedish	fader
Danish	fader
Norwegian	far
Polish	ojciec
Czech	otec
Serbo-Croat.	otac
Hungarian	atya
Finnish	isä
Turkish	baba
Indonesian	ajah, bapak
Esperanto	patro
Russian	atyéts
Greek	pate'ras
Arabic	ab
Hebrew	av
Yiddish	foter
Japanese	chichi
Swahili	baba

370 February

French	février
Spanish	febrero
Italian	febbraio
Portuguese	fevereiro
Rumanian	februarie
German	Februar
Dutch	Februari
Swedish	februari
Danish	februar
Norwegian	februar
Polish	luty
Czech	únor
Serbo-Croat.	veljača
Hungarian	febru ár
Finnish	helmikuu
Turkish	şubat
Indonesian	Februari
Esperanto	Februaro
Russian	fevrál
Greek	Fevroua'rios
Arabic	fibrayer
Hebrew	februar
Yiddish	februar
Japanese	nigwatsu
Swahili	Februari

371 ferry

French	bac
Spanish	barca
Italian	traghetto
Portuguese	passagem
Rumanian	feribot
German	Fähre
Dutch	veer
Swedish	färja
Danish	færge
Norwegian	ferge
Polish	prom
Czech	převoz
Serbo-Croat.	skela
Hungarian	komp
Finnish	lautta
Turkish	sal, feribot
Indonesian	tambangan
Esperanto	pramo
Russian	paróm
Greek	porthmi'on
Arabic	miadiyya
Hebrew	magboret
Yiddish	prohss
Japanese	watashibune
Swahili	kivuko

372 few

French	peu
Spanish	poco
Italian	pochi
Portuguese	pouco
Rumanian	puţine
German	wenig
Dutch	weinig
Swedish	få
Danish	få
Norwegian	få
Polish	mało
Czech	málo
Serbo-Croat.	malo
Hungarian	kevés
Finnish	harvat
Turkish	az
Indonesian	sedikit
Esperanto	mal'multaj
Russian	málo
Greek	li'gi
Arabic	qalil
Hebrew	meatim
Yiddish	venig
Japanese	shoosuu
Swahili	-chache

373 fifteen

French	quinze
Spanish	quince
Italian	quindici
Portuguese	quinze
Rumanian	cincisprezece
German	fünfzehn
Dutch	vijftien
Swedish	femton
Danish	femten
Norwegian	femten
Polish	piętnaście
Czech	patnáct
Serbo-Croat.	petnaest
Hungarian	tizenöt
Finnish	viisitoista
Turkish	on beş
Indonesian	lima belas
Esperanto	dek kvin
Russian	pitnátset
Greek	dekapen'te
Arabic	chamsat ashar
Hebrew	chamischah assar
Yiddish	fuftsehn
Japanese	juugo
Swahili	kumi na tano

374 fifty

French	cinquante
Spanish	cincuenta
Italian	cinquanta
Portuguese	cinqüenta
Rumanian	cincizeci
German	fünfzig
Dutch	vijftig
Swedish	femtio
Danish	halvtreds
Norwegian	femti
Polish	pięćdziesiąt
Czech	padesát
Serbo-Croat.	pedeset
Hungarian	ötven
Finnish	viisikymmentä
Turkish	elli
Indonesian	lima pulah
Esperanto	kvin'dek
Russian	pitdesyát
Greek	penin'ta
Arabic	chamsoun
Hebrew	chamischim
Yiddish	fuftsig
Japanese	gojuu
Swahili	hamsini

375 fig

French	figue
Spanish	higo
Italian	fico
Portuguese	figo
Rumanian	smochină
German	Feige
Dutch	vijg
Swedish	fikon
Danish	figen
Norwegian	fiken
Polish	figa
Czech	fík
Serbo-Croat.	smokva
Hungarian	füge
Finnish	viikuna
Turkish	incir
Indonesian	ara
Esperanto	figo
Russian	smókva, fíga
Greek	si'kon
Arabic	tin
Hebrew	teenah
Yiddish	fajg
Japanese	ichijiku
Swahili	tini

376 find

French	trouver
Spanish	hallar
Italian	trovare
Portuguese	achar
Rumanian	găsi
German	finden
Dutch	vinden
Swedish	finna
Danish	finde
Norwegian	finne
Polish	znajdować
Czech	nalézti, najiti
Serbo-Croat.	naći
Hungarian	talál
Finnish	löytää
Turkish	bulmak
Indonesian	dapat, tjahari
Esperanto	trovi
Russian	nakhadít
Greek	vri'sko
Arabic	yagid
Hebrew	matsa
Yiddish	gefinen
Japanese	miidasu
Swahili	kuta

377 finger

French	doigt
Spanish	dedo
Italian	dito
Portuguese	dedo
Rumanian	deget
German	Finger
Dutch	vinger
Swedish	finger
Danish	finger
Norwegian	finger
Polish	palec
Czech	prst
Serbo-Croat.	prst
Hungarian	ujj
Finnish	sormi
Turkish	parmak
Indonesian	djari
Esperanto	fingro
Russian	pálets
Greek	dak'tilo
Arabic	isbaa
Hebrew	etsba
Yiddish	finger
Japanese	yubi
Swahili	kidole

378 fingernail

French	ongle
Spanish	uña
Italian	unghia
Portuguese	unha
Rumanian	unghi
German	Fingernagel
Dutch	nagel
Swedish	fingernagel
Danish	fingernegl
Norwegian	negl
Polish	paznokieć
Czech	nehet
Serbo-Croat.	nokat
Hungarian	köröm
Finnish	kynsi
Turkish	tırnak
Indonesian	kuku
Esperanto	ungo
Russian	nógot
Greek	ni'chi
Arabic	izfar
Hebrew	tsiporen
Yiddish	fingernogel
Japanese	tsume
Swahili	kucha

379 fire

French	feu
Spanish	fuego
Italian	fuoco
Portuguese	fogo
Rumanian	foc
German	Feuer
Dutch	vuur
Swedish	eld
Danish	ild
Norwegian	ild
Polish	ogień
Czech	oheň
Serbo-Croat.	vatra
Hungarian	tüz
Finnish	tuli
Turkish	ateş
Indonesian	api
Esperanto	fajro
Russian	agón
Greek	fotia'
Arabic	nar
Hebrew	esch
Yiddish	sreife
Japanese	hi
Swahili	moto

380 fish

French	poisson
Spanish	pescado
Italian	pesce
Portuguese	peixe
Rumanian	peşte
German	Fisch
Dutch	vis
Swedish	fisk
Danish	fisk
Norwegian	fisk
Polish	ryba
Czech	ryba
Serbo-Croat.	riba
Hungarian	hal
Finnish	kala
Turkish	balık
Indonesian	ikan
Esperanto	fiŝo
Russian	ríba
Greek	psa'ri
Arabic	samak
Hebrew	dag
Yiddish	fisch
Japanese	sakana
Swahili	samaki

381 fist

French	poing
Spanish	puño
Italian	pugno
Portuguese	punho
Rumanian	pumn
German	Faust
Dutch	vuist
Swedish	näve
Danish	næve
Norwegian	neve
Polish	pięść
Czech	pěst
Serbo-Croat.	pesnica
Hungarian	ököl
Finnish	nyrkki
Turkish	yumruk
Indonesian	tindju, genggam
Esperanto	pugno
Russian	kulák
Greek	pigmi'
Arabic	qabda
Hebrew	egrof
Yiddish	kulak
Japanese	kobushi
Swahili	ngumi

382 five

French	cinq
Spanish	cinco
Italian	cinque
Portuguese	cinco
Rumanian	cinci
German	fünf
Dutch	vijf
Swedish	fem
Danish	fem
Norwegian	fem
Polish	pięć
Czech	pět
Serbo-Croat.	pet
Hungarian	öt
Finnish	viisi
Turkish	beş
Indonesian	lima
Esperanto	kvin
Russian	pyát
Greek	pen'te
Arabic	chams
Hebrew	chamischah
Yiddish	finef
Japanese	go
Swahili	tano

383 flat

French	plat
Spanish	plano
Italian	piatto
Portuguese	plano
Rumanian	plat
German	flach
Dutch	vlak
Swedish	flat
Danish	flad
Norwegian	flat
Polish	płaski
Czech	plochý
Serbo-Croat.	ravan
Hungarian	lapos
Finnish	litteä
Turkish	düz
Indonesian	rato,datar
Esperanto	ebena
Russian	plóski
Greek	epi'pedos
Arabic	mounbasit
Hebrew	schatuach
Yiddish	platschik
Japanese	tairana
Swahili	sawa

384 flax

French	lin
Spanish	lino
Italian	lino
Portuguese	linho
Rumanian	in
German	Flachs
Dutch	vlas
Swedish	lin
Danish	hør
Norwegian	lin
Polish	len
Czech	len
Serbo-Croat.	lan
Hungarian	len
Finnish	pellava
Turkish	keten
Indonesian	rami
Esperanto	lino
Russian	lyón
Greek	lina'ri
Arabic	kittan, qinnab
Hebrew	pischtan
Yiddish	flaks
Japanese	ama
Swahili	kitani

385 flea

French	puce
Spanish	pulga
Italian	pulce
Portuguese	pulga
Rumanian	purice
German	Floh
Dutch	vlo
Swedish	loppa
Danish	loppe
Norwegian	loppe
Polish	pchła
Czech	blecha
Serbo-Croat.	buha
Hungarian	bolha
Finnish	kirppu
Turkish	pire
Indonesian	pindjal
Esperanto	pulo
Russian	blokhá
Greek	psi'los
Arabic	barghouts
Hebrew	parosch
Yiddish	floy
Japanese	nomi
Swahili	kiroboto

386 floor

French	plancher
Spanish	suelo
Italian	pavimento
Portuguese	soalho
Rumanian	pardoseală
German	Fussboden
Dutch	vloer
Swedish	golv
Danish	gulv
Norwegian	gulv
Polish	podłoga
Czech	podlaha
Serbo-Croat.	pod
Hungarian	padló
Finnish	lattia
Turkish	döşeme
Indonesian	lantai
Esperanto	planko
Russian	pol
Greek	pa'toma
Arabic	ard al-hougra
Hebrew	ritspah
Yiddish	podloge
Japanese	yuka
Swahili	sakafu

387 flour

French	farine
Spanish	harina
Italian	farina
Portuguese	farinha
Rumanian	făină
German	Mehl
Dutch	meel
Swedish	mjöl
Danish	mel
Norwegian	mel
Polish	mąka
Czech	mouka
Serbo-Croat.	brašno
Hungarian	liszt
Finnish	jauho
Turkish	un
Indonesian	tepung
Esperanto	faruno
Russian	muká
Greek	alev'ri
Arabic	daqiq
Hebrew	kemach
Yiddish	mehl
Japanese	komugiko
Swahili	unga

388 flower

French	fleur
Spanish	flor
Italian	fiore
Portuguese	flôr
Rumanian	floare
German	Blume
Dutch	bloem
Swedish	blomma
Danish	blomst
Norwegian	blomst
Polish	kwiat
Czech	květina
Serbo-Croat.	cvjet
Hungarian	virág
Finnish	kukka
Turkish	çiçek
Indonesian	bunga
Esperanto	floro
Russian	tsvetók
Greek	loulou'di
Arabic	zahra
Hebrew	perach
Yiddish	blum
Japanese	hana
Swahili	ua

389 flute

French	flûte
Spanish	flauta
Italian	flauto
Portuguese	flauta
Rumanian	flaut
German	Flöte
Dutch	fluit
Swedish	fljöt
Danish	fløjte
Norwegian	fløyte
Polish	flet
Czech	flétna
Serbo-Croat.	flauta
Hungarian	fuvola
Finnish	huilu
Turkish	flüt
Indonesian	suling
Esperanto	fluto
Russian	fléyta
Greek	fla'outo
Arabic	naye
Hebrew	chalil
Yiddish	flejt
Japanese	yokobue
Swahili	filimbi

390 fly

French	mouche
Spanish	mosca
Italian	mosca
Portuguese	mosca
Rumanian	muscă
German	Fliege
Dutch	vlieg
Swedish	fluga
Danish	flue
Norwegian	flue
Polish	mucha
Czech	moucha
Serbo-Croat.	muha
Hungarian	légy
Finnish	kärpänen
Turkish	sinek
Indonesian	lalta, laler
Esperanto	mûso
Russian	múkha
Greek	mi'ya
Arabic	doubaba
Hebrew	svuv
Yiddish	flieg
Japanese	hae
Swahili	inzi

391 food

French	nourriture
Spanish	alimento
Italian	alimento
Portuguese	alimento
Rumanian	aliment
German	Nahrung
Dutch	voedsel
Swedish	näring
Danish	næring
Norwegian	næring
Polish	żywność
Czech	potrava, jídlo
Serbo-Croat.	hrana
Hungarian	táplálék
Finnish	ruoka
Turkish	gıda
Indonesian	makanan
Esperanto	nutr'aĵo
Russian	píshcha
Greek	trofi'
Arabic	ghitzaa
Hebrew	maachol
Yiddish	schpeis
Japanese	shokumotsu
Swahili	chakula

392 foot

French	pied
Spanish	pie
Italian	piede
Portuguese	pé
Rumanian	picior
German	Fuss
Dutch	voet
Swedish	fot
Danish	fod
Norwegian	fot
Polish	stopa
Czech	noha
Serbo-Croat.	stopalo
Hungarian	láb
Finnish	jalka
Turkish	ayak
Indonesian	kaki
Esperanto	piedo
Russian	nagá
Greek	po'di
Arabic	qadam
Hebrew	regel
Yiddish	fuss
Japanese	ashi
Swahili	mguu

393 football

French	football
Spanish	fútbol
Italian	calcio
Portuguese	futebol
Rumanian	fotbal
German	Fussball
Dutch	voetbal
Swedish	fotboll
Danish	fodbold
Norwegian	fotball
Polish	piłka nożna
Czech	kopaná
Serbo-Croat.	futbal
Hungarian	labdarúgás
Finnish	jalkapallo
Turkish	futbol
Indonesian	bola sepak
Esperanto	pied'pilko
Russian	futból
Greek	podo'sferon
Arabic	kourat al-qadam
Hebrew	kaduregel
Yiddish	fussbail
Japanese	futtobooru
Swahili	futboli

394 forbidden

French	défendu
Spanish	prohibido
Italian	vietato
Portuguese	proibido
Rumanian	interzice
German	verboten
Dutch	verboden
Swedish	förbjuden
Danish	forbyde
Norwegian	forbudt
Polish	zakazany
Czech	zakázaný
Serbo-Croat.	zabranjeno
Hungarian	tilos
Finnish	kielletty
Turkish	yasak
Indonesian	pantang, larang
Esperanto	mal'permesi
Russian	zapreshchénni
Greek	apagorevme'nos
Arabic	mamnoua
Hebrew	assur
Yiddish	asseren
Japanese	kinji rareta
Swahili	marufuku

395 foreign

French	étranger
Spanish	extranjero
Italian	straniero
Portuguese	estrangeiro
Rumanian	străin
German	fremd
Dutch	vreemd
Swedish	utländsk
Danish	fremmed
Norwegian	fremmed
Polish	obcokrajowy
Czech	zahranični
Serbo-Croat.	stran
Hungarian	külföldi
Finnish	ulkomainen
Turkish	ecnebi
Indonesian	asing, luar
Esperanto	fremda
Russian	innastránni
Greek	xe'nos
Arabic	gharib
Hebrew	nachri
Yiddish	fremd
Japanese	gwaikoku no
Swahili	-geni

396 forget

French	oublier
Spanish	olvidar
Italian	dimenticare
Portuguese	esquecer
Rumanian	uita
German	vergessen
Dutch	vergeten
Swedish	glömma
Danish	glemme
Norwegian	glemme
Polish	zapomnieć
Czech	zapomenouti
Serbo-Croat.	zaboraviti
Hungarian	elfelejt
Finnish	unohtaa
Turkish	unutmak
Indonesian	luna
Esperanto	forgesi
Russian	zabít
Greek	xechno'
Arabic	yansa
Hebrew	schachach
Yiddish	fergessen
Japanese	wasureru
Swahili	sahau

397 fork

French	fourchette
Spanish	tenedor
Italian	forchetta
Portuguese	garfo
Rumanian	furculiţă
German	Gabel
Dutch	vork
Swedish	gaffel
Danish	gaffel
Norwegian	gaffel
Polish	widelec
Czech	vidlička
Serbo-Croat.	viljuška
Hungarian	villa
Finnish	haarukka
Turkish	çatal
Indonesian	garpu
Esperanto	forko
Russian	vílka
Greek	pirou'ni
Arabic	shouka
Hebrew	masleg
Yiddish	gopel
Japanese	fooku
Swahili	uma

398 forty

French	quarante
Spanish	cuarenta
Italian	quaranta
Portuguese	quarenta
Rumanian	patruzeci
German	vierzig
Dutch	veertig
Swedish	fyrtio
Danish	fyrre
Norwegian	førti
Polish	czterdzieści
Czech	čtyřicet
Serbo-Croat.	četrdeset
Hungarian	negyven
Finnish	neljäkymmentä
Turkish	kırk
Indonesian	empat pulah
Esperanto	kvar'dek
Russian	sórak
Greek	saran'ta
Arabic	arbaoun
Hebrew	arbaim
Yiddish	fertsig
Japanese	yonjuu
Swahili	arobaini

399 fountain pen

French	stylo
Spanish	pluma estilográfica
Italian	penna stilografica
Portuguese	caneta-tinteiro
Rumanian	stilou
German	Füllfederhalter
Dutch	vulpen
Swedish	reservoar-penna
Danish	fyldepen
Norwegian	fyllepenn
Polish	wieczne pióro
Czech	plnicí pero
Serbo-Croat.	stilo
Hungarian	töltötoll
Finnish	täytekynä
Turkish	dolma kalem
Indonesian	pupeén
Esperanto	font'plumo
Russian	véchnoye peró
Greek	stilogra'fos
Arabic	qalam hibr
Hebrew	et novea
Yiddish	filfeder
Japanese	man'nen-hitsu
Swahili	kalamu ya wino

400 four

French	quatre
Spanish	cuatro
Italian	quattro
Portuguese	quatro
Rumanian	patru
German	vier
Dutch	vier
Swedish	fyra
Danish	fire
Norwegian	fire
Polish	cztery
Czech	čtyri
Serbo-Croat.	četiri
Hungarian	négy
Finnish	neljä
Turkish	dört
Indonesian	empot
Esperanto	kvar
Russian	chetírye
Greek	te'sera
Arabic	arbaa
Hebrew	arba
Yiddish	fier
Japanese	shi
Swahili	nne

401 fourteen

French	quatorze
Spanish	catorce
Italian	quattordici
Portuguese	catorze
Rumanian	patrusprezece
German	vierzehn
Dutch	veertien
Swedish	fjorton
Danish	fjorten
Norwegian	fjorten
Polish	czternaśćie
Czech	čtrnáct
Serbo-Croat.	četrnaest
Hungarian	tizennégy
Finnish	neljätoista
Turkish	on dört
Indonesian	empat belas
Esperanto	dek kvar
Russian	chetírnatsit
Greek	dekate'ssara
Arabic	arbaat ashar
Hebrew	arba esreh
Yiddish	fertsen
Japanese	juushi
Swahili	kumi na nne

402 fox

French	renard
Spanish	zorra
Italian	volpe
Portuguese	raposa
Rumanian	vulpe
German	Fuchs
Dutch	vos
Swedish	räv
Danish	ræv
Norwegian	rev
Polish	lis
Czech	liška
Serbo-Croat.	lisica
Hungarian	róka
Finnish	kettu
Turkish	tilki
Indonesian	tubah
Esperanto	vulpo
Russian	lisítsa
Greek	alepou'
Arabic	tsalab
Hebrew	schual
Yiddish	fuks
Japanese	kitsune
Swahili	mbweha

403 fragile

French	fragile
Spanish	frágil
Italian	fragile
Portuguese	frágil
Rumanian	fragil
German	zerbrechlich
Dutch	breekbaar
Swedish	bräcklig
Danish	skrøbelig
Norwegian	skjør
Polish	kruchy
Czech	křehký
Serbo-Croat.	loman
Hungarian	törékeny
Finnish	särkyvä
Turkish	kırılır
Indonesian	rangup
Esperanto	delikata
Russian	khrúpki
Greek	ef'thrafstos
Arabic	hash, qabil lilkasr
Hebrew	schabir
Yiddish	tserbrechlech
Japanese	koware-yasui
Swahili	-a kuvunjika upesi

404 free

French	libre
Spanish	libre
Italian	libero
Portuguese	livre
Rumanian	liber
German	frei
Dutch	vrij
Swedish	fri
Danish	fri
Norwegian	fri
Polish	wolny
Czech	volný
Serbo-Croat.	slobodan
Hungarian	szabad
Finnish	vapaa
Turkish	serbest
Indonesian	bebas
Esperanto	libera
Russian	svabódni
Greek	elef'theros
Arabic	hour
Hebrew	chafschie
Yiddish	frei
Japanese	jiyuu no
Swahili	huru

405 fresh

French	frais
Spanish	fresco
Italian	fresco
Portuguese	fresco
Rumanian	proaspăt
German	frisch
Dutch	vers
Swedish	färsk
Danish	frisk
Norwegian	frisk
Polish	świeży
Czech	čerstvý
Serbo-Croat.	svjež
Hungarian	friss, új
Finnish	raikas
Turkish	taze
Indonesian	baru
Esperanto	freŝa
Russian	svyézhi
Greek	fres'kos
Arabic	tazig
Hebrew	tari
Yiddish	frisch
Japanese	shinsen na
Swahili	-bichi

406 Friday

French	vendredi
Spanish	viernes
Italian	venerdi
Portuguese	sexta-feira
Rumanian	vineri
German	Freitag
Dutch	Vrijdag
Swedish	fredag
Danish	fredag
Norwegian	fredag
Polish	piątek
Czech	pátek
Serbo-Croat.	petak
Hungarian	péntek
Finnish	perjantai
Turkish	cuma
Indonesian	Djumahat
Esperanto	vendredo
Russian	pyátnitsa
Greek	Paraskevi'
Arabic	al goumaa
Hebrew	yom schischi
Yiddish	freitog
Japanese	kin'yoobi
Swahili	Ijumaa

407 fried fish

French	poisson frit
Spanish	pescado frito
Italian	pesce fritto
Portuguese	peixe frito
Rumanian	peşte prăjiti
German	Bratfisch
Dutch	gebakken vis
Swedish	stekt fisk
Danish	stegt fisk
Norwegian	stekt fisk
Polish	pieczona ryba
Czech	pečená ryba
Serbo-Croat.	pržena riba
Hungarian	sült hal
Finnish	paistettu kala
Turkish	kızarmış balik
Indonesian	ikan goreng
Esperanto	fiŝ'idoj
Russian	zhárenaya ríba
Greek	tiganito' psa'ri
Arabic	samak maqli
Hebrew	dagim metuganim
Yiddish	gebrotene fisch
Japanese	abura de ageta sakana
Swahili	samaki iliokaangua

408 friend

French	ami
Spanish	amigo
Italian	amico
Portuguese	amigo
Rumanian	prieten
German	Freund
Dutch	vriend
Swedish	vän
Danish	ven
Norwegian	venn
Polish	przyjaciel
Czech	přítel
Serbo-Croat.	prijatelj
Hungarian	barát
Finnish	ystävä
Turkish	dost
Indonesian	sahabat
Esperanto	amiko
Russian	druk
Greek	fi'los
Arabic	sadiq
Hebrew	yedid
Yiddish	chaver
Japanese	tomodachi
Swahili	rafiki

409 frog

French	grenouille
Spanish	rana
Italian	rana
Portuguese	rã
Rumanian	broască
German	Frosch
Dutch	kikvors
Swedish	groda
Danish	frø
Norwegian	frosk
Polish	żaba
Czech	žába
Serbo-Croat.	žaba
Hungarian	béka
Finnish	sammakko
Turkish	kurbağa
Indonesian	katak
Esperanto	rano
Russian	lyagúshka
Greek	va'trachos
Arabic	doufdaa
Hebrew	tsefardea
Yiddish	dsabe
Japanese	kaeru
Swahili	chura

410 from

French	de
Spanish	de
Italian	da
Portuguese	de
Rumanian	de
German	von
Dutch	van
Swedish	från
Danish	fra
Norwegian	fra
Polish	od
Czech	od, z
Serbo-Croat.	od
Hungarian	-bol, -tól, -ról
Finnish	luota
Turkish	-dan
Indonesian	dari
Esperanto	de
Russian	ot
Greek	apo'
Arabic	min
Hebrew	min
Yiddish	fun
Japanese	kara
Swahili	kwa

411 front

French	façade
Spanish	frente
Italian	fronte
Portuguese	frente
Rumanian	faţă
German	Vorderseite
Dutch	voorkant
Swedish	framsida
Danish	forside
Norwegian	forside
Polish	przód
Czech	předná strana
Serbo-Croat.	fasada
Hungarian	homlok
Finnish	etupuoli
Turkish	önünde
Indonesian	muka
Esperanto	fronto
Russian	fasát
Greek	me'topon
Arabic	amam
Hebrew	metsach
Yiddish	fornt
Japanese	shoomen
Swahili	upande wa mbele

412 fruit

French	fruit
Spanish	fruta
Italian	frutta
Portuguese	fruta
Rumanian	fruct
German	Obst
Dutch	vrucht
Swedish	frukt
Danish	frugt
Norwegian	frukt
Polish	owoc
Czech	ovoce
Serbo-Croat.	voće
Hungarian	gyümölcs
Finnish	hedelmä
Turkish	meyve
Indonesian	buah
Esperanto	frukto
Russian	frukt
Greek	frou'to
Arabic	fakiha
Hebrew	prie
Yiddish	frucht
Japanese	kudamono
Swahili	matunda

413 funeral

French	funérailles
Spanish	funeral
Italian	funerale
Portuguese	funeral
Rumanian	funeralii
German	Begräbnis
Dutch	begrafenis
Swedish	begravning
Danish	begravelse
Norwegian	begravelse
Polish	pogrzeb
Czech	pohřeb
Serbo-Croat.	pogreb
Hungarian	temetés
Finnish	hautaus
Turkish	cenaze
Indonesian	pemakaman
Esperanto	funeralo
Russian	pókharani
Greek	kidi'a
Arabic	ganaza
Hebrew	levayah
Yiddish	levaye
Japanese	sooshiki
Swahili	maziko

414 fur coat

French	manteau de fourrure
Spanish	abrigo de pieles
Italian	pelliccia
Portuguese	casaco de pele
Rumanian	blană
German	Pelzmantel
Dutch	bontjas
Swedish	päls
Danish	pels
Norwegian	pels
Polish	futro
Czech	kožich
Serbo-Croat.	bunda
Hungarian	bunda
Finnish	turkki
Turkish	kürk
Indonesian	mantel bulu binatang
Esperanto	pelto
Russian	myékh
Greek	gou'nino palto'
Arabic	mitaf min al-fira
Hebrew	aderes sear
Yiddish	pelts
Japanese	kegawa no kooto
Swahili	koti ya manyoya

415 gain

French	gagner
Spanish	ganar
Italian	guadagnare
Portuguese	ganhar
Rumanian	cîştiga
German	gewinnen
Dutch	verkrijgen
Swedish	vinna
Danish	vinde
Norwegian	vinne, oppnå
Polish	zyskać
Czech	ziskati
Serbo-Croat.	dobiti
Hungarian	nyer
Finnish	voittaa
Turkish	kazanmak
Indonesian	peroleh
Esperanto	gajni
Russian	dobivát
Greek	kerdi'zo
Arabic	yaksab
Hebrew	hirviach
Yiddish	gevinen
Japanese	uru
Swahili	faidi

416 game

French	jeu
Spanish	juego
Italian	giuoco
Portuguese	jôgo
Rumanian	joc
German	Spiel
Dutch	spel
Swedish	spel
Danish	leg
Norwegian	lek
Polish	zabawa
Czech	hra
Serbo-Croat.	igra
Hungarian	játék
Finnish	peli
Turkish	oyun
Indonesian	main
Esperanto	ludo
Russian	igrá
Greek	pechni'di
Arabic	louaba
Hebrew	mischak
Yiddish	schpiel
Japanese	shiai
Swahili	mchezo

417 garden

French	jardin
Spanish	jardín
Italian	giardino
Portuguese	jardim
Rumanian	grădina
German	Garten
Dutch	tuin
Swedish	trädgård
Danish	have
Norwegian	hage
Polish	ogród
Czech	zahrada
Serbo-Croat.	vrt
Hungarian	kert
Finnish	puutarha
Turkish	bahçe
Indonesian	kebun
Esperanto	ĝardeno
Russian	sat
Greek	ki'pos
Arabic	hadiqa
Hebrew	gan
Yiddish	gorten
Japanese	niwa
Swahili	bustani

418 garlic

French	ail
Spanish	ajo
Italian	aglio
Portuguese	alho
Rumanian	usturoi
German	Knoblauch
Dutch	knoflook
Swedish	vitlök
Danish	hvidløg
Norwegian	hvitløk
Polish	czosnek
Czech	česnek
Serbo-Croat.	beli luk
Hungarian	fokhagyma
Finnish	valkosipuli
Turkish	sarmısak
Indonesian	bawang putih
Esperanto	ajlo
Russian	chesnók
Greek	skor'don
Arabic	tsoum
Hebrew	schum
Yiddish	knobel
Japanese	nin'niku
Swahili	kitunguu saumu

419 garter

French	jarretière
Spanish	liga
Italian	giarrettiera
Portuguese	jarreteira
Rumanian	jartieră
German	Strumpfband
Dutch	kouseband
Swedish	strumpeband
Danish	sokkeholder
Norwegian	strømpebånd
Polish	podwiązka
Czech	podvazek
Serbo-Croat.	podvezica
Hungarian	harisnyakötő
Finnish	sukkanauha
Turkish	çorap băgı
Indonesian	ikat kaos
Esperanto	ŝtrump'zono
Russian	padvyáska
Greek	kaltsode'ta
Arabic	roubat ap-soq
Hebrew	birit
Yiddish	podviaske
Japanese	kutsushita-dome
Swahili	ukanda wa kuzuia soksi

420 gasoline

French	essence
Spanish	gasolina
Italian	benzina
Portuguese	gasolina
Rumanian	benzină
German	Benzin
Dutch	benzine
Swedish	bensin
Danish	benzin
Norwegian	bensin
Polish	benzyna
Czech	benzin
Serbo-Croat.	benzin
Hungarian	benzin
Finnish	bensiini
Turkish	benzin
Indonesian	bénsin
Esperanto	benzino
Russian	benzín
Greek	gazoli'ni
Arabic	ghazoulin
Hebrew	gasolin
Yiddish	bentsin
Japanese	gasorin
Swahili	petroli

421 gauge

French	jauge
Spanish	medida
Italian	misura
Portuguese	instrumento de medida
Rumanian	calibru
German	Mass
Dutch	peil
Swedish	mått
Danish	mål
Norwegian	mål
Polish	miara
Czech	míra
Serbo-Croat.	mjera
Hungarian	mérték
Finnish	mitta
Turkish	mikyas
Indonesian	ukuran
Esperanto	mezuro
Russian	myéra
Greek	metri'tis
Arabic	miayar
Hebrew	midah
Yiddish	mos
Japanese	keiki
Swahili	kipimio

422 general delivery

French	poste restante
Spanish	lista de correos
Italian	fermo-posta
Portuguese	posta-restante
Rumanian	postrestant
German	postlagernd
Dutch	poste-restante
Swedish	postlagrande
Danish	poste restante
Norwegian	poste restante
Polish	poste restante
Czech	poste restante
Serbo-Croat.	poste restante
Hungarian	postán maradó
Finnish	noudettava
Turkish	post restant
Indonesian	pos restant
Esperanto	poŝto rest'anta
Russian	do vastryébovaniye
Greek	post restant'
Arabic	tawzi aam
Hebrew	tevat doar
Yiddish	postfach
Japanese	yuubinbutsu kyokuwatashi
Swahili	postarestanti

423 gift

French	cadeau
Spanish	regalo
Italian	dono
Portuguese	presente
Rumanian	dar
German	Geschenk
Dutch	cadeau
Swedish	gåva
Danish	gave
Norwegian	gave
Polish	podarek
Czech	dar
Serbo-Croat.	dar
Hungarian	ajándék
Finnish	lahja
Turkish	hediye
Indonesian	hadoliah
Esperanto	donaco
Russian	padárok
Greek	do'ron
Arabic	hadiya
Hebrew	matan
Yiddish	matune
Japanese	okurimono
Swahili	zawadi

424 girl

French	jeune fille
Spanish	muchacha
Italian	ragazza
Portuguese	menina
Rumanian	fată
German	Mädchen
Dutch	meisje
Swedish	flicka
Danish	pige
Norwegian	pike
Polish	dziewczyna
Czech	děvče
Serbo-Croat.	devojka
Hungarian	leány
Finnish	tyttö
Turkish	kız
Indonesian	gadis
Esperanto	knab'ino
Russian	dyévushka
Greek	kori'tsi
Arabic	bint
Hebrew	naarah
Yiddish	maidel
Japanese	on'na no ko
Swahili	msichana

425 give

French	donner
Spanish	dar
Italian	dare
Portuguese	dar
Rumanian	da
German	geben
Dutch	geven
Swedish	giva
Danish	give
Norwegian	gi
Polish	dać
Czech	dáti
Serbo-Croat.	dati
Hungarian	ad
Finnish	antaa
Turkish	vermek
Indonesian	beri
Esperanto	doni
Russian	dát
Greek	di'no
Arabic	yuti
Hebrew	natan
Yiddish	geben
Japanese	ataeru
Swahili	toa

426 glad

French	heureux
Spanish	alegre
Italian	lieto
Portuguese	contente
Rumanian	bucuros
German	froh
Dutch	blij
Swedish	glad
Danish	glad
Norwegian	glad
Polish	szczęśliwy
Czech	potěšen, radostný
Serbo-Croat.	veseo
Hungarian	boldog
Finnish	iloinen
Turkish	memnun
Indonesian	suka hati
Esperanto	ĝoja
Russian	rádosni
Greek	efcharistime'nos
Arabic	said
Hebrew	sameach
Yiddish	derfreyt
Japanese	ureshii
Swahili	-a furaha

427 glass

French	verre
Spanish	vidrio
Italian	vetro
Portuguese	vidro
Rumanian	sticlă
German	Glas
Dutch	glas
Swedish	glas
Danish	glas
Norwegian	glass
Polish	szkło
Czech	sklo
Serbo-Croat.	staklo
Hungarian	pohár
Finnish	lasi
Turkish	cam
Indonesian	katja
Esperanto	vitro
Russian	stekló
Greek	poti'ri
Arabic	zougag
Hebrew	sechuchit
Yiddish	glos
Japanese	garasu
Swahili	kioo

428 glove

French	gant
Spanish	guante
Italian	guanto
Portuguese	luva
Rumanian	manuşă
German	Handschuh
Dutch	handschoen
Swedish	handske
Danish	handske
Norwegian	hanske
Polish	rękawiczka
Czech	rukavice
Serbo-Croat.	rukavica
Hungarian	kesztyü
Finnish	hansikas
Turkish	eldiven
Indonesian.	sarung tangan
Esperanto	ganto
Russian	perchátka
Greek	gan'ti
Arabic	qouffaz
Hebrew	kefafah
Yiddish	hendschke
Japanese	tebukuro
Swahili	mfuko wa mkono

429 glue

French	colle
Spanish	cola
Italian	colla
Portuguese	cola
Rumanian	clei
German	Klebstoff
Dutch	lijm
Swedish	klister
Danish	lim
Norwegian	lim
Polish	klej
Czech	lepidlo, klih
Serbo-Croat.	lepak
Hungarian	enyv
Finnish	liima
Turkish	tutkal, zamk
Indonesian	lem
Esperanto	gluo
Russian	klyéy
Greek	ko'lla
Arabic	samgh
Hebrew	devek
Yiddish	kleb
Japanese	nikawa
Swahili	sherizi

430 go

French	aller
Spanish	ir
Italian	andare
Portuguese	ir
Rumanian	merge
German	gehen
Dutch	gaan
Swedish	gå
Danish	gå
Norwegian	gå
Polish	iść
Czech	jíti, choditi
Serbo-Croat.	ići
Hungarian	megy
Finnish	mennä
Turkish	gitmek
Indonesian	pergi
Esperanto	iri
Russian	ití
Greek	piye'no
Arabic	yatzhab
Hebrew	halach
Yiddish	gehn
Japanese	yuku
Swahili	enda

431 goat

French	chèvre
Spanish	cabra
Italian	capra
Portuguese	cabra
Rumanian	capră
German	Ziege
Dutch	geit
Swedish	get
Danish	ged
Norwegian	geit
Polish	koza
Czech	koza
Serbo-Croat.	koza
Hungarian	kecske
Finnish	vuohi
Turkish	keçi
Indonesian	kambing
Esperanto	kapro
Russian	kazá
Greek	katsi'ka
Arabic	gidye
Hebrew	ez
Yiddish	koze
Japanese	yagi
Swahili	mbuzi

432 God

French	Dieu
Spanish	Dios
Italian	Dio
Portuguese	Deus
Rumanian	dumnezeu
German	Gott
Dutch	God
Swedish	Gud
Danish	Gud
Norwegian	Gud
Polish	Bóg
Czech	bůh
Serbo-Croat.	bog
Hungarian	isten
Finnish	Jumala
Turkish	Allah, tanri
Indonesian	Tuhan, Allah
Esperanto	dio
Russian	bokh
Greek	Theos'
Arabic	ilah
Hebrew	el
Yiddish	got
Japanese	kami
Swahili	Mungu

433 gold

French	or
Spanish	oro
Italian	oro
Portuguese	ouro
Rumanian	aur
German	Gold
Dutch	goud
Swedish	guld
Danish	guld
Norwegian	gull
Polish	złoto
Czech	zlato
Serbo-Croat.	zlato
Hungarian	arany
Finnish	kulta
Turkish	altın
Indonesian	emas
Esperanto	oro
Russian	zólato
Greek	chrisos'
Arabic	tzahab
Hebrew	zahav
Yiddish	gold
Japanese	kin
Swahili	dhahabu

434 good

French	bon
Spanish	bueno
Italian	buono
Portuguese	bom
Rumanian	bun
German	gut
Dutch	goed
Swedish	god
Danish	god
Norwegian	god
Polish	dobrze
Czech	dobrý
Serbo-Croat.	dobro
Hungarian	jó
Finnish	hyvä
Turkish	iyi
Indonesian	baik
Esperanto	bona
Russian	kharóshi
Greek	kalos'
Arabic	gayid
Hebrew	tov
Yiddish	gut
Japanese	yoi
Swahili	-ema

435 goodby

French	au revoir
Spanish	adíos
Italian	addio
Portuguese	adeus
Rumanian	adio
German	auf Wiedersehen
Dutch	dag
Swedish	adjö
Danish	farvel
Norwegian	farvel
Polish	do widzenia
Czech	sbohem
Serbo-Croat.	zbogom
Hungarian	istenhozzád
Finnish	hyvästi
Turkish	allaha ısmarladık
Indonesian	selemat tinggal
Esperanto	adiaŭ
Russian	do zvidániya
Greek	andi'o
Arabic	ila al-laqaa
Hebrew	schalom
Yiddish	seid gezund
Japanese	sayoonara
Swahili	kwaheri

436 goose

French	oie
Spanish	ganso
Italian	oca
Portuguese	ganso
Rumanian	gîscă
German	Gans
Dutch	gans
Swedish	gås
Danish	gås
Norwegian	gås
Polish	gęś
Czech	husa
Serbo-Croat.	guska
Hungarian	liba
Finnish	hanhi
Turkish	kaz
Indonesian	angsa, gangsa
Esperanto	ansero
Russian	gus
Greek	chi'na
Arabic	wizzah
Hebrew	avazah
Yiddish	gands
Japanese	gachoo
Swahili	bata bukini

437 gooseberry

French	groseille
Spanish	grosella
Italian	ribes
Portuguese	groselha
Rumanian	coacăză
German	Stachelbeere
Dutch	kruisbes
Swedish	krusbär
Danish	stikkelsbær
Norwegian	stikkelsabær
Polish	agrest
Czech	angrešt
Serbo-Croat.	ogrozd
Hungarian	egres
Finnish	karviaismarja
Turkish	bektaşi üzümü
Indonesian	gusbai
Esperanto	groso
Russian	krishóvnik
Greek	frankosta'filon
Arabic	inab al-tsalab
Hebrew	akavit
Yiddish	agress
Japanese	suguri
Swahili	namna ya tunda

438 government

French	gouvernement
Spanish	gobierno
Italian	governo
Portuguese	govêrno
Rumanian	guvern
German	Regierung
Dutch	regering
Swedish	styrelse
Danish	regering
Norwegian	regjering
Polish	rząd
Czech	vláda
Serbo-Croat.	vlada
Hungarian	kormány
Finnish	hallitus
Turkish	hükûmet
Indonesian	permerintah
Esperanto	registaro
Russian	pravítelstvo
Greek	kiver'nisis
Arabic	houkouma
Hebrew	memschalah
Yiddish	regierung
Japanese	seifu
Swahili	serikali

439 grape

French	raisin
Spanish	uva
Italian	uva
Portuguese	uva
Rumanian	strugur
German	Weintraube
Dutch	druif
Swedish	druva
Danish	drue
Norwegian	drue
Polish	winogrono
Czech	hrozen
Serbo-Croat.	grožđje
Hungarian	szellő
Finnish	viinirypäle
Turkish	üzüm
Indonesian	buah anggur
Esperanto	vin'bero
Russian	vinagrát
Greek	stafi'li
Arabic	inab
Hebrew	enav
Yiddish	veintroib
Japanese	budoo
Swahili	zabibu

440 grapefruit

French	pamplemousse
Spanish	toronja
Italian	pompelmo
Portuguese	toronja
Rumanian	grepfrut
German	Pompelmuse
Dutch	pompelmoes
Swedish	grapefruit
Danish	grapefrugt
Norwegian	grapefrukt
Polish	grapefruit
Czech	druh pomeranče
Serbo-Croat.	grejpfrut
Hungarian	grépfrút
Finnish	greippi
Turkish	grepfrut
Indonesian	buah djeruk
Esperanto	pampelmo
Russian	gréypfrut
Greek	greip-frout'
Arabic	laymoun hindi
Hebrew	eschkolit
Yiddish	grepfrucht
Japanese	gureepu fruutsu
Swahili	balungi

441 grass

French	herbe
Spanish	hierba
Italian	erba
Portuguese	erva
Rumanian	iarbă
German	Gras
Dutch	gras
Swedish	gräss
Danish	græs
Norwegian	gress
Polish	trawa
Czech	tráva
Serbo-Croat.	trava
Hungarian	fű
Finnish	ruoho
Turkish	çimen
Indonesian	rumput
Esperanto	herbo
Russian	travá
Greek	grasi'di
Arabic	hashish
Hebrew	essev
Yiddish	groz
Japanese	kusa
Swahili	majani

442 gravy

French	sauce
Spanish	salsa
Italian	sugo
Portuguese	môlho
Rumanian	sos
German	Sosse
Dutch	jus
Swedish	sås
Danish	sovs
Norwegian	saus
Polish	sos
Czech	omáčka
Serbo-Croat.	sos
Hungarian	mártás
Finnish	kastike
Turkish	salça
Indonesian	saos, kuah
Esperanto	suko
Russian	padlífka, sóus
Greek	sal'tsa
Arabic	salsa
Hebrew	rotev
Yiddish	soss
Japanese	nikujiru
Swahili	mchuzi

443 green

French	vert
Spanish	verde
Italian	verde
Portuguese	verde
Rumanian	verde
German	grün
Dutch	groen
Swedish	grön
Danish	grøn
Norwegian	grønn
Polish	zielony
Czech	zelený
Serbo-Croat.	zeleno
Hungarian	zöld
Finnish	vihreä
Turkish	yeşil
Indonesian	hidjah
Esperanto	verda
Russian	zelyóni
Greek	pra'sinos
Arabic	achdar
Hebrew	yarok
Yiddish	grien
Japanese	midori'iro
Swahili	rangi ya majani

444 grey

French	gris
Spanish	gris
Italian	grigio
Portuguese	cinzento
Rumanian	gri
German	grau
Dutch	grijs
Swedish	grå
Danish	grå
Norwegian	grå
Polish	szary
Czech	šedivý
Serbo-Croat.	siv
Hungarian	szürke
Finnish	harmaa
Turkish	gri
Indonesian	kelabu
Esperanto	griza
Russian	syéri
Greek	gri'zos
Arabic	ramadi
Hebrew	afor
Yiddish	groi
Japanese	hai'iro
Swahili	rangi ya majivu

445 grow

French	croître
Spanish	crecer
Italian	crescere
Portuguese	crescer
Rumanian	creşte
German	wachsen
Dutch	groeien
Swedish	växa
Danish	vokse
Norwegian	vokse
Polish	rosnąć
Czech	růsti
Serbo-Croat.	rasti
Hungarian	nő
Finnish	kasvaa
Turkish	büyümek
Indonesian	tumbuh
Esperanto	kreski
Russian	rastí
Greek	megalo'no
Arabic	yazdad
Hebrew	gadal
Yiddish	vaksen
Japanese	seichoo suru
Swahili	kua

446 guard

French	garde
Spanish	guardia
Italian	guardia
Portuguese	guarda
Rumanian	gardă
German	Wache
Dutch	wacht
Swedish	vakt
Danish	vagt
Norwegian	vakt
Polish	straż
Czech	stráž
Serbo-Croat.	čuvar
Hungarian	őr
Finnish	vartio
Turkish	bekçi
Indonesian	kawal
Esperanto	gardo
Russian	strázha
Greek	fi'lakas
Arabic	haris
Hebrew	mischmar
Yiddish	vach
Japanese	goei
Swahili	hadhari

447 guest

French	invité
Spanish	convidado
Italian	ospite
Portuguese	convidado
Rumanian	mosafir
German	Gast
Dutch	gast
Swedish	gäst
Danish	gæst
Norwegian	gjest
Polish	gość
Czech	host
Serbo-Croat.	gost
Hungarian	vendég
Finnish	vieras
Turkish	misafir
Indonesian	tamu
Esperanto	gasto
Russian	gost
Greek	filoxenou'menos
Arabic	dayf
Hebrew	oreach
Yiddish	gast
Japanese	kyaku
Swahili	mgeni

448 guide

French	guide
Spanish	guía
Italian	guida
Portuguese	guia
Rumanian	ghid
German	Führer
Dutch	gids
Swedish	förare
Danish	fører
Norwegian	fører
Polish	przewodnik
Czech	vůdce
Serbo-Croat.	vodič
Hungarian	vezető
Finnish	opas
Turkish	kılavuz
Indonesian	pandu
Esperanto	gvid'anto
Russian	provodník
Greek	xenagos'
Arabic	mourshid
Hebrew	madrich
Yiddish	vegweiser
Japanese	an'naisha
Swahili	kiongozi

449 guilty

French	coupable
Spanish	culpable
Italian	colpevole
Portuguese	culpado
Rumanian	vinovat
German	schuldig
Dutch	schuldig
Swedish	skyldig
Danish	skyldig
Norwegian	skyldig
Polish	winny
Czech	vinný
Serbo-Croat.	kriv
Hungarian	bűnös
Finnish	syyllinen
Turkish	suçlu
Indonesian	bersalan, berdosa
Esperanto	kulpa
Russian	vinóvni
Greek	e'nochos
Arabic	moutznib
Hebrew	chayav
Yiddish	chayif
Japanese	tsumi aru
Swahili	-enye hatia

450 gun

French	arme de feu
Spanish	arma
Italian	arma
Portuguese	arma de fogo
Rumanian	puşcă
German	Waffe
Dutch	geweer
Swedish	vapen
Danish	våben
Norwegian	våpen
Polish	strzelba
Czech	zbraň
Serbo-Croat.	puška
Hungarian	fegyver
Finnish	ase
Turkish	ateş silâhı
Indonesian	sendjita
Esperanto	paf'ilo
Russian	arúzhiye
Greek	op'lon
Arabic	mousadas
Hebrew	klay-zayin
Yiddish	klay-zayin
Japanese	juu
Swahili	bunduki

451 gymnastics

French	gymnastique
Spanish	gimnasia
Italian	ginnastica
Portuguese	ginástica
Rumanian	gimnastică
German	Turnen
Dutch	gymnastiek
Swedish	gymnastik
Danish	gymnastik
Norwegian	gymnastikk
Polish	gimnastyka
Czech	tělocvik
Serbo-Croat.	gimnastika
Hungarian	torna
Finnish	voimistella
Turkish	cimnastik
Indonesian	gerak badan
Esperanto	gimnastiko
Russian	gimnástika
Greek	yimnastiki'
Arabic	riyadah
Hebrew	hitamlut
Yiddish	gimnastike
Japanese	taisoo
Swahili	zoezi kwa mwili

452 hail

French	grêle
Spanish	granizo
Italian	grandine
Portuguese	granizo
Rumanian	grindină
German	Hagel
Dutch	hagel
Swedish	hagel
Danish	hagl
Norwegian	hagl
Polish	grad
Czech	kroupy
Serbo-Croat.	grad
Hungarian	jégeső
Finnish	rakeet
Turkish	dolu
Indonesian	hujan es
Esperanto	hajlo
Russian	grat
Greek	chala'zi
Arabic	barad
Hebrew	barad
Yiddish	hogel
Japanese	arare
Swahili	mvua ya mawe

453 hair

French	cheveux
Spanish	pelo
Italian	capello
Portuguese	cabelo
Rumanian	păr
German	Haar
Dutch	haar
Swedish	hår
Danish	hår
Norwegian	hår
Polish	włosy
Czech	vlas
Serbo-Croat.	kosa
Hungarian	haj
Finnish	tukka
Turkish	saç
Indonesian	rambut
Esperanto	haro
Russian	vólasi
Greek	mallia'
Arabic	shaar
Hebrew	saarot
Yiddish	hoor
Japanese	ke
Swahili	nywele

454 hairdresser

French	coiffeur
Spanish	peluquero
Italian	parrucchiere
Portuguese	cabeleireiro
Rumanian	coafor
German	Friseur
Dutch	kapper
Swedish	frisör
Danish	frisør
Norwegian	frisør
Polish	fryzjer
Czech	kadeřník, holič
Serbo-Croat.	frizer
Hungarian	fodrász
Finnish	parturi
Turkish	berber
Indonesian	tukang rambut
Esperanto	friz'isto
Russian	parikmákher
Greek	komo'tria
Arabic	mizayen
Hebrew	sapar
Yiddish	frizejr
Japanese	kamiyui
Swahili	kinyozi

455 half

French	demi
Spanish	medio
Italian	mezzo
Portuguese	meio
Rumanian	jumătate
German	halb
Dutch	half
Swedish	hälft
Danish	halv
Norwegian	halv
Polish	połowa
Czech	poloviční, půl
Serbo-Croat.	polovina
Hungarian	fél
Finnish	puoli
Turkish	yarım
Indonesian	setengah
Esperanto	du'one
Russian	palavína
Greek	misos'
Arabic	nisf
Hebrew	chatsi
Yiddish	halb
Japanese	hanbun
Swahili	nusu

456 ham

French	jambon
Spanish	jamón
Italian	prosciutto
Portuguese	presunto
Rumanian	şuncă
German	Schinken
Dutch	ham
Swedish	skinka
Danish	skinke
Norwegian	skinke
Polish	szynka
Czech	šunka
Serbo-Croat.	šunka
Hungarian	sonka
Finnish	kinkku
Turkish	jambon
Indonesian	ham
Esperanto	ŝinko
Russian	vechiná
Greek	zambon'
Arabic	fachtz chanzir
Hebrew	schok chasir
Yiddish	schunken
Japanese	hamu
Swahili	paja ya nguruwe

457 hammer

French	marteau
Spanish	martillo
Italian	martello
Portuguese	martelo
Rumanian	ciocan
German	Hammer
Dutch	hamer
Swedish	hammare
Danish	hammer
Norwegian	hammer
Polish	młot
Czech	kladivo
Serbo-Croat.	čekić
Hungarian	kalapács
Finnish	vasara
Turkish	çekiç
Indonesian	martil, tukul
Esperanto	martelo
Russian	mólot
Greek	sfiri',
Arabic	matraqa
Hebrew	patisch
Yiddish	hammer
Japanese	kanazuchi
Swahili	nyundo

458 hand

French	main
Spanish	mano
Italian	mano
Portuguese	mão
Rumanian	mînă
German	Hand
Dutch	hand
Swedish	hand
Danish	hånd
Norwegian	hånd
Polish	ręka
Czech	ruka
Serbo-Croat.	ruka
Hungarian	kéz
Finnish	käsi
Turkish	el
Indonesian	tangan
Esperanto	mano
Russian	ruká
Greek	che'ri
Arabic	yad
Hebrew	yad
Yiddish	hand
Japanese	te
Swahili	mkono

459 handkerchief

French	mouchoir
Spanish	pañuelo
Italian	fazzoletto
Portuguese	lenço
Rumanian	batistă
German	Taschentuch
Dutch	zakdoek
Swedish	näsduk
Danish	lommetørklæde
Norwegian	lommetørkle
Polish	chusteczka
Czech	kapesník
Serbo-Croat.	maramica
Hungarian	zsebkendő
Finnish	nenäliina
Turkish	mendil
Indonesian	sapu tangan
Esperanto	poŝ'tuko
Russian	nasavóy platók
Greek	manti'li
Arabic	mandil
Hebrew	mitpachat
Yiddish	fatscheile
Japanese	hankachi
Swahili	kitambaa

460 hang

French	pendre
Spanish	colgar
Italian	pendere
Portuguese	pendurar
Rumanian	atirna
German	hängen
Dutch	hangen
Swedish	hänga
Danish	hænge
Norwegian	henge
Polish	wieszać
Czech	věsiti
Serbo-Croat.	obesiti
Hungarian	akaszt
Finnish	ripustaa
Turkish	asmak
Indonesian	gantung
Esperanto	pendi
Russian	vyéshat
Greek	kremo'
Arabic	yashnouq
Hebrew	talah
Yiddish	hengen
Japanese	kakeru
Swahili	angika

461 harbor

French	port
Spanish	puerto
Italian	porto
Portuguese	pôrto
Rumanian	port
German	Hafen
Dutch	haven
Swedish	hamn
Danish	havn
Norwegian	havn
Polish	przystań
Czech	přísta
Serbo-Croat.	pristanište
Hungarian	kikötő
Finnish	satama
Turkish	liman
Indonesian	labuhan
Esperanto	haveno
Russian	gávan
Greek	lima'ni
Arabic	tsaghr
Hebrew	namal
Yiddish	hafen
Japanese	minato
Swahili	bandari

462 hard

French	dur
Spanish	duro
Italian	duro
Portuguese	duro
Rumanian	dur
German	hart
Dutch	hard
Swedish	hård
Danish	hård
Norwegian	hard
Polish	twardy
Czech	tvrdý
Serbo-Croat.	tvrd
Hungarian	kemény
Finnish	kova
Turkish	sert
Indonesian	keras
Esperanto	malmola
Russian	tvyórdi
Greek	skliros'
Arabic	gamid
Hebrew	kascheh
Yiddish	hart
Japanese	katai
Swahili	-gumu

463 harvest

French	moisson
Spanish	cosecha
Italian	raccolta
Portuguese	colheita
Rumanian	recoltă
German	Ernte
Dutch	oogst
Swedish	skörd
Danish	høst
Norwegian	høst, avl
Polish	żniwo
Czech	sklizeň
Serbo-Croat.	žetva
Hungarian	aratás
Finnish	sato
Turkish	hasat
Indonesian	penén
Esperanto	rikolto
Russian	zhátva
Greek	singomidi'
Arabic	hisad
Hebrew	katsir
Yiddish	ernte
Japanese	shuukwaku
Swahili	mavuno

464 hat

French	chapeau
Spanish	sombrero
Italian	cappello
Portuguese	chapéu
Rumanian	palărie
German	Hut
Dutch	hoed
Swedish	hatt
Danish	hat
Norwegian	hatt
Polish	kapelusz
Czech	klobouk
Serbo-Croat.	šesir
Hungarian	kalap
Finnish	hattu
Turkish	şapka
Indonesian	topi
Esperanto	ĉapelo
Russian	shlyápa
Greek	kape'llo
Arabic	qoubaa
Hebrew	kova
Yiddish	kapelusch
Japanese	booshi
Swahili	kofia

465 hate

French	haïr
Spanish	odiar
Italian	odiare
Portuguese	odiar
Rumanian	urî
German	hassen
Dutch	haten
Swedish	hata
Danish	hade
Norwegian	hate
Polish	nienawidzieć
Czech	nenáviděti
Serbo-Croat.	mrzeti
Hungarian	gyűlöl
Finnish	vihata
Turkish	nefret etmek
Indonesian	bentji
Esperanto	mal'ami
Russian	nenavídet
Greek	miso'
Arabic	kourh
Hebrew	sane
Yiddish	feint hoben
Japanese	kirau
Swahili	chukia

466 have

French	avoir
Spanish	tener
Italian	avere
Portuguese	ter
Rumanian	avea
German	haben
Dutch	hebben
Swedish	hava
Danish	have
Norwegian	ha
Polish	mieć
Czech	míti
Serbo-Croat.	imati
Hungarian	vmje van
Finnish	omata
Turkish	malik olmak
Indonesian	punjai
Esperanto	havi
Russian	imyét
Greek	e'cho
Arabic	ind : indy
Hebrew	haya l . . .
Yiddish	hoben
Japanese	motsu
Swahili	-wa na

467 he

French	il
Spanish	él
Italian	egli
Portuguese	êle
Rumanian	el
German	er
Dutch	hij
Swedish	han
Danish	han
Norwegian	han
Polish	on
Czech	on
Serbo-Croat.	on
Hungarian	ő
Finnish	hän
Turkish	o
Indonesian	dia
Esperanto	li
Russian	on
Greek	aftos'
Arabic	houwa
Hebrew	hu
Yiddish	er
Japanese	kare
Swahili	yeye

468 head

French	tête
Spanish	cabeza
Italian	testa
Portuguese	cabeça
Rumanian	cap
German	Kopf
Dutch	hoofd
Swedish	huvud
Danish	hoved
Norwegian	hode
Polish	głowa
Czech	hlava
Serbo-Croat.	glava
Hungarian	fej
Finnish	pää
Turkish	baş
Indonesian	kepala
Esperanto	kapo
Russian	galavá
Greek	kefa'li
Arabic	raas
Hebrew	rosch
Yiddish	kop
Japanese	atama
Swahili	kichwa

469 health

French	santé
Spanish	salud
Italian	salute
Portuguese	saúde
Rumanian	sănătate
German	Gesundheit
Dutch	gezondheid
Swedish	hälsa
Danish	sundhed
Norwegian	helse
Polish	zdrowie
Czech	zdraví
Serbo-Croat.	zdravlje
Hungarian	egészség
Finnish	terveys
Turkish	sıhhat
Indonesian	keséhat
Esperanto	sano
Russian	zdaróvye
Greek	iyi'a
Arabic	siha
Hebrew	briut
Yiddish	gezundheit
Japanese	kenkoo
Swahili	uzima

470 hear

French	entendre
Spanish	oír
Italian	udire
Portuguese	ouvir
Rumanian	asculta
German	hören
Dutch	horen
Swedish	höra
Danish	høre
Norwegian	høre
Polish	słyszeć
Czech	slyšeti
Serbo-Croat.	čuti
Hungarian	hall
Finnish	kuulla
Turkish	duymak
Indonesian	dengar
Esperanto	aŭdi
Russian	slíshat
Greek	akou'o
Arabic	yasmaa
Hebrew	schamah
Yiddish	heren
Japanese	kiku
Swahili	sikia

471 heart

French	cœur
Spanish	corazón
Italian	cuore
Portuguese	coraçao
Rumanian	inimă
German	Herz
Dutch	hart
Swedish	hjärta
Danish	hjerte
Norwegian	hjerte
Polish	serce
Czech	srdce
Serbo-Croat.	srce
Hungarian	szív
Finnish	sydän
Turkish	kalb
Indonesian	annutdjg
Esperanto	koro
Russian	syértse
Greek	kardia'
Arabic	qalb
Hebrew	lev
Yiddish	herts
Japanese	shinzoo
Swahili	moyo

472 heavy

French	lourd
Spanish	pesado
Italian	pesante
Portuguese	pesado
Rumanian	greu
German	schwer
Dutch	zwaar
Swedish	tung
Danish	tung
Norwegian	tung
Polish	ciężki
Czech	těžký
Serbo-Croat.	težak
Hungarian	nehéz
Finnish	raskas
Turkish	ağır
Indonesian	berat
Esperanto	peza
Russian	tyazhóli
Greek	varis'
Arabic	tsaqil
Hebrew	kavet
Yiddish	schver
Japanese	omoi
Swahili	-zito

473 heel

French	talon
Spanish	talón
Italian	calcagno
Portuguese	calcanhar
Rumanian	călcîi
German	Ferse
Dutch	hiel
Swedish	häl
Danish	hæl
Norwegian	hæl
Polish	pięta
Czech	pata
Serbo-Croat.	peta
Hungarian	sarok
Finnish	kantapää
Turkish	ökçe
Indonesian	tumit
Esperanto	kalkano
Russian	pyatá
Greek	pter'na
Arabic	kaab
Hebrew	akev
Yiddish	pjate
Japanese	kakato
Swahili	kifundo cha mguu

474 help

French	aider
Spanish	ayudar
Italian	aiutare
Portuguese	ajudar
Rumanian	ajuta
German	helfen
Dutch	helpen
Swedish	hjälpa
Danish	hjælpe
Norwegian	hjelpe
Polish	pomoc
Czech	pomoci
Serbo-Croat.	pomóći
Hungarian	segít
Finnish	auttaa
Turkish	yardim etmek
Indonesian	tolong
Esperanto	helpi
Russian	pomagát
Greek	voitha'o
Arabic	youin
Hebrew	asar
Yiddish	helfen
Japanese	tasukeru
Swahili	saidia

475 here

French	ici
Spanish	aquí
Italian	qui
Portuguese	aqui
Rumanian	aici
German	hier
Dutch	hier
Swedish	här
Danish	her
Norwegian	her
Polish	tutaj
Czech	zde
Serbo-Croat.	ovdje
Hungarian	itt
Finnish	täällä
Turkish	burada
Indonesian	sini
Esperanto	tie ĉi
Russian	zdyés
Greek	edo'
Arabic	houna
Hebrew	kan
Yiddish	do
Japanese	koko
Swahili	hapa

476 herring

French	hareng
Spanish	arenque
Italian	aringa
Portuguese	arenque
Rumanian	hering
German	Hering
Dutch	haring
Swedish	sill
Danish	sild
Norwegian	sild
Polish	śledź
Czech	sled', slaneček
Serbo-Croat.	haringa
Hungarian	hering
Finnish	silli
Turkish	ringa balığı
Indonesian	haring
Esperanto	haringo
Russian	selyótka
Greek	ren'ga
Arabic	ringa
Hebrew	dagmeluach
Yiddish	hering
Japanese	nishin
Swahili	namna ya samaki

477 highway

French	route
Spanish	carretera
Italian	strada maestra
Portuguese	estrada
Rumanian	şosea
German	Landstrasse
Dutch	grote weg
Swedish	landsväg
Danish	landevej
Norwegian	landevei
Polish	szosa
Czech	silnice
Serbo-Croat.	drum
Hungarian	országút
Finnish	maantie
Turkish	cadde
Indonesian	djalan raja
Esperanto	vojo
Russian	daróga
Greek	leofo'ros
Arabic	tariq
Hebrew	kvisch
Yiddish	fuhrveg
Japanese	koosoku dooro
Swahili	barabara

478 hole

French	trou
Spanish	agujero
Italian	buco
Portuguese	buraco
Rumanian	gaură
German	Loch
Dutch	gat
Swedish	hål
Danish	hul
Norwegian	hull
Polish	dziura
Czech	díra
Serbo-Croat.	rupa
Hungarian	lyuk
Finnish	reikä
Turkish	çukur
Indonesian	lobang
Esperanto	truo
Russian	dirá
Greek	tri'pa
Arabic	tsouqb
Hebrew	nekev
Yiddish	loch
Japanese	ana
Swahili	tundu

479 holiday

French	fête
Spanish	fiesta
Italian	festa
Portuguese	feriado
Rumanian	sărbatoare
German	Feiertag
Dutch	vacantie
Swedish	ferie
Danish	helligdag
Norwegian	ferie
Polish	święto
Czech	svaték
Serbo-Croat.	praznik
Hungarian	ünnep
Finnish	juhlapäivä
Turkish	tatil günü
Indonesian	liburan, pakansi
Esperanto	ferio
Russian	práznik
Greek	eorti'
Arabic	ıd
Hebrew	chag
Yiddish	yomtof
Japanese	saijitsu
Swahili	sikukuu

480 honey

French	miel
Spanish	miel
Italian	miele
Portuguese	mel
Rumanian	miere
German	Honig
Dutch	honing
Swedish	honung
Danish	honning
Norwegian	honning
Polish	miód
Czech	med
Serbo-Croat.	med
Hungarian	méz
Finnish	hunaja
Turkish	bal
Indonesian	mada
Esperanto	mielo
Russian	myot
Greek	me'li
Arabic	aasal
Hebrew	dvasch
Yiddish	honig
Japanese	hachimitsu
Swahili	asali

481 horse

French	cheval
Spanish	caballo
Italian	cavallo
Portuguese	cavalo
Rumanian	cal
German	Pferd
Dutch	paard
Swedish	häst
Danish	hest
Norwegian	hest
Polish	koń
Czech	kůň
Serbo-Croat.	konj
Hungarian	ló
Finnish	hevonen
Turkish	at
Indonesian	kuda
Esperanto	ĉevalo
Russian	lózhat
Greek	a'logo
Arabic	hisan
Hebrew	sus
Yiddish	ferd
Japanese	uma
Swahili	farasi

482 horserace

French	course de chevaux
Spanish	carrera de caballos
Italian	corsa di cavalli
Portuguese	corrida de cavalo
Rumanian	cursă de cai
German	Pferderennen
Dutch	wedren
Swedish	ridtävling
Danish	hestevæddeløb
Norwegian	hesteveddeløp
Polish	wiścigi konne
Czech	koňské dostihy
Serbo-Croat.	konjske trke
Hungarian	lóverseny
Finnish	ratsastuskilpailut
Turkish	at yarışı
Indonesian	patjuan kuda
Esperanto	ĉeval'kur'ado
Russian	skáchki
Greek	ippodromi'a
Arabic	sibaq ap-chail
Hebrew	hitcharah susim
Yiddish	ferdgeloif
Japanese	keiba
Swahili	shindano ya farasi

483 hospital

French	hôpital
Spanish	hospital
Italian	ospedale
Portuguese	hospital
Rumanian	spital
German	Krankenhaus
Dutch	ziekenhuis
Swedish	sjukhus
Danish	hospital
Norwegian	sykehus
Polish	szpital
Czech	nemocnice
Serbo-Croat.	bolnica
Hungarian	kórház
Finnish	sairaala
Turkish	hastane
Indonesian	tumah sakit
Esperanto	hospitalo
Russian	balnítsa
Greek	nosokomi'on
Arabic	moustashfa
Hebrew	beth-cholim
Yiddish	schpitol
Japanese	byooin
Swahili	hospitali

484 hotel

French	hôtel
Spanish	hotel
Italian	albergo
Portuguese	hotel
Rumanian	hotel
German	Hotel
Dutch	hotel
Swedish	hotell
Danish	hotel
Norwegian	hotell
Polish	hotel
Czech	hotel
Serbo-Croat.	hotel
Hungarian	szálloda
Finnish	hotelli
Turkish	otel
Indonesian	hotél
Esperanto	hotelo
Russian	gastínitsa
Greek	xenodochi'on
Arabic	lukanda
Hebrew	malon
Yiddish	hotel
Japanese	hoteru
Swahili	hoteli

485 hour

French	heure
Spanish	hora
Italian	ora
Portuguese	hora
Rumanian	oră
German	Stunde
Dutch	uur
Swedish	timme
Danish	time
Norwegian	time
Polish	godzina
Czech	hodina
Serbo-Croat.	čas
Hungarian	óra
Finnish	tunti
Turkish	saat
Indonesian	djam
Esperanto	horo
Russian	chas
Greek	o'ra
Arabic	saah
Hebrew	schaah
Yiddish	schuh
Japanese	ichijikan
Swahili	saa

486 house

French	maison
Spanish	casa
Italian	casa
Portuguese	casa
Rumanian	casă
German	Haus
Dutch	huis
Swedish	hus
Danish	hus
Norwegian	hus
Polish	dom
Czech	dům
Serbo-Croat.	kuća
Hungarian	ház
Finnish	talo
Turkish	ev
Indonesian	rumah
Esperanto	domo
Russian	dom
Greek	spi'ti
Arabic	bayt
Hebrew	bayit
Yiddish	hois
Japanese	ie
Swahili	nyumba

487 hundred

French	cent
Spanish	ciento
Italian	cento
Portuguese	cem
Rumanian	sută
German	hundert
Dutch	honderd
Swedish	hundra
Danish	hundrede
Norwegian	hundre
Polish	sto
Czech	sto
Serbo-Croat.	sto
Hungarian	száz
Finnish	sata
Turkish	yüz
Indonesian	seratus
Esperanto	cento
Russian	sto
Greek	ekaton'
Arabic	maah
Hebrew	meah
Yiddish	hundert
Japanese	hyaku
Swahili	mia

488 hungry

French	affamé
Spanish	hambriento
Italian	affamato
Portuguese	faminto
Rumanian	flămînd
German	hungrig
Dutch	hongerig
Swedish	hungrig
Danish	sulten
Norwegian	sulten
Polish	głodny
Czech	hladový
Serbo-Croat.	gladan
Hungarian	éhes
Finnish	nälkäinen
Turkish	aç
Indonesian	lapar
Esperanto	mal'sata
Russian	galódni
Greek	pinasme'nos
Arabic	gawaan
Hebrew	raev
Yiddish	hungerig
Japanese	ueta
Swahili	-enye njaa

489 hunt

French	chasser
Spanish	cazar
Italian	cacciare
Portuguese	caçar
Rumanian	vîna
German	jagen
Dutch	jagen
Swedish	jaga
Danish	jage
Norwegian	jage
Polish	polować
Czech	loviti
Serbo-Croat.	loviti
Hungarian	vadászik
Finnish	metsästää
Turkish	avlamak
Indonesian	pemburan
Esperanto	ĉasi
Russian	akhótitsa
Greek	kinigo'
Arabic	yastad
Hebrew	tsayid
Yiddish	yogen
Japanese	karu
Swahili	winda

490 husband

French	mari
Spanish	marido
Italian	sposo
Portuguese	marido
Rumanian	soţ
German	Ehemann
Dutch	echtgenoot
Swedish	make
Danish	ægtemand
Norwegian	ektemann
Polish	mąż
Czech	manžel
Serbo-Croat.	muž
Hungarian	férj
Finnish	mies
Turkish	koca
Indonesian	laki
Esperanto	edzo
Russian	mush, suprúk
Greek	si'zigos
Arabic	zawg
Hebrew	baal
Yiddish	man
Japanese	otto
Swahili	mume

491 ice

French	glace
Spanish	hielo
Italian	ghiaccio
Portuguese	gêlo
Rumanian	gheaţă
German	Eis
Dutch	ijs
Swedish	is
Danish	is
Norwegian	is
Polish	lód
Czech	led
Serbo-Croat.	led
Hungarian	jég
Finnish	jää
Turkish	buz
Indonesian	és
Esperanto	glacio
Russian	lyót
Greek	pa'gos
Arabic	tsalg
Hebrew	kerach
Yiddish	eis
Japanese	koori
Swahili	barafu

492 ice cream

French	glace
Spanish	helado
Italian	gelato
Portuguese	sorvete
Rumanian	îngheţată
German	Speiseeis
Dutch	roomijs
Swedish	glass
Danish	flødeis
Norwegian	iskrem
Polish	lody
Czech	zmrzlina
Serbo-Croat.	sladoled
Hungarian	fagylalt
Finnish	jäätelö
Turkish	dondurma
Indonesian	áskrim
Esperanto	glaci'aĵo
Russian	marózhenoye
Greek	pagoton'
Arabic	jilati, bouza
Hebrew	glidah
Yiddish	gefroirenes
Japanese	aisukuriimu
Swahili	aisi krimi

493 illegal

French	illégal
Spanish	ilegal
Italian	illegale
Portuguese	ilegal
Rumanian	ilegal
German	ungesetzlich
Dutch	onwettelijk
Swedish	olaglig
Danish	ulovlig
Norwegian	ulovlig
Polish	nielegalny
Czech	nezákonný, ilegální
Serbo-Croat.	nezakonit
Hungarian	törvénytelen
Finnish	laiton
Turkish	gayrı meşru
Indonesian	melanggar hukum
Esperanto	kontraŭ'leĝa
Russian	nezakónni
Greek	para'nomos
Arabic	ghair qanouni
Hebrew	bilti chuki
Yiddish	ungesetslich
Japanese	ihoo no
Swahili	-sio haki

494 import

French	importation
Spanish	importación
Italian	importazione
Portuguese	importação
Rumanian	import
German	Einfuhr
Dutch	invoer
Swedish	import
Danish	import
Norwegian	import
Polish	przywóz
Czech	dovoz, import
Serbo-Croat.	uvoz
Hungarian	behozatal
Finnish	tuonti
Turkish	ithalât
Indonesian	impor
Esperanto	importo
Russian	impórt, vvos
Greek	isagoge'
Arabic	istirad
Hebrew	yevu
Yiddish	einfuhr
Japanese	yunyuu
Swahili	bidhaa zinazoingia

495 industry

French	industrie
Spanish	industria
Italian	industria
Portuguese	industria
Rumanian	industrie
German	Gewerbe, Industrie
Dutch	industrie
Swedish	industri
Danish	industri
Norwegian	industri
Polish	przemysł
Czech	průmysl, živnost
Serbo-Croat.	industrija
Hungarian	ipar
Finnish	teollisuus
Turkish	endüstri
Indonesian	industri
Esperanto	industrio
Russian	pramíshlenost
Greek	viomichani'a
Arabic	sinaa
Hebrew	taasiah
Yiddish	industrie
Japanese	sangyoo
Swahili	uchumi

496 inflation

French	inflation
Spanish	inflación
Italian	inflazione
Portuguese	inflação
Rumanian	inflaţie
German	Entwertung
Dutch	inflatie
Swedish	inflation
Danish	inflation
Norwegian	inflasjon
Polish	inflacja
Czech	inflace
Serbo-Croat.	inflacija
Hungarian	infláció
Finnish	inflatio
Turkish	enflâsyon
Indonesian	inflasi
Esperanto	ŝvel'igio
Russian	inflátsiya
Greek	plithorismos'
Arabic	tadchoum mali
Hebrew	nipuach
Yiddish	inflatsye
Japanese	infureeshyon
Swahili	kupandisha bei ya vitu

497 information

French	information
Spanish	información
Italian	informazione
Portuguese	informação
Rumanian	informaţie
German	Auskunft
Dutch	inlichting
Swedish	upplysning
Danish	oplysning
Norwegian	opplysning
Polish	informacja
Czech	informace
Serbo-Croat.	obavještenje
Hungarian	felvilágosítás
Finnish	tieto
Turkish	malûmat
Indonesian	keterangan
Esperanto	informo
Russian	spráfka
Greek	plirofori'a
Arabic	istilamat
Hebrew	yediah
Yiddish	informatsye
Japanese	tsuuchi
Swahili	-maarifa

498 ink

French	encre
Spanish	tinta
Italian	inchiostro
Portuguese	tinta
Rumanian	cerneală
German	Tinte
Dutch	inkt
Swedish	bläck
Danish	blæk
Norwegian	blekk
Polish	atrament
Czech	inkoust
Serbo-Croat.	tinta
Hungarian	tinta
Finnish	muste
Turkish	mürekkep
Indonesian	tinta, dawat
Esperanto	inko
Russian	cherníla
Greek	mela'ni
Arabic	hibr
Hebrew	diyo
Yiddish	tint
Japanese	inki
Swahili	wino

499 insect

French	insecte
Spanish	insecto
Italian	insetto
Portuguese	inseto
Rumanian	insectă
German	Insekt
Dutch	insekt
Swedish	insekt
Danish	insekt
Norwegian	insekt
Polish	owad
Czech	hmyz
Serbo-Croat.	insekt
Hungarian	rovar
Finnish	hyönteinen
Turkish	haşere
Indonesian	serangga
Esperanto	insekto
Russian	nasekómoye
Greek	en'tomon
Arabic	hashara
Hebrew	scherets
Yiddish	insek
Japanese	konchuu
Swahili	mdudu

500 insurance

French	assurance
Spanish	seguro
Italian	assicurazione
Portuguese	seguro
Rumanian	asiguare
German	Versicherung
Dutch	verzekering
Swedish	försäkring
Danish	forsikring
Norwegian	forsikkring
Polish	ubezpieczenie
Czech	pojištění
Serbo-Croat.	osiguranje
Hungarian	biztosítás
Finnish	vakuutus
Turkish	sigorta
Indonesian	asuransi
Esperanto	asekuro
Russian	strakhaványiye
Greek	asfa'lia
Arabic	taamin
Hebrew	bituach
Yiddish	assekurants
Japanese	hoken
Swahili	bima

501 interest

French	intérêt
Spanish	rédito
Italian	interessi
Portuguese	interêsse
Rumanian	dobîndă
German	Zins
Dutch	rente
Swedish	ränta
Danish	rente
Norwegian	rente
Polish	odsetki
Czech	úrok
Serbo-Croat.	interes
Hungarian	kamat
Finnish	korko
Turkish	faiz
Indonesian	untung
Esperanto	procento
Russian	pratsént
Greek	endiafe'ron
Arabic	faida
Hebrew	ribit
Yiddish	pretsent
Japanese	rishi
Swahili	faida

502 interpreter

French	interprète
Spanish	intérprete
Italian	interprete
Portuguese	intárprete
Rumanian	interpret
German	Dolmetscher
Dutch	vertolker
Swedish	tolk
Danish	tolk
Norwegian	tolk
Polish	tłumacz
Czech	tlumočník
Serbo-Croat.	tumač
Hungarian	tolmács
Finnish	tulkki
Turkish	tercüman
Indonesian	tafsir
Esperanto	interpret'isto
Russian	perevótchik
Greek	dierminefs'
Arabic	moutargim
Hebrew	turgeman
Yiddish	dolmetscher
Japanese	tsuuyaku
Swahili	mkalimani

503 invention

French	invention
Spanish	invención
Italian	invenzione
Portuguese	invenção
Rumanian	invenţie
German	Erfindung
Dutch	uitvinding
Swedish	uppfinning
Danish	opfindelse
Norwegian	oppfinnelse
Polish	wynalazek
Czech	vynaález
Serbo-Croat.	pronalazak
Hungarian	feltalálás
Finnish	keksintö
Turkish	icat
Indonesian	ráka
Esperanto	invento
Russian	izabretyéniye
Greek	efev'resis
Arabic	ichtiraa
Hebrew	hamtsaah
Yiddish	erfindung
Japanese	hatsumei
Swahili	ubuni

504 iron

French	fer
Spanish	hierro
Italian	ferro
Portuguese	ferro
Rumanian	fier
German	Eisen
Dutch	ijzer
Swedish	järn
Danish	jern
Norwegian	jern
Polish	żelazo
Czech	železo
Serbo-Croat.	železo
Hungarian	vas
Finnish	rauta
Turkish	demir
Indonesian	besi
Esperanto	fero
Russian	zhelyéso
Greek	si'dero
Arabic	hadid
Hebrew	barsel
Yiddish	eisen
Japanese	tetsu
Swahili	chuma

505 ironing

French	repasser
Spanish	planchar
Italian	stirare
Portuguese	passar a ferro
Rumanian	călca
German	bügeln
Dutch	strijken
Swedish	pressa
Danish	stryge
Norwegian	stryke
Polish	prasować
Czech	žehliti
Serbo-Croat.	glačati
Hungarian	vasal
Finnish	silitys
Turkish	ütülemek
Indonesian	menjeterika
Esperanto	gladi
Russian	gládit
Greek	sidero'no
Arabic	yakwi
Hebrew	gihuts
Yiddish	biglen
Japanese	airon o kakeru
Swahili	piga pasi

506 island

French	île
Spanish	isla
Italian	isola
Portuguese	ilha
Rumanian	insulă
German	Insel
Dutch	eiland
Swedish	ö
Danish	ø
Norwegian	øy
Polish	wyspa
Czech	ostrov
Serbo-Croat.	ostrvo
Hungarian	sziget
Finnish	saari
Turkish	ada
Indonesian	pulau
Esperanto	insulo
Russian	óstraf
Greek	nisi'
Arabic	gazira
Hebrew	iy
Yiddish	insel
Japanese	shima
Swahili	kisiwa

507 January

French	janvier
Spanish	enero
Italian	gennaio
Portuguese	janeiro
Rumanian	ianuarie
German	Januar
Dutch	Januari
Swedish	januari
Danish	januar
Norwegian	januar
Polish	styczeń
Czech	leden
Serbo-Croat.	siječanj
Hungarian	január
Finnish	tammikuu
Turkish	ocak
Indonesian	Djanuari
Esperanto	Januaro
Russian	yanvár
Greek	Ianoua'rios
Arabic	yanayir
Hebrew	yanuar
Yiddish	yanuar
Japanese	ichigwatsu
Swahili	Januari

508 jealous

French	jaloux
Spanish	celoso
Italian	geloso
Portuguese	ciumento
Rumanian	gelos
German	eifersüchtig
Dutch	jaloers
Swedish	avundsjuk
Danish	skinsyg
Norwegian	skinnsyk
Polish	zazdrosny
Czech	žárlivý
Serbo-Croat.	zavidljiv
Hungarian	féltékeny
Finnish	mustasukkainen
Turkish	kıskanç
Indonesian	tjemburu
Esperanto	ĵaluza
Russian	revnívi
Greek	zilia'ris
Arabic	ghayour
Hebrew	mekane
Yiddish	mekane
Japanese	shitto bukai
Swahili	-wivu

509 jewel

French	bijou
Spanish	joya
Italian	gioiello
Portuguese	jóia
Rumanian	guivaer
German	Juwel
Dutch	juweel
Swedish	juvel
Danish	juvel
Norwegian	juvel
Polish	klejnot
Czech	klenot
Serbo-Croat.	dragulj
Hungarian	ékszer
Finnish	jalokivi
Turkish	mücevher
Indonesian	djauhar
Esperanto	gemo
Russian	dragatsénast
Greek	bizou'
Arabic	hilya
Hebrew	tachschit
Yiddish	tsiering
Japanese	hooseki
Swahili	kito

510 joke

French	plaisanterie
Spanish	chiste
Italian	scherzo
Portuguese	gracejo
Rumanian	glumă
German	Scherz
Dutch	grap
Swedish	skämt
Danish	spøg
Norwegian	spøk
Polish	żart
Czech	žert, vtip
Serbo-Croat.	šala
Hungarian	tréfa
Finnish	pila
Turkish	şaka
Indonesian	lawak, sendajgurau
Esperanto	šerco
Russian	shútka
Greek	asti'on
Arabic	mizah
Hebrew	halatsah
Yiddish	schpass
Japanese	joodan
Swahili	mzaha

511 July

French	juillet
Spanish	julio
Italian	luglio
Portuguese	julho
Rumanian	iulie
German	Juli
Dutch	Juli
Swedish	juli
Danish	juli
Norwegian	juli
Polish	lipiec
Czech	červenec
Serbo-Croat.	srpanj
Hungarian	július
Finnish	heinäkuu
Turkish	temmuz
Indonesian	Djui
Esperanto	Julio
Russian	yúl
Greek	Iou'lios
Arabic	youlya
Hebrew	yuli
Yiddish	yuli
Japanese	shichigwatsu
Swahili	Julai

512 June

French	juin
Spanish	junio
Italian	giugno
Portuguese	junho
Rumanian	iunie
German	Juni
Dutch	Juni
Swedish	juni
Danish	juni
Norwegian	juni
Polish	czerwiec
Czech	červen
Serbo-Croat.	lipanj
Hungarian	június
Finnish	kesäkuu
Turkish	haziran
Indonesian	Djuni
Esperanto	Junio
Russian	yún
Greek	Iou'nios
Arabic	younya
Hebrew	yuni
Yiddish	yuni
Japanese	rokugwatsu
Swahili	Juni

513 key

French	clef
Spanish	llave
Italian	chiave
Portuguese	chave
Rumanian	cheie
German	Schlüssel
Dutch	sleutel
Swedish	nyckel
Danish	nøgle
Norwegian	nøkkel
Polish	klucz
Czech	klíč
Serbo-Croat.	ključ
Hungarian	kulcs
Finnish	avain
Turkish	anahtar
Indonesian	kuntji
Esperanto	ŝlos'ilo
Russian	klyuch
Greek	klidi'
Arabic	mouftah
Hebrew	mafteach
Yiddish	schlissel
Japanese	kagi
Swahili	ufunguo

514 kidney

French	rein
Spanish	riñon
Italian	rene
Portuguese	rim
Rumanian	rinichi
German	Niere
Dutch	nier
Swedish	njure
Danish	nyre
Norwegian	nyre
Polish	nerka
Czech	ledvina
Serbo-Croat.	bubreg
Hungarian	vese
Finnish	munuainen
Turkish	böbrek
Indonesian	gindjal
Esperanto	reno
Russian	póchka
Greek	nefro'
Arabic	kilya
Hebrew	kilyah
Yiddish	nieren
Japanese	jinzoo
Swahili	figo

515 king

French	roi
Spanish	rey
Italian	re
Portuguese	rei
Rumanian	rege
German	König
Dutch	koning
Swedish	kung
Danish	konge
Norwegian	konge
Polish	król
Czech	král
Serbo-Croat.	kralj
Hungarian	király
Finnish	kuningas
Turkish	kıral
Indonesian	radja
Esperanto	reĝo
Russian	karól
Greek	vasilefs'
Arabic	malik
Hebrew	melech
Yiddish	melech
Japanese	oo
Swahili	mfalme

516 kiss

French	baiser
Spanish	beso
Italian	bacio
Portuguese	beijo
Rumanian	sărut
German	Kuss
Dutch	kus
Swedish	kyss
Danish	kys
Norwegian	kyss
Polish	pocałunek
Czech	polibek
Serbo-Croat.	poljubac
Hungarian	csók
Finnish	suudelma
Turkish	buse
Indonesian	tjium, ketjup
Esperanto	kiso
Russian	patselúi
Greek	fili'
Arabic	qoubla
Hebrew	neschikah
Yiddish	kisch
Japanese	seppun
Swahili	busu

517 kitchen

French	cuisine
Spanish	cocina
Italian	cucina
Portuguese	cozinha
Rumanian	bucătărie
German	Küche
Dutch	keuken
Swedish	kök
Danish	køkken
Norwegian	kjøkken
Polish	kuchnia
Czech	kuchyně
Serbo-Croat.	kuhinja
Hungarian	konyha
Finnish	keittiö
Turkish	mutfak
Indonesian	dapur
Esperanto	kuir'ejo
Russian	kúkhnya
Greek	kouzi'na
Arabic	matbach
Hebrew	mitbach
Yiddish	kich
Japanese	daidokoro
Swahili	jikoni

518 knapsack

French	havresac
Spanish	mochila
Italian	zàino
Portuguese	mochila de soldado
Rumanian	raniţă
German	Rucksack
Dutch	ransel
Swedish	ränsel
Danish	tornyster
Norwegian	ryggsekk
Polish	plecak
Czech	batoh
Serbo-Croat.	ranac
Hungarian	hátizsák
Finnish	selkäreppu
Turkish	torba
Indonesian	buntil, boktja
Esperanto	tornistro
Russian	ránets
Greek	yilios'
Arabic	garabandiya
Hebrew	tarmil
Yiddish	ranets
Japanese	hainoo
Swahili	shanta

519 knee

French	genou
Spanish	rodilla
Italian	ginocchio
Portuguese	joelho
Rumanian	genunchi
German	Knie
Dutch	knie
Swedish	knä
Danish	knæ
Norwegian	kne
Polish	kolano
Czech	koleno
Serbo-Croat.	koljeno
Hungarian	térd
Finnish	polvi
Turkish	diz
Indonesian	lutat
Esperanto	genuo
Russian	kalyéno
Greek	go'nato
Arabic	roukba
Hebrew	berech
Yiddish	knie
Japanese	hiza
Swahili	goti

520 knife

French	couteau
Spanish	cuchillo
Italian	coltello
Portuguese	faca
Rumanian	cuţit
German	Messer
Dutch	mes
Swedish	kniv
Danish	kniv
Norwegian	kniv
Polish	nóż
Czech	nůž
Serbo-Croat.	nož
Hungarian	kés
Finnish	veitsi
Turkish	bıçak
Indonesian	pisau
Esperanto	tranĉ'ilo
Russian	nosh
Greek	mache'ri
Arabic	sikkin
Hebrew	sakin
Yiddish	messer
Japanese	naifu
Swahili	kisu

521 lace

French	dentelle
Spanish	encaje
Italian	merletto
Portuguese	renda
Rumanian	dantelă
German	Spitzen
Dutch	kant
Swedish	spets
Danish	knipling
Norwegian	kniplinger
Polish	koronka
Czech	krajka
Serbo-Croat.	čipka
Hungarian	csipke
Finnish	pitsi
Turkish	dantelâ
Indonesian	rénda
Esperanto	punto
Russian	krúzhevo
Greek	dante'la
Arabic	dantilla
Hebrew	tachrim
Yiddish	schpitserei
Japanese	reesu
Swahili	nguo ya kimia

522 ladder

French	échelle
Spanish	escalera
Italian	scala a piuoli
Portuguese	escada de mão
Rumanian	scară
German	Leiter
Dutch	ladder
Swedish	stege
Danish	stige
Norwegian	stige
Polish	drabina
Czech	žebřík
Serbo-Croat.	lestve
Hungarian	létra
Finnish	tikapuut
Turkish	merdiven
Indonesian	tangga
Esperanto	ŝtup'et'aro
Russian	lyésnitsa
Greek	ska'la
Arabic	sillim
Hebrew	sulam
Yiddish	leiter
Japanese	hashigo
Swahili	ngazi

523 lake

French	lac
Spanish	lago
Italian	lago
Portuguese	lago
Rumanian	lac
German	See
Dutch	meer
Swedish	insjö
Danish	sø
Norwegian	innsjø
Polish	jezioro
Czech	jezero
Serbo-Croat.	jezero
Hungarian	tó
Finnish	järvi
Turkish	göl
Indonesian	telaga
Esperanto	lago
Russian	ózero
Greek	lim'ni
Arabic	bouhayra
Hebrew	agam
Yiddish	osyere
Japanese	mizu'umi
Swahili	ziwa la maji

524 lamb

French	agneau
Spanish	cordero
Italian	agnello
Portuguese	cordeiro
Rumanian	miel
German	Lamm
Dutch	lam
Swedish	lamm
Danish	lam
Norwegian	lam
Polish	baranek
Czech	jehně
Serbo-Croat.	jagnje
Hungarian	bárány
Finnish	karitsa
Turkish	kuzu
Indonesian	anak domba
Esperanto	ŝaf'ido
Russian	yagyónak
Greek	arni'
Arabic	daan
Hebrew	seh
Yiddish	lamm
Japanese	kohitsuji
Swahili	kikondoo

525 language

French	langue
Spanish	lengua
Italian	lingua
Portuguese	língua
Rumanian	limbă
German	Sprache
Dutch	taal
Swedish	språk
Danish	sprog
Norwegian	språk
Polish	mowa
Czech	jazyk
Serbo-Croat.	jezik
Hungarian	nyelv
Finnish	kieli
Turkish	lisan
Indonesian	bahasa
Esperanto	lingvo
Russian	yasík
Greek	glo'ssa
Arabic	lougha
Hebrew	laschon
Yiddish	luschon
Japanese	gengo
Swahili	lugha

526 large

French	grand
Spanish	grande
Italian	largo
Portuguese	grande
Rumanian	mare
German	gross
Dutch	groot
Swedish	stor
Danish	stor
Norwegian	stor
Polish	wielki
Czech	velký
Serbo-Croat.	veliki
Hungarian	nagy
Finnish	suuri
Turkish	büyük
Indonesian	besar
Esperanto	granda
Russian	balshóy
Greek	mega'los
Arabic	kabir
Hebrew	gadol
Yiddish	groiss
Japanese	ooki'i
Swahili	-kubwa

527 late

French	tard
Spanish	tarde
Italian	tardi
Portuguese	tarde
Rumanian	tîrziu
German	spät
Dutch	laat
Swedish	sen
Danish	sen
Norwegian	sen
Polish	późno
Czech	pozdní
Serbo-Croat.	pozno
Hungarian	késő
Finnish	myöhään
Turkish	geç
Indonesian	lambat
Esperanto	mal'frua
Russian	pózno
Greek	arga'
Arabic	moutaachir
Hebrew	meuchar
Yiddish	schpet
Japanese	osoi
Swahili	kawia

528 laugh

French	rire
Spanish	reír
Italian	ridere
Portuguese	rir
Rumanian	rîde
German	lachen
Dutch	lachen
Swedish	skratta
Danish	le
Norwegian	le
Polish	śmiać się
Czech	smáti
Serbo-Croat.	smejati
Hungarian	nevet
Finnish	nauraa
Turkish	gülmek
Indonesian	tertawa
Esperanto	ridi
Russian	smeyátsa
Greek	yela'o
Arabic	yadhak
Hebrew	tsachak
Yiddish	lachn
Japanese	warau
Swahili	cheka

529 laundry

French	blanchisserie
Spanish	lavanderia
Italian	lavanderia
Portuguese	lavandaria
Rumanian	spălătorie
German	Wäscherei
Dutch	wasgoed
Swedish	tvättinrättning
Danish	vaskeri
Norwegian	vaskeri
Polish	pralnia
Czech	prádelna
Serbo-Croat.	vešernica
Hungarian	mosoda
Finnish	pesulaitos
Turkish	çamaşır
Indonesian	tjutjian
Esperanto	lesiv'ejo
Russian	práchechnaya
Greek	plinti'rion
Arabic	maghsal
Hebrew	machbesah
Yiddish	vescherei
Japanese	sentakuya
Swahili	kiwanda cha dobi

530 lawyer

French	avocat
Spanish	abogado
Italian	avvocato
Portuguese	advogado
Rumanian	avocat
German	Rechtsanwalt
Dutch	advocaat
Swedish	advokat
Danish	advokat
Norwegian	advokat
Polish	adwokat
Czech	právník
Serbo-Croat.	advokat
Hungarian	ügyvéd
Finnish	asianajaja
Turkish	avukat
Indonesian	apokat
Esperanto	leĝ'isto
Russian	advakát
Greek	dikigo'ros
Arabic	mouhami
Hebrew	orech din
Yiddish	advokat
Japanese	bengoshi
Swahili	mwanasheria

531 lazy

French	paresseux
Spanish	perezoso
Italian	pigro
Portuguese	preguiçoso
Rumanian	leneş
German	faul
Dutch	lui
Swedish	lat
Danish	doven
Norwegian	doven
Polish	leniwy
Czech	liný
Serbo-Croat.	lenj
Hungarian	lusta
Finnish	laiska
Turkish	tembel
Indonesian	malas
Esperanto	mal'labor'ema
Russian	lenívi
Greek	tebe'lis
Arabic	kaslan
Hebrew	atsel
Yiddish	foil
Japanese	taida na
Swahili	vivu

532 lead

French	plomb
Spanish	plomo
Italian	piombo
Portuguese	chumbo
Rumanian	plumb
German	Blei
Dutch	lood
Swedish	bly
Danish	bly
Norwegian	bly
Polish	ołów
Czech	olovo
Serbo-Croat.	olovo
Hungarian	ólom
Finnish	lyijy
Turkish	kurşun
Indonesian	timal hitam
Esperanto	plumbo
Russian	svinyéts
Greek	mo'lyvos
Arabic	rousas
Hebrew	ofereth
Yiddish	blei
Japanese	namari
Swahili	risasi

533 leaf

French	feuille
Spanish	hoja
Italian	foglia
Portuguese	fôlha
Rumanian	frunză
German	Blatt
Dutch	blad
Swedish	blad
Danish	blad
Norwegian	blad
Polish	liść
Czech	list
Serbo-Croat.	list
Hungarian	levél
Finnish	lehti
Turkish	yaprak
Indonesian	daun
Esperanto	folio
Russian	list
Greek	fi'lon
Arabic	waraqa
Hebrew	aleh
Yiddish	blatt
Japanese	ha
Swahili	jani

534 learn

French	apprendre
Spanish	aprender
Italian	imparare
Portuguese	aprender
Rumanian	învăţa
German	lernen
Dutch	leren
Swedish	lära
Danish	lære
Norwegian	lære
Polish	uczyć się
Czech	učiti
Serbo-Croat.	učiti
Hungarian	tanul
Finnish	oppia
Turkish	öğrenmek
Indonesian	beladjar
Esperanto	lerni
Russian	uchítsa
Greek	mathe'no
Arabic	yataalam
Hebrew	lamat
Yiddish	lernen
Japanese	manabu
Swahili	jifunza

535 leather

French	cuir
Spanish	cuero
Italian	cuoio
Portuguese	couro
Rumanian	piele
German	Leder
Dutch	leer
Swedish	läder
Danish	læder
Norwegian	læ
Polish	skóra
Czech	kůže
Serbo-Croat.	koža
Hungarian	bőr
Finnish	nahka
Turkish	deri
Indonesian	kulit
Esperanto	ledo
Russian	kózha
Greek	der'ma
Arabic	gild
Hebrew	or
Yiddish	leder
Japanese	nameshigawa
Swahili	ngozi

536 leave

French	laisser
Spanish	dejar
Italian	lasciare
Portuguese	deixar
Rumanian	pleca
German	verlassen
Dutch	vertrekken
Swedish	länna
Danish	forlade
Norwegian	forlate
Polish	odejść
Czech	opustiti
Serbo-Croat.	ostaviti
Hungarian	elhagy
Finnish	lähteä
Turkish	terketmek
Indonesian	pergi
Esperanto	lasi
Russian	ukhodít
Greek	afi'no
Arabic	yousafir
Hebrew	asav
Yiddish	ferlosen
Japanese	saru
Swahili	toka katika

537 left

French	gauche
Spanish	izquierdo
Italian	sinistro
Portuguese	esquerda
Rumanian	stîng
German	links
Dutch	links
Swedish	vänster
Danish	venstre
Norwegian	venstre
Polish	na lewo
Czech	nalevo
Serbo-Croat.	levo
Hungarian	balra
Finnish	vasen
Turkish	sol
Indonesian	kiri
Esperanto	mal'dekstra
Russian	nalyévo
Greek	aristeros'
Arabic	shamal
Hebrew	smali
Yiddish	links
Japanese	hidari no
Swahili	-a kushota

538 leg

French	jambe
Spanish	pierna
Italian	gamba
Portuguese	perna
Rumanian	picior
German	Bein
Dutch	been
Swedish	ben
Danish	ben
Norwegian	ben
Polish	noga
Czech	noha
Serbo-Croat.	noga
Hungarian	lábszár
Finnish	sääri
Turkish	bacak
Indonesian	gagi
Esperanto	kruro
Russian	nagá
Greek	po'di
Arabic	saq
Hebrew	regel
Yiddish	fuss
Japanese	ashi
Swahili	mguu

539 legal

French	légal
Spanish	legal
Italian	legale
Portuguese	legal
Rumanian	legal
German	gesetzlich
Dutch	wettelijk
Swedish	laglig
Danish	retmæessig
Norwegian	lær
Polish	prawny
Czech	zákonný
Serbo-Croat.	zakonit
Hungarian	törvényes
Finnish	laillinen
Turkish	meşru
Indonesian	sah
Esperanto	legitima
Russian	zakónni
Greek	no'mimos
Arabic	qanouni
Hebrew	chukki
Yiddish	gesetslech
Japanese	goohooteki na
Swahili	-a sheria

540 lemon

French	citron
Spanish	limón
Italian	limone
Portuguese	limão
Rumanian	lămîie
German	Zitrone
Dutch	citroen
Swedish	citron
Danish	citron
Norwegian	sitron
Polish	cytryna
Czech	citrón
Serbo-Croat.	limun
Hungarian	citrom
Finnish	sitruuna
Turkish	limon
Indonesian	limau, djeruk
Esperanto	citrono
Russian	limón
Greek	lemo'ni
Arabic	laymoun
Hebrew	limon
Yiddish	limene
Japanese	remon
Swahili	limao

541 lens

French	lentille
Spanish	lente
Italian	lente
Portuguese	lente
Rumanian	lentilă
German	Linse
Dutch	lens
Swedish	lins
Danish	linse
Norwegian	linse
Polish	soczewka
Czech	čočka
Serbo-Croat.	sočivo
Hungarian	lencse
Finnish	linssi
Turkish	adese
Indonesian	léns
Esperanto	lenso
Russian	línsa
Greek	fakos'
Arabic	adasa
Hebrew	adascha
Yiddish	lens
Japanese	renzu
Swahili	kioo

542 letter

French	lettre
Spanish	carta
Italian	lettera
Portuguese	carta
Rumanian	scrisoare
German	Brief
Dutch	brief
Swedish	brev
Danish	brev
Norwegian	brev
Polish	list
Czech	dopis
Serbo-Croat.	pismo
Hungarian	levél
Finnish	kirje
Turkish	mektup
Indonesian	suart
Esperanto	letero
Russian	pismó
Greek	gra'ma
Arabic	chitab
Hebrew	michtav
Yiddish	brief
Japanese	tegami
Swahili	barua

543 library

French	bibliothèque
Spanish	biblioteca
Italian	biblioteca
Portuguese	biblioteca
Rumanian	bibliotecă
German	Bibliothek
Dutch	leeszaal
Swedish	bibliotek
Danish	bibliotek
Norwegian	bibliotek
Polish	biblioteka
Czech	knihovna
Serbo-Croat.	biblioteka
Hungarian	könyvtár
Finnish	kirjasto
Turkish	kütüphane
Indonesian	perpustakam
Esperanto	biblioteko
Russian	bibliatyéka
Greek	vivliothi'ki
Arabic	maktaba
Hebrew	sifriyah
Yiddish	biblotek
Japanese	toshokwan
Swahili	maktaba

544 life

French	vie
Spanish	vida
Italian	vita
Portuguese	vida
Rumanian	viaţă
German	Leben
Dutch	leven
Swedish	liv
Danish	liv
Norwegian	liv
Polish	życie
Czech	život
Serbo-Croat.	život
Hungarian	élet
Finnish	elämä
Turkish	hayat
Indonesian	hidup
Esperanto	vivo
Russian	zhisn
Greek	zo-i'
Arabic	haya
Hebrew	chayim
Yiddish	leben
Japanese	inochi
Swahili	uzima

545 life belt

French	ceinture de sauvetage
Spanish	salvavidas
Italian	salvagente
Portuguese	salva-vidas
Rumanian	colac de salvare
German	Rettungsgürtel
Dutch	reddings gordel
Swedish	livbälte
Danish	redningsbælte
Norwegian	livbelte
Polish	pas ratunkowy
Czech	záchranný pás
Serbo-Croat.	pojas za spasavanje
Hungarian	mentőöv
Finnish	pelastusvyö
Turkish	cankurtaran kemeri
Indonesian	pelampung berenang
Esperanto	sav'zono
Russian	spasátelni póyas
Greek	sosi'vion
Arabic	tawq al-nagda
Hebrew	chagorahatsalah
Yiddish	rettungsgartel
Japanese	anzenberuto
Swahili	mshipi kwa kuelea

546 light

French	lumière
Spanish	luz
Italian	luce
Portuguese	luz
Rumanian	lumină
German	Licht
Dutch	licht
Swedish	ljus
Danish	lys
Norwegian	lys
Polish	światło
Czech	světlo
Serbo-Croat.	svjetlost
Hungarian	fény
Finnish	valo
Turkish	ışık
Indonesian	tjahaja
Esperanto	lumo
Russian	svyét
Greek	fos'
Arabic	moudi
Hebrew	or
Yiddish	licht
Japanese	hikari
Swahili	nuru

547 lightning

French	éclair
Spanish	relámpago
Italian	fulmine
Portuguese	relâmpago
Rumanian	fulger
German	Blitz
Dutch	bliksem
Swedish	blixt
Danish	lyn
Norwegian	lyn
Polish	błyskawica
Czech	blesk
Serbo-Croat.	munja
Hungarian	villám
Finnish	salama
Turkish	şimşek
Indonesian	kilat
Esperanto	fulmo
Russian	mólniya
Greek	astrapi'
Arabic	barq
Hebrew	barak
Yiddish	blits
Japanese	denkoo
Swahili	umeme

548 lilac

French	lilas
Spanish	lila
Italian	lilla
Portuguese	lilás
Rumanian	liliac
German	Flieder
Dutch	sering
Swedish	syren
Danish	syren
Norwegian	syrin
Polish	bez
Czech	bez
Serbo-Croat.	jorgovan
Hungarian	orgona
Finnish	sireeni
Turkish	leylâk
Indonesian	lilak
Esperanto	lilako
Russian	siryén
Greek	paschalia'
Arabic	banafsigi
Hebrew	lilach
Yiddish	flieder
Japanese	murasaki-hashidoi
Swahili	namna ya ua

549 lime

French	chaux
Spanish	cal
Italian	calce
Portuguese	cal
Rumanian	var
German	Kalk
Dutch	kalk
Swedish	kalk
Danish	kalk
Norwegian	kalk
Polish	wapno
Czech	vápno
Serbo-Croat.	vapno
Hungarian	mész
Finnish	kalkki
Turkish	kireç
Indonesian	kapur
Esperanto	kalko
Russian	ízvyest
Greek	asvesto'lithos
Arabic	gir
Hebrew	siyd
Yiddish	kalech
Japanese	sekkwai
Swahili	chokaa

550 linen

French	toile de lin
Spanish	lino
Italian	tela
Portuguese	tela
Rumanian	pînză
German	Leinen
Dutch	linnen
Swedish	linne
Danish	lærred
Norwegian	lin
Polish	płótno
Czech	plátno
Serbo-Croat.	platno
Hungarian	vászon
Finnish	liina
Turkish	keten
Indonesian	linan
Esperanto	tolo
Russian	palatnó
Greek	linon'
Arabic	bayadat
Hebrew	pischton
Yiddish	leivend
Japanese	asanuno
Swahili	kitani

551 lion

French	lion
Spanish	león
Italian	leone
Portuguese	leão
Rumanian	leu
German	Löwe
Dutch	leeuw
Swedish	lejon
Danish	løve
Norwegian	løve
Polish	lew
Czech	lev
Serbo-Croat.	lav
Hungarian	oroszlán
Finnish	leijona
Turkish	aslan
Indonesian	singa
Esperanto	leono
Russian	lyéf
Greek	lionta'ri
Arabic	asad
Hebrew	lavie
Yiddish	leib
Japanese	raion
Swahili	simba

552 lip

French	lèvre
Spanish	labio
Italian	labbro
Portuguese	lábio
Rumanian	buză
German	Lippe
Dutch	lip
Swedish	läpp
Danish	læbe
Norwegian	leppe
Polish	warga
Czech	ret
Serbo-Croat.	usna
Hungarian	ajak
Finnish	huuli
Turkish	dudak
Indonesian	bibir
Esperanto	lipo
Russian	gubá
Greek	chi'li
Arabic	shifah
Hebrew	safah
Yiddish	lip
Japanese	kuchibiru
Swahili	mdomo

553 liqueur

French	liqueur
Spanish	licor
Italian	liquore
Portuguese	licor
Rumanian	lichior
German	Likör
Dutch	likeur
Swedish	sprit
Danish	likør
Norwegian	likør
Polish	likier
Czech	lihovina
Serbo-Croat.	liker
Hungarian	likőr
Finnish	likööri
Turkish	likör
Indonesian	sopi manis
Esperanto	likvoro
Russian	likyór
Greek	liker'
Arabic	mashroub rawhy
Hebrew	maschke charif
Yiddish	bronfen
Japanese	rikyuurushu
Swahili	maji tamu na kileo

554 liquid

French	liquide
Spanish	líquido
Italian	liquido
Portuguese	líquido
Rumanian	lichid
German	flüssig
Dutch	voleibaar
Swedish	flytande
Danish	flydende
Norwegian	flytende
Polish	płynny
Czech	tekutý
Serbo-Croat.	tečan
Hungarian	folyékony
Finnish	nestemäinen
Turkish	sıvı
Indonesian	tjair
Esperanto	likva
Russian	zhítki
Greek	igro'
Arabic	sail
Hebrew	nozel
Yiddish	flissik
Japanese	ekitai
Swahili	-a maji

555 liver

French	foie
Spanish	hígado
Italian	fegato
Portuguese	fígado
Rumanian	ficat
German	Leber
Dutch	lever
Swedish	lever
Danish	lever
Norwegian	lever
Polish	wątroba
Czech	játra
Serbo-Croat.	jetra
Hungarian	máj
Finnish	maksa
Turkish	karaciğer
Indonesian	hati
Esperanto	hepato
Russian	pyéchen
Greek	syko'ti
Arabic	kabid
Hebrew	kaved
Yiddish	leber
Japanese	kanzoo
Swahili	ini

556 living room

French	salon
Spanish	sala
Italian	salotto
Portuguese	sala de visitas
Rumanian	salon
German	Wohnzimmer
Dutch	woonkamer
Swedish	salong
Danish	opholdsstue
Norwegian	dagligstue
Polish	pokój mieszkalny
Czech	obytný pokoj
Serbo-Croat.	dnevna soba
Hungarian	nappali
Finnish	olohuone
Turkish	oturma odası
Indonesian	kamar duduk
Esperanto	ĉambro
Russian	gastínaya
Greek	kathimerino'
Arabic	hougrat al-istjqbal
Hebrew	cheder schachun
Yiddish	wointsimer
Japanese	ima
Swahili	sebule

557 lobster

French	homard
Spanish	langosta
Italian	aragosta
Portuguese	lagosta
Rumanian	homar
German	Hummer
Dutch	zeekreeft
Swedish	hummer
Danish	hummer
Norwegian	hummer
Polish	homar
Czech	humr
Serbo-Croat.	jastog
Hungarian	homár
Finnish	hummeri
Turkish	ıstakoz
Indonesian	udang karang
Esperanto	omaro
Russian	amár
Greek	astakos'
Arabic	langoust
Hebrew	sarton yam
Yiddish	krebs
Japanese	ebi
Swahili	kamba

558 lock

French	serrure
Spanish	cerradura
Italian	serratura
Portuguese	fechadura
Rumanian	broască
German	Schloss
Dutch	slot
Swedish	lås
Danish	lås
Norwegian	lås
Polish	zamek
Czech	zámek
Serbo-Croat.	brava
Hungarian	lakat
Finnish	lukko
Turkish	kilit
Indonesian	ibu kuntji
Esperanto	seruro
Russian	zamók
Greek	klidonia'
Arabic	kaloun
Hebrew	manul
Yiddish	schloss
Japanese	joo
Swahili	kufuli

559 long

French	long
Spanish	largo
Italian	lungo
Portuguese	comprido
Rumanian	lung
German	lang
Dutch	lang
Swedish	lång
Danish	lang
Norwegian	lang
Polish	długi
Czech	dlouhý
Serbo-Croat.	dugo
Hungarian	hosszú
Finnish	pitkä
Turkish	uzun
Indonesian	pandjang
Esperanto	longa
Russian	dlíni
Greek	makris'
Arabic	tawil
Hebrew	aroch
Yiddish	lang
Japanese	nagai
Swahili	-refu

560 loom

French	métier à tisser
Spanish	telar
Italian	telaio
Portuguese	tear
Rumanian	război
German	Webstuhl
Dutch	los
Swedish	vävstol
Danish	væverstol
Norwegian	vevstol
Polish	warsztat tkacki
Czech	tkalcovský stav
Serbo-Croat.	stan za tkanje
Hungarian	szövőszék
Finnish	kangaspuut
Turkish	dokuma tezgâhı
Indonesian	perkakas tenun
Esperanto	teks'maŝino
Russian	tkátski stanók
Greek	argalios'
Arabic	nol
Hebrew	nol
Yiddish	veberschtuhl
Japanese	hataoriki
Swahili	kitanda cha mfumi

561 loss

French	perte
Spanish	pérdida
Italian	perdita
Portuguese	perda
Rumanian	pierdere
German	Verlust
Dutch	verlies
Swedish	förlust
Danish	tab
Norwegian	tap
Polish	strata
Czech	ztráta
Serbo-Croat.	izgubiti
Hungarian	veszteség
Finnish	menetys
Turkish	kayıp
Indonesian	rugi
Esperanto	perdo
Russian	patyérya
Greek	apo'lia
Arabic	chisara
Hebrew	hefssed
Yiddish	schoden
Japanese	sonshitsu
Swahili	hasara

562 love

French	amour
Spanish	amor
Italian	amore
Portuguese	amor
Rumanian	iubire
German	Liebe
Dutch	liefde
Swedish	kärlek
Danish	elskov
Norwegian	kjærlighet
Polish	miłość
Czech	láska
Serbo-Croat.	ljubav
Hungarian	szeretet
Finnish	rakkaus
Turkish	aşk, sevgi
Indonesian	tjinta
Esperanto	amo
Russian	lyubóf
Greek	aga'pi
Arabic	houb
Hebrew	ahavah
Yiddish	libe
Japanese	ai
Swahili	upendo

563 luck

French	chance
Spanish	suerte
Italian	fortuna
Portuguese	sorte
Rumanian	noroc
German	Glück
Dutch	geluk
Swedish	lycka
Danish	lykke
Norwegian	lykke
Polish	szczęście
Czech	štěstí
Serbo-Croat.	sreća
Hungarian	szerencse
Finnish	onni
Turkish	talih
Indonesian	untung
Esperanto	ŝanco
Russian	schástye
Greek	ti'chi
Arabic	haz
Hebrew	masal
Yiddish	mazel
Japanese	un
Swahili	bahati

564 luggage

French	bagages
Spanish	equipaje
Italian	bagaglio
Portuguese	bagagem
Rumanian	bagaj
German	Gepäck
Dutch	bagage
Swedish	bagage
Danish	bagage
Norwegian	bagasje
Polish	bagaż
Czech	zavazadla
Serbo-Croat.	prtljag
Hungarian	podgyász
Finnish	matkatavarat
Turkish	bagaj
Indonesian	bagasi
Esperanto	pak'aĵoj
Russian	bagásh
Greek	aposkeve'
Arabic	amtiat al-mousafir
Hebrew	misvadoth
Yiddish	bagasch
Japanese	tenimotsu
Swahili	mizigo

565 lung

French	poumon
Spanish	pulmón
Italian	polmone
Portuguese	pulmão
Rumanian	plămîn
German	Lunge
Dutch	long
Swedish	lunga
Danish	lunge
Norwegian	lunge
Polish	płuca
Czech	plíce
Serbo-Croat.	pluće
Hungarian	tüdő
Finnish	keuhko
Turkish	akciğer
Indonesian	paru-paru
Esperanto	pulmo
Russian	lyókhkoye
Greek	pnev'monas
Arabic	ria
Hebrew	reah
Yiddish	lung
Japanese	hai
Swahili	pafu

566 machine

French	machine
Spanish	máquina
Italian	macchina
Portuguese	máquina
Rumanian	maşină
German	Maschine
Dutch	machine
Swedish	maskin
Danish	maskine
Norwegian	maskin
Polish	maszyna
Czech	stroj
Serbo-Croat.	mašina
Hungarian	gép
Finnish	kone
Turkish	makina
Indonesian	mesin
Esperanto	maŝino
Russian	mashína
Greek	michani'
Arabic	makina
Hebrew	mechonah
Yiddish	maschin
Japanese	kikai
Swahili	mashine

567 magazine

French	revue
Spanish	revista
Italian	rivista
Portuguese	revista
Rumanian	revistă
German	Zeitschrift
Dutch	tijdschrift
Swedish	tidskrift
Danish	tidsskrift
Norwegian	tidskrift
Polish	czasopismo
Czech	časopis
Serbo-Croat.	časopis
Hungarian	folyóirat
Finnish	aikakauslehti
Turkish	mecmua
Indonesian	madjalah
Esperanto	gazeto
Russian	zhurnál
Greek	periodikon'
Arabic	migala
Hebrew	tekufon
Yiddish	dzurnal
Japanese	zasshi
Swahili	kitabu kama gazeti

568 magic

French	magie
Spanish	magia
Italian	magia
Portuguese	mágico
Rumanian	magie
German	Zauber
Dutch	toverkunst
Swedish	magi
Danish	trylleri
Norwegian	magisk
Polish	magja
Czech	kouzlo
Serbo-Croat.	čarobija
Hungarian	varázs
Finnish	noituus
Turkish	sihir
Indonesian	sihir, gaib
Esperanto	magio
Russian	mágiya
Greek	magei'a
Arabic	sihr
Hebrew	kischuf
Yiddish	kischuf
Japanese	majutsu
Swahili	uchawi

569 maid

French	servante
Spanish	criada
Italian	serva
Portuguese	servente
Rumanian	servitoare
German	Dienstmädchen
Dutch	meisje
Swedish	piga
Danish	tjenestepige
Norwegian	hushjelp
Polish	służąca
Czech	služebná
Serbo-Croat.	sluškinja
Hungarian	cselédlány
Finnish	palvelustyttö
Turkish	hizmetci
Indonesian	babu
Esperanto	serv'ist'ino
Russian	slushánka
Greek	ipire'tria
Arabic	chadima
Hebrew	mescharetet
Yiddish	dienstmedel
Japanese	jochuu
Swahili	mtumishi wa kike

570 mail

French	poste
Spanish	correo
Italian	posta
Portuguese	correio
Rumanian	poştă
German	Post
Dutch	post
Swedish	post
Danish	post
Norwegian	post
Polish	poczta
Czech	pošta
Serbo-Croat.	pošta
Hungarian	posta
Finnish	posti
Turkish	posta
Indonesian	pos
Esperanto	poŝto
Russian	póchta
Greek	alilografi'a
Arabic	barid
Hebrew	doar
Yiddish	post
Japanese	yuubinbutsu
Swahili	barua za posta

571 make

French	faire
Spanish	hacer
Italian	fare
Portuguese	fazer
Rumanian	face
German	machen
Dutch	maken
Swedish	göra
Danish	gøre
Norwegian	gjøre
Polish	zrobić
Czech	dělati
Serbo-Croat.	činiti
Hungarian	czinál
Finnish	tehdä
Turkish	yapmak
Indonesian	buatan
Esperanto	fari
Russian	dyélat
Greek	ka'no
Arabic	yasnaa
Hebrew	assah
Yiddish	machen
Japanese	tsukuru
Swahili	fanya

572 malignant

French	malin
Spanish	maligno
Italian	maligno
Portuguese	maligno
Rumanian	rău
German	bösartig
Dutch	kwaadaardig
Swedish	elak
Danish	ondartet
Norwegian	ondartet
Polish	złośliwy
Czech	zlý
Serbo-Croat.	zloban
Hungarian	roszindulatú
Finnish	pahanlaatuinen
Turkish	uğursuz
Indonesian	djahat
Esperanto	malica
Russian	zlóstni
Greek	kakoe'this
Arabic	chabitse
Hebrew	mamir
Yiddish	beishaft
Japanese	akusei
Swahili	-ovu

573 man

French	homme
Spanish	hombre
Italian	uomo
Portuguese	homem
Rumanian	om
German	Mensch
Dutch	man
Swedish	människa
Danish	menneske
Norwegian	menneske
Polish	człowiek
Czech	člověk
Serbo-Croat.	čovjek
Hungarian	ember
Finnish	ihminen
Turkish	insan
Indonesian	manusi
Esperanto	homo
Russian	chilovyék
Greek	an'thropos
Arabic	ragoul
Hebrew	adam
Yiddish	mensch
Japanese	otoko no hito
Swahili	mtu

574 map

French	carte
Spanish	mapa
Italian	mappa
Portuguese	mapa
Rumanian	hartă
German	Landkarte
Dutch	landkaart
Swedish	karta
Danish	kort
Norwegian	kart
Polish	mapa
Czech	mapa
Serbo-Croat.	mapa
Hungarian	térkép
Finnish	kartta
Turkish	harita
Indonesian	peta
Esperanto	karto
Russian	kárta
Greek	char'tis
Arabic	charita
Hebrew	mapah
Yiddish	map
Japanese	chizu
Swahili	ramani

575 March

French	mars
Spanish	marzo
Italian	marzo
Portuguese	março
Rumanian	martie
German	März
Dutch	Maart
Swedish	mars
Danish	marts
Norwegian	mars
Polish	marzec
Czech	březen
Serbo-Croat.	ožujak
Hungarian	március
Finnish	maaliskuu
Turkish	mart ayı
Indonesian	Maret
Esperanto	Marto
Russian	mart
Greek	Mar'tios
Arabic	maris
Hebrew	merts
Yiddish	merts
Japanese	sangwatsu
Swahili	Machi

576 market

French	marché
Spanish	mercado
Italian	mercato
Portuguese	mercado
Rumanian	piaţă
German	Markt
Dutch	markt
Swedish	torg
Danish	marked
Norwegian	torg
Polish	targ
Czech	trh
Serbo-Croat.	trg
Hungarian	piac
Finnish	tori
Turkish	çarşı
Indonesian	pasar
Esperanto	bazaro
Russian	bazár
Greek	agora'
Arabic	souq
Hebrew	schuk
Yiddish	yerid
Japanese	ichiba
Swahili	soko

577 marmalade

French	marmelade
Spanish	mermelada
Italian	marmellata
Portuguese	marmelada
Rumanian	marmeladă
German	Marmelade
Dutch	marmelade
Swedish	marmelad
Danish	marmelade
Norwegian	marmelade
Polish	marmelada
Czech	zavařenina
Serbo-Croat.	marmalada
Hungarian	gyümölcsiz
Finnish	marmelaadi
Turkish	marmelât
Indonesian	marmalada, selé
Esperanto	marmelado
Russian	marmelát
Greek	marmela'da
Arabic	mourabba
Hebrew	ribah
Yiddish	eingemachts
Japanese	maamareedo
Swahili	mraba

578 maroon

French	marron
Spanish	marron
Italian	castagno
Portuguese	côr de vinho
Rumanian	castaniu
German	kastanienbraun
Dutch	kastanjebruin
Swedish	rödbrun
Danish	rødbrun
Norwegian	rødbrun
Polish	kasztanowaty
Czech	kaštanihnedý
Serbo-Croat.	kestenjavo
Hungarian	vörösesbarna
Finnish	kastaniruskea
Turkish	maron
Indonesian	merah tua
Esperanto	brun'purpura
Russian	kashtánovi
Greek	vyssini'
Arabic	bouni
Hebrew	chom kearmoni
Yiddish	kaschtanbroin
Japanese	kuri'iro
Swahili	rangi kama nyekunde nyeusi

579 marriage

French	mariage
Spanish	matrimonio
Italian	matrimonio
Portuguese	matrimônio
Rumanian	căsătorie
German	Heirat
Dutch	huwelijk
Swedish	äktenskap
Danish	giftermål
Norwegian	ekteskap
Polish	małżeństwo
Czech	sňatek
Serbo-Croat.	brak
Hungarian	házasság
Finnish	avioliitto
Turkish	evlenme
Indonesian	kawin
Esperanto	edz'igo
Russian	brak
Greek	ga'mos
Arabic	zawag
Hebrew	nessuim
Yiddish	heirat
Japanese	kekkon
Swahili	ndoa

580 match

French	allumette
Spanish	fósforo
Italian	fiammifero
Portuguese	fósforo
Rumanian	chibrit
German	Zündholz
Dutch	lucifer
Swedish	tändsticka
Danish	tændstik
Norwegian	fyrstikk
Polish	zapałka
Czech	zápalka
Serbo-Croat.	šibica
Hungarian	gyufa
Finnish	tulitikku
Turkish	kibrit
Indonesian	korék api
Esperanto	alumeto
Russian	spíchka
Greek	spir'to
Arabic	tsiqab
Hebrew	gaphrur
Yiddish	schvebele
Japanese	macchi
Swahili	kiberiti

581 mattress

French	matelas
Spanish	colchón
Italian	materasso
Portuguese	colchão
Rumanian	saltea
German	Matratze
Dutch	matras
Swedish	madrass
Danish	madras
Norwegian	madrass
Polish	materac
Czech	matrace
Serbo-Croat.	madrac
Hungarian	ágybetét
Finnish	patja
Turkish	şilte
Indonesian	tilam
Esperanto	matraco
Russian	tyufyák
Greek	stro'ma
Arabic	martaba
Hebrew	misran
Yiddish	matrats
Japanese	futon
Swahili	godoro

582 May

French	mai
Spanish	mayo
Italian	maggio
Portuguese	maio
Rumanian	mai
German	Mai
Dutch	Mei
Swedish	maj
Danish	maj
Norwegian	mai
Polish	maj
Czech	květen
Serbo-Croat.	svibanj
Hungarian	május
Finnish	toukokuu
Turkish	mayıs ayı
Indonesian	Mai
Esperanto	Majo
Russian	may
Greek	ma'-ios
Arabic	mayo
Hebrew	may
Yiddish	mai
Japanese	gogwatsu
Swahili	Mei

583 maybe

French	peut-être
Spanish	quizá
Italian	forse
Portuguese	talvez
Rumanian	poate
German	vielleicht
Dutch	misschien
Swedish	kanske
Danish	måske
Norwegian	kanskje
Polish	może
Czech	možná
Serbo-Croat.	možda
Hungarian	talán
Finnish	ehkä
Turkish	belki
Indonesian	barangkali
Esperanto	eble
Russian	mózhet bit
Greek	i'sos
Arabic	roubama
Hebrew	efscher
Yiddish	efschar
Japanese	tabun
Swahili	labda

584 meal

French	repas
Spanish	comida
Italian	pasto
Portuguese	refeição
Rumanian	masă
German	Mahlzeit
Dutch	maaltijd
Swedish	måltid
Danish	måltid
Norwegian	måltid
Polish	obiad
Czech	jídlo
Serbo-Croat.	obrok
Hungarian	étkezés
Finnish	ateria
Turkish	yemek
Indonesian	seantapan
Esperanto	manĝo
Russian	yedá
Greek	fayiton
Arabic	wagba
Hebrew	seudah
Yiddish	mohltseit
Japanese	shokuji
Swahili	chakula

585 meat

French	viande
Spanish	carne
Italian	carne
Portuguese	carne
Rumanian	carne
German	Fleisch
Dutch	vlees
Swedish	kött
Danish	kød
Norwegian	kjøtt
Polish	mięso
Czech	maso
Serbo-Croat.	meso
Hungarian	hús
Finnish	liha
Turkish	et
Indonesian	daging
Esperanto	viando
Russian	myáso
Greek	kre'as
Arabic	lahm
Hebrew	bassar
Yiddish	fleisch
Japanese	niku
Swahili	nyama

586 medicine

French	médicament
Spanish	medicina
Italian	medicina
Portuguese	medicina
Rumanian	medicină
German	Medizin
Dutch	medicijn
Swedish	medicin
Danish	medicin
Norwegian	medisin
Polish	lekarstwo
Czech	lék
Serbo-Croat.	medecina
Hungarian	orvosság
Finnish	lääke
Turkish	ilâç
Indonesian	obat
Esperanto	medikamento
Russian	lekárstvo
Greek	far'makon
Arabic	dawaa
Hebrew	refuah
Yiddish	meditsin
Japanese	kusuri
Swahili	dawa

587 meet

French	rencontrer
Spanish	encontrar
Italian	incontrare
Portuguese	encontrar
Rumanian	întîlni
German	treffen
Dutch	ontmoeten
Swedish	möta
Danish	møde
Norwegian	møte
Polish	spotkać
Czech	potkati
Serbo-Croat.	sresti
Hungarian	találkozik
Finnish	kohdata
Turkish	rasgelmek
Indonesian	bertemu
Esperanto	renkonti
Russian	fstryétit
Greek	sinanto'
Arabic	youqabil
Hebrew	pagasch
Yiddish	treffen
Japanese	au
Swahili	kuta

588 melon

French	melon
Spanish	melón
Italian	melone
Portuguese	melão
Rumanian	pepene
German	Melone
Dutch	meloen
Swedish	melon
Danish	melon
Norwegian	melon
Polish	melon
Czech	meloun
Serbo-Croat.	dinja
Hungarian	dinnye
Finnish	meloni
Turkish	kawun
Indonesian	semangka
Esperanto	melono
Russian	dínya
Greek	pepo'ni
Arabic	shammam
Hebrew	melon
Yiddish	melon
Japanese	meron
Swahili	tikiti (maji)

589 memorial

French	monument
Spanish	monumento
Italian	monumento
Portuguese	memorial
Rumanian	monument
German	Denkmal
Dutch	gedenkstuk
Swedish	minnesmärke
Danish	mindesmærke
Norwegian	minnesmerke
Polish	pomnik
Czech	pomník
Serbo-Croat.	spomjenik
Hungarian	emlékmű
Finnish	muistomerkki
Turkish	âbide
Indonesian	ingatan
Esperanto	memor'aĵo
Russian	pámyatnik
Greek	mnimo'sinon
Arabic	nasb titzkari
Hebrew	secher
Yiddish	gedenkschtein
Japanese	kinenbutsu
Swahili	nguzo ya kumbukumbu

590 merchant

French	commerçant
Spanish	mercader
Italian	mercante
Portuguese	comerciante
Rumanian	comerciant
German	Kaufmann
Dutch	koopman
Swedish	köpman
Danish	købmand
Norwegian	kjøpmann
Polish	kupiec
Czech	obchodník
Serbo-Croat.	trgovac
Hungarian	kereskedő
Finnish	kauppias
Turkish	tüccar
Indonesian	saudagar
Esperanto	komerc'isto
Russian	kupyéts
Greek	em'poros
Arabic	tagir
Hebrew	socher
Yiddish	soicher
Japanese	shoonin
Swahili	mfanyi biashara

591 merry

French	gai
Spanish	alegre
Italian	allegro
Portuguese	alegre
Rumanian	vesel
German	lustig
Dutch	vrolijk
Swedish	munter
Danish	lystig
Norwegian	lystig
Polish	wesoły
Czech	veselý
Serbo-Croat.	veselo
Hungarian	vidám
Finnish	iloinen
Turkish	şen
Indonesian	ria
Esperanto	gaja
Russian	vesýoli
Greek	charou'menos
Arabic	marih
Hebrew	alis
Yiddish	lustig
Japanese	tanoshii
Swahili	-a furaha nyingi

592 metal

French	métal
Spanish	metal
Italian	metallo
Portuguese	metal
Rumanian	metal
German	Metall
Dutch	metaal
Swedish	metall
Danish	metal
Norwegian	metall
Polish	metal
Czech	kov
Serbo-Croat.	metal
Hungarian	fém
Finnish	metalli
Turkish	maden
Indonesian	logam
Esperanto	metalo
Russian	metál
Greek	me'talon
Arabic	maadin
Hebrew	matechet
Yiddish	metal
Japanese	kinzoku
Swahili	madini

593 milk

French	lait
Spanish	leche
Italian	latte
Portuguese	leite
Rumanian	lapte
German	Milch
Dutch	melk
Swedish	mjölk
Danish	mælk
Norwegian	melk
Polish	mleko
Czech	mléko
Serbo-Croat.	mlijeko
Hungarian	tej
Finnish	maito
Turkish	süt
Indonesian	susu
Esperanto	lakto
Russian	malakó
Greek	ga'la
Arabic	laban
Hebrew	chalav
Yiddish	milech
Japanese	gyuunyuu
Swahili	maziwa

594 minute

French	minute
Spanish	minuto
Italian	minuto
Portuguese	minuto
Rumanian	minut
German	Minute
Dutch	minuut
Swedish	minut
Danish	minut
Norwegian	minutt
Polish	minuta
Czech	minuta
Serbo-Croat.	minuta
Hungarian	perc
Finnish	minuutti
Turkish	dakika
Indonesian	menit
Esperanto	minuto
Russian	minúta
Greek	lepton
Arabic	daqiqa
Hebrew	rega
Yiddish	rege
Japanese	fun
Swahili	dakika

595 mistake

French	erreur
Spanish	error
Italian	errore
Portuguese	êrro
Rumanian	greşeală
German	Irrtum
Dutch	fout
Swedish	misstag
Danish	fejltagelse
Norwegian	feil, mistak
Polish	błąd
Czech	omyl
Serbo-Croat.	greška
Hungarian	tévedés
Finnish	erehdys
Turkish	yanlış
Indonesian	salah
Esperanto	eraro
Russian	ashípka
Greek	la'thos
Arabic	ghalta
Hebrew	tauth
Yiddish	tuis
Japanese	machigai
Swahili	kosa

596 mix

French	mélanger
Spanish	mezclar
Italian	mischiare
Portuguese	misturar
Rumanian	amesteca
German	mischen
Dutch	mengen
Swedish	blanda
Danish	blande
Norwegian	blande
Polish	mieszać
Czech	míchati
Serbo-Croat.	pomješati
Hungarian	kever
Finnish	sekoittaa
Turkish	karıştırmak
Indonesian	tjampur
Esperanto	miksi
Russian	smeshát
Greek	anamigni'o
Arabic	youmzig
Hebrew	irbev
Yiddish	mischen
Japanese	mazeru
Swahili	changa

597 Monday

French	lundi
Spanish	lunes
Italian	lunedi
Portuguese	segunda-feira
Rumanian	luni
German	Montag
Dutch	Maandag
Swedish	måndag
Danish	mandag
Norwegian	mandag
Polish	poniedziałek
Czech	pondělí
Serbo-Croat.	ponjedeljak
Hungarian	hétfő
Finnish	maanantai
Turkish	pazartesi
Indonesian	Senin
Esperanto	lundo
Russian	panidyélnik
Greek	Defte'ra
Arabic	youm al-itsnain
Hebrew	yom scheni
Yiddish	montog
Japanese	getsuyoobi
Swahili	Jumatatu

598 money

French	argent
Spanish	dinero
Italian	denaro
Portuguese	dinheiro
Rumanian	bani
German	Geld
Dutch	geld
Swedish	pengar
Danish	penge
Norwegian	penger
Polish	pieniądze
Czech	peníze
Serbo-Croat.	novac
Hungarian	pénz
Finnish	raha
Turkish	para
Indonesian	uang
Esperanto	mono
Russian	dyéngi
Greek	lepta'
Arabic	nouqoud
Hebrew	mamon
Yiddish	geld
Japanese	kinsen
Swahili	fedha

599 month

French	mois
Spanish	mes
Italian	mese
Portuguese	mês
Rumanian	lună
German	Monat
Dutch	maand
Swedish	månad
Danish	måned
Norwegian	måned
Polish	miesiąc
Czech	mésíc
Serbo-Croat.	mjesec
Hungarian	hónap
Finnish	kuukausi
Turkish	ay
Indonesian	bulan
Esperanto	monato
Russian	myésats
Greek	mi'nas
Arabic	shahr
Hebrew	chodesch
Yiddish	choidesch
Japanese	tsuki
Swahili	mwezi

600 moon

French	lune
Spanish	luna
Italian	luna
Portuguese	lua
Rumanian	lună
German	Mond
Dutch	maan
Swedish	måne
Danish	måne
Norwegian	måne
Polish	księżyc
Czech	komár
Serbo-Croat.	mjesec
Hungarian	hold
Finnish	kuu
Turkish	ay
Indonesian	bulan
Esperanto	luno
Russian	luná
Greek	fenga'ri
Arabic	qamar
Hebrew	levanah
Yiddish	levoneh
Japanese	tsuki
Swahili	mwezi

601 morning

French	matin
Spanish	mañana
Italian	mattina
Portuguese	manhã
Rumanian	dimineaţa
German	Morgen
Dutch	morgen
Swedish	morgon
Danish	morgen
Norwegian	morgen
Polish	rano
Czech	ráno
Serbo-Croat.	jutro
Hungarian	reggel
Finnish	aamu
Turkish	sabah
Indonesian	pagi
Esperanto	mateno
Russian	útro
Greek	pro-i'
Arabic	soubh
Hebrew	boker
Yiddish	friehmorgen
Japanese	asa
Swahili	asubuhi

602 mosquito

French	moustique
Spanish	mosquito
Italian	zanzara
Portuguese	mosquito
Rumanian	ţînţar
German	Mücke
Dutch	mug
Swedish	mygga
Danish	myg
Norwegian	mygg
Polish	komar
Czech	komár, moskyt
Serbo-Croat.	komarac
Hungarian	szúnyog
Finnish	sääski
Turkish	sivrisinek
Indonesian	njamuk
Esperanto	moskito
Russian	kamár
Greek	kounou'pi
Arabic	namousa
Hebrew	yitusch
Yiddish	komare
Japanese	ka
Swahili	mbu

603 mother

French	mère
Spanish	madre
Italian	madre
Portuguese	mãe
Rumanian	mamă
German	Mutter
Dutch	moeder
Swedish	moder
Danish	moder
Norwegian	mor
Polish	matka
Czech	matka
Serbo-Croat.	majka
Hungarian	anya
Finnish	äiti
Turkish	anne
Indonesian	induk
Esperanto	patr'ino
Russian	mat
Greek	mite'ra
Arabic	oum
Hebrew	em
Yiddish	muter
Japanese	haha
Swahili	mama

604 mountain

French	montagne
Spanish	montaña
Italian	montagna
Portuguese	montanha
Rumanian	munte
German	Berg
Dutch	berg
Swedish	berg
Danish	bjerg
Norwegian	fjell
Polish	góra
Czech	hora
Serbo-Croat.	gora
Hungarian	hegy
Finnish	vuori
Turkish	dağ
Indonesian	gunung
Esperanto	monto
Russian	gorá
Greek	vouno'
Arabic	gabal
Hebrew	har
Yiddish	berg
Japanese	yama
Swahili	mlima

605 mouse

French	souris
Spanish	ratón
Italian	topo
Portuguese	camundongo
Rumanian	şoarece
German	Maus
Dutch	muis
Swedish	mus
Danish	mus
Norwegian	mus
Polish	mysz
Czech	myš
Serbo-Croat.	miš
Hungarian	egér
Finnish	hiiri
Turkish	fare
Indonesian	tikus
Esperanto	muso
Russian	mish
Greek	pontikos'
Arabic	faar
Hebrew	achbar
Yiddish	moys
Japanese	hatsuka-nezumi
Swahili	panya mdogo

606 mouth

French	bouche
Spanish	boca
Italian	bocca
Portuguese	bôca
Rumanian	gură
German	Mund
Dutch	mond
Swedish	mun
Danish	mund
Norwegian	munn
Polish	usta
Czech	ústa
Serbo-Croat.	usta
Hungarian	száj
Finnish	suu
Turkish	ağiz
Indonesian	mulut
Esperanto	buŝo
Russian	rot
Greek	sto'ma
Arabic	fam
Hebrew	peh
Yiddish	moil
Japanese	kuchi
Swahili	kinywa

607 mouthwash

French	rince-bouche
Spanish	enjuague
Italian	acqua per la bocca
Portuguese	gargarejo
Rumanian	clăti gura
German	Mundwasser
Dutch	mondspoeling
Swedish	munvatten
Danish	mundvand
Norwegian	munnvann
Polish	woda do ust
Czech	ústí voda
Serbo-Croat.	voda za usta
Hungarian	szájvíz
Finnish	suuvesi
Turkish	ağiz yıkayıcı
Indonesian	obat pembersih gigi
Esperanto	dent'pur'ig'aĵo
Russian	palaskániye
Greek	odonto'krema
Arabic	ghasi lil-fam
Hebrew	megirgur
Yiddish	mundwasser
Japanese	hamigaki-eki
Swahili	maji kwa kusafisha kinywa

608 move

French	mouvoir
Spanish	mover
Italian	muovere
Portuguese	mover
Rumanian	mişca
German	bewegen
Dutch	bewegen
Swedish	flytta
Danish	bevæge
Norwegian	bevege
Polish	ruszać
Czech	pohnuti
Serbo-Croat.	kretati
Hungarian	mozgat
Finnish	liikuttaa
Turkish	hareket etmek
Indonesian	bergerak
Esperanto	movi
Russian	dvígat
Greek	kino'
Arabic	youharik
Hebrew	henia
Yiddish	bewegen
Japanese	ugokasu
Swahili	sogeza

609 movie

French	cinéma
Spanish	cine
Italian	cinema
Portuguese	cinema
Rumanian	cinema
German	Kino
Dutch	film
Swedish	biograf
Danish	biograf
Norwegian	kino
Polish	kino
Czech	kino
Serbo-Croat.	kino
Hungarian	mozi
Finnish	elokuvat
Turkish	sinema
Indonesian	bioskop
Esperanto	cinemo
Russian	kinó
Greek	kinimatogra'fos
Arabic	sinima
Hebrew	kolnoa
Yiddish	kinema
Japanese	eiga
Swahili	sinema

610 much

French	beaucoup
Spanish	mucho
Italian	molto
Portuguese	muito
Rumanian	mult
German	viel
Dutch	veel
Swedish	mycket
Danish	megen
Norwegian	megen
Polish	dużo
Czech	mnoho
Serbo-Croat.	mnogo
Hungarian	sok
Finnish	paljo
Turkish	çok
Indonesian	banjak
Esperanto	multo
Russian	mnógo
Greek	poli', pola'
Arabic	katsir
Hebrew	harbeh
Yiddish	assach
Japanese	takusan no
Swahili	-ingi

611 municipality

French	municipalité
Spanish	municipio
Italian	municipio
Portuguese	municipalidade
Rumanian	municipalitate
German	Gemeinde
Dutch	gemeente
Swedish	kommun
Danish	kommune
Norwegian	bykommune
Polish	gmina
Czech	obec
Serbo-Croat.	opština
Hungarian	község
Finnish	kaupunkikunta
Turkish	belediye
Indonesian	kotapradja
Esperanto	municipalo
Russian	obshchína
Greek	dimarchi'a
Arabic	dar al-baladiya
Hebrew	iriyah
Yiddish	gemine
Japanese	jichitai
Swahili	baraza ya mji

612 mushroom

French	champignon
Spanish	seta
Italian	fungo
Portuguese	cogumelo
Rumanian	ciupercă
German	Pilz
Dutch	paddestoel
Swedish	svamp
Danish	svamp
Norwegian	sopp
Polish	grzyb
Czech	houba
Serbo-Croat.	glijva
Hungarian	gomba
Finnish	sieni
Turkish	mantar
Indonesian	tjendawan
Esperanto	agariko
Russian	grib
Greek	manita'ri
Arabic	ish al-ghourab
Hebrew	pitriah
Yiddish	schwemel
Japanese	kinoko
Swahili	kiyoga

613 mustard

French	moutarde
Spanish	mostaza
Italian	mostarda
Portuguese	mostarda
Rumanian	muştar
German	Senf
Dutch	mosterd
Swedish	senap
Danish	sennep
Norwegian	sennep
Polish	musztarda
Czech	hořčice
Serbo-Croat.	gorušica
Hungarian	mustár
Finnish	mustard
Turkish	hardal
Indonesian	moster
Esperanto	mustardo
Russian	garchítsa
Greek	musta'rda
Arabic	kardal
Hebrew	chardal
Yiddish	gortschitse
Japanese	karashi
Swahili	haradali

614 mute

French	muet
Spanish	mudo
Italian	muto
Portuguese	mudo
Rumanian	mut
German	stumm
Dutch	stom
Swedish	stum
Danish	stum
Norwegian	stum
Polish	niemy
Czech	němý
Serbo-Croat.	nem
Hungarian	néma
Finnish	mykkä
Turkish	dilsiz
Indonesian	bisu
Esperanto	muta
Russian	nemóy
Greek	vovos'
Arabic	samit
Hebrew	ilem
Yiddish	schtum
Japanese	oshi no
Swahili	kimya

615 mutual

French	mutuel
Spanish	mutuo
Italian	mutuo
Portuguese	mútuo
Rumanian	mutual
German	gemeinsam
Dutch	wederkerig
Swedish	ömsesidig
Danish	fælles
Norwegian	gjensidig
Polish	wzajemny
Czech	vzájemný
Serbo-Croat.	uzajaman
Hungarian	kölcsönös
Finnish	keskinäinen
Turkish	karşılıklı
Indonesian	saling
Esperanto	komuna
Russian	vzaímni
Greek	amive'os
Arabic	moutabadal
Hebrew	hadadi
Yiddish	tsusamen
Japanese	soogo no
Swahili	-a wao kwa wao

616 nail

French	clou
Spanish	clavo
Italian	chiodo
Portuguese	prego
Rumanian	cui
German	Nagel
Dutch	spijker
Swedish	spik
Danish	søm
Norwegian	spiker
Polish	gwóźdź
Czech	hřebík
Serbo-Croat.	ekser
Hungarian	szeg
Finnish	naula
Turkish	çivi
Indonesian	paku
Esperanto	najlo
Russian	gvost
Greek	karfi'
Arabic	mismar
Hebrew	massmer
Yiddish	tschvek
Japanese	kugi
Swahili	msumari

617 nail file

French	lime à ongles
Spanish	lima
Italian	lima da unghie
Portuguese	limpador de unhas
Rumanian	pilă
German	Nagelfeile
Dutch	nagelvijl
Swedish	nagelfil
Danish	neglefil
Norwegian	neglefil
Polish	pilniczek do paznokci
Czech	pilníček na nehty
Serbo-Croat.	turpija za note
Hungarian	körömreszelő
Finnish	kynsiviila
Turkish	tırnak törpüsü
Indonesian	kikir kuku
Esperanto	fajlilo por ungo
Russian	pílochka
Greek	li'ma nichion'
Arabic	mibrad azafir
Hebrew	schofin letsiporen
Yiddish	nogelfeil
Japanese	tsume yasuri
Swahili	tupa ya ukucha

618 name

French	nom
Spanish	nombre
Italian	nome
Portuguese	nome
Rumanian	nume
German	Name
Dutch	naam
Swedish	namn
Danish	navn
Norwegian	navn
Polish	nazwisko
Czech	jméno
Serbo-Croat.	ime
Hungarian	név
Finnish	nimi
Turkish	isim
Indonesian	nama
Esperanto	nomo
Russian	ímya
Greek	o'noma
Arabic	ism
Hebrew	schem
Yiddish	nomen
Japanese	na
Swahili	jina

619 nature

French	nature
Spanish	naturaleza
Italian	natura
Portuguese	natureza
Rumanian	natură
German	Natur
Dutch	natuur
Swedish	natur
Danish	natur
Norwegian	natur
Polish	przyroda
Czech	příroda
Serbo-Croat.	priroda
Hungarian	természet
Finnish	luonto
Turkish	tabiat
Indonesian	alam
Esperanto	naturo
Russian	priróda
Greek	phi'sis
Arabic	tabiaa
Hebrew	teva
Yiddish	natur
Japanese	shizen
Swahili	tabia

620 near

French	près
Spanish	cerca
Italian	prossimo
Portuguese	próximo
Rumanian	apropiat
German	neben
Dutch	dichtbij
Swedish	nära
Danish	nær
Norwegian	nær
Polish	blisko
Czech	blízký
Serbo-Croat.	blizu
Hungarian	közel
Finnish	lähellä
Turkish	yakın
Indonesian	dekat
Esperanto	apude
Russian	blísko
Greek	konta'
Arabic	qarib
Hebrew	etsel
Yiddish	nohent
Japanese	chikai
Swahili	karibu

621 neck

French	cou
Spanish	cuello
Italian	collo
Portuguese	pescoço
Rumanian	gît
German	Nacken
Dutch	hals
Swedish	nacke
Danish	hals
Norwegian	hals
Polish	kark
Czech	krk
Serbo-Croat.	vrat
Hungarian	nyak
Finnish	kaula
Turkish	boyun
Indonesian	léhér
Esperanto	kolo
Russian	shéya
Greek	lemos'
Arabic	raqaba
Hebrew	tsavar
Yiddish	karek
Japanese	kubi
Swahili	shingo

622 necklace

French	collier
Spanish	collar
Italian	collana
Portuguese	colar
Rumanian	colier
German	Halskette
Dutch	halssnoer
Swedish	halsband
Danish	halskæde
Norwegian	halsbånd
Polish	naszyjnik
Czech	náhrdelníka
Serbo-Croat.	orglica
Hungarian	nyaklánc
Finnish	kaulakoriste
Turkish	gerdanlık
Indonesian	kalung
Esperanto	kol'ringo
Russian	azheryéliye
Greek	peride'reon
Arabic	iqd
Hebrew	tsavaron
Yiddish	halsbendel
Japanese	kubikazari
Swahili	mkufu

623 needle

French	aiguille
Spanish	aguja
Italian	ago
Portuguese	agulha
Rumanian	ac
German	Nadel
Dutch	naald
Swedish	nål
Danish	nål
Norwegian	nål
Polish	igła
Czech	jehla
Serbo-Croat.	igla
Hungarian	tű
Finnish	neula
Turkish	iğne
Indonesian	djarum
Esperanto	nadlo
Russian	iglá
Greek	velo'na
Arabic	ibra
Hebrew	machat
Yiddish	nodel
Japanese	hari
Swahili	sindano

624 neighbor

French	voisin
Spanish	vecino
Italian	vicino
Portuguese	vizinho
Rumanian	vecin
German	Nachbar
Dutch	buur
Swedish	granne
Danish	nabo
Norwegian	nabo
Polish	sąsiad
Czech	soused
Serbo-Croat.	susjed
Hungarian	szomszéd
Finnish	naapuri
Turkish	komşu
Indonesian	tetangga
Esperanto	najbaro
Russian	sasyét
Greek	yi'tonas
Arabic	gar
Hebrew	schachen
Yiddish	schochen
Japanese	rinjin
Swahili	jirani

625 nervous

French	nerveux
Spanish	nervioso
Italian	nervoso
Portuguese	nervoso
Rumanian	nervos
German	nervös
Dutch	zenuwachtig
Swedish	nervös
Danish	nervøs
Norwegian	nervøs
Polish	nerwowy
Czech	nervózni
Serbo-Croat.	nervozan
Hungarian	ideges
Finnish	hermostunut
Turkish	sinirli
Indonesian	gugup
Esperanto	nerva
Russian	nérvni
Greek	nevrikos'
Arabic	asabi
Hebrew	atsbani
Yiddish	nerves
Japanese	shinkei-kwabin no
Swahili	-epesi kushtuka

626 neutral

French	neutre
Spanish	neutral
Italian	neutrale
Portuguese	neutro
Rumanian	neutru
German	neutral
Dutch	neutraal
Swedish	neutral
Danish	neutral
Norwegian	nøytral
Polish	neutralny
Czech	neutrálni
Serbo-Croat.	neutralan
Hungarian	semleges
Finnish	puolueeton
Turkish	bitaraf
Indonesian	nétral
Esperanto	neŭtrala
Russian	neitrálni
Greek	oude'teros
Arabic	mouhayid
Hebrew	chiyud
Yiddish	umparteiish
Japanese	chuuritsu no
Swahili	wala hivi wala hivi

627 never

French	jamais
Spanish	nunca
Italian	mai
Portuguese	nunca
Rumanian	niciodată
German	niemals
Dutch	nooit
Swedish	aldrig
Danish	aldrig
Norwegian	aldri
Polish	nigdy
Czech	nikdy
Serbo-Croat.	nikad
Hungarian	soha
Finnish	ei koskaan
Turkish	hiç
Indonesian	tidak pernah
Esperanto	neniam
Russian	nikagdá
Greek	pote'
Arabic	abadan
Hebrew	meolam lo
Yiddish	kenmohl
Japanese	kesshite . . . nai
Swahili	si . . . kamwe

628 new

French	nouveau
Spanish	nuevo
Italian	nuovo
Portuguese	novo
Rumanian	nou
German	neu
Dutch	nieuw
Swedish	ny
Danish	ny
Norwegian	ny
Polish	nowy
Czech	nový
Serbo-Croat.	nov
Hungarian	új
Finnish	uusi
Turkish	yeni
Indonesian	baru
Esperanto	nova
Russian	nóvi
Greek	kenou'rios
Arabic	gadid
Hebrew	chatasch
Yiddish	nai
Japanese	atarashii
Swahili	-pya

629 newspaper

French	journal
Spanish	periódico
Italian	giornale
Portuguese	jornal
Rumanian	ziar
German	Zeitung
Dutch	krant
Swedish	tidning
Danish	avis
Norwegian	avis
Polish	gazeta
Czech	noviny
Serbo-Croat.	novine
Hungarian	újság
Finnish	sanomalehti
Turkish	gazete
Indonesian	surat kabar
Esperanto	ĵurnalo
Russian	gazyéta
Greek	efimeri'da
Arabic	garida
Hebrew	iton
Yiddish	tseitung
Japanese	shinbun
Swahili	gazeti

630 night

French	nuit
Spanish	noche
Italian	notte
Portuguese	noite
Rumanian	noapte
German	Nacht
Dutch	nacht
Swedish	natt
Danish	nat
Norwegian	natt
Polish	noc
Czech	noc
Serbo-Croat.	noć
Hungarian	éjszaka
Finnish	yö
Turkish	gece
Indonesian	malam
Esperanto	nokto
Russian	noch
Greek	ni'chta
Arabic	layla
Hebrew	laylah
Yiddish	nacht
Japanese	yoru
Swahili	usiku

631 nine

French	neuf
Spanish	nueve
Italian	nove
Portuguese	nove
Rumanian	nouă
German	neun
Dutch	negen
Swedish	nio
Danish	ni
Norwegian	ni
Polish	dziewięć
Czech	devět
Serbo-Croat.	devet
Hungarian	kilenc
Finnish	yhdeksän
Turkish	dokuz
Indonesian	sembilan
Esperanto	naŭ
Russian	dyévyat
Greek	enne'a
Arabic	tisaa
Hebrew	tischah
Yiddish	nein
Japanese	ku
Swahili	tisa

632 nineteen

French	dix-neuf
Spanish	diecinueve
Italian	diciannove
Portuguese	dezenove
Rumanian	nouăsprezece
German	neunzehn
Dutch	negentien
Swedish	nitton
Danish	nitten
Norwegian	nitten
Polish	dziewiętnaście
Czech	devatenáct
Serbo-Croat.	devetnaest
Hungarian	tizenkilenc
Finnish	yhdeksäntoista
Turkish	on dokuz
Indonesian	sembilan belas
Esperanto	dek naŭ
Russian	devatnátsat
Greek	dekaenne'a
Arabic	tisaat ashar
Hebrew	tischah assar
Yiddish	neintsehn
Japanese	juuku
Swahili	kumi na tisa

633 ninety

French	quatre-vingt-dix
Spanish	noventa
Italian	novanta
Portuguese	noventa
Rumanian	nouăzeci
German	neunzig
Dutch	negentig
Swedish	nittio
Danish	halvfems
Norwegian	nitty
Polish	dziewięćdziesiąt
Czech	devadesát
Serbo-Croat.	devedeset
Hungarian	kilencven
Finnish	yhdeksänkymmentä
Turkish	doksan
Indonesian	sembilan puluh
Esperanto	naŭ'dek
Russian	devinósto
Greek	enenin'ta
Arabic	tisoun
Hebrew	tischim
Yiddish	neintsig
Japanese	kyuujuu
Swahili	tisini

634 no

French	non
Spanish	no
Italian	no
Portuguese	não
Rumanian	nu
German	nein
Dutch	neen
Swedish	nej
Danish	nej
Norwegian	nei
Polish	nie
Czech	ne
Serbo-Croat.	ne
Hungarian	nem
Finnish	ei
Turkish	hayır
Indonesian	tidak
Esperanto	ne
Russian	nyet
Greek	o'chi
Arabic	la
Hebrew	lo
Yiddish	nit
Japanese	iya
Swahili	hapana

635 noise

French	bruit
Spanish	ruido
Italian	chiasso
Portuguese	barulho
Rumanian	zgomot
German	Lärm
Dutch	lawaai
Swedish	larm
Danish	støj
Norwegian	larm
Polish	hałas
Czech	hluk
Serbo-Croat.	buka
Hungarian	zaj, lárma
Finnish	melu
Turkish	gürültü
Indonesian	gaduh, ribut
Esperanto	bruo
Russian	shum
Greek	tho'rivos
Arabic	dawdaa
Hebrew	raasch
Yiddish	gereisch
Japanese	sawagi
Swahili	sauti

636 noodle

French	nouille
Spanish	tallarín
Italian	tagliatelle
Portuguese	macarrão
Rumanian	ţăieţei
German	Nudeln
Dutch	vermicelli
Swedish	nudlar
Danish	nudel
Norwegian	nudel
Polish	makaron
Czech	nudle
Serbo-Croat.	rezanci
Hungarian	metélt
Finnish	makarooni
Turkish	şehriye
Indonesian	mi
Esperanto	naiv'ulo
Russian	lapshá
Greek	chilopi'tta
Arabic	achraq
Hebrew	itriyah
Yiddish	lokschen
Japanese	udon
Swahili	tambi

637 noon

French	midi
Spanish	mediodía
Italian	mezzogiorno
Portuguese	meio dia
Rumanian	amiaza
German	mittags
Dutch	middag
Swedish	middagstid
Danish	middag
Norwegian	middag
Polish	południe
Czech	poledne
Serbo-Croat.	podne
Hungarian	dél
Finnish	puolipäivä
Turkish	öğle
Indonesian	tengah hari
Esperanto	tag'mezo
Russian	póldyen
Greek	mesime'ri
Arabic	zuhr
Hebrew	tsaharaim
Yiddish	mittog
Japanese	shoogo
Swahili	adhuhuri

639 nose

French	nez
Spanish	nariz
Italian	naso
Portuguese	nariz
Rumanian	nas
German	Nase
Dutch	neus
Swedish	näsa
Danish	næse
Norwegian	nese
Polish	nos
Czech	nos
Serbo-Croat.	nos
Hungarian	orr
Finnish	nenä
Turkish	burun
Indonesian	hidung
Esperanto	nazo
Russian	nos
Greek	mi'ti
Arabic	anf
Hebrew	af
Yiddish	nos
Japanese	hana
Swahili	pua

638 north

French	nord
Spanish	norte
Italian	nord
Portuguese	norte
Rumanian	nord
German	Norden
Dutch	noord
Swedish	nord
Danish	nord
Norwegian	nord
Polish	pólnoc
Czech	sever
Serbo-Croat.	sjever
Hungarian	észak
Finnish	pohjoinen
Turkish	kuzey
Indonesian	utara
Esperanto	nordo
Russian	séver
Greek	voras'
Arabic	shamal
Hebrew	tsafon
Yiddish	tsufenseit
Japanese	kita
Swahili	kaskazini

640 November

French	novembre
Spanish	noviembre
Italian	novembre
Portuguese	novembro
Rumanian	noiembrie
German	November
Dutch	November
Swedish	november
Danish	november
Norwegian	november
Polish	listopad
Czech	listopad
Serbo-Croat.	studeni
Hungarian	november
Finnish	marraskuu
Turkish	kasım
Indonesian	Nopémber
Esperanto	Novembro
Russian	nayábr
Greek	Noem'vrios
Arabic	nouvembar
Hebrew	november
Yiddish	november
Japanese	juuichigwatsu
Swahili	Novemba

641 now

French	maintenant
Spanish	ahora
Italian	adesso
Portuguese	agora
Rumanian	acum
German	jetzt
Dutch	nu
Swedish	nu
Danish	nu
Norwegian	nå
Polish	teraz
Czech	nyní
Serbo-Croat.	sada
Hungarian	most
Finnish	nyt
Turkish	şimdi
Indonesian	kini
Esperanto	nun
Russian	tepyér
Greek	to'ra
Arabic	al-an
Hebrew	atah
Yiddish	itst
Japanese	ima
Swahili	sasa

642 number

French	nombre
Spanish	número
Italian	numero
Portuguese	número
Rumanian	număr
German	Zahl
Dutch	nummer
Swedish	tal
Danish	nummer
Norwegian	nummer
Polish	numer
Czech	čislo
Serbo-Croat.	broj
Hungarian	szám
Finnish	numero
Turkish	numara
Indonesian	romor
Esperanto	nombro
Russian	chisló
Greek	arithmos'
Arabic	adad
Hebrew	mispar
Yiddish	numer
Japanese	suu
Swahili	namba

643 nurse

French	infirmière
Spanish	enfermera
Italian	infermiera
Portuguese	enfermeira
Rumanian	infirmieră
German	Krankenschwester
Dutch	verpleegster
Swedish	sköterska
Danish	sygeplejerske
Norwegian	skepleierske
Polish	pielęgniarka
Czech	ošetřovatelka
Serbo-Croat.	bolničarka
Hungarian	ápolónő
Finnish	sairaanhoitaja
Turkish	hemşire
Indonesian	djura rawat
Esperanto	fleg'isto
Russian	sidyélka
Greek	nosoko'mos
Arabic	moumarida
Hebrew	achot
Yiddish	verterin
Japanese	kangofu
Swahili	mwuguzi

644 nut

French	noix
Spanish	nuez
Italian	noce
Portuguese	noz
Rumanian	nucă
German	Nuss
Dutch	noot
Swedish	nöt
Danish	nød
Norwegian	nøtt
Polish	orzech
Czech	ořech
Serbo-Croat.	orah
Hungarian	dió
Finnish	pähkinä
Turkish	fındık
Indonesian	njiur
Esperanto	nuk'so
Russian	aryékh
Greek	kari'di
Arabic	miksarat
Hebrew	egoz
Yiddish	nus
Japanese	kenkwa
Swahili	kokwa

645 oak

French	chêne
Spanish	roble
Italian	quercia
Portuguese	carvalho
Rumanian	stejar
German	Eiche
Dutch	eik
Swedish	ek
Danish	eg
Norwegian	eik
Polish	dąb
Czech	dub
Serbo-Croat.	hrast
Hungarian	tölgy
Finnish	tammi
Turkish	meşe
Indonesian	ék
Esperanto	kverko
Russian	dup
Greek	velanidia'
Arabic	ballout
Hebrew	alon
Yiddish	demb
Japanese	kashi
Swahili	namna ya mti

646 oar

French	rame
Spanish	remo
Italian	remo
Portuguese	remo
Rumanian	vîslă
German	Ruder
Dutch	roeiriem
Swedish	åra
Danish	åre
Norwegian	åre
Polish	wiosło
Czech	veslo
Serbo-Croat.	veslo
Hungarian	evező
Finnish	airo
Turkish	kürek
Indonesian	dajung
Esperanto	rem'ilo
Russian	vesló
Greek	koupi'
Arabic	miqdaf
Hebrew	maschot
Yiddish	viosle
Japanese	kai
Swahili	kasia

647 oats

French	avoine
Spanish	avena
Italian	avena
Portuguese	aveia
Rumanian	ovăz
German	Hafer
Dutch	haver
Swedish	havre
Danish	havre
Norwegian	havre
Polish	owies
Czech	oves
Serbo-Croat.	zob
Hungarian	zab
Finnish	kaura
Turkish	yulaf
Indonesian	haver
Esperanto	aveno
Russian	avyós
Greek	vro'mi
Arabic	shoufan
Hebrew	schibolet schual
Yiddish	hober
Japanese	karasumugi
Swahili	nafaka kama shayiri

648 occupy

French	occuper
Spanish	ocupar
Italian	occupare
Portuguese	ocupar
Rumanian	ocupa
German	besetzen
Dutch	bewonen
Swedish	besätta
Danish	besætte
Norwegian	besette
Polish	zająć
Czech	obsaditi
Serbo-Croat.	zauzeti
Hungarian	elfolglal
Finnish	viedä
Turkish	işgal etmek
Indonesian	duduki
Esperanto	okupi
Russian	zanyát
Greek	apascholo'
Arabic	yashghil
Hebrew	lachad
Yiddish	farnumen
Japanese	shimeru
Swahili	kaa

649 October

French	octobre
Spanish	octubre
Italian	ottobre
Portuguese	outubro
Rumanian	octombrie
German	Oktober
Dutch	Oktober
Swedish	oktober
Danish	oktober
Norwegian	oktober
Polish	październik
Czech	řijen
Serbo-Croat.	listopad
Hungarian	október
Finnish	lokakuu
Turkish	ekim
Indonesian	Oktober
Esperanto	Oktobro
Russian	aktyábr
Greek	Okto'vrios
Arabic	oktobar
Hebrew	oktober
Yiddish	oktober
Japanese	juugwatsu
Swahili	Oktoba

650 office

French	bureau
Spanish	oficina
Italian	ufficio
Portuguese	escritório
Rumanian	birou
German	Büro
Dutch	kantoor
Swedish	kontor
Danish	kontor
Norwegian	kontor
Polish	biuro
Czech	úřad
Serbo-Croat.	kancelarija
Hungarian	iroda
Finnish	toimisto
Turkish	büro
Indonesian	kantor
Esperanto	ofic'ejo
Russian	byuró
Greek	grafi'on
Arabic	maktab
Hebrew	misrad
Yiddish	biro
Japanese	jimusho
Swahili	afisi

651 oil

French	huile
Spanish	aceite
Italian	olio
Portuguese	óleo
Rumanian	ulei
German	Öl
Dutch	olie
Swedish	olja
Danish	olie
Norwegian	olje
Polish	olej
Czech	olej
Serbo-Croat.	ulje
Hungarian	olaj
Finnish	öljy
Turkish	yağ
Indonesian	minjak
Esperanto	oleo
Russian	máslo
Greek	la'di
Arabic	zayt
Hebrew	schemen
Yiddish	el
Japanese	abura
Swahili	mafuta

652 old

French	vieux
Spanish	viejo
Italian	vecchio
Portuguese	velho
Rumanian	vechi
German	alt
Dutch	oud
Swedish	gammal
Danish	gammel
Norwegian	gammel
Polish	stary
Czech	starý
Serbo-Croat.	star
Hungarian	öreg
Finnish	vanha
Turkish	eski
Indonesian	tua
Esperanto	mal'nova
Russian	stári
Greek	pali-os'
Arabic	qadim
Hebrew	yaschan
Yiddish	alt
Japanese	oita
Swahili	-zee

653 olive

French	olive
Spanish	oliva
Italian	oliva
Portuguese	azeitona
Rumanian	maslină
German	Olive
Dutch	olijf
Swedish	oliv
Danish	oliven
Norwegian	oliven
Polish	oliwka
Czech	oliva
Serbo-Croat.	maslina
Hungarian	olajbogyó
Finnish	oliivi
Turkish	zeytin
Indonesian	zait
Esperanto	olivo
Russian	alíva
Greek	eli-a'
Arabic	zaytoun
Hebrew	sayit
Yiddish	olif
Japanese	oriibu
Swahili	zeituni

654 one

French	un
Spanish	uno
Italian	uno
Portuguese	um
Rumanian	un
German	eins
Dutch	een
Swedish	en
Danish	én, ét
Norwegian	en
Polish	jeden
Czech	jeden
Serbo-Croat.	jedan
Hungarian	egy
Finnish	yksi
Turkish	bir
Indonesian	satu
Esperanto	unu
Russian	adín
Greek	e'na
Arabic	wahid
Hebrew	echad
Yiddish	ein
Japanese	ichi
Swahili	-moja

655 onion

French	oignon
Spanish	cebolla
Italian	cipolla
Portuguese	cebola
Rumanian	ceapă
German	Zwiebel
Dutch	ui
Swedish	lök
Danish	løg
Norwegian	løk
Polish	cebula
Czech	cibule
Serbo-Croat.	luk
Hungarian	hagyma
Finnish	sipuli
Turkish	soğan
Indonesian	bawang
Esperanto	cepo
Russian	luk
Greek	kremi'di
Arabic	basal
Hebrew	batsal
Yiddish	tsibele
Japanese	tamanegi
Swahili	kitunguu

656 open

French	ouvert
Spanish	abierto
Italian	aperto
Portuguese	aberto
Rumanian	deschis
German	offen
Dutch	open
Swedish	öppen
Danish	åben
Norwegian	åpen
Polish	otwarty
Czech	otevřený
Serbo-Croat.	otvoren
Hungarian	nyílt
Finnish	auki
Turkish	açık
Indonesian	buka
Esperanto	ne'ferm'ita
Russian	atkríti
Greek	aniktos'
Arabic	maftouh
Hebrew	patuach
Yiddish	ofen
Japanese	hiraita
Swahili	wazi

657 orange

French	orange
Spanish	naranja
Italian	arancia
Portuguese	laranja
Rumanian	portocală
German	Apfelsine
Dutch	sinaasappel
Swedish	apelsin
Danish	appelsin
Norwegian	appelsin
Polish	pomarańcza
Czech	pomeranč
Serbo-Croat.	pomorandža
Hungarian	narancs
Finnish	appelsiini
Turkish	portakal
Indonesian	djeruk manis
Esperanto	orango
Russian	apelsín
Greek	portoka'li
Arabic	bourtouqal
Hebrew	tapus
Yiddish	marants
Japanese	orenji
Swahili	chungwa

658 ore

French	minerai
Spanish	mineral
Italian	minerale
Portuguese	minério
Rumanian	minereu
German	Erz
Dutch	erts
Swedish	malm
Danish	malm
Norwegian	malm
Polish	ruda
Czech	ruda
Serbo-Croat.	ruda
Hungarian	érc
Finnish	malmi
Turkish	maden
Indonesian	bidjih
Esperanto	mineralo
Russian	rudá
Greek	meta'levma
Arabic	maadin cham
Hebrew	afrah
Yiddish	erts
Japanese	kooseki
Swahili	mawe yenye madini

659 outside

French	dehors
Spanish	fuera
Italian	fuori
Portuguese	de fora
Rumanian	exterior
German	aussen
Dutch	buiten
Swedish	utanför
Danish	udenfor
Norwegian	utenfor
Polish	zewnątrz
Czech	vnější
Serbo-Croat.	spolja
Hungarian	külső
Finnish	ulkona
Turkish	dış
Indonesian	luar
Esperanto	ekstera
Russian	na dvaryé
Greek	e'xo
Arabic	charig
Hebrew	bachuts
Yiddish	droyssen
Japanese	sotogawa no
Swahili	nje

660 ox

French	boeuf
Spanish	buey
Italian	bue
Portuguese	boi
Rumanian	bou
German	Ochse
Dutch	os
Swedish	oxe
Danish	okse
Norwegian	okse
Polish	wół
Czech	vůl
Serbo-Croat.	vo
Hungarian	ökör
Finnish	härkä
Turkish	öküz
Indonesian	sapi kebiri
Esperanto	bovo
Russian	vol
Greek	vo'di
Arabic	tsor
Hebrew	schor
Yiddish	oks
Japanese	kyoseioushi
Swahili	maksai

661 pain

French	douleur
Spanish	dolor
Italian	dolore
Portuguese	dor
Rumanian	durere
German	Schmerz
Dutch	pijn
Swedish	smärta
Danish	smerte
Norwegian	smerte
Polish	ból
Czech	bolest
Serbo-Croat.	bol
Hungarian	fájdalom
Finnish	kipu
Turkish	ağrı
Indonesian	sakit, susah
Esperanto	doloro
Russian	bol
Greek	po'nos
Arabic	alam
Hebrew	keev
Yiddish	tsar
Japanese	kutsuu
Swahili	maumivu

662 painting

French	peinture
Spanish	pintura
Italian	pittura
Portuguese	pintura
Rumanian	tablou
German	Gemälde
Dutch	schilderij
Swedish	målning
Danish	maleri
Norwegian	maleri
Polish	malowidło
Czech	malba
Serbo-Croat.	slikanje
Hungarian	festmény
Finnish	maalaus
Turkish	resim
Indonesian	lukisan
Esperanto	pentr'ado
Russian	zhívopis
Greek	zografiki'
Arabic	sourabilalwan
Hebrew	tmunah
Yiddish	gemelde
Japanese	kwaiga
Swahili	picha ya rangi

663 pair

French	paire
Spanish	pareja
Italian	paio
Portuguese	par
Rumanian	pereche
German	Paar
Dutch	paar
Swedish	par
Danish	par
Norwegian	par
Polish	para
Czech	pár
Serbo-Croat.	par
Hungarian	pár
Finnish	pari
Turkish	çift
Indonesian	pasang
Esperanto	paro
Russian	pára
Greek	zev'gos
Arabic	zoug
Hebrew	sug
Yiddish	puer
Japanese	tsui
Swahili	jozi

664 pancake

French	crêpe
Spanish	tortilla
Italian	frittella
Portuguese	panqueca
Rumanian	clătită
German	Pfannkuchen
Dutch	pannekoek
Swedish	pannkaka
Danish	pandekage
Norwegian	pannekake
Polish	naleśnik
Czech	lívanec
Serbo-Croat.	palačinka
Hungarian	palacsinta
Finnish	pannukakku
Turkish	gözleme
Indonesian	panekuk, dadar
Esperanto	pat'kuko
Russian	blin
Greek	tigani'ta
Arabic	fatira
Hebrew	levivah
Yiddish	blintse
Japanese	hottokeeki
Swahili	andazi kama kitumbua

665 panic

French	panique
Spanish	pánico
Italian	panico
Portuguese	pânico
Rumanian	panică
German	Schreck
Dutch	paniek
Swedish	panik
Danish	panik
Norwegian	panikk
Polish	popłoch
Czech	ponika
Serbo-Croat.	panika
Hungarian	rémület
Finnish	pakokauhu
Turkish	panik
Indonesian	panik, dahsjat
Esperanto	paniko
Russian	pánika
Greek	panikos'
Arabic	gazaa
Hebrew	behalah
Yiddish	schreck
Japanese	kyookoo
Swahili	woga mkubwa

666 paper

French	papier
Spanish	papel
Italian	carta
Portuguese	papel
Rumanian	hîrtie
German	Papier
Dutch	papier
Swedish	papper
Danish	papir
Norwegian	papir
Polish	papier
Czech	papír
Serbo-Croat.	hartija
Hungarian	papír
Finnish	paperi
Turkish	kâğıt
Indonesian	kertas
Esperanto	papero
Russian	bumága
Greek	charti'
Arabic	waraq
Hebrew	neyar
Yiddish	papir
Japanese	kami
Swahili	karatasi

667 parachute

French	parachute
Spanish	paracaídas
Italian	paracadute
Portuguese	paraquedas
Rumanian	paraşută
German	Fallschirm
Dutch	parachute
Swedish	fallskärm
Danish	faldskærm
Norwegian	fallskjerm
Polish	spadochron
Czech	padák
Serbo-Croat.	padobran
Hungarian	ejtőernyő
Finnish	rauha
Turkish	paraşüt
Indonesian	pajung udara
Esperanto	paraŝuto
Russian	parashyút
Greek	alexi'ptoto
Arabic	barashout
Hebrew	matsneach
Yiddish	fallschirm
Japanese	rakkagasa
Swahili	mwavuli kuelea hewani

668 parcel

French	paquet
Spanish	paquete
Italian	pacco
Portuguese	pacote
Rumanian	pachet
German	Paket
Dutch	pakje
Swedish	paket
Danish	pakke
Norwegian	pakke
Polish	pakiet
Czech	balík
Serbo-Croat.	paket
Hungarian	csomag
Finnish	paketti
Turkish	paket
Indonesian	pakét
Esperanto	pak'eto
Russian	pakyét
Greek	pake'to
Arabic	tard
Hebrew	chavilah
Yiddish	pekel
Japanese	kozutsumi
Swahili	kifurushi

669 parents

French	parents
Spanish	padres
Italian	genitori
Portuguese	pais
Rumanian	părinţi
German	Eltern
Dutch	ouders
Swedish	föräldrar
Danish	forældre
Norwegian	foreldre
Polish	rodzice
Czech	rodiče
Serbo-Croat.	roditelji
Hungarian	szülő
Finnish	vanhemmat
Turkish	ebeveyn
Indonesian	ibu bapa
Esperanto	ge'patroj
Russian	radítyeli
Greek	gonis'
Arabic	al-walidain
Hebrew	horim
Yiddish	tate-mame
Japanese	oya
Swahili	wazazi

670 parking

French	parking
Spanish	estacíonar
Italian	parcare
Portuguese	estacionamento
Rumanian	staţiona
German	parken
Dutch	park
Swedish	parkera
Danish	parkere
Norwegian	parkering
Polish	stawać
Czech	parkovati
Serbo-Croat.	parkiranje
Hungarian	parkol
Finnish	puisto
Turkish	oto parki
Indonesian	memarkir
Esperanto	parki
Russian	stayát
Greek	stath'mefsis
Arabic	moutanazah
Hebrew	chanuyah
Yiddish	opschtellen
Japanese	chuusha
Swahili	weka katika kiwanja

671 parsley

French	persil
Spanish	perejil
Italian	prezzemolo
Portuguese	salsa
Rumanian	pătrunjel
German	Petersilie
Dutch	peterselie
Swedish	persilja
Danish	persille
Norwegian	persille
Polish	pietruszka
Czech	petržel
Serbo-Croat.	peršun
Hungarian	petrezselyem
Finnish	persilja
Turkish	maydanoz
Indonesian	peétérséli
Esperanto	petroselo
Russian	petrúshka
Greek	ma-intanos'
Arabic	maqdounis
Hebrew	karpas
Yiddish	petruschke
Japanese	paseri
Swahili	mboga kama majani

672 part

French	part
Spanish	parte
Italian	parte
Portuguese	parte
Rumanian	parte
German	Teil
Dutch	gedeelte
Swedish	del
Danish	del
Norwegian	del
Polish	część
Czech	část
Serbo-Croat.	deo
Hungarian	rész
Finnish	osa
Turkish	kısım
Indonesian	bagian
Esperanto	parto
Russian	chast
Greek	me'ros
Arabic	gouza
Hebrew	chelek
Yiddish	chelik
Japanese	bubun
Swahili	sehemu

673 partridge

French	perdrix
Spanish	perdiz
Italian	pernice
Portuguese	perdiz
Rumanian	potîrniche
German	Rebhuhn
Dutch	patrijs
Swedish	rapphöna
Danish	agerhøne
Norwegian	åkerhøne
Polish	kuropatwa
Czech	koroptev
Serbo-Croat.	jarebica
Hungarian	fogoly
Finnish	peltopyy
Turkish	keklik
Indonesian	ajam hutan
Esperanto	perdriko
Russian	kurapátka
Greek	per'dika
Arabic	siman
Hebrew	chaglah
Yiddish	kurapatke
Japanese	shako
Swahili	kwale

674 passport

French	passeport
Spanish	pasaporte
Italian	passaporto
Portuguese	passaporte
Rumanian	paşaport
German	Pass
Dutch	paspoort
Swedish	pass
Danish	pas
Norwegian	pass
Polish	paszport
Czech	cestovní pas
Serbo-Croat.	pasoš
Hungarian	útlevél
Finnish	passi
Turkish	pasaport
Indonesian	sunrat pas
Esperanto	pasporto
Russian	pásport
Greek	diavati'rio
Arabic	gawaz safar
Hebrew	darkon
Yiddish	pasport
Japanese	ryoken
Swahili	cheti cha njia

675 pay

French	payer
Spanish	pagar
Italian	pagare
Portuguese	pagar
Rumanian	plăti
German	zahlen
Dutch	betalen
Swedish	betala
Danish	betale
Norwegian	betale
Polish	płacić
Czech	platiti
Serbo-Croat.	platiti
Hungarian	fizet
Finnish	maksaa
Turkish	ödemek
Indonesian	bajar
Esperanto	pagi
Russian	platít
Greek	pliro'no
Arabic	yadfaa
Hebrew	schilam
Yiddish	tsohlen
Japanese	shiharau
Swahili	lipa

676 pea

French	pois
Spanish	guisante
Italian	pisello
Portuguese	ervilha
Rumanian	mazăre
German	Erbse
Dutch	erwt
Swedish	ärt
Danish	ært
Norwegian	ert
Polish	groch
Czech	hrách
Serbo-Croat.	grašak
Hungarian	borsó
Finnish	herne
Turkish	bezelye
Indonesian	katjang
Esperanto	pizo
Russian	garókh
Greek	bize'li
Arabic	bisila
Hebrew	afunah
Yiddish	arbes
Japanese	endoo
Swahili	njegere

677 peace

French	paix
Spanish	paz
Italian	pace
Portuguese	paz
Rumanian	pace
German	Frieden
Dutch	vrede
Swedish	fred
Danish	fred
Norwegian	fred
Polish	pokój
Czech	mír
Serbo-Croat.	mir
Hungarian	béke
Finnish	ruaha
Turkish	sulh
Indonesian	perdamaian
Esperanto	paco
Russian	mir
Greek	iri'ni
Arabic	salam
Hebrew	schalom
Yiddish	scholim
Japanese	heiwa
Swahili	amani

678 pear

French	poire
Spanish	pera
Italian	pera
Portuguese	pera
Rumanian	pară
German	Birne
Dutch	peer
Swedish	päron
Danish	pære
Norwegian	pære
Polish	gruszka
Czech	hruška
Serbo-Croat.	kruška
Hungarian	körte
Finnish	päärynä
Turkish	armut
Indonesian	pér
Esperanto	piro
Russian	grúsha
Greek	achla'di
Arabic	koumitsra
Hebrew	anas
Yiddish	barne
Japanese	nashi
Swahili	tunda kama pęra

679 peasant

French	paysan
Spanish	campesino
Italian	contadino
Portuguese	camponês
Rumanian	ţăran
German	Bauer
Dutch	boer
Swedish	bonde
Danish	bonde
Norwegian	bonde
Polish	chłop
Czech	sedlák
Serbo-Croat.	seljak
Hungarian	paraszt
Finnish	talonpoika
Turkish	köylü
Indonesian	petani
Esperanto	kamp'ar'ano
Russian	krestyánin
Greek	choria'tis
Arabic	falah
Hebrew	ikar
Yiddish	poyr
Japanese	noofu
Swahili	mkulima

680 pen

French	plume
Spanish	pluma
Italian	penna
Portuguese	pena
Rumanian	toc
German	Federhalter
Dutch	pen
Swedish	penna
Danish	pen
Norwegian	penn
Polish	pióro
Czech	pero
Serbo-Croat.	pero
Hungarian	toll
Finnish	kynä
Turkish	kalem
Indonesian	péna, kalam
Esperanto	plumo
Russian	piró
Greek	pen'na
Arabic	risha
Hebrew	et
Yiddish	pen
Japanese	pen
Swahili	kalamu ya wino

681 pencil

French	crayon
Spanish	lápiz
Italian	matita
Portuguese	lápis
Rumanian	creion
German	Bleistift
Dutch	potlood
Swedish	blyertspenna
Danish	blyant
Norwegian	blyant
Polish	ołówek
Czech	tužka
Serbo-Croat.	olovka
Hungarian	ceruza
Finnish	lyijykynä
Turkish	kurşun kalem
Indonesian	patlot
Esperanto	krajono
Russian	karandásh
Greek	moli'vi
Arabic	qalam
Hebrew	iparon
Yiddish	bleischtift
Japanese	enpitsu
Swahili	kalamu ya risasi

682 pepper

French	poivre
Spanish	pimienta
Italian	pepe
Portuguese	pimenta
Rumanian	piper
German	Pfeffer
Dutch	peper
Swedish	peppar
Danish	peber
Norwegian	pepper
Polish	pieprz
Czech	pepř
Serbo-Croat.	biber
Hungarian	bors
Finnish	pippuri
Turkish	biber
Indonesian	lada, meritja
Esperanto	pipro
Russian	pyérets
Greek	pipe'ri
Arabic	filfil
Hebrew	pilpel
Yiddish	fefer
Japanese	koshoo
Swahili	pilipili

683 permitted

French	permis
Spanish	permitido
Italian	permesso
Portuguese	licito
Rumanian	permis
German	erlaubt
Dutch	veroorloofd
Swedish	tillåtet
Danish	tilladt
Norwegian	tillatt
Polish	dozwolony
Czech	devoleno
Serbo-Croat.	dozvoljeno
Hungarian	szabad
Finnish	sallittu
Turkish	caiz
Indonesian	izin, lulusan
Esperanto	permesa
Russian	pazvalítelni
Greek	epitrepo'menos
Arabic	masmouh
Hebrew	mutar
Yiddish	derloibt
Japanese	yurusareta
Swahili	halali

684 pharmacy

French	pharmacie
Spanish	farmacia
Italian	farmacia
Portuguese	farmácia
Rumanian	farmacie
German	Apotheke
Dutch	apotheek
Swedish	apotek
Danish	apotek
Norwegian	apotek
Polish	apteka
Czech	lékarna
Serbo-Croat.	apoteka
Hungarian	gyógyszertár
Finnish	apteekki
Turkish	eczane
Indonesian	apotek, rumah obat
Esperanto	apoteko
Russian	aptyéka
Greek	farmaki'on
Arabic	agzachana
Hebrew	beth mirkachat
Yiddish	aptek
Japanese	yakkyoku
Swahili	duka la dawa

685 phonograph

French	phonographe
Spanish	fonógrafo
Italian	fonografa
Portuguese	fonógrafo
Rumanian	gramofon
German	Grammophon
Dutch	grammofoon
Swedish	grammofon
Danish	grammofon
Norwegian	grammofon
Polish	gramofon
Czech	gramafon
Serbo-Croat.	gramofon
Hungarian	gramofon
Finnish	gramofoni
Turkish	fonograf
Indonesian	gramofon
Esperanto	fonografo
Russian	gramafón
Greek	fono'grafos
Arabic	founoughraf
Hebrew	makol
Yiddish	fonograf
Japanese	chikuonki
Swahili	mashine kucheza muziki

686 physician

French	médecin
Spanish	médico
Italian	medico
Portuguese	médico
Rumanian	medic
German	Arzt
Dutch	dokter
Swedish	läkare
Danish	læge
Norwegian	læge
Polish	lekarz
Czech	lékář
Serbo-Croat.	ljekar
Hungarian	orvos
Finnish	lääkäri
Turkish	doktor
Indonesian	tabib, dokter
Esperanto	kurac'isto
Russian	vrach
Greek	yatros'
Arabic	tabib
Hebrew	rofe
Yiddish	dokter
Japanese	ishi
Swahili	daktari

687 piano

French	piano
Spanish	piano
Italian	pianoforte
Portuguese	piano
Rumanian	piano
German	Klavier
Dutch	piano
Swedish	piano
Danish	klaver
Norwegian	piano
Polish	fortepian
Czech	klavir
Serbo-Croat.	klavir
Hungarian	zongora
Finnish	piano
Turkish	piyano
Indonesian	piano
Esperanto	piano
Russian	pianíno
Greek	pia'no
Arabic	bayan
Hebrew	psanter
Yiddish	klavir
Japanese	piano
Swahili	kinanda

688 picture

French	tableau
Spanish	retrato
Italian	quadro
Portuguese	quadro
Rumanian	poză
German	Bild
Dutch	afbeelding
Swedish	bild
Danish	billede
Norwegian	bilde
Polish	obraz
Czech	obraz
Serbo-Croat.	slika
Hungarian	kép
Finnish	kuva
Turkish	tasvir
Indonesian	gambar
Esperanto	bildo
Russian	kartína
Greek	iko'na
Arabic	lawha
Hebrew	tmunah
Yiddish	bild
Japanese	e
Swahili	picha

689 pig

French	cochon
Spanish	cerdo
Italian	porco
Portuguese	porco
Rumanian	porc
German	Schwein
Dutch	varken
Swedish	svin
Danish	svin
Norwegian	gris
Polish	świnia
Czech	prase
Serbo-Croat.	svinja
Hungarian	disznó
Finnish	sika
Turkish	domuz
Indonesian	babi
Esperanto	porko
Russian	svinyá
Greek	chi'ros
Arabic	chanzir
Hebrew	chasir
Yiddish	schvein
Japanese	buta
Swahili	nguruwe

690 pigeon

French	pigeon
Spanish	pichón
Italian	piccione
Portuguese	pombo
Rumanian	porumbel
German	Taube
Dutch	duif
Swedish	duva
Danish	due
Norwegian	due
Polish	gołąb
Czech	holub
Serbo-Croat.	golub
Hungarian	galamb
Finnish	kyyhkynen
Turkish	güvercin
Indonesian	merpati, burung dara
Esperanto	kolombo
Russian	gólup
Greek	periste'ri
Arabic	hamama
Hebrew	yonah
Yiddish	tob
Japanese	hato
Swahili	njiwa

691 pillow

French	oreiller
Spanish	almohada
Italian	cuscino
Portuguese	almofada
Rumanian	pernă
German	Kissen
Dutch	kussen
Swedish	kudde
Danish	pude
Norwegian	pute
Polish	poduszka
Czech	polštář
Serbo-Croat.	jastuk
Hungarian	párna
Finnish	pielus
Turkish	yastık
Indonesian	bantal
Esperanto	kap'kuseno
Russian	padúshka
Greek	maxila'ri
Arabic	michada
Hebrew	kesset
Yiddish	kuschen
Japanese	makura
Swahili	mto

692 pilot

French	pilote
Spanish	piloto
Italian	pilota
Portuguese	pilôto
Rumanian	pilot
German	Lotse
Dutch	piloot
Swedish	pilot
Danish	lods
Norwegian	los
Polish	pilot
Czech	lodivod
Serbo-Croat.	pilot
Hungarian	pilóta
Finnish	luotsi
Turkish	kılavuz
Indonesian	pilot, pandu
Esperanto	piloto
Russian	pilót
Greek	pilo'tos
Arabic	roubban
Hebrew	navat
Yiddish	steierman
Japanese	mizusako-an'nai
Swahili	rubani

693 pin

French	épingle
Spanish	alfiler
Italian	spillo
Portuguese	alfinete
Rumanian	ac
German	Stecknadel
Dutch	speld
Swedish	knappnål
Danish	knappenål
Norwegian	knappenål
Polish	szpilka
Czech	špendlík
Serbo-Croat.	pribarača
Hungarian	gombostű
Finnish	nuppineula
Turkish	iğne
Indonesian	peniti
Esperanto	pinglo
Russian	buláfka
Greek	karfi'tsa
Arabic	dabbous
Hebrew	prifah
Yiddish	schpilke
Japanese	pin
Swahili	pini

694 pine tree

French	pin
Spanish	pino
Italian	pino
Portuguese	pinheiro
Rumanian	pin
German	Fichte
Dutch	pijnboom
Swedish	tall
Danish	fyrretræ
Norwegian	nåletre
Polish	sosna
Czech	smrk
Serbo-Croat.	bor
Hungarian	fenyő
Finnish	mänty
Turkish	çam
Indonesian	tjemara
Esperanto	pino
Russian	sasná
Greek	pef'ko
Arabic	shagarat sonobar
Hebrew	oren
Yiddish	sossne
Japanese	matsu
Swahili	mti kama msunobari

695 pink

French	rose
Spanish	rosado
Italian	rosa
Portuguese	côr de rosa
Rumanian	roz
German	rosa
Dutch	rose
Swedish	skär
Danish	blegrød
Norwegian	rosa
Polish	różowy
Czech	růžový
Serbo-Croat.	ružičast
Hungarian	rózsaszinű
Finnish	neilikka
Turkish	pembe
Indonesian	mérah diambu
Esperanto	roz'koloro
Russian	rózavi
Greek	roz'
Arabic	bambi
Hebrew	varod
Yiddish	roza
Japanese	momoiro
Swahili	-ekundu -eupe

696 pipe

French	tuyau
Spanish	tubo
Italian	tubo
Portuguese	tubo
Rumanian	tub
German	Rohr
Dutch	buis
Swedish	rör
Danish	rør
Norwegian	rør
Polish	rura
Czech	roura
Serbo-Croat.	cev
Hungarian	cső
Finnish	putki
Turkish	boru
Indonesian	pipa
Esperanto	tubo
Russian	trubá
Greek	pi'pa
Arabic	masour.
Hebrew	tsinor
Yiddish	rehr
Japanese	paipu
Swahili	mwanzi

697 plant

French	plante
Spanish	planta
Italian	planta
Portuguese	planta
Rumanian	plantă
German	Pflanze
Dutch	plant
Swedish	växt
Danish	plante
Norwegian	plante
Polish	roślina
Czech	rostlina
Serbo-Croat.	biljka
Hungarian	növény
Finnish	kasvi
Turkish	nebat
Indonesian	tanaman
Esperanto	planto
Russian	rastyéniye
Greek	fiton'
Arabic	nabat
Hebrew	tsemach
Yiddish	geweks
Japanese	shokubutsu
Swahili	mmea

698 platform

French	quai
Spanish	andén
Italian	piattaforma
Portuguese	plataforma
Rumanian	peron
German	Bahnsteig
Dutch	perron
Swedish	perrong
Danish	perron
Norwegian	perrong
Polish	peron
Czech	nástupiště
Serbo-Croat.	peron
Hungarian	peron
Finnish	asemasilta
Turkish	peron
Indonesian	péron
Esperanto	perono
Russian	perón
Greek	exe'dra
Arabic	rasif
Hebrew	duchan
Yiddish	peron
Japanese	dan
Swahili	gati

699 play

French	jouer
Spanish	jugar
Italian	giocare
Portuguese	jogar
Rumanian	juca
German	spielen
Dutch	spelen
Swedish	spela
Danish	spil
Norwegian	spill
Polish	grać
Czech	hrátí
Serbo-Croat.	igrati
Hungarian	játszik
Finnish	leikkiä
Turkish	oynamak
Indonesian	main
Esperanto	ludo
Russian	igrát
Greek	pe'zo
Arabic	yalaab
Hebrew	hischtaascha
Yiddish	schpielen
Japanese	asobu
Swahili	cheza

700 playing card

French	carte à jouer
Spanish	baraja
Italian	carta da giuoco
Portuguese	carta de jogas
Rumanian	carte de joc
German	Spielkarte
Dutch	speelkaart
Swedish	spelkort
Danish	spillekort
Norwegian	spillkort
Polish	karta
Czech	hrací karta
Serbo-Croat.	karta
Hungarian	játekkártya
Finnish	pelikortti
Turkish	oyun kâğıdı
Indonesian	kartu main
Esperanto	ludcarto
Russian	igrálnaya kárta
Greek	kar'ta pechnidiou'
Arabic	warag koutshina
Hebrew	kartim
Yiddish	korten
Japanese	toranpu
Swahili	karata

701 please

French	s'il vous plaît
Spanish	por favor
Italian	prego
Portuguese	por favor
Rumanian	poftim
German	bitte
Dutch	alstublieu
Swedish	var så god
Danish	vær så god
Norwegian	vær så god
Polish	proszę
Czech	prosím
Serbo-Croat.	molim
Hungarian	kérem
Finnish	olkaa hyvä
Turkish	lûtfen
Indonesian	silakan
Esperanto	se plaĉas
Russian	pashálsta
Greek	parakalo'
Arabic	min faḍlak
Hebrew	bewakaschah
Yiddish	seit azoi gut
Japanese	doozo
Swahili	tafadhali

702 pleasure

French	plaisir
Spanish	placer
Italian	piacere
Portuguese	prazer
Rumanian	plăcere
German	Vergnügen
Dutch	plezier
Swedish	nöje
Danish	fornøjelse
Norwegian	fornøyelse
Polish	przyjemność
Czech	radost
Serbo-Croat.	zadovoljsto
Hungarian	öröm
Finnish	huvi
Turkish	safa
Indonesian	kesukaan
Esperanto	plezuro
Russian	udavólstviye
Greek	efcharis'tisis
Arabic	sourour
Hebrew	hanaha
Yiddish	hanuhe
Japanese	tanoshimi
Swahili	furaha

703 plum

French	prune
Spanish	ciruela
Italian	susina
Portuguese	ameixa
Rumanian	prună
German	Pflaume
Dutch	pruim
Swedish	plommon
Danish	blomme
Norwegian	plomme
Polish	śliwka
Czech	švestka
Serbo-Croat.	šljiva
Hungarian	szilva
Finnish	luumu
Turkish	erik
Indonesian	prém
Esperanto	pruno
Russian	slíva
Greek	damas'kinon
Arabic	qarasia
Hebrew	schasif
Yiddish	floim
Japanese	ume
Swahili	tunda kama zambarau

704 pocket

French	poche
Spanish	bolsillo
Italian	tasca
Portuguese	bolso
Rumanian	buzunar
German	Tasche
Dutch	zak
Swedish	ficka
Danish	lomme
Norwegian	lomme
Polish	kieszeń
Czech	kapsa
Serbo-Croat.	džep
Hungarian	zseb
Finnish	tasku
Turkish	cep
Indonesian	saku, kantong
Esperanto	poŝo
Russian	karmán
Greek	tse'pi
Arabic	gib
Hebrew	kiss
Yiddish	keschene
Japanese	poketto
Swahili	mfuko

705 point

French	point
Spanish	punto
Italian	punto
Portuguese	ponto
Rumanian	punct
German	Punkt
Dutch	punt
Swedish	punkt
Danish	punkt
Norwegian	punkt
Polish	kropka
Czech	bod
Serbo-Croat.	točka
Hungarian	pont
Finnish	piste
Turkish	nokta
Indonesian	noktah, titik
Esperanto	punkto
Russian	tóchka
Greek	simi'on
Arabic	nouqta
Hebrew	dagesch
Yiddish	pintel
Japanese	ten
Swahili	nukta

706 poison

French	poison
Spanish	veneno
Italian	veleno
Portuguese	veneno
Rumanian	otravă
German	Gift
Dutch	vergif
Swedish	gift
Danish	gift
Norwegian	gift
Polish	trucizna
Czech	jed
Serbo-Croat.	otrov
Hungarian	méreg
Finnish	myrkky
Turkish	zehir
Indonesian	ratjum
Esperanto	veneno
Russian	yát
Greek	diliti'rion
Arabic	samak
Hebrew	sam
Yiddish	ssam
Japanese	doku
Swahili	sumu

707 poor

French	pauvre
Spanish	pobre
Italian	povero
Portuguese	pobre
Rumanian	sărac
German	arm
Dutch	arm
Swedish	fattig
Danish	fattig
Norwegian	fattig
Polish	biedny
Czech	chudý
Serbo-Croat.	siromašan
Hungarian	szegény
Finnish	köyhä
Turkish	fakir
Indonesian	papa, miskin
Esperanto	mal'riĉa
Russian	byédni
Greek	ptochos'
Arabic	faqir
Hebrew	ani
Yiddish	orim
Japanese	mazushii
Swahili	maskini

708 pork

French	porc
Spanish	puerco
Italian	carne di porco
Portuguese	carne de porco
Rumanian	carne de porc
German	Schweinefleisch
Dutch	varkensvlees
Swedish	fläsk
Danish	svinekød
Norwegian	svinekjøtt
Polish	wieprzowina
Czech	vepřové maso
Serbo-Croat.	svinjetina
Hungarian	sertéshús
Finnish	sianliha
Turkish	domuz eti
Indonesian	daging babi
Esperanto	pork'viando
Russian	svinína
Greek	chirinon' kre'as
Arabic	lahm chanzir
Hebrew	besar-chasir
Yiddish	chazerfleisch
Japanese	butaniku
Swahili	nyama ya nuruwe

709 portable

French	portatif
Spanish	portátil
Italian	portabile
Portuguese	portátil
Rumanian	portabil
German	tragbar
Dutch	draagbaar
Swedish	bärbar
Danish	transportabel
Norwegian	transportabel
Polish	przenośny
Czech	přenosný
Serbo-Croat.	prenosiv
Hungarian	hordozható
Finnish	kannettava
Turkish	taşınabilir
Indonesian	dapat dibawa
Esperanto	port'ebla
Russian	pirinósni
Greek	foritos'
Arabic	sahl al-haml
Hebrew	mitaltel
Yiddish	trogbar
Japanese	keitai no
Swahili	-a kuchukulika

710 porter

French	porteur
Spanish	mozo
Italian	facchino
Portuguese	carregador
Rumanian	hamal
German	Gepäckträger
Dutch	kruier
Swedish	stadsbud
Danish	drager
Norwegian	bærer
Polish	tragarz
Czech	nosič
Serbo-Croat.	vratar
Hungarian	hordár
Finnish	kantaja
Turkish	hamal
Indonesian	kuli pemikul barang
Esperanto	port'isto
Russian	nasílshchik
Greek	achthofo'ros
Arabic	hammal
Hebrew	sabal
Yiddish	treger
Japanese	akaboo
Swahili	mchukuzi

711 postcard

French	carte postale
Spanish	tarjeta postal
Italian	cartolina postale
Portuguese	cartão postal
Rumanian	carte poştala
German	Postkarte
Dutch	briefkaart
Swedish	brevkort
Danish	brevkort
Norwegian	brevkort
Polish	pocztówka
Czech	dopisnice
Serbo-Croat.	dopisnica
Hungarian	levelezőlap
Finnish	postikortti
Turkish	kart postal
Indonesian	kartu pos
Esperanto	poŝt'karto
Russian	atkrítka
Greek	kart' postal'
Arabic	kart postal
Hebrew	geluyah
Yiddish	postkartel
Japanese	yuubin-hagaki
Swahili	kąrata kama barua

712 post office

French	bureau de poste
Spanish	correos
Italian	ufficio postale
Portuguese	correio
Rumanian	poştă
German	Postamt
Dutch	postkantoor
Swedish	postkontor
Danish	postkontor
Norwegian	postkontor
Polish	poczta
Czech	poštovní úřad
Serbo-Croat.	poštanski ured
Hungarian	postahivatal
Finnish	postikonttori
Turkish	postane
Indonesian	kantor pos
Esperanto	poŝtejo
Russian	pochtámt
Greek	tachidromi'on
Arabic	maktab al-barid
Hebrew	beth doar
Yiddish	post
Japanese	yuubinkyoku
Swahili	nyumba ya posta

713 pot

French	pot
Spanish	olla
Italian	pentola
Portuguese	panela
Rumanian	oală
German	Topf
Dutch	pot
Swedish	gryta
Danish	potte
Norwegian	gryte, potte
Polish	garnek
Czech	hrnec
Serbo-Croat.	lonac
Hungarian	fazék
Finnish	ruukku
Turkish	tencere
Indonesian	periuk
Esperanto	poto
Russian	garshók
Greek	dochi'o
Arabic	waa
Hebrew	kederah
Yiddish	top
Japanese	nabe
Swahili	kopo

714 potato

French	pomme de terre
Spanish	patata
Italian	patata
Portuguese	batata
Rumanian	cartof
German	Kartoffel
Dutch	aardappel
Swedish	potatis
Danish	kartoffel
Norwegian	potet
Polish	ziemniak
Czech	brambor
Serbo-Croat.	krompir
Hungarian	burgonya, krumpli
Finnish	peruna
Turkish	patates
Indonesian	kentang
Esperanto	terpomo
Russian	kartófel
Greek	pata'ta
Arabic	batatis
Hebrew	tapuach adamah
Yiddish	erdepel
Japanese	jagwaimo
Swahili	kiazi

715 powder

French	poudre
Spanish	polvo
Italian	polvere
Portuguese	pó
Rumanian	praf
German	Pulver
Dutch	poeder
Swedish	pulver
Danish	pulver
Norwegian	pulver
Polish	proch
Czech	pudr
Serbo-Croat.	prašak
Hungarian	por
Finnish	pulveri
Turkish	toz
Indonesian	bubuk, bedak
Esperanto	pulvoro
Russian	parashók
Greek	pou'dra
Arabic	mashouq
Hebrew	avak
Yiddish	puder
Japanese	kona
Swahili	uvumbi

716 price

French	prix
Spanish	precio
Italian	prezzo
Portuguese	preço
Rumanian	pret
German	Preis
Dutch	prijs
Swedish	pris
Danish	pris
Norwegian	pris
Polish	cena
Czech	cena
Serbo-Croat.	cjena
Hungarian	ár
Finnish	hinta
Turkish	fiyat
Indonesian	harga
Esperanto	prezo
Russian	tsená
Greek	timi'
Arabic	tsaman
Hebrew	mechir
Yiddish	preis
Japanese	nedan
Swahili	bei

717 print

French	imprimer
Spanish	imprimir
Italian	stampare
Portuguese	imprimir
Rumanian	tipărire
German	drucken
Dutch	drukken
Swedish	trycka
Danish	trykke
Norwegian	trykke
Polish	drukować
Czech	tisknouti
Serbo-Croat.	tiskanje
Hungarian	nyomtat
Finnish	painaa
Turkish	matbaacılık
Indonesian	tjétak
Esperanto	presi
Russian	pechátat
Greek	tipo'no
Arabic	yatbaa
Hebrew	dafas
Yiddish	druken
Japanese	insatsu
Swahili	piga chapa

718 prison

French	prison
Spanish	cárcel
Italian	prigione
Portuguese	prisão
Rumanian	închisoare
German	Gefängnis
Dutch	gevangenis
Swedish	fängelse
Danish	fængsel
Norwegian	fengsel
Polish	więzienie
Czech	vězení
Serbo-Croat.	zatvor
Hungarian	fogház
Finnish	vankila
Turkish	hapisane
Indonesian	penjara
Esperanto	mal'liber'ejo
Russian	tyurmá
Greek	filaki'
Arabic	sign
Hebrew	ssohar
Yiddish	kriminal
Japanese	keimusho
Swahili	kifungo

719 profession

French	profession
Spanish	profesión
Italian	professione
Portuguese	profissão
Rumanian	meserie
German	Beruf
Dutch	beroep
Swedish	yrke
Danish	profession
Norwegian	yrke
Polish	zawód
Czech	povolání
Serbo-Croat.	zanimanje
Hungarian	hivatás
Finnish	ammatti
Turkish	meslek
Indonesian	pekerdjaan
Esperanto	profesio
Russian	prafyésia
Greek	epan'gelma
Arabic	mihna
Hebrew	miktsoa
Yiddish	professye
Japanese	shokugyoo
Swahili	uchumi

720 property

French	propriété
Spanish	propiedad
Italian	proprietà
Portuguese	propriedade
Rumanian	proprietate
German	Eigentum
Dutch	eigendom
Swedish	egendom
Danish	ejendom
Norwegian	eiendom
Polish	własność
Czech	majetek
Serbo-Croat.	vlasništvo
Hungarian	tulajdon
Finnish	omaisuus
Turkish	mal
Indonesian	milik
Esperanto	posedaĵo
Russian	sóbstvenost
Greek	periousi'a
Arabic	milk
Hebrew	rechusch
Yiddish	eigentum
Japanese	zaisan
Swahili	mali

721 purse

French	porte-monnaie
Spanish	bolsillo
Italian	portamonete
Portuguese	bôlsa para dinheiro
Rumanian	portmoneu
German	Geldtasche
Dutch	portemonnaie
Swedish	portmonnä
Danish	pung
Norwegian	pung
Polish	portmonetka
Czech	peněženka
Serbo-Croat.	novčanik
Hungarian	pénztárca
Finnish	kukkaro
Turkish	para kesesi
Indonesian	dompét
Esperanto	mon'ujo
Russian	kashelyók
Greek	portofo'li
Arabic	hafiza
Hebrew	arnak
Yiddish	geldbeitel
Japanese	saifu
Swahili	kifuko

722 quarter

French	quart
Spanish	cuarto
Italian	quarto
Portuguese	quarto
Rumanian	sfert
German	viertel
Dutch	kwart
Swedish	fjärdedel
Danish	fjerdedel
Norwegian	fjerdedel
Polish	ćwierć
Czech	čtvrt
Serbo-Croat.	četvrtina
Hungarian	negyed
Finnish	neljäsosa
Turkish	çeyrek
Indonesian	suku
Esperanto	kvar'ono
Russian	chétvert
Greek	te'tarton
Arabic	rouba
Hebrew	reva
Yiddish	firtel
Japanese	yonbun no ichi
Swahili	robo

723 queen

French	reine
Spanish	reina
Italian	regina
Portuguese	rainha
Rumanian	regină
German	Königin
Dutch	koningin
Swedish	drottning
Danish	dronning
Norwegian	dronning
Polish	królowa
Czech	královna
Serbo-Croat.	kraljica
Hungarian	királynő
Finnish	kuningatar
Turkish	kıraliçe
Indonesian	radio perempuan
Esperanto	reĝ'ino
Russian	karalyéva
Greek	vasi'lissa
Arabic	malika
Hebrew	malkah
Yiddish	malke
Japanese	jo'oo
Swahili	malkia

724 question

French	question
Spanish	pregunta
Italian	domanda
Portuguese	pergunta
Rumanian	întrebare
German	Frage
Dutch	vraag
Swedish	fråga
Danish	spørgsmål
Norwegian	spørsmål
Polish	pytanie
Czech	otázka
Serbo-Croat.	pitanje
Hungarian	kérdés
Finnish	kysymys
Turkish	sual
Indonesian	pertanjaan
Esperanto	demando
Russian	vaprós
Greek	ero'tisis
Arabic	soual
Hebrew	scheelah
Yiddish	kasche
Japanese	shitsumon
Swahili	swali

725 quick

French	vite
Spanish	pronto
Italian	pronto
Portuguese	depressa
Rumanian	iute, repede
German	rasch
Dutch	vlug
Swedish	kvick
Danish	rask
Norwegian	kvikk
Polish	szybki
Czech	rychlý
Serbo-Croat.	brz
Hungarian	hamar
Finnish	nopea
Turkish	çabuk
Indonesian	tjepat, ladju
Esperanto	rapida
Russian	bístri
Greek	gri'goros
Arabic	saria
Hebrew	maher
Yiddish	schnell
Japanese	hayai
Swahili	-epesi

726 quiet

French	tranquille
Spanish	tranquilo
Italian	quieto
Portuguese	quieto
Rumanian	liniştit
German	ruhig
Dutch	rustig
Swedish	stilla
Danish	stille
Norwegian	stille
Polish	cicho
Czech	klidný
Serbo-Croat.	miran
Hungarian	csendes
Finnish	tyyni
Turkish	sessiz
Indonesian	teduh, tenang
Esperanto	silenta
Russian	tíkhi
Greek	i'sichos
Arabic	hadi
Hebrew	schaket
Yiddish	spokoine
Japanese	shizuka na
Swahili	-liotulia

727 rabbit

French	lapin
Spanish	conejo
Italian	coniglio
Portuguese	coelho
Rumanian	iepure
German	Kaninchen
Dutch	konijn
Swedish	kanin
Danish	kanin
Norwegian	kanin
Polish	królik
Czech	králík
Serbo-Croat.	kunić
Hungarian	házinyúl
Finnish	kaniini
Turkish	ada tavşanı
Indonesian	terwélu, kelintji
Esperanto	kuniklo
Russian	królik
Greek	koune'li
Arabic	arnab
Hebrew	schafan
Yiddish	krolik
Japanese	usagi
Swahili	sungura

728 radio

French	T.S.F.
Spanish	radio
Italian	radio
Portuguese	rádio
Rumanian	radio
German	Radio
Dutch	radio
Swedish	radio
Danish	radio
Norwegian	radio
Polish	radjo
Czech	rádio
Serbo-Croat.	radio
Hungarian	rádio
Finnish	radio
Turkish	radyo
Indonesian	radio
Esperanto	radio
Russian	rádio
Greek	radio'fonon
Arabic	radio
Hebrew	radyo
Yiddish	radyo
Japanese	rajio
Swahili	radio

729 rag

French	chiffon
Spanish	trapo
Italian	cencio
Portuguese	trapo
Rumanian	zdreanţă
German	Lappen
Dutch	lomp
Swedish	trasa
Danish	klud
Norwegian	klut
Polish	szmata
Czech	hadr
Serbo-Croat.	krpa
Hungarian	rongy
Finnish	lumppu
Turkish	paçavra
Indonesian	kain robék
Esperanto	ĉifono
Russian	tryápka
Greek	koure'li
Arabic	kirka
Hebrew	smartut
Yiddish	smatte
Japanese	boro
Swahili	kitambaa

730 rain

French	pluie
Spanish	lluvia
Italian	pioggia
Portuguese	chuva
Rumanian	ploaie
German	Regen
Dutch	regen
Swedish	regn
Danish	regn
Norwegian	regn
Polish	deszcz
Czech	dešt'
Serbo-Croat.	kiša
Hungarian	eső
Finnish	sade
Turkish	yağmur
Indonesian	hudjan
Esperanto	pluvo
Russian	dozht
Greek	vrochi'
Arabic	matar
Hebrew	geschem
Yiddish	regen
Japanese	ame
Swahili	mvua

731 raincoat

French	imperméable
Spanish	impermeable
Italian	impermeabile
Portuguese	impermeável
Rumanian	impermeabil
German	Regenmantel
Dutch	regenjas
Swedish	regnkappa
Danish	regnfrakke
Norwegian	regnfrakke
Polish	płaszcz deszczowny
Czech	plást' do deště
Serbo-Croat.	kišni kaput
Hungarian	esőköpeny
Finnish	sadetakki
Turkish	yağmurluk
Indonesian	djas hudjan
Esperanto	pluv'mantelo
Russian	dozhdevík
Greek	adia'vrochon
Arabic	mitaf matar
Hebrew	meil geschem
Yiddish	regenmantel
Japanese	reinkooto
Swahili	koti la mvua

732 raspberry

French	framboise
Spanish	frambuesa
Italian	lampone
Portuguese	framboesa
Rumanian	zmeură
German	Himbeere
Dutch	framboos
Swedish	hallon
Danish	hindbær
Norwegian	bringebær
Polish	malina
Czech	malina
Serbo-Croat.	malina
Hungarian	málna
Finnish	vadelma
Turkish	ahududu
Indonesian	rasbai
Esperanto	frambo
Russian	malína
Greek	vato'mouro
Arabic	tout
Hebrew	petel
Yiddish	maline
Japanese	kiichigo
Swahili	namna ya tunda

733 rat

French	rat
Spanish	rata
Italian	ratto
Portuguese	rato
Rumanian	şobolan
German	Ratte
Dutch	rat
Swedish	råtta
Danish	rotte
Norwegian	rotte
Polish	szczur
Czech	krysa
Serbo-Croat.	pacov
Hungarian	patkány
Finnish	rotta
Turkish	sıçan
Indonesian	tikus besar
Esperanto	rato
Russian	krísa
Greek	aroure'os
Arabic	far
Hebrew	achbrosch
Yiddish	schtshur
Japanese	nezumi
Swahili	panya

734 razor

French	rasoir
Spanish	navaja
Italian	rasoio
Portuguese	navalha de barbear
Rumanian	brici
German	Rasiermesser
Dutch	scheermes
Swedish	rakkniv
Danish	barberkniv
Norwegian	barberkniv
Polish	brzytwa
Czech	břitva
Serbo-Croat.	britva
Hungarian	borotva
Finnish	partaveitsi
Turkish	ustura
Indonesian	pisau tjukur
Esperanto	raz'ilo
Russian	brítva
Greek	xira'fi
Arabic	mous hilaqa
Hebrew	taargiluach
Yiddish	britve
Japanese	kamisori
Swahili	wembe

735 read

French	lire
Spanish	leer
Italian	leggere
Portuguese	ler
Rumanian	citi
German	lesen
Dutch	lezen
Swedish	läsa
Danish	læse
Norwegian	lese
Polish	czytać
Czech	čisti
Serbo-Croat.	čitati
Hungarian	olvas
Finnish	lukea
Turkish	okumak
Indonesian	batja
Esperanto	legi
Russian	chitát
Greek	diava'zo
Arabic	yaqra
Hebrew	kara
Yiddish	leinen
Japanese	yomu
Swahili	soma

736 receipt

French	reçu
Spanish	recibo
Italian	ricevuta
Portuguese	recibo
Rumanian	chitanţă
German	Quittung
Dutch	ontvangstbewijs
Swedish	kvitto
Danish	kvittering
Norwegian	kvittering
Polish	pokwitowanie
Czech	stvrzenka
Serbo-Croat.	potvrda
Hungarian	nyugta
Finnish	kuitti
Turkish	makbuz
Indonesian	kwitansi
Esperanto	kvitanco
Russian	kvitántsiya
Greek	apo'dixis
Arabic	isal
Hebrew	kabalah
Yiddish	kvittung
Japanese	ryooshuusho
Swahili	hati

737 red

French	rouge
Spanish	rojo
Italian	rosso
Portuguese	vermelho
Rumanian	roşu
German	rot
Dutch	rood
Swedish	röd
Danish	rød
Norwegian	rød
Polish	czerwony
Czech	červený
Serbo-Croat.	crven
Hungarian	piros
Finnish	punainen
Turkish	kırmızı
Indonesian	mérah
Esperanto	ruĝa
Russian	krásni
Greek	ko'kinos
Arabic	ahmar
Hebrew	adom
Yiddish	roit
Japanese	akai
Swahili	-ekundu

738 reduce

French	réduire
Spanish	reducir
Italian	ridurre
Portuguese	reduzir
Rumanian	reduce
German	herabsetzen
Dutch	verminderen
Swedish	minska
Danish	formindske
Norwegian	forminske
Polish	redukować
Czech	snížiti
Serbo-Croat.	smanjiti
Hungarian	scökkent
Finnish	supistaa
Turkish	azaltmak
Indonesian	susut
Esperanto	mal'pli'igi
Russian	umenishát
Greek	mio'no
Arabic	youchafid
Hebrew	hifchit
Yiddish	mindern
Japanese	shukushoo suru
Swahili	punguza

739 register

French	enregistrer
Spanish	registrar
Italian	registrare
Portuguese	registrar
Rumanian	înregistra
German	einschreiben
Dutch	registreren
Swedish	registrera
Danish	indskrive
Norwegian	innskrive
Polish	rejestrować
Czech	zapsati
Serbo-Croat.	registar
Hungarian	bejelent
Finnish	kirjata
Turkish	kaydetmek
Indonesian	daftar
Esperanto	registri
Russian	registríravat
Greek	katachoro'
Arabic	yousagil
Hebrew	rascham
Yiddish	registrirn
Japanese	tooroku suru
Swahili	andika katika kitabu

740 religion

French	religion
Spanish	religión
Italian	religione
Portuguese	religião
Rumanian	religie
German	Religion
Dutch	godsdienst
Swedish	religion
Danish	religion
Norwegian	religion
Polish	religia
Czech	náboženství
Serbo-Croat.	vera
Hungarian	vallás
Finnish	uskonto
Turkish	din
Indonesian	agama
Esperanto	religio
Russian	relígiya
Greek	thriski'a
Arabic	din
Hebrew	dat
Yiddish	religye
Japanese	shuukyoo
Swahili	dini

741 rent

French	loyer
Spanish	alquiler
Italian	affitto
Portuguese	aluguel
Rumanian	chirie
German	Miete
Dutch	huur
Swedish	hyra
Danish	leje
Norwegian	husleie
Polish	komorne
Czech	nájemné
Serbo-Croat.	stanarina
Hungarian	lakbér
Finnish	vuokra
Turkish	kira
Indonesian	séwa
Esperanto	lu'prezo
Russian	kvartírnaya pláta
Greek	eni'kion
Arabic	igar
Hebrew	charirah
Yiddish	direh-geld
Japanese	yachin
Swahili	kodi ya nyumba

742 repeat

French	répéter
Spanish	repetir
Italian	ripetere
Portuguese	repetir
Rumanian	repeta
German	wiederholen
Dutch	herhalen
Swedish	upprepa
Danish	gentage
Norwegian	gjenta
Polish	powtórzyć
Czech	opakovati
Serbo-Croat.	ponoviti
Hungarian	ismétel
Finnish	toistaa
Turkish	tekrarlamak
Indonesian	ulangi
Esperanto	ripeti
Russian	paftarít
Greek	epanalamva'no
Arabic	youid
Hebrew	chasar
Yiddish	iberchazern
Japanese	hanpuku suru
Swahili	sema/fanya tena

743 rest

French	reposer
Spanish	descansar
Italian	riposare
Portuguese	descansar
Rumanian	odihni
German	rasten
Dutch	rust
Swedish	rasta
Danish	hvile
Norwegian	hvile
Polish	odpoczywać
Czech	odpočinouti
Serbo-Croat.	odmor
Hungarian	pihen
Finnish	levöhtää
Turkish	dinlemek
Indonesian	istirahat
Esperanto	ripozi
Russian	otdikhát
Greek	xekoura'zome
Arabic	raha
Hebrew	nach
Yiddish	ruhen
Japanese	yasumu
Swahili	pumzika

744 restaurant

French	restaurant
Spanish	restaurante
Italian	ristorante
Portuguese	restaurante
Rumanian	restaurant
German	Gasthaus
Dutch	restaurant
Swedish	restaurang
Danish	restaurant
Norwegian	restaurant
Polish	restauracja
Czech	restaurace
Serbo-Croat.	restoran
Hungarian	étterem
Finnish	ravintola
Turkish	restoran
Indonesian	réstoran
Esperanto	restoracio
Russian	restarán
Greek	estiato'rion
Arabic	mataam
Hebrew	missadah
Yiddish	restorant
Japanese	resutoran
Swahili	hoteli

745 rice

French	riz
Spanish	arroz
Italian	riso
Portuguese	arroz
Rumanian	orez
German	Reis
Dutch	rijst
Swedish	ris
Danish	ris
Norwegian	ris
Polish	ryż
Czech	rýže
Serbo-Croat.	riža
Hungarian	rizs
Finnish	riisi
Turkish	pirinç
Indonesian	padi, nasi
Esperanto	rizo
Russian	ris
Greek	ri'zi
Arabic	ourz
Hebrew	ores
Yiddish	reis
Japanese	kome
Swahili	mchele

746 rich

French	riche
Spanish	rico
Italian	ricco
Portuguese	rico
Rumanian	bogat
German	reich
Dutch	rijk
Swedish	rik
Danish	rig
Norwegian	rik
Polish	bogaty
Czech	bohatý
Serbo-Croat.	bogat
Hungarian	gazdag
Finnish	rikas
Turkish	zengin
Indonesian	kaja
Esperanto	riĉa
Russian	bagáti
Greek	plou'sios
Arabic	ghani
Hebrew	aschir
Yiddish	reich
Japanese	ton da
Swahili	-enye mali

747 rifle

French	fusil
Spanish	fusil
Italian	carabina
Portuguese	espingarda
Rumanian	carabină
German	Gewehr
Dutch	geweer
Swedish	gevär
Danish	gevær
Norwegian	gevær
Polish	karabin
Czech	puška
Serbo-Croat.	vojnička puška
Hungarian	puska
Finnish	kivääri
Turkish	tüfek
Indonesian	bedil, senapang
Esperanto	riflo
Russian	ruzhyó
Greek	toufe'ki
Arabic	boundouqiya
Hebrew	rove
Yiddish	biks
Japanese	shoojuu
Swahili	bunduki

748 right

French	droit
Spanish	derecha
Italian	destra
Portuguese	direita
Rumanian	drept
German	rechts
Dutch	rechts
Swedish	höger
Danish	højre
Norwegian	høyre
Polish	prawo
Czech	napravo
Serbo-Croat.	desno
Hungarian	jobbra
Finnish	oikealla
Turkish	sağ
Indonesian	kanan
Esperanto	dekstra
Russian	naprávo
Greek	dexia'
Arabic	yamin
Hebrew	yemani
Yiddish	rechts
Japanese	migi no
Swahili	-a kulia

749 ring

French	bague
Spanish	sortija
Italian	anello
Portuguese	anel
Rumanian	inel
German	Ring
Dutch	ring
Swedish	ring
Danish	ring
Norwegian	ring
Polish	pierścień
Czech	prsten
Serbo-Croat.	prsten
Hungarian	gyürü
Finnish	sormus
Turkish	yüzük
Indonesian	tjintjin
Esperanto	ringo
Russian	kaltsó
Greek	daktili'di
Arabic	chatim
Hebrew	tabaat
Yiddish	ring
Japanese	yubiwa
Swahili	pete

750 ripe

French	mûr
Spanish	maduro
Italian	maturo
Portuguese	maduro
Rumanian	copt
German	reif
Dutch	rijp
Swedish	mogen
Danish	moden
Norwegian	moden
Polish	dojrzały
Czech	zralý
Serbo-Croat.	zreo
Hungarian	érett
Finnish	kypsä
Turkish	olgun
Indonesian	masak, matang
Esperanto	matura
Russian	zryéli
Greek	o'rimos
Arabic	nadig
Hebrew	baschel
Yiddish	reif
Japanese	jukushita
Swahili	-bivu

751 risk

French	risque
Spanish	riesgo
Italian	rischio
Portuguese	risco
Rumanian	risc
German	Risiko
Dutch	risico
Swedish	risk
Danish	risiko
Norwegian	risiko
Polish	ryzyko
Czech	riziko
Serbo-Croat.	opasnost
Hungarian	kockázat
Finnish	uskalias
Turkish	riziko
Indonesian	risiko, bahaja
Esperanto	risko
Russian	risk
Greek	kin'dinos
Arabic	mouchatara
Hebrew	sikun
Yiddish	risike
Japanese	kiken
Swahili	hatari

752 river

French	fleuve
Spanish	río
Italian	fiume
Portuguese	rio
Rumanian	rîu
German	Fluss
Dutch	rivier
Swedish	flod
Danish	flod
Norwegian	flod
Polish	rzeka
Czech	řeka
Serbo-Croat.	rijeka
Hungarian	folyó
Finnish	joki
Turkish	nehir
Indonesian	sungai, kali
Esperanto	rivero
Russian	reká
Greek	potamos'
Arabic	nahr
Hebrew	nahar
Yiddish	fluss
Japanese	kawa
Swahili	mto

753 roast

French	rôtir
Spanish	asar
Italian	arrostire
Portuguese	assar
Rumanian	frige
German	braten
Dutch	braden
Swedish	steka
Danish	stege
Norwegian	steke
Polish	piec
Czech	péci
Serbo-Croat.	pržiti
Hungarian	süt
Finnish	paistaa
Turkish	kızartmak
Indonesian	panggang
Esperanto	rosti
Russian	zhárit
Greek	psi'no
Arabic	yashwi
Hebrew	tsalah
Yiddish	broten
Japanese	aburu
Swahili	oka

754 roast beef

French	rosbif
Spanish	rosbif
Italian	rosbif
Portuguese	rosbife
Rumanian	rosbif
German	Rinderbraten
Dutch	rosbief
Swedish	oxstek
Danish	oksesteg
Norwegian	oksestek
Polish	pieczeń wołowa
Czech	pečeně
Serbo-Croat.	pečena govedina
Hungarian	marhasült
Finnish	paisti
Turkish	kebap
Indonesian	ros bief
Esperanto	rostbefo
Russian	róstbif
Greek	psito' vodino'
Arabic	shiwa
Hebrew	eschpar
Yiddish	rinderbraten
Japanese	yakigyuuniku
Swahili	ubavu wa ng'ombe oka

755 roll

French	petit pain
Spanish	panecillo
Italian	panino
Portuguese	pãozinho
Rumanian	chiflă
German	Semmel
Dutch	broodje
Swedish	bulle
Danish	rundstykke
Norwegian	bolle
Polish	bułka
Czech	houska
Serbo-Croat.	kifla
Hungarian	zsemle
Finnish	sämpylä
Turkish	francala
Indonesian	roti ketgil
Esperanto	bulko
Russian	búlka
Greek	koulou'ri
Arabic	sandwitsh
Hebrew	lachmaniah
Yiddish	semel
Japanese	roorupan
Swahili	mkate mdogo

756 roof

French	toit
Spanish	tejado
Italian	tetto
Portuguese	telhado
Rumanian	acoperiş
German	Dach
Dutch	dak
Swedish	tak
Danish	tag
Norwegian	tak
Polish	dach
Czech	střecha
Serbo-Croat.	krov
Hungarian	tető
Finnish	katto
Turkish	dam
Indonesian	atap
Esperanto	tegmento
Russian	krísha
Greek	ste'gi
Arabic	saqf
Hebrew	gag
Yiddish	dach
Japanese	yane
Swahili	paa

757 room

French	chambre
Spanish	cuarto
Italian	camera
Portuguese	quarto
Rumanian	cameră
German	Zimmer
Dutch	kamer
Swedish	rum
Danish	værelse
Norwegian	rom
Polish	pokój
Czech	pokoj
Serbo-Croat.	soba
Hungarian	szoba
Finnish	huone
Turkish	oda
Indonesian	kamar, bilik
Esperanto	ĉambro
Russian	kómnata
Greek	doma'tion
Arabic	hougra
Hebrew	cheder
Yiddish	tsimer
Japanese	heya
Swahili	chumba

758 root

French	racine
Spanish	raíz
Italian	radice
Portuguese	raiz
Rumanian	radacină
German	Wurzel
Dutch	wortel
Swedish	rot
Danish	rod
Norwegian	rot
Polish	korzeń
Czech	kořen
Serbo-Croat.	koren
Hungarian	gyökér
Finnish	juuri
Turkish	kök
Indonesian	akar
Esperanto	radiko
Russian	kóren
Greek	ri'za
Arabic	gizr
Hebrew	schoresch
Yiddish	vortsel
Japanese	ne
Swahili	shina

759 rope

French	corde
Spanish	cuerda
Italian	corda
Portuguese	corda
Rumanian	frînghie
German	Seil
Dutch	touw
Swedish	rep
Danish	reb
Norwegian	reip, tau
Polish	sznur
Czech	provaz
Serbo-Croat.	uže
Hungarian	kötél
Finnish	köysi
Turkish	ip
Indonesian	tali
Esperanto	ŝnuro
Russian	veryófka
Greek	s-chini'
Arabic	habl
Hebrew	chevel
Yiddish	schtrik
Japanese	nawa
Swahili	kamba

760 round

French	rond
Spanish	redondo
Italian	rotondo
Portuguese	redondo
Rumanian	rotund
German	rund
Dutch	rond
Swedish	rund
Danish	rund
Norwegian	reip
Polish	okrągły
Czech	kulatý
Serbo-Croat.	okrugao
Hungarian	kerek
Finnish	pyöreä
Turkish	yuvarlak
Indonesian	bulat
Esperanto	ronda
Russian	krúgli
Greek	strongilos'
Arabic	moustadir
Hebrew	agol
Yiddish	keilechdik
Japanese	marui
Swahili	-a mviringo

761 rubber

French	caoutchouc
Spanish	caucho
Italian	gomma
Portuguese	borracha
Rumanian	gumă
German	Gummi
Dutch	gomelastik
Swedish	gummi
Danish	gummi
Norwegian	gummi
Polish	kauczuk
Czech	kaučuk
Serbo-Croat.	guma
Hungarian	gumi
Finnish	kumi
Turkish	kauçuk
Indonesian	karét
Esperanto	kaŭčuko
Russian	rezína
Greek	las'tichon
Arabic	mattat
Hebrew	tsemeg
Yiddish	gumilastik
Japanese	gomu
Swahili	mpiva

762 run

French	courir
Spanish	correr
Italian	correre
Portuguese	correr
Rumanian	alerga
German	laufen
Dutch	rennen
Swedish	springa
Danish	rende
Norwegian	løpe
Polish	biec
Czech	běžeti
Serbo-Croat.	trčati
Hungarian	szalad
Finnish	juosta
Turkish	koşmak
Indonesian	lari
Esperanto	kuri
Russian	bezhát
Greek	tre'cho
Arabic	yagri
Hebrew	rats
Yiddish	loifen
Japanese	hashiru
Swahili	enda mbio

763 rust

French	rouille
Spanish	moho
Italian	ruggine
Portuguese	ferrugem
Rumanian	rugină
German	Rost
Dutch	roest
Swedish	rost
Danish	rust
Norwegian	rust
Polish	rdza
Czech	rez
Serbo-Croat.	rdja
Hungarian	rozsda
Finnish	ruoste
Turkish	pas
Indonesian	karat, tahi besi
Esperanto	rusto
Russian	rsháfchina
Greek	skouria'
Arabic	sada
Hebrew	chaludah
Yiddish	dzavert
Japanese	sabi
Swahili	kutu

764 rye

French	seigle
Spanish	centeno
Italian	segala
Portuguese	centeio
Rumanian	secară
German	Roggen
Dutch	rogge
Swedish	råg
Danish	rug
Norwegian	rug
Polish	żyto
Czech	žito
Serbo-Croat.	raž
Hungarian	rozs
Finnish	ruis
Turkish	çavdar
Indonesian	ganrum hitam
Esperanto	sekalo
Russian	rosh
Greek	si'kalis
Arabic	shair
Hebrew	schipon
Yiddish	korn
Japanese	rai-mugi
Swahili	nafaka kama ngano

765 sad

French	triste
Spanish	triste
Italian	triste
Portuguese	triste
Rumanian	trist
German	traurig
Dutch	droevig
Swedish	sorglig
Danish	trist
Norwegian	sturen
Polish	smutny
Czech	smutný
Serbo-Croat.	tužan
Hungarian	szomorú
Finnish	surullinen
Turkish	hazin
Indonesian	sedih
Esperanto	grava
Russian	pechálni
Greek	lipime'nos
Arabic	hazin
Hebrew	atsuf
Yiddish	troirig
Japanese	kanashii
Swahili	-a huzuni

766 saddle

French	selle
Spanish	silla de montar
Italian	sella
Portuguese	sela
Rumanian	şa
German	Sattel
Dutch	zadel
Swedish	sadel
Danish	sadel
Norwegian	sal
Polish	siodło
Czech	sedlo
Serbo-Croat.	sjedlo
Hungarian	nyereg
Finnish	satula
Turkish	eyer
Indonesian	séla, pelana
Esperanto	selo
Russian	sedló
Greek	se'la
Arabic	bardaa
Hebrew	ukaf
Yiddish	sottel
Japanese	kura
Swahili	tandiko

767 safety

French	sûreté
Spanish	seguridad
Italian	sicurezza
Portuguese	segurança
Rumanian	siguranţă
German	Sicherheit
Dutch	veiligheid
Swedish	säkerhet
Danish	sikkerhed
Norwegian	sikkerhet
Polish	bezpieczeństwo
Czech	bezpečnost
Serbo-Croat.	sigurnost
Hungarian	biztonság
Finnish	turvallisuus
Turkish	emniyet
Indonesian	keamanan
Esperanto	sekur'eco
Russian	bezapásnost
Greek	asfa'lia
Arabic	aman
Hebrew	bitachon
Yiddish	sicherheit
Japanese	anzen
Swahili	salama

768 sailor

French	marin
Spanish	marinero
Italian	marinaio
Portuguese	marinheiro
Rumanian	marinar
German	Matrose
Dutch	matroos
Swedish	matros
Danish	matros
Norwegian	sjømann
Polish	marynarz
Czech	námořník
Serbo-Croat.	mornar
Hungarian	matróz
Finnish	matruusi
Turkish	denizci
Indonesian	kelasi, orang kapal
Esperanto	mar'isto
Russian	matrós
Greek	naftikos'
Arabic	bahhar
Hebrew	sapan
Yiddish	matroiz
Japanese	suifu
Swahili	bahari

769 salt

French	sel
Spanish	sal
Italian	sale
Portuguese	sal
Rumanian	sare
German	Salz
Dutch	zout
Swedish	salt
Danish	salt
Norwegian	salt
Polish	sól
Czech	sůl
Serbo-Croat.	so
Hungarian	só
Finnish	suola
Turkish	tuz
Indonesian	garam, asin
Esperanto	salo
Russian	sol
Greek	ala'ti
Arabic	malh
Hebrew	melach
Yiddish	salts
Japanese	shio
Swahili	chumvi

770 sample

French	échantillon
Spanish	muestra
Italian	campione
Portuguese	amostra
Rumanian	mostră
German	Muster
Dutch	monster
Swedish	mönster
Danish	prøve
Norwegian	mønster
Polish	próbka
Czech	vzorek
Serbo-Croat.	uzorak
Hungarian	minta
Finnish	näytte
Turkish	örnek
Indonesian	tjontoh
Esperanto	specimeno
Russian	abrazyéts
Greek	dig'ma
Arabic	mostara
Hebrew	dugmah
Yiddish	muster
Japanese	mihon
Swahili	namna

771 sand

French	sable
Spanish	arena
Italian	sabbia
Portuguese	areia
Rumanian	nisip
German	Sand
Dutch	zand
Swedish	sand
Danish	sand
Norwegian	sand
Polish	piasek
Czech	písek
Serbo-Croat.	pjesak
Hungarian	homok
Finnish	hiekka
Turkish	kum
Indonesian	pasir
Esperanto	sablo
Russian	pesók
Greek	a'mos
Arabic	rimal
Hebrew	chol
Yiddish	samd
Japanese	suna
Swahili	mchanga

772 Saturday

French	samedi
Spanish	sábado
Italian	sabato
Portuguese	sabado
Rumanian	sîmbătă
German	Samstag
Dutch	Zaterdag
Swedish	lördag
Danish	lørdag
Norwegian	lørdag
Polish	sobota
Czech	sobota
Serbo-Croat.	subota
Hungarian	szombat
Finnish	lauantai
Turkish	cumartesi
Indonesian	Sabtu
Esperanto	sabato
Russian	subóta
Greek	Sa-vvaton
Arabic	al-sabt
Hebrew	schabat
Yiddish	schabbes
Japanese	doyoobi
Swahili	Jumamosi

773 sausage

French	saucisse
Spanish	salchicha
Italian	salsiccia
Portuguese	chouriço
Rumanian	cîrnat
German	Wurst
Dutch	worst
Swedish	korv
Danish	pølse
Norwegian	pølse
Polish	kiełbasa
Czech	klobása
Serbo-Croat.	kobasica
Hungarian	kolbász
Finnish	makkara
Turkish	sucuk
Indonesian	sosis
Esperanto	kolbaso
Russian	kalbasá
Greek	louka'niko
Arabic	sougou
Hebrew	naknik
Yiddish	kolbasse
Japanese	choozume
Swahili	nyama hatika utumbo

774 scarf

French	cache-nez
Spanish	bufanda
Italian	sciarpa
Portuguese	chale
Rumanian	eşarfă
German	Halstuch
Dutch	sjaal
Swedish	halsduk
Danish	halstørklæde
Norwegian	skjerf
Polish	szalik
Czech	šála
Serbo-Croat.	šal
Hungarian	sál
Finnish	kaulaliina
Turkish	boyun atkısı
Indonesian	sjal
Esperanto	skarpo
Russian	sharf
Greek	esar'pa
Arabic	isharb
Hebrew	redid
Yiddish	halstuch
Japanese	erimaki
Swahili	shali

775 school

French	école
Spanish	escuela
Italian	scuola
Portuguese	escola
Rumanian	şcoală
German	Schule
Dutch	school
Swedish	skola
Danish	skole
Norwegian	skole
Polish	szkoła
Czech	škola
Serbo-Croat.	škola
Hungarian	iskola
Finnish	koulu
Turkish	okul
Indonesian	sekolah
Esperanto	lern'ejo
Russian	shkóla
Greek	s-choli'on
Arabic	madrasa
Hebrew	beth sefer
Yiddish	schule
Japanese	gakkoo
Swahili	skuli

776 science

French	science
Spanish	ciencia
Italian	scienza
Portuguese	ciência
Rumanian	ştiinţă
German	Wissenschaft
Dutch	wetenschap
Swedish	vetenskap
Danish	videnskab
Norwegian	vitenskap
Polish	nauka
Czech	věda
Serbo-Croat.	nauka
Hungarian	tudomány
Finnish	tiede
Turkish	fen
Indonesian	ilmu
Esperanto	scienco
Russian	naúka
Greek	episti'mi
Arabic	ilm
Hebrew	mada
Yiddish	vissenschaft
Japanese	kwagaku
Swahili	elimu

777 scissors

French	ciseaux
Spanish	tijeras
Italian	forbici
Portuguese	tesouras
Rumanian	foarfece
German	Schere
Dutch	schaar
Swedish	sax
Danish	saks
Norwegian	saks
Polish	nożyczki
Czech	nůžky
Serbo-Croat.	škare
Hungarian	olló
Finnish	sakset
Turkish	makas
Indonesian	gunting
Esperanto	tond'ilo
Russian	nózhnitsi
Greek	psali'di
Arabic	miqas
Hebrew	missparaim
Yiddish	scheer
Japanese	hasami
Swahili	mkasi

778 scrambled eggs

French	oeufs brouillés
Spanish	huevos revueltos
Italian	uova strapazzate
Portuguese	ovos mexidos
Rumanian	oua jumări
German	Rührei
Dutch	roereieren
Swedish	äggröra
Danish	rØræg
Norwegian	eggerØre
Polish	jajecznica
Czech	míchaná vejce
Serbo-Croat.	pržiti jaja
Hungarian	rántotta
Finnish	munakokkeli
Turkish	çalkalanıp yumurta
Indonesian	mengaduk telur
Esperanto	ovo batita
Russian	yayíchnitsa
Greek	omele'ta
Arabic	bayd madroub
Hebrew	taraf beytsim
Yiddish	jeischnitse
Japanese	iritamago
Swahili	mayai mavuruga

779 screw

French	vis
Spanish	tornillo
Italian	vite
Portuguese	parafuso
Rumanian	şurub
German	Schraube
Dutch	schroef
Swedish	skruv
Danish	skrue
Norwegian	skrue
Polish	śruba
Czech	šroub
Serbo-Croat.	šaraf
Hungarian	csavar
Finnish	ruuvi
Turkish	vida
Indonesian	sekerup
Esperanto	ŝraŭbo
Russian	vint
Greek	vi'da
Arabic	mosmar alaouz
Hebrew	boreg
Yiddish	schroif
Japanese	neji
Swahili	skrubu

780 sea

French	mer
Spanish	mar
Italian	mare
Portuguese	mar
Rumanian	mare
German	Meer
Dutch	zee
Swedish	hav
Danish	hav
Norwegian	hav
Polish	morze
Czech	moře
Serbo-Croat.	more
Hungarian	tenger
Finnish	meri
Turkish	deniz
Indonesian	laut
Esperanto	maro
Russian	mórye
Greek	tha'lassa
Arabic	bahr
Hebrew	yam
Yiddish	yam
Japanese	umi
Swahili	bahari

781 see

French	voir
Spanish	ver
Italian	vedere
Portuguese	ver
Rumanian	vedea
German	sehen
Dutch	zien
Swedish	se
Danish	se
Norwegian	se
Polish	widzieć
Czech	vidéti
Serbo-Croat.	videti
Hungarian	lát
Finnish	nähdä
Turkish	görmek
Indonesian	lihat
Esperanto	vidi
Russian	vídit
Greek	vle'po
Arabic	yara
Hebrew	raha
Yiddish	sehen
Japanese	miru
Swahili	ona

782 sell

French	vendre
Spanish	vender
Italian	vendere
Portuguese	vender
Rumanian	vinde
German	verkaufen
Dutch	verkopen
Swedish	sälja
Danish	sælge
Norwegian	selge
Polish	sprzedawać
Czech	prodávati
Serbo-Croat.	prodati
Hungarian	elad
Finnish	myydää
Turkish	satmak
Indonesian	djual
Esperanto	vendi
Russian	pradát
Greek	poula'o
Arabic	yabi
Hebrew	machar
Yiddish	ferkoifen
Japanese	uru
Swahili	uza

783 send

French	envoyer
Spanish	enviar
Italian	mandare
Portuguese	enviar
Rumanian	trimite
German	senden
Dutch	zenden
Swedish	sända
Danish	sende
Norwegian	sende
Polish	posyłać
Czech	poslati
Serbo-Croat.	poslati
Hungarian	küld
Finnish	lähettäö
Turkish	göndermek
Indonesian	kirim
Esperanto	sendi
Russian	paslát
Greek	ste'lo
Arabic	yoursil
Hebrew	schalach
Yiddish	schicken
Japanese	okuru
Swahili	peleka

784 September

French	septembre
Spanish	septiembre
Italian	settembre
Portuguese	setembro
Rumanian	septembrie
German	September
Dutch	September
Swedish	september
Danish	september
Norwegian	september
Polish	wrzesień
Czech	září
Serbo-Croat.	rujan
Hungarian	szeptember
Finnish	syyskuu
Turkish	eylûl
Indonesian	Séptémber
Esperanto	Septembro
Russian	sintyábr
Greek	Septem'vrios
Arabic	sebtembar
Hebrew	september
Yiddish	september
Japanese	kugwatsu
Swahili	Septemba

785 seven

French	sept
Spanish	siete
Italian	sette
Portuguese	sete
Rumanian	şapte
German	sieben
Dutch	zeven
Swedish	sju
Danish	syv
Norwegian	sju
Polish	siedem
Czech	sedm
Serbo-Croat.	sedam
Hungarian	hét
Finnish	seitsemän
Turkish	yedi
Indonesian	tudjuh
Esperanto	sep
Russian	syém
Greek	epta'
Arabic	sabaa
Hebrew	schivah
Yiddish	sibben
Japanese	shichi
Swahili	saba

786 seventeen

French	dix-sept
Spanish	diecisiete
Italian	diciassette
Portuguese	dezessete
Rumanian	şaptesprezece
German	siebzehn
Dutch	zeventien
Swedish	sjutton
Danish	sytten
Norwegian	sytten
Polish	siedemnaście
Czech	sedmnáct
Serbo-Croat.	sedamnaest
Hungarian	tizenhét
Finnish	seitsemäntoista
Turkish	on yedi
Indonesian	tutjuh belas
Esperanto	dek sep
Russian	semnátset
Greek	dekaepta'
Arabic	sabaat ashar
Hebrew	schivah assar
Yiddish	sibentsen
Japanese	juushichi
Swahili	kumi na saba

787 seventy

French	soixante-dix
Spanish	setenta
Italian	settanta
Portuguese	setenta
Rumanian	şaptezeci
German	siebzig
Dutch	zeventig
Swedish	sjuttio
Danish	halvfjerds
Norwegian	sytti
Polish	siedemdziesiąt
Czech	sedmdesát
Serbo-Croat.	sedamdeset
Hungarian	hetven
Finnish	seitsemänkymmentä
Turkish	yetmiş
Indonesian	tudjuh pulu
Esperanto	sep'dek
Russian	syémdesat
Greek	evdomin'ta
Arabic	saboun
Hebrew	schivim
Yiddish	sibetsig
Japanese	shichijuu
Swahili	sabini

788 sew

French	coudre
Spanish	coser
Italian	cucire
Portuguese	coser
Rumanian	coase
German	nähen
Dutch	naaien
Swedish	sy
Danish	sy
Norwegian	sy
Polish	szyć
Czech	šíti
Serbo-Croat.	šiti
Hungarian	varr
Finnish	ommella
Turkish	dikiş dikmek
Indonesian	djahit
Esperanto	kudri
Russian	shit
Greek	ra'vo
Arabic	youhik
Hebrew	chiyet
Yiddish	nehen
Japanese	nuu
Swahili	shona

789 shave

French	raser
Spanish	afeitar
Italian	radere
Portuguese	barbear
Rumanian	bărbieri
German	rasieren
Dutch	scheren
Swedish	raka
Danish	barbere
Norwegian	barbere
Polish	golić
Czech	holiti
Serbo-Croat.	brijati
Hungarian	borotvál
Finnish	ajaaparta
Turkish	tıraş
Indonesian	tjukur
Esperanto	razi
Russian	brit
Greek	xiri'zo
Arabic	yahliq
Hebrew	gilach
Yiddish	golen
Japanese	soru
Swahili	nyoa

790 sheep

French	mouton
Spanish	oveja
Italian	pecora
Portuguese	ovelha
Rumanian	oaie
German	Schaf
Dutch	schaap
Swedish	får
Danish	får
Norwegian	sau
Polish	owca
Czech	ovce
Serbo-Croat.	ovca
Hungarian	juh
Finnish	lammas
Turkish	koyun
Indonesian	domba
Esperanto	ŝafo
Russian	aftsá
Greek	pro'vaton
Arabic	charouf
Hebrew	tson
Yiddish	scheps
Japanese	hitsuji
Swahili	kondoo

791 shirt

French	chemise
Spanish	camisa
Italian	camicia
Portuguese	camisa
Rumanian	cămaşă
German	Hemd
Dutch	overhemd
Swedish	skjorta
Danish	skjorte
Norwegian	skjorte
Polish	koszula
Czech	košile
Serbo-Croat.	košulja
Hungarian	ing
Finnish	paita
Turkish	gömlek
Indonesian	kemédja
Esperanto	ĉemizo
Russian	rubáshka
Greek	pouka'mison
Arabic	qamis
Hebrew	kutonet
Yiddish	hemd
Japanese	shatsu
Swahili	shati

792 shoe

French	soulier
Spanish	zapato
Italian	scarpa
Portuguese	sapato
Rumanian	pantof
German	Schuh
Dutch	schoen
Swedish	sko
Danish	sko
Norwegian	sko
Polish	but
Czech	střevíc
Serbo-Croat.	cipela
Hungarian	cipő
Finnish	kenkä
Turkish	ayakkabı
Indonesian	sepatu
Esperanto	ŝuo
Russian	bashmák
Greek	papou'tsi
Arabic	hitza
Hebrew	naal
Yiddish	schiech
Japanese	kutsu
Swahili	kiatu

793 short

French	court
Spanish	corto
Italian	corto
Portuguese	curto
Rumanian	scurt
German	kurz
Dutch	kort
Swedish	kort
Danish	kort
Norwegian	kort
Polish	krótki
Czech	krátký
Serbo-Croat.	kratak
Hungarian	rövid
Finnish	lyhyt
Turkish	kısa
Indonesian	péndák
Esperanto	mal'longa
Russian	karótki
Greek	kondos'
Arabic	qasir
Hebrew	katsar
Yiddish	kurts
Japanese	mijikai
Swahili	-fupi

794 shoulder

French	épaule
Spanish	hombro
Italian	spalla
Portuguese	ombro
Rumanian	umăr
German	Schulter
Dutch	schouder
Swedish	skuldra
Danish	skulder
Norwegian	skulder
Polish	ramię
Czech	rameno
Serbo-Croat.	rame
Hungarian	váll
Finnish	hartia
Turkish	omuz
Indonesian	bahu, pundak
Esperanto	ŝultro
Russian	plechó
Greek	o'mos
Arabic	katif
Hebrew	katef
Yiddish	aksl
Japanese	kata
Swahili	bega

795 sick

French	malade
Spanish	enfermo
Italian	ammalato
Portuguese	doente
Rumanian	bolnav
German	krank
Dutch	ziek
Swedish	sjuk
Danish	syg
Norwegian	syk
Polish	chory
Czech	nemocný
Serbo-Croat.	bolestan
Hungarian	beteg
Finnish	sairas
Turkish	hasta
Indonesian	sakit
Esperanto	mal'sana
Russian	balnóy
Greek	a'rostos
Arabic	marid
Hebrew	choleh
Yiddish	krank
Japanese	byooki no
Swahili	-gonjwa

796 signature

French	signature
Spanish	firma
Italian	firma
Portuguese	assinatura
Rumanian	semnatură
German	Unterschrift
Dutch	handtekening
Swedish	underskrift
Danish	underskrift
Norwegian	underskrift
Polish	podpis
Czech	podpis
Serbo-Croat.	potpis
Hungarian	aláírás
Finnish	allekirjoitus
Turkish	imza
Indonesian	tanda tangan
Esperanto	sub'skribo
Russian	pótpis
Greek	ipografi'
Arabic	imda
Hebrew	chatimah
Yiddish	chsime
Japanese	shomei
Swahili	sahihi

797 silk

French	soie
Spanish	seda
Italian	seta
Portuguese	sêda
Rumanian	mătase
German	Seide
Dutch	zijde
Swedish	silke
Danish	silke
Norwegian	silke
Polish	jedwab
Czech	hedvábí
Serbo-Croat.	svila
Hungarian	selyem
Finnish	silkki
Turkish	ipek
Indonesian	sutera
Esperanto	silko
Russian	sholk
Greek	meta'xi
Arabic	harir
Hebrew	meschi
Yiddish	seid
Japanese	kinu
Swahili	hariri

798 silver

French	argent
Spanish	plata
Italian	argento
Portuguese	prata
Rumanian	argint
German	Silber
Dutch	zilver
Swedish	silver
Danish	sølv
Norwegian	sølv
Polish	srebro
Czech	stříbro
Serbo-Croat.	srebro
Hungarian	ezüst
Finnish	hopea
Turkish	gümüs
Indonesian	párak
Esperanto	arĝento
Russian	serebró
Greek	asi'mi
Arabic	fida
Hebrew	kessef
Yiddish	silber
Japanese	gin
Swahili	fedha

799 sing

French	chanter
Spanish	cantar
Italian	cantare
Portuguese	cantar
Rumanian	cînta
German	singen
Dutch	zingen
Swedish	sjunga
Danish	synge
Norwegian	synge
Polish	śpiewać
Czech	zpívati
Serbo-Croat.	pjevati
Hungarian	énekel
Finnish	laulaa
Turkish	şarkı söylemek
Indonesian	njanji
Esperanto	kanti
Russian	pyét
Greek	tragouda'o
Arabic	youghanni
Hebrew	simer
Yiddish	singen
Japanese	utau
Swahili	imba

800 sister

French	sœur
Spanish	hermana
Italian	sorella
Portuguese	irmã
Rumanian	soră
German	Schwester
Dutch	zuster
Swedish	syster
Danish	søster
Norwegian	søster
Polish	siostra
Czech	sestra
Serbo-Croat.	sestra
Hungarian	nővér
Finnish	sisar
Turkish	kızkardeş
Indonesian	saudara perempuan
Esperanto	frat'ino
Russian	sestrá
Greek	adelfi'
Arabic	oucht
Hebrew	achot
Yiddish	schvester
Japanese	shimai
Swahili	dada

801 sit

French	(être) assis
Spanish	sentarse
Italian	sedere
Portuguese	assentar
Rumanian	şedea
German	sitzen
Dutch	zitten
Swedish	sitta
Danish	sidde
Norwegian	sitte
Polish	siedzieć
Czech	seděti
Serbo-Croat.	sjedeti
Hungarian	ül
Finnish	istua
Turkish	oturmak
Indonesian	dudak
Esperanto	sidi
Russian	sidyét
Greek	ka'thome
Arabic	yaqoud
Hebrew	yaschav
Yiddish	sitsen
Japanese	suwaru
Swahili	kaa

802 six

French	six
Spanish	seis
Italian	sei
Portuguese	seis
Rumanian	şase
German	sechs
Dutch	zes
Swedish	sex
Danish	seks
Norwegian	seks
Polish	sześć
Czech	šest
Serbo-Croat.	šest
Hungarian	hat
Finnish	kuusi
Turkish	altı
Indonesian	enam
Esperanto	ses
Russian	shest
Greek	e'xi
Arabic	sitta
Hebrew	schischăh
Yiddish	seks
Japanese	roku
Swahili	sita

803 sixteen

French	seize
Spanish	dieciseis
Italian	sedici
Portuguese	dezesseis
Rumanian	şaisprezece
German	sechzehn
Dutch	zestien
Swedish	sexton
Danish	seksten
Norwegian	seksten
Polish	szesnaście
Czech	šestnáct
Serbo-Croat.	šestanaest
Hungarian	tizenhat
Finnish	kuusitoista
Turkish	on altı
Indonesian	enam belas
Esperanto	dek ses
Russian	shestnátsit
Greek	deka-e'xi
Arabic	sittata ashar
Hebrew	schischah assar
Yiddish	sechtsen
Japanese	juuroku
Swahili	kumi na sita

804 sixty

French	soixante
Spanish	sesenta
Italian	sessanta
Portuguese	sessenta
Rumanian	şaizeci
German	sechzig
Dutch	zestig
Swedish	sextio
Danish	tres
Norwegian	seksti
Polish	sześćdziesiąt
Czech	šedesát
Serbo-Croat.	šezdeset
Hungarian	hatvan
Finnish	kuusikymmentä
Turkish	altmıs
Indonesian	enam pulah
Esperanto	ses'dek
Russian	shestdesyát
Greek	exin'ta
Arabic	sittoun
Hebrew	schischim
Yiddish	sechtsig
Japanese	rokujuu
Swahili	sitini

805 skin

French	peau
Spanish	piel
Italian	pelle
Portuguese	pele
Rumanian	piele
German	Haut
Dutch	huid
Swedish	skinn
Danish	hud
Norwegian	hud
Polish	skóra
Czech	kůže
Serbo-Croat.	koža
Hungarian	bőr
Finnish	iho
Turkish	deri
Indonesian	kulit
Esperanto	haŭto
Russian	kózha
Greek	der'ma
Arabic	gild
Hebrew	geled
Yiddish	skure
Japanese	kawa
Swahili	ngozi

806 skis

French	skis
Spanish	esquís
Italian	sci
Portuguese	esqui
Rumanian	schi
German	Schi
Dutch	skis
Swedish	skidor
Danish	ski
Norwegian	ski
Polish	narty
Czech	lyže
Serbo-Croat.	ski
Hungarian	sí
Finnish	suksi
Turkish	kayak
Indonesian	ski
Esperanto	skio
Russian	lízhi
Greek	ski'
Arabic	ski, mazlag al-galid
Hebrew	miglaschim
Yiddish	nartes
Japanese	sukii
Swahili	ski

807 sky

French	ciel
Spanish	cielo
Italian	cielo
Portuguese	céu
Rumanian	cer
German	Himmel
Dutch	lucht
Swedish	himmel
Danish	himmel
Norwegian	himmel
Polish	niebo
Czech	nebe
Serbo-Croat.	nebo
Hungarian	ég
Finnish	taivas
Turkish	gök
Indonesian	langit
Esperanto	ĉielo
Russian	nyébo
Greek	ouranos'
Arabic	sama
Hebrew	rakia
Yiddish	himel
Japanese	sora
Swahili	mbingu

808 sled

French	traineau
Spanish	trineo
Italian	slitta
Portuguese	trenó
Rumanian	sanie
German	Schlitten
Dutch	slee
Swedish	släde
Danish	slæde
Norwegian	slede
Polish	sanie
Czech	sáně
Serbo-Croat.	saone
Hungarian	szánko
Finnish	reki
Turkish	kızak
Indonesian	pengérétan
Esperanto	sledo
Russian	sáni
Greek	e'lkithron
Arabic	mizlaga, zahhafa
Hebrew	mischeleth
Yiddish	schlitten
Japanese	sori
Swahili	gari kwa theluji

809 sleep

French	dormir
Spanish	dormir
Italian	dormire
Portuguese	dormir
Rumanian	dormi
German	schlafen
Dutch	slapen
Swedish	sova
Danish	sove
Norwegian	sove
Polish	spać
Czech	spáti
Serbo-Croat.	spavati
Hungarian	alszik
Finnish	nukkua
Turkish	uyku
Indonesian	tidur
Esperanto	dormi
Russian	spát
Greek	kima'me
Arabic	yanam
Hebrew	yaschan
Yiddish	schlofen
Japanese	nemuru
Swahili	lala

810 slowly

French	lentement
Spanish	despacio
Italian	adagio
Portuguese	vagarosamente
Rumanian	lent
German	langsam
Dutch	langzaam
Swedish	långsam
Danish	langsom
Norwegian	langsom
Polish	powoli
Czech	pomalý
Serbo-Croat.	polagano
Hungarian	lassan
Finnish	hidas
Turkish	yavaş
Indonesian	perlahan-lahan
Esperanto	mal'rapida
Russian	myédlenno
Greek	siga'
Arabic	biboute
Hebrew	leat leat
Yiddish	povole
Japanese	osoi
Swahili	pole pole

811 small

French	petit
Spanish	pequeño
Italian	piccolo
Portuguese	pequeno
Rumanian	mic
German	klein
Dutch	klein
Swedish	liten
Danish	lille
Norwegian	litten
Polish	mały
Czech	malý
Serbo-Croat.	mali
Hungarian	kis
Finnish	pieni
Turkish	küçük
Indonesian	ketjil
Esperanto	mal'granda
Russian	málenki
Greek	mikros'
Arabic	saghir
Hebrew	katan
Yiddish	klein
Japanese	chiisai
Swahili	-dogo

812 smell

French	sentir
Spanish	oler
Italian	odorare
Portuguese	cheirar
Rumanian	miros
German	riechen
Dutch	reuk
Swedish	lukta
Danish	lugte
Norwegian	lukte
Polish	wąchać
Czech	čichati
Serbo-Croat.	mirisati
Hungarian	szagol
Finnish	haistaa
Turkish	kokmak
Indonesian	bau
Esperanto	odori
Russian	pákhnut
Greek	miri'zo
Arabic	yashim
Hebrew	reyach
Yiddish	schmeken
Japanese	kagu
Swahili	sikia harufu

813 smoke

French	fumée
Spanish	humo
Italian	fumo
Portuguese	fumo
Rumanian	fum
German	Rauch
Dutch	rook
Swedish	rök
Danish	røg
Norwegian	røk
Polish	dym
Czech	kouř
Serbo-Croat.	dim
Hungarian	füst
Finnish	savu
Turkish	duman
Indonesian	asap
Esperanto	fumo
Russian	dim
Greek	kapnos'
Arabic	douchan
Hebrew	aschan
Yiddish	rojech
Japanese	kemuri
Swahili	moshi

814 snake

French	serpent
Spanish	serpiente
Italian	serpente
Portuguese	cobra
Rumanian	şarpe
German	Schlange
Dutch	slang
Swedish	orm
Danish	slange
Norwegian	orm
Polish	wąż
Czech	had
Serbo-Croat.	zmija
Hungarian	kígyó
Finnish	käärme
Turkish	yılan
Indonesian	ular
Esperanto	serpento
Russian	zmeyá
Greek	fi'di
Arabic	tsouban
Hebrew	nachasch
Yiddish	schlang
Japanese	hebi
Swahili	nyoka

815 snow

French	neige
Spanish	nieve
Italian	neve
Portuguese	neve
Rumanian	zăpadă
German	Schnee
Dutch	sneeuw
Swedish	snö
Danish	sne
Norwegian	snø
Polish	śnieg
Czech	sníh
Serbo-Croat.	snijeg
Hungarian	hó
Finnish	lumi
Turkish	kar
Indonesian	saldju
Esperanto	neĝo
Russian	snyék
Greek	chio'ni
Arabic	galid
Hebrew	scheleg
Yiddish	schnee
Japanese	yuki
Swahili	theluji

816 soap

French	savon
Spanish	jabón
Italian	sapone
Portuguese	sabão
Rumanian	săpun
German	Seife
Dutch	zeep
Swedish	tvål
Danish	sæbe
Norwegian	såpe
Polish	mydło
Czech	mýdlo
Serbo-Croat.	sapun
Hungarian	szappan
Finnish	saippua
Turkish	sabun
Indonesian	sabun
Esperanto	sapo
Russian	mílo
Greek	sapou'ni
Arabic	saboun
Hebrew	sabon
Yiddish	seif
Japanese	sekken
Swahili	sabuni

817 socks

French	chaussettes
Spanish	calcetines
Italian	calzetti
Portuguese	peúgas
Rumanian	ciorapi
German	Socken
Dutch	sokken
Swedish	strumpa
Danish	sok
Norwegian	sokker
Polish	skarpetki
Czech	ponožky
Serbo-Croat.	čarape
Hungarian	zokni
Finnish	sukka
Turkish	çorap
Indonesian	kaus
Esperanto	ŝtrump'eto
Russian	noskí
Greek	kal'tses
Arabic	gawrab
Hebrew	gerev
Yiddish	skarpetke
Japanese	kutsushita
Swahili	soksi

818 sofa

French	sofa
Spanish	sofá
Italian	sofà
Portuguese	sofá
Rumanian	sofa
German	Sofa
Dutch	canapé
Swedish	soffa
Danish	sofa
Norwegian	sofa
Polish	sofa
Czech	pohovka
Serbo-Croat.	sofa
Hungarian	pamlag
Finnish	sohva
Turkish	kanape
Indonesian	bangku
Esperanto	kanapo
Russian	diván
Greek	kanapes'
Arabic	arika
Hebrew	sapah
Yiddish	kanape
Japanese	nagaisu
Swahili	kiti kirefu

819 soft

French	mou
Spanish	blando
Italian	molle
Portuguese	macio
Rumanian	moale
German	weich
Dutch	zacht
Swedish	mjuk
Danish	blød
Norwegian	bløt
Polish	miękki
Czech	měkký
Serbo-Croat.	mjekan
Hungarian	puha
Finnish	pehmeä
Turkish	yumuşak
Indonesian	lembék
Esperanto	mola
Russian	myákhki
Greek	malakos'
Arabic	layin
Hebrew	rach
Yiddish	veyech
Japanese	yawarakai
Swahili	-ororo

820 soldier

French	soldat
Spanish	soldado
Italian	soldato
Portuguese	soldado
Rumanian	soldat
German	Soldat
Dutch	soldaat
Swedish	soldat
Danish	soldat
Norwegian	soldat
Polish	żołnierz
Czech	voják
Serbo-Croat.	vojnik
Hungarian	katona
Finnish	sotilas
Turkish	asker
Indonesian	serdadu
Esperanto	soldato
Russian	soldát
Greek	stratio'tis
Arabic	goundi
Hebrew	chayal
Yiddish	selner
Japanese	gunjin
Swahili	askari

821 solution

French	solution
Spanish	solución
Italian	soluzione
Portuguese	solução
Rumanian	soluţie
German	Lösung
Dutch	oplossing
Swedish	lösning
Danish	løsning
Norwegian	oppløsning
Polish	rozwiązanie
Czech	roztok
Serbo-Croat.	rešenje
Hungarian	oldat
Finnish	liuos
Turkish	erime
Indonesian	larutan
Esperanto	solvo
Russian	reshénye
Greek	li'sis
Arabic	hal
Hebrew	pitron
Yiddish	oiflezung
Japanese	yookai
Swahili	ufumbuzi

822 son

French	fils
Spanish	hijo
Italian	figlio
Portuguese	filho
Rumanian	fiu
German	Sohn
Dutch	zoon
Swedish	son
Danish	søn
Norwegian	sønn
Polish	syn
Czech	syn
Serbo-Croat.	sin
Hungarian	fiú
Finnish	poika
Turkish	oğul
Indonesian	anak laki-laki
Esperanto	filo
Russian	sin
Greek	yi-os'
Arabic	ibn
Hebrew	ben
Yiddish	suhn
Japanese	musuko
Swahili	mwana

823 sorrow

French	chagrin
Spanish	dolor
Italian	dolore
Portuguese	dor
Rumanian	mihnire
German	Kummer
Dutch	droefheid
Swedish	sorg
Danish	kummer
Norwegian	sorg
Polish	smutek
Czech	hoře
Serbo-Croat.	tuga
Hungarian	szomorúság
Finnish	suru
Turkish	keder
Indonesian	dukatjita
Esperanto	malĝojo
Russian	pechál
Greek	li'pi
Arabic	yasaf
Hebrew	tsaar
Yiddish	agmass nefesch
Japanese	kanashimi
Swahili	sikitiko

824 sound

French	sain
Spanish	sano
Italian	sano
Portuguese	são
Rumanian	sănătos
German	gesund
Dutch	gezond
Swedish	frisk
Danish	sund
Norwegian	frisk
Polish	zdrowy
Czech	zdravý
Serbo-Croat.	zdrav
Hungarian	egészséges
Finnish	terve
Turkish	sağlam
Indonesian	segar
Esperanto	sen'difekta
Russian	zdaróvi
Greek	i'chos
Arabic	sahih
Hebrew	barie
Yiddish	gesund
Japanese	kenzen na
Swahili	mlio

825 soup

French	potage
Spanish	sopa
Italian	minestra
Portuguese	sopa
Rumanian	supă
German	Suppe
Dutch	soep
Swedish	soppa
Danish	suppe
Norwegian	suppe
Polish	zupa
Czech	polévka
Serbo-Croat.	juha
Hungarian	leves
Finnish	keitto
Turkish	çorba
Indonesian	sop
Esperanto	supo
Russian	sup
Greek	sou'pa
Arabic	shourba
Hebrew	marak
Yiddish	yoich
Japanese	suupu
Swahili	mchuzi

826 sour

French	aigre
Spanish	agrio
Italian	agro
Portuguese	azêdo
Rumanian	acru
German	sauer
Dutch	zuur
Swedish	sur
Danish	sur
Norwegian	sur
Polish	kwaśny
Czech	kyselý
Serbo-Croat.	kiseo
Hungarian	savanyú
Finnish	hapan
Turkish	ekşi
Indonesian	asam
Esperanto	acida
Russian	kísli
Greek	xinos'
Arabic	hamid
Hebrew	chamuts
Yiddish	zoyer
Japanese	suppai
Swahili	-chungu

827 south

French	sud
Spanish	sur
Italian	sud
Portuguese	sul
Rumanian	sud
German	Süden
Dutch	zuid
Swedish	söder
Danish	syd
Norwegian	syd
Polish	południe
Czech	jižní
Serbo-Croat.	jug
Hungarian	dél
Finnish	etelä
Turkish	güney
Indonesian	selatan
Esperanto	sudo
Russian	yuk
Greek	no'tos
Arabic	ganoub
Hebrew	darom
Yiddish	dorim
Japanese	minami
Swahili	kusini

828 space

French	espace
Spanish	espacio
Italian	spazio
Portuguese	espaço
Rumanian	spaţiu
German	Raum
Dutch	ruimte
Swedish	rymd
Danish	rum
Norwegian	rom
Polish	przestrzeń
Czech	prostor
Serbo-Croat.	prostor
Hungarian	tér
Finnish	avaruus
Turkish	saha
Indonesian	luas, spasi
Esperanto	spaco
Russian	prastránstvo
Greek	cho'ros
Arabic	fada
Hebrew	revach
Yiddish	plats
Japanese	kuukan
Swahili	nafasi

829 speak

French	parler
Spanish	hablar
Italian	parlare
Portuguese	falar
Rumanian	vorbi
German	sprechen
Dutch	spreken
Swedish	tala
Danish	tale
Norwegian	tale
Polish	mówić
Czech	mluviti
Serbo-Croat.	govoriti
Hungarian	beszél
Finnish	puhua
Turkish	konuşmak
Indonesian	berbitjara
Esperanto	paroli
Russian	gavarít
Greek	mila'o
Arabic	yatakalam
Hebrew	diber
Yiddish	reden
Japanese	hanasu
Swahili	nena

830 special

French	spécial
Spanish	especial
Italian	speciale
Portuguese	especial
Rumanian	special
German	besonders
Dutch	speciaal
Swedish	speciell
Danish	speciel
Norwegian	spesiell
Polish	specjalny
Czech	zvláštni
Serbo-Croat.	poseban
Hungarian	különleges
Finnish	erikoinen
Turkish	hususi
Indonesian	sépesial
Esperanto	speciala
Russian	spetsiálni
Greek	idikos'
Arabic	chas
Hebrew	bifrat
Yiddish	basunder
Japanese	tokubetsu
Swahili	-a namna

831 spice

French	épice
Spanish	especia
Italian	spezie
Portuguese	especiaria
Rumanian	condiment
German	Gewürz
Dutch	specerij
Swedish	krydda
Danish	krydderi
Norwegian	kryddek
Polish	przyprawa
Czech	koření
Serbo-Croat.	začin
Hungarian	fűszer
Finnish	mauste
Turkish	bahar
Indonesian	rempah, bumbu
Esperanto	spico
Russian	pryánosti
Greek	bachariko
Arabic	tawabil
Hebrew	tevel
Yiddish	gevirts
Japanese	yakumi
Swahili	kiungo cha kunukia

832 spoon

French	cuiller
Spanish	cuchara
Italian	cucchiaio
Portuguese	colher
Rumanian	lingură
German	Löffel
Dutch	lepel
Swedish	sked
Danish	ske
Norwegian	skje
Polish	łyżka
Czech	lžíce
Serbo-Croat.	kašika
Hungarian	kanál
Finnish	lusikka
Turkish	kaşık
Indonesian	séndok
Esperanto	kulero
Russian	lóshka
Greek	kouta'li
Arabic	milaaqa
Hebrew	kaff
Yiddish	leffel
Japanese	saji
Swahili	kijiko

833 spring

French	printemps
Spanish	primavera
Italian	primavera
Portuguese	primavera
Rumanian	primăvară
German	Frühling
Dutch	voorjaar
Swedish	vår
Danish	forår
Norwegian	vår
Polish	wiosna
Czech	jaro
Serbo-Croat.	proljeće
Hungarian	tavasz
Finnish	kevät
Turkish	ilkbahar
Indonesian	musim bunga
Esperanto	printempo
Russian	vesná
Greek	a'nixis
Arabic	rabi
Hebrew	aviv
Yiddish	frihling
Japanese	haru
Swahili	miwezi Machi-Juni

834 stable

French	écurie
Spanish	establo
Italian	stalla
Portuguese	estável
Rumanian	staul
German	Stall
Dutch	stal
Swedish	stall
Danish	stald
Norwegian	stall
Polish	stajnia
Czech	stáj
Serbo-Croat.	štala
Hungarian	istálló
Finnish	talli
Turkish	ahır
Indonesian	kanlang
Esperanto	stalo
Russian	konyúshnya
Greek	sta'vlos
Arabic	istabl
Hebrew	urva
Yiddish	schtal
Japanese	umaya
Swahili	banda la wanyama

835 staircase

French	escalier
Spanish	escalera
Italian	scala
Portuguese	escada
Rumanian	scară
German	Treppe
Dutch	trap
Swedish	trappupgång
Danish	trappe
Norwegian	trappe
Polish	schody
Czech	schody
Serbo-Croat.	stepenice
Hungarian	lepcső
Finnish	portaat
Turkish	merdiven
Indonesian	tangga
Esperanto	ŝtup'aro
Russian	lésnitsa
Greek	ska'la
Arabic	darag
Hebrew	madregot
Yiddish	trep
Japanese	kaidan
Swahili	madaraja

836 stamp (mail)

French	timbre
Spanish	sello de correos
Italian	francobollo
Portuguese	sêlo
Rumanian	timbru
German	Briefmarke
Dutch	postzegel
Swedish	frimärke
Danish	frimærke
Norwegian	frimerke
Polish	znaczek
Czech	známka poštovní
Serbo-Croat.	marka
Hungarian	bélyeg
Finnish	merkki
Turkish	pul
Indonesian	perangko
Esperanto	poŝt'marko
Russian	pochtaváya márka
Greek	gramato'simon
Arabic	warqat bousta
Hebrew	bull
Yiddish	marken
Japanese	kitte
Swahili	tikiti ya posta

837 stamp (seal)

French	cachet
Spanish	sello
Italian	sigillo
Portuguese	carimbo
Rumanian	sigiliu
German	Stempel
Dutch	stempelen
Swedish	stämpel
Danish	stempel
Norwegian	stempel
Polish	pieczęć
Czech	razítko
Serbo-Croat.	pečat
Hungarian	pecsét
Finnish	leima
Turkish	mühür
Indonesian	ségel
Esperanto	stamp'ilo
Russian	pechát
Greek	sfragi'da
Arabic	chitm al-barid
Hebrew	chotam
Yiddish	sigel
Japanese	in
Swahili	chapa

838 stand

French	être debout
Spanish	estar de pie
Italian	stare in piedi
Portuguese	estar de pe
Rumanian	sta
German	stehen
Dutch	staan
Swedish	stå
Danish	stå
Norwegian	stå
Polish	stać
Czech	státi
Serbo-Croat.	stajati
Hungarian	áll
Finnish	seisoa
Turkish	ayakta durmak
Indonesian	berdiri
Esperanto	stari
Russian	stoyát
Greek	ste'kome
Arabic	yaqif
Hebrew	amad
Yiddish	schtehn
Japanese	tatsu
Swahili	simama

839 star

French	étoile
Spanish	estrella
Italian	stella
Portuguese	estrêla
Rumanian	astru
German	Stern
Dutch	ster
Swedish	stjärna
Danish	stjerne
Norwegian	stjerne
Polish	gwiazda
Czech	hvězda
Serbo-Croat.	zvjezda
Hungarian	csillag
Finnish	tähti
Turkish	yıldız
Indonesian	bintang
Esperanto	stelo
Russian	zvezdá
Greek	astir'
Arabic	nagm
Hebrew	kochav
Yiddish	schtern
Japanese	hoshi
Swahili	nyota

840 starch

French	amidon
Spanish	almidón
Italian	amido
Portuguese	amido
Rumanian	amidon
German	Stärke
Dutch	stijven
Swedish	stärkelse
Danish	stivelse
Norwegian	stivelse
Polish	krochmal
Czech	škrob
Serbo-Croat.	štirak
Hungarian	keményítő
Finnish	tärkkelys
Turkish	kola
Indonesian	pati, kandji
Esperanto	amelo
Russian	krakhmál
Greek	a'milon
Arabic	nisha
Hebrew	amilan
Yiddish	krochmal
Japanese	nori
Swahili	wanga

841 station

French	gare
Spanish	estación
Italian	stazione
Portuguese	estacão
Rumanian	staţiune
German	Bahnhof
Dutch	station
Swedish	station
Danish	station
Norwegian	stasjon
Polish	stacja
Czech	nádraží
Serbo-Croat.	stanica
Hungarian	állomás
Finnish	asema
Turkish	istasyon
Indonesian	stasium
Esperanto	stacio
Russian	stántsiya
Greek	stathmos'
Arabic	mihatta
Hebrew	tachanah
Yiddish	voksal
Japanese	eki
Swahili	stesheni

842 steal

French	voler
Spanish	robar
Italian	rubare
Portuguese	roubar
Rumanian	fura
German	stehlen
Dutch	stelen
Swedish	stjäla
Danish	stjæle
Norwegian	stjele
Polish	kraść
Czech	krásti
Serbo-Croat.	krasti
Hungarian	lop
Finnish	varastaa
Turkish	çalmak
Indonesian	tjuri
Esperanto	šteli
Russian	krást
Greek	kle'vo
Arabic	yasriq
Hebrew	ganav
Yiddish	ganvenen
Japanese	nusumu
Swahili	iba

843 steel

French	acier
Spanish	acero
Italian	acciaio
Portuguese	aço
Rumanian	oţel
German	Stahl
Dutch	staal
Swedish	stål
Danish	stål
Norwegian	stål
Polish	stal
Czech	ocel
Serbo-Croat.	čelik
Hungarian	acél
Finnish	teräs
Turkish	çelik
Indonesian	wadja, badja
Esperanto	štalo
Russian	stal
Greek	cha'livas
Arabic	soulb
Hebrew	peladah
Yiddish	schtohl
Japanese	kootetsu
Swahili	pua

844 stick

French	bâton
Spanish	palo
Italian	bastone
Portuguese	pau
Rumanian	băţ
German	Stock
Dutch	stok
Swedish	käpp
Danish	stok
Norwegian	stokk
Polish	kij
Czech	hůl
Serbo-Croat.	štap
Hungarian	bot
Finnish	sauva
Turkish	baston
Indonesian	batang
Esperanto	bastono
Russian	pálka
Greek	ravdi'
Arabic	asa
Hebrew	makel
Yiddish	schtekken
Japanese	tsue
Swahili	fimbo

845 sting

French	piquer
Spanish	picar
Italian	pungere
Portuguese	picar
Rumanian	înțepa
German	stechen
Dutch	steken
Swedish	sticka
Danish	stikke
Norwegian	stikke
Polish	kłuć
Czech	píchnouti
Serbo-Croat.	bosti
Hungarian	szúr
Finnish	pistää
Turkish	sokmak
Indonesian	sengat
Esperanto	piki
Russian	zhálit
Greek	kentri'zo
Arabic	yaldagh
Hebrew	akats
Yiddish	schtechen
Japanese	sasu
Swahili	uma

846 stock exchange

French	bourse
Spanish	bolsa
Italian	borsa valori
Portuguese	bolsa de valores
Rumanian	bursă
German	Börse
Dutch	effectenbeurs
Swedish	börs
Danish	børsen
Norwegian	børs
Polish	giełda
Czech	burza
Serbo-Croat.	berza
Hungarian	tőzsde
Finnish	pörssi
Turkish	borsa
Indonesian	pasar uang
Esperanto	borso
Russian	bírzha
Greek	chrimatisti'rion
Arabic	boursa
Hebrew	burssah
Yiddish	berze
Japanese	kabushiki torihiki jo
Swahili	bursa

847 stomach

French	estomac
Spanish	estómago
Italian	stomaco
Portuguese	estômago
Rumanian	stomac
German	Magen
Dutch	maag
Swedish	mage
Danish	mave
Norwegian	mage
Polish	żołądek
Czech	žaludek
Serbo-Croat.	želudac
Hungarian	gyomor
Finnish	maha
Turkish	mide
Indonesian	lambung
Esperanto	stomako
Russian	zhelúdok
Greek	stoma'chi
Arabic	maida
Hebrew	keivah
Yiddish	mogen
Japanese	i
Swahili	tumbo

848 stone

French	pierre
Spanish	piedra
Italian	pietra
Portuguese	pedra
Rumanian	piatră
German	Stein
Dutch	steen
Swedish	sten
Danish	sten
Norwegian	stein
Polish	kamień
Czech	kámen
Serbo-Croat.	kamen
Hungarian	kő
Finnish	kivi
Turkish	taş
Indonesian	batu
Esperanto	štono
Russian	kámen
Greek	pet'ra
Arabic	hagar
Hebrew	even
Yiddish	schtein
Japanese	ishi
Swahili	jiwe

849 stop

French	arrêt
Spanish	parada
Italian	fermata
Portuguese	paragem
Rumanian	oprire
German	Haltestelle
Dutch	stoppen
Swedish	hållplats
Danish	stoppested
Norwegian	stans
Polish	przystanek
Czech	zastávka
Serbo-Croat.	svršetak
Hungarian	megállóhely
Finnish	seis
Turkish	durak
Indonesian	henti
Esperanto	halto
Russian	astanófka
Greek	sta'sis
Arabic	youqif
Hebrew	hifsik
Yiddish	opschtel
Japanese	teishi
Swahili	ngojo

850 store

French	magasin
Spanish	tienda
Italian	magazzino
Portuguese	loja
Rumanian	prăvălie
German	Laden
Dutch	winkel
Swedish	butik
Danish	butik
Norwegian	buttik
Polish	sklep
Czech	sklad
Serbo-Croat.	radnja
Hungarian	bolt
Finnish	kauppauoti
Turkish	dükkân
Indonesian	toko
Esperanto	butiko
Russian	láfka
Greek	magazi'
Arabic	mahal
Hebrew	machsan
Yiddish	gevelb
Japanese	mise
Swahili	duka

851 storm

French	orage
Spanish	tormenta
Italian	tempesta
Portuguese	tempestade
Rumanian	furtună
German	Sturm
Dutch	storm
Swedish	storm
Danish	storm
Norwegian	storm
Polish	burza
Czech	bouře
Serbo-Croat.	bura
Hungarian	vihar
Finnish	myrsky
Turkish	fırtına
Indonesian	angin ribut
Esperanto	ŝtormo
Russian	búrya
Greek	thi'ela
Arabic	asifa
Hebrew	saar
Yiddish	schturm
Japanese	arashi
Swahili	dhoruba

852 stove

French	poêle
Spanish	estufa
Italian	stufa
Portuguese	fogão
Rumanian	sobă
German	Ofen
Dutch	fornuis
Swedish	ugn
Danish	ovn
Norwegian	ovn
Polish	piec
Czech	kamna
Serbo-Croat.	peć
Hungarian	kályha
Finnish	komiina
Turkish	fırın
Indonesian	kompor
Esperanto	forno
Russian	pyéch
Greek	therma'stra
Arabic	mawqid
Hebrew	kirah
Yiddish	pjekelek
Japanese	sutoobu
Swahili	jiko

853 strawberry

French	fraise
Spanish	fresa
Italian	fragola
Portuguese	morango
Rumanian	fragă
German	Erdbeere
Dutch	aardbei
Swedish	jordgubbe
Danish	jorbær
Norwegian	jordbær
Polish	poziomka
Czech	jahoda
Serbo-Croat.	jagoda
Hungarian	földieper
Finnish	mansikka
Turkish	çilek
Indonesian	arbai, arbén
Esperanto	frago
Russian	klubníka
Greek	fra'oula
Arabic	farawla
Hebrew	tut sadeh
Yiddish	posjemke
Japanese	ichigo
Swahili	namna ya tunda

854 street

French	rue
Spanish	calle
Italian	via
Portuguese	rua
Rumanian	stradă
German	Strasse
Dutch	straat
Swedish	gata
Danish	gade
Norwegian	gate
Polish	ulica
Czech	ulice
Serbo-Croat.	ulica
Hungarian	útca
Finnish	katu
Turkish	sokak
Indonesian	djjajljan
Esperanto	strato
Russian	úlitsa
Greek	dro'mos
Arabic	sharia
Hebrew	rechov
Yiddish	gass
Japanese	gairo
Swahili	njia ya mji

855 strong

French	fort
Spanish	fuerte
Italian	forte
Portuguese	forte
Rumanian	puternic
German	stark
Dutch	sterk
Swedish	stark
Danish	stærk
Norwegian	sterk
Polish	silny
Czech	silný
Serbo-Croat.	jak
Hungarian	erős
Finnish	vahva
Turkish	kuvvetli
Indonesian	kuat
Esperanto	forta
Russian	sílni
Greek	dinatos'
Arabic	qawi
Hebrew	chazak
Yiddish	schtark
Japanese	tsuyoi
Swahili	-a nguvu

856 student

French	étudiant
Spanish	estudiante
Italian	studente
Portuguese	estudante
Rumanian	student
German	Schüler
Dutch	student
Swedish	student
Danish	student
Norwegian	student
Polish	student
Czech	student
Serbo-Croat.	student
Hungarian	diák
Finnish	oppilas
Turkish	talebe
Indonesian	peladjar, siswa
Esperanto	studento
Russian	studyént
Greek	spoudastis'
Arabic	talib
Hebrew	talmid
Yiddish	schtudent
Japanese	gakusei
Swahili	mwanafunzi

857 sugar

French	sucre
Spanish	azúcar
Italian	zucchero
Portuguese	açúcar
Rumanian	zahăr
German	Zucker
Dutch	suiker
Swedish	socker
Danish	sukker
Norwegian	sukker
Polish	cukier,
Czech	cukr
Serbo-Croat.	šećer
Hungarian	cukor
Finnish	sokeri
Turkish	şeker
Indonesian	gula, sakar
Esperanto	sukero
Russian	sákhar
Greek	za'chari
Arabic	soukar
Hebrew	sukkar
Yiddish	tsukker
Japanese	satoo
Swahili	sukari

858 summer

French	été
Spanish	verano
Italian	estate
Portuguese	verão
Rumanian	vară
German	Sommer
Dutch	zomer
Swedish	sommar
Danish	sommer
Norwegian	sommer
Polish	lato
Czech	léto
Serbo-Croat.	ljeto
Hungarian	nyár
Finnish	kesä
Turkish	yaz
Indonesian	musim panas
Esperanto	somero
Russian	lyéto
Greek	kaloke'ri
Arabic	sayf
Hebrew	kayits
Yiddish	sumer
Japanese	natsu
Swahili	wakati wa jua kali

859 sun

French	soleil
Spanish	sol
Italian	sole
Portuguese	sol
Rumanian	soare
German	Sonne
Dutch	zon
Swedish	sol
Danish	sol
Norwegian	sol
Polish	słońce
Czech	slunce
Serbo-Croat.	sunce
Hungarian	nap
Finnish	aurinko
Turkish	güneş
Indonesian	matahari, suria
Esperanto	suno
Russian	sóntse
Greek	i'lios
Arabic	shams
Hebrew	schemesch
Yiddish	sun
Japanese	taiyoo
Swahili	jua

860 Sunday

French	dimanche
Spanish	domingo
Italian	domenica
Portuguese	domingo
Rumanian	duminică
German	Sonntag
Dutch	Zondag
Swedish	söndag
Danish	søndag
Norwegian	søndag
Polish	niedziela
Czech	neděle
Serbo-Croat.	nedelja
Hungarian	vasárnap
Finnish	sunnuntai
Turkish	pazar
Indonesian	Ahad
Esperanto	dimanĉo
Russian	voskresyénye
Greek	Kyriaki'
Arabic	al-ahad
Hebrew	yom rischon
Yiddish	suntog
Japanese	nichiyoobi
Swahili	Jumapili

861 supper

French	souper
Spanish	cena
Italian	cena
Portuguese	ceia
Rumanian	cină
German	Abendessen
Dutch	avondeten
Swedish	kvällsmat
Danish	aftensmad
Norwegian	kveldsmat
Polish	kolacja
Czech	večeře
Serbo-Croat.	večera
Hungarian	vacsora
Finnish	illallinen
Turkish	akşam yemeği
Indonesian	makanaan malam
Esperanto	vesper'manĝo
Russian	úzhin
Greek	di'pnon
Arabic	asha
Hebrew	aruchat erev
Yiddish	vetschere
Japanese	yuushoku
Swahili	chakula cha usiku

862 surprise

French	surprendre
Spanish	sorprender
Italian	sorprendere
Portuguese	surpreender
Rumanian	surprinde
German	überraschen
Dutch	verrassen
Swedish	överraska
Danish	overraske
Norwegian	overraske
Polish	zdziwić
Czech	překvapiti
Serbo-Croat.	iznenaditi
Hungarian	meglep
Finnish	yllättää
Turkish	şaşurtmak
Indonesian	hérankan
Esperanto	surprizi
Russian	izumlyát
Greek	ekpli'sso
Arabic	moufagaa
Hebrew	hiftia
Yiddish	iberraschen
Japanese	odoroku
Swahili	shangaza

863 suspenders

French	bretelles
Spanish	tirantes
Italian	bretelle
Portuguese	suspensório
Rumanian	bretele
German	Hosenträger
Dutch	bretels
Swedish	hängslen
Danish	seler
Norwegian	bukseseler
Polish	szelki
Czech	šle
Serbo-Croat.	podvezice
Hungarian	nadrágtartó
Finnish	housunkannattimet
Turkish	pantolon askısı
Indonesian	bretél
Esperanto	ŝelko
Russian	patyáshki
Greek	tira'ntes
Arabic	hamalat
Hebrew	ketefot
Yiddish	schelkes
Japanese	zubon-tsuri
Swahili	ukanda wa kuzuia suruali

864 sweet

French	doux
Spanish	dulce
Italian	dolce
Portuguese	doce
Rumanian	dulce
German	süss
Dutch	zoet
Swedish	söt
Danish	sød
Norwegian	søt
Polish	słodki
Czech	sladký
Serbo-Croat.	sladak
Hungarian	édes
Finnish	makea
Turkish	tatlı
Indonesian	manis
Esperanto	dolĉa
Russian	sládki
Greek	glikos'
Arabic	atzb
Hebrew	matok
Yiddish	sies
Japanese	amai
Swahili	-tamu

865 swim

French	nager
Spanish	nadar
Italian	nuotare
Portuguese	nadar
Rumanian	înota
German	schwimmen
Dutch	zwemmen
Swedish	simma
Danish	svømme
Norwegian	svømme
Polish	pływać
Czech	plavati
Serbo-Croat.	plivati
Hungarian	úszik
Finnish	uida
Turkish	yüzmek
Indonesian	berenang
Esperanto	naĝi
Russian	plávat
Greek	kolimbo'
Arabic	yaoum
Hebrew	sachah
Yiddish	schvimmen
Japanese	oyogu
Swahili	ogelea

866 table

French	table
Spanish	mesa
Italian	tavola
Portuguese	mesa
Rumanian	masă
German	Tisch
Dutch	tafel
Swedish	bord
Danish	bord
Norwegian	bord
Polish	stół
Czech	stůl
Serbo-Croat.	sto
Hungarian	asztal
Finnish	pöytä
Turkish	masa
Indonesian	medja
Esperanto	tablo
Russian	stol
Greek	trape'zi
Arabic	mindada
Hebrew	schulchan
Yiddish	tisch
Japanese	shokutaku
Swahili	meza

867 tail

French	queue
Spanish	rabo
Italian	coda
Portuguese	cauda
Rumanian	coadă
German	Schwanz
Dutch	staart
Swedish	svans
Danish	hale
Norwegian	hale
Polish	ogon
Czech	ocas
Serbo-Croat.	rjep
Hungarian	farok
Finnish	häntä
Turkish	kuyruk
Indonesian	ékor
Esperanto	fin'aĵo
Russian	khvost
Greek	oura'
Arabic	tzayl
Hebrew	sanav
Yiddish	vejdel
Japanese	o
Swahili	mkią

868 tailor

French	tailleur
Spanish	sastre
Italian	sarto
Portuguese	alfaiate
Rumanian	croitor
German	Schneider
Dutch	kleermaker
Swedish	skräddare
Danish	skrædder
Norwegian	skredder
Polish	krawiec
Czech	krejčí
Serbo-Croat.	krojač
Hungarian	szabó
Finnish	räätäli
Turkish	terzi
Indonesian	tukang djahit
Esperanto	tajloro
Russian	partnóy
Greek	raf'tis
Arabic	chayyat
Hebrew	chayat
Yiddish	schneider
Japanese	shitateya
Swahili	mshoni

869 take

French	prendre
Spanish	tomar
Italian	prendere
Portuguese	tomar
Rumanian	lua
German	nehmen
Dutch	nemen
Swedish	taga
Danish	tage
Norwegian	ta
Polish	wziąć
Czech	vzíti
Serbo-Croat.	uzeti
Hungarian	vesz
Finnish	ottaa
Turkish	almak
Indonesian	ambil
Esperanto	preni
Russian	vzyat
Greek	per'no
Arabic	yachoutz
Hebrew	lakach
Yiddish	nehmen
Japanese	toru
Swahili	kamata

870 talk

French	parler
Spanish	hablar
Italian	parlare
Portuguese	falar
Rumanian	vorbi
German	reden
Dutch	praten
Swedish	tala
Danish	snakke
Norwegian	snakke
Polish	rozmawiać
Czech	hovořiti
Serbo-Croat.	govariti
Hungarian	társalog
Finnish	puhua
Turkish	konuşma
Indonesian	tjakap
Esperanto	paroli
Russian	skazát
Greek	mila'o
Arabic	yatakalam
Hebrew	diber
Yiddish	redden
Japanese	hanasu
Swahili	nena

871 tall

French	haut
Spanish	alto
Italian	alto
Portuguese	alto
Rumanian	înalt
German	hoch
Dutch	lang
Swedish	hög
Danish	høj
Norwegian	høy
Polish	wysoki
Czech	vysoký
Serbo-Croat.	visok
Hungarian	magas
Finnish	korkea
Turkish	uzun boylu
Indonesian	tinggi
Esperanto	alta
Russian	visóki
Greek	psilos'
Arabic	tawil
Hebrew	gavoha
Yiddish	hoich
Japanese	tak ai
Swahili	-refu

872 taste

French	goût
Spanish	gusto
Italian	gusto
Portuguese	sabor
Rumanian	gust
German	Geschmack
Dutch	smaak
Swedish	smak
Danish	smag
Norwegian	smak
Polish	smak
Czech	vkus
Serbo-Croat.	ukus
Hungarian	íz
Finnish	maku
Turkish	lezzet
Indonesian	rasa
Esperanto	gusto
Russian	fkus
Greek	gou'sto
Arabic	tzawq
Hebrew	taam
Yiddish	taam
Japanese	aji
Swahili	ladha

873 tax

French	impôt
Spanish	impuesto
Italian	imposta
Portuguese	taxa
Rumanian	impozit
German	Steuer
Dutch	belasting
Swedish	skatt
Danish	skat
Norwegian	skatt
Polish	podatek
Czech	daň
Serbo-Croat.	porez
Hungarian	adó
Finnish	vero
Turkish	vergi
Indonesian	padjak
Esperanto	imposto
Russian	nalók
Greek	fo'ros
Arabic	dariba
Hebrew	mass
Yiddish	schteier
Japanese	zei
Swahili	kodi

874 tea

French	thé
Spanish	té
Italian	tè
Portuguese	chá
Rumanian	ceai
German	Tee
Dutch	thee
Swedish	te
Danish	te
Norwegian	te
Polish	herbata
Czech	čaj
Serbo-Croat.	čaj
Hungarian	tea
Finnish	tee
Turkish	çay
Indonesian	téh
Esperanto	teo
Russian	cháy
Greek	tsa'-i
Arabic	shaye
Hebrew	teh
Yiddish	tay
Japanese	cha
Swahili	chai

875 teacher

French	instituteur
Spanish	maestro
Italian	insegnante
Portuguese	professor
Rumanian	învăţător
German	Lehrer
Dutch	onderwijzer
Swedish	lärare
Danish	lærer
Norwegian	lærer
Polish	nauczyciel
Czech	učitel
Serbo-Croat.	nastavnik
Hungarian	tanító
Finnish	opettaja
Turkish	öğretmen
Indonesian	gura
Esperanto	instru'isto
Russian	uchítel
Greek	das'kalos
Arabic	moualim, moudaris
Hebrew	moreh
Yiddish	lehrer
Japanese	kyooshi
Swahili	mwalimu

876 tedious

French	ennuyeux
Spanish	aburrido
Italian	tedioso
Portuguese	aborrecido
Rumanian	plicticos
German	langweilig
Dutch	saai
Swedish	tråkig
Danish	kedelig
Norwegian	kjedelig
Polish	nudny
Czech	nudný
Serbo-Croat.	dosadan
Hungarian	unalmas
Finnish	ikävä
Turkish	usandırıcı
Indonesian	bojak, djemu
Esperanto	teda
Russian	skúchni
Greek	aniaros'
Arabic	moumil
Hebrew	meyagea
Yiddish	nudne
Japanese	taikutsu
Swahili	-a kuchosha

877 television

French	télévision
Spanish	televisión
Italian	televisione
Portuguese	televisão
Rumanian	televiziune
German	Fernsehen
Dutch	televisie
Swedish	television
Danish	fjernsyn
Norwegian	fjernsyn
Polish	telewizja
Czech	televize
Serbo-Croat.	televizja
Hungarian	televízió
Finnish	televisio
Turkish	televizyon
Indonesian	televisi
Esperanto	televid'ado
Russian	televidyéniye
Greek	tileo'rasis
Arabic	telefizion
Hebrew	sikayon
Yiddish	televizje
Japanese	terebijon
Swahili	televisioni

878 ten

French	dix
Spanish	diez
Italian	dieci
Portuguese	dez
Rumanian	zece
German	zehn
Dutch	tien
Swedish	tio
Danish	ti
Norwegian	ti
Polish	dziesięć
Czech	deset
Serbo-Croat.	deset
Hungarian	tíz
Finnish	kymmenen
Turkish	on
Indonesian	sepuluh
Esperanto	dek
Russian	dyésit
Greek	de'ka
Arabic	ashara
Hebrew	asarah
Yiddish	tsehn
Japanese	juu
Swahili	kuma

879 tent

French	tente
Spanish	tienda
Italian	tenda
Portuguese	tenda
Rumanian	cort
German	Zelt
Dutch	tent
Swedish	tält
Danish	telt
Norwegian	telt
Polish	namiot
Czech	stan
Serbo-Croat.	šator
Hungarian	sátor
Finnish	teltta
Turkish	çadır
Indonesian	kémah
Esperanto	tendo
Russian	palátka
Greek	ten'ta
Arabic	chayma
Hebrew	ohel
Yiddish	getselt
Japanese	tento
Swahili	hema

880 test

French	test
Spanish	prueba
Italian	prova
Portuguese	prova
Rumanian	probă
German	Prüfung
Dutch	proef
Swedish	prov
Danish	prøve
Norwegian	prøve
Polish	próba
Czech	zkouška
Serbo-Croat.	proba
Hungarian	vizsga
Finnish	testi
Turkish	deneme
Indonesian	udjian
Esperanto	provo
Russian	eksámen
Greek	a'skisis
Arabic	imtihan
Hebrew	nissayon
Yiddish	eksamin
Japanese	shiken
Swahili	jaribu

881 thanks

French	merci
Spanish	gracias
Italian	grazie
Portuguese	obrigado
Rumanian	mulţumiri
German	danke
Dutch	dank
Swedish	tack
Danish	tak
Norwegian	takk
Polish	dziękuje
Czech	děkuji
Serbo-Croat.	hvala
Hungarian	köszönöm
Finnish	kiitos
Turkish	teşekkür
Indonesian	terima kasih
Esperanto	dankon
Russian	spasíbo
Greek	efcharisto'
Arabic	shoukran
Hebrew	todah
Yiddish	dank
Japanese	kansha suru
Swahili	asante

882 theater

French	théâtre
Spanish	teatro
Italian	teatro
Portuguese	teatro
Rumanian	teatru
German	Theater
Dutch	schouwburg
Swedish	teater
Danish	teater
Norwegian	teater
Polish	teatr
Czech	divadlo
Serbo-Croat.	kozalište
Hungarian	színház
Finnish	teatteri
Turkish	tiyatro
Indonesian	rumah komidi
Esperanto	teatro
Russian	teátr
Greek	the'atron
Arabic	masrah
Hebrew	teatron
Yiddish	teater
Japanese	gekijoo
Swahili	nyumba ya vishikesho

883 there

French	là
Spanish	allí
Italian	là
Portuguese	alí
Rumanian	acolo
German	dort
Dutch	daar
Swedish	där
Danish	der
Norwegian	der
Polish	tam
Czech	tam
Serbo-Croat.	tamo
Hungarian	ott
Finnish	siellä
Turkish	orada
Indonesian	situ, sana
Esperanto	tie
Russian	tam
Greek	eki'
Arabic	hounak
Hebrew	scham
Yiddish	dorten
Japanese	soko ni
Swahili	pale

884 thick

French	épais
Spanish	espeso
Italian	spesso
Portuguese	espêsso
Rumanian	gros
German	dick
Dutch	dik
Swedish	tjock
Danish	tyk
Norwegian	tykk
Polish	gruby
Czech	tlustý
Serbo-Croat.	debeo
Hungarian	vastag
Finnish	paksu
Turkish	kalın
Indonesian	tebal
Esperanto	dika
Russian	tólsti
Greek	piknos'
Arabic	katsif
Hebrew	aveh
Yiddish	grob
Japanese	atsui
Swahili	-zito

885 thief

French	voleur
Spanish	ladrón
Italian	ladro
Portuguese	ladrão
Rumanian	hoţ
German	Dieb
Dutch	dief
Swedish	tjuv
Danish	tyv
Norwegian	tyv
Polish	złodziej
Czech	zloděj
Serbo-Croat.	kradljvac
Hungarian	tolvaj
Finnish	varas
Turkish	hırsız
Indonesian	maling, pentjuri
Esperanto	ŝtel'isto
Russian	vor
Greek	klef'tis
Arabic	liss
Hebrew	ganav
Yiddish	ganev
Japanese	nusubito
Swahili	mwivi

886 thigh

French	cuisse
Spanish	muslo
Italian	coscia
Portuguese	coxa
Rumanian	coapsă
German	Oberschenkel
Dutch	dij
Swedish	lår
Danish	lår
Norwegian	lår
Polish	udo
Czech	stehno
Serbo-Croat.	bjedro
Hungarian	comb
Finnish	reisi
Turkish	uyluk
Indonesian	paha
Esperanto	femuro
Russian	bedró
Greek	miros'
Arabic	fachtz
Hebrew	yarech
Yiddish	diech
Japanese	momo
Swahili	upaja

887 thin

French	mince
Spanish	delgado
Italian	sottile
Portuguese	delgado
Rumanian	subţire
German	dünn
Dutch	dun
Swedish	tunn
Danish	tynd
Norwegian	tynn
Polish	cienki
Czech	tenký
Serbo-Croat.	tanak
Hungarian	vékony
Finnish	ohut
Turkish	ince
Indonesian	tipis, kurus
Esperanto	mal'dika
Russian	tónki
Greek	leptos'
Arabic	nahif
Hebrew	dak
Yiddish	din
Japanese	usui
Swahili	-embamba

888 think

French	penser
Spanish	pensar
Italian	pensare
Portuguese	pensar
Rumanian	gîndi
German	denken
Dutch	denken
Swedish	tänka
Danish	tænke
Norwegian	tenke
Polish	myśleć
Czech	mysliti
Serbo-Croat.	misliti
Hungarian	gondol
Finnish	ajatella
Turkish	düsünmek
Indonesian	pikir
Esperanto	pensi
Russian	dúmat
Greek	nomi'zo, skep'tome
Arabic	youfakir
Hebrew	chaschav
Yiddish	trachten
Japanese	omou
Swahili	fikiri

889 thirst

French	soif
Spanish	sed
Italian	sete
Portuguese	sêde
Rumanian	sete
German	Durst
Dutch	dorst
Swedish	törst
Danish	tørst
Norwegian	tørst
Polish	pragnienie
Czech	žizeň
Serbo-Croat.	žed
Hungarian	szomjúság
Finnish	jano
Turkish	suszluk
Indonesian	haus
Esperanto	soifo
Russian	zházhda
Greek	di'psa
Arabic	atash
Hebrew	tsama
Yiddish	darscht
Japanese	kawaki
Swahili	kiu

890 thirteen

French	treize
Spanish	trece
Italian	tredici
Portuguese	treze
Rumanian	treisprezece
German	dreizehn
Dutch	dertien
Swedish	tretton
Danish	tretten
Norwegian	tretten
Polish	trzynaście
Czech	třináct
Serbo-Croat.	trinaest
Hungarian	tizenhárom
Finnish	kolmetoista
Turkish	on üç
Indonesian	tigabelas
Esperanto	dek tri
Russian	trinátsit
Greek	dekatri'a
Arabic	tsalatsat ashar
Hebrew	schloschah assar
Yiddish	dreitsen
Japanese	juusan
Swahili	kumi na tatu

891 thirty

French	trente
Spanish	treinta
Italian	trenta
Portuguese	trinta
Rumanian	treizeci
German	dreissig
Dutch	dertig
Swedish	trettio
Danish	tredive
Norwegian	tredve
Polish	trzydzieści
Czech	třicet
Serbo-Croat.	trideset
Hungarian	harminc
Finnish	kolmekymmentä
Turkish	otuz
Indonesian	tigapulah
Esperanto	tri'dek
Russian	trítset
Greek	trian'ta
Arabic	tsalatsoun
Hebrew	schloschim
Yiddish	dreissig
Japanese	sanjuu
Swahili	thelathini

892 thousand

French	mille
Spanish	mil
Italian	mille
Portuguese	mil
Rumanian	mie
German	tausend
Dutch	duizend
Swedish	tusen
Danish	tusind
Norwegian	tusen
Polish	tysiąc
Czech	tisíc
Serbo-Croat.	hiljada
Hungarian	ezer
Finnish	tuhat
Turkish	bin
Indonesian	seribu
Esperanto	mil
Russian	tísicha
Greek	chi'lia
Arabic	alf
Hebrew	elef
Yiddish	toisend
Japanese	sen
Swahili	elfu

893 thread

French	fil
Spanish	hilo
Italian	filo
Portuguese	fio
Rumanian	aţă
German	Faden
Dutch	draad
Swedish	tråd
Danish	tråd
Norwegian	tråd
Polish	nitka
Czech	nit
Serbo-Croat.	nit
Hungarian	cérna
Finnish	lanka
Turkish	iplik
Indonesian	benang
Esperanto	fadeno
Russian	nítka
Greek	klosti'
Arabic	chayt
Hebrew	chut
Yiddish	fodim
Japanese	ito
Swahili	uzi

894 three

French	trois
Spanish	tres
Italian	tre
Portuguese	três
Rumanian	trei
German	drei
Dutch	drie
Swedish	tre
Danish	tre
Norwegian	tre
Polish	trzy
Czech	tři
Serbo-Croat.	tri
Hungarian	három
Finnish	kolme
Turkish	üç
Indonesian	tiga
Esperanto	tri
Russian	tri
Greek	tri'a
Arabic	tsalatsa
Hebrew	schloschah
Yiddish	drei
Japanese	san
Swahili	tatu

895 throat

French	gorge
Spanish	garganta
Italian	gola
Portuguese	garganta
Rumanian	gîtlej
German	Kehle
Dutch	keel
Swedish	strupe
Danish	strube
Norwegian	strupe
Polish	gardło
Czech	hrdlo
Serbo-Croat.	grlo
Hungarian	torok
Finnish	kurkku
Turkish	boğaz
Indonesian	kerongkongan
Esperanto	gorĝo
Russian	górlo
Greek	lemos'
Arabic	halq
Hebrew	garon
Yiddish	halts
Japanese	nodo
Swahili	koo

896 throw

French	jeter
Spanish	arrojar
Italian	gettare
Portuguese	lançar
Rumanian	arunca
German	werfen
Dutch	worp
Swedish	kasta
Danish	kaste
Norwegian	kaste
Polish	rzucać
Czech	hoditi
Serbo-Croat.	bacati
Hungarian	dob
Finnish	heittää
Turkish	atmak
Indonesian	lémpar
Esperanto	ĵeti
Russian	brasát
Greek	ri'chno
Arabic	yarmi
Hebrew	sarak
Yiddish	varfen
Japanese	nageru
Swahili	tupa

897 thumb

French	pouce
Spanish	pulgar
Italian	pollice
Portuguese	polegar
Rumanian	degetul mare
German	Daumen
Dutch	duim
Swedish	tumme
Danish	tommelfinger
Norwegian	tommelfinger
Polish	kciuk
Czech	palec
Serbo-Croat.	palac
Hungarian	hüvelykujj
Finnish	peukalo
Turkish	baş parmak
Indonesian	djempol, ibu djari
Esperanto	polekso
Russian	bolshóy pálets
Greek	anti'chir
Arabic	ibham al-yad
Hebrew	bohen
Yiddish	doimen
Japanese	oyayubi
Swahili	kidole cha gumba

898 thunder

French	tonnerre
Spanish	trueno
Italian	tuono
Portuguese	trovão
Rumanian	tunet
German	Donner
Dutch	donder
Swedish	åska
Danish	torden
Norwegian	torden
Polish	grzmot
Czech	hrom
Serbo-Croat.	grom
Hungarian	mennydörgés
Finnish	ukkonen
Turkish	gök gürlemesi
Indonesian	guntur, gurah
Esperanto	tondro
Russian	grom
Greek	keravnos'
Arabic	raad
Hebrew	raam
Yiddish	dunner
Japanese	raimei
Swahili	radi

899 Thursday

French	jeudi
Spanish	jueves
Italian	giovedi
Portuguese	quinta-feira
Rumanian	joi
German	Donnerstag
Dutch	Donderdag
Swedish	torsdag
Danish	torsdag
Norwegian	torsdag
Polish	czwartek
Czech	čtvrtek
Serbo-Croat.	četvrtak
Hungarian	csütörtök
Finnish	torstai
Turkish	perşembe
Indonesian	Kemis
Esperanto	ĵaŭdo
Russian	chetvérk
Greek	Pem'pti
Arabic	youm al-chamis
Hebrew	yom chamischi
Yiddish	donnerschtog
Japanese	mokuyoobi
Swahili	Alhamjsi

900 ticket

French	billet
Spanish	billete
Italian	biglietto
Portuguese	bilhete
Rumanian	bilet
German	Fahrkarte
Dutch	kaartje
Swedish	biljett
Danish	billet
Norwegian	billet
Polish	bilet
Czech	vstupenka
Serbo-Croat.	ulaznica
Hungarian	jegy
Finnish	lippu
Turkish	bilet
Indonesian	kartjis, teket
Esperanto	bileto
Russian	bilyét
Greek	isiti'rion
Arabic	tatzkara
Hebrew	kartis
Yiddish	bilet
Japanese	kippu
Swahili	tikiti

901 tie

French	cravate
Spanish	corbata
Italian	cravatta
Portuguese	gravata
Rumanian	cravată
German	Krawatte
Dutch	das
Swedish	slips
Danish	slips
Norwegian	slips
Polish	krawat
Czech	kravata
Serbo-Croat.	kravata
Hungarian	nyakkendő
Finnish	kravatti
Turkish	kravat
Indonesian	dasi
Esperanto	kravato
Russian	gálstuk
Greek	grava'ta
Arabic	roubat al-ounouq
Hebrew	anivah
Yiddish	kravat
Japanese	nekutai
Swahili	kitambaa cha shingoni

902 tiger

French	tigre
Spanish	tigre
Italian	tigre
Portuguese	tigre
Rumanian	tigru
German	Tiger
Dutch	tijger
Swedish	tiger
Danish	tiger
Norwegian	tiger
Polish	tygrys
Czech	tygr
Serbo-Croat.	tigar
Hungarian	tigris
Finnish	tiikeri
Turkish	kaplan
Indonesian	harimau
Esperanto	tigro
Russian	tigr
Greek	ti'gris
Arabic	nimr
Hebrew	namer
Yiddish	tiger
Japanese	tora
Swahili	mnyama kama chui mkubwa

903 time

French	temps
Spanish	tiempo
Italian	tempo
Portuguese	tempo
Rumanian	timp
German	Zeit
Dutch	tijd
Swedish	tid
Danish	tid
Norwegian	tid
Polish	czas
Czech	čas
Serbo-Croat.	vrijeme
Hungarian	idő
Finnish	aika
Turkish	saat
Indonesian	waktu
Esperanto	tempo
Russian	vryémya
Greek	chro'nos
Arabic	waqt
Hebrew	sman
Yiddish	tseit
Japanese	jikan
Swahili	wakati

904 timetable

French	horaire
Spanish	horario
Italian	orario
Portuguese	horário
Rumanian	orar
German	Fahrplan
Dutch	dienstregeling
Swedish	tidtabell
Danish	køreplan
Norwegian	timetabell
Polish	rozkład
Czech	jízdni řád
Serbo-Croat.	vozni red
Hungarian	menetrend
Finnish	aikataulu
Turkish	tarife
Indonesian	buk sepur
Esperanto	hor'aro
Russian	raspisánye
Greek	dromolo'gion
Arabic	gadwal al-tawqit
Hebrew	luach haschaot
Yiddish	fohrplan
Japanese	jikanhyoo
Swahili	orodha ya saa

905 tin

French	étain
Spanish	estaño
Italian	stagno
Portuguese	estanho
Rumanian	cositor
German	Zinn
Dutch	tin
Swedish	tenn
Danish	tin, blik
Norwegian	blikk
Polish	cyna
Czech	cín
Serbo-Croat.	kalaj
Hungarian	ón
Finnish	tina
Turkish	teneke
Indonesian	timah
Esperanto	stano
Russian	ólovo
Greek	kassi'teros
Arabic	safih
Hebrew	pach
Yiddish	blech
Japanese	suzu
Swahili	bati

906 tire

French	pneu
Spanish	neumático
Italian	pneumatico
Portuguese	pneu
Rumanian	anvelopă
German	Reifen
Dutch	band
Swedish	däck
Danish	dæk
Norwegian	dekk
Polish	opona
Czech	pneumatika
Serbo-Croat.	gumeni obruč
Hungarian	pneumatik
Finnish	pyörän rengas
Turkish	lâstik
Indonesian	ban roda
Esperanto	bendo
Russian	shína
Greek	las'ticho aftikini'tou
Arabic	itar
Hebrew	tsamig
Yiddish	reifen
Japanese	taiya
Swahili	mpira

907 tired

French	fatigué
Spanish	cansado
Italian	stanco
Portuguese	cansado
Rumanian	obosit
German	müde
Dutch	vermoeid
Swedish	trött
Danish	træt
Norwegian	trøtt
Polish	zmęczony
Czech	unavený
Serbo-Croat.	umoran
Hungarian	fáradt
Finnish	väsynyt
Turkish	yorgun
Indonesian	penat
Esperanto	laca
Russian	ustáli
Greek	kourasme'nos
Arabic	moutaab
Hebrew	ayef
Yiddish	mied
Japanese	tsukareta
Swahili	chovu

908 toast

French	toast
Spanish	tostada
Italian	crostino
Portuguese	torrada
Rumanian	pîine prăjita
German	Geröstetes Brot
Dutch	geroosterd brood
Swedish	rostat bröd
Danish	ristet brød
Norwegian	ristet brød
Polish	grzanka
Czech	opékaný chléb
Serbo-Croat.	prženi hlijeb
Hungarian	pirítós
Finnish	paahtoleipä
Turkish	kızarmış ekmek
Indonesian	roti panggang
Esperanto	rost'pano
Russian	grenkí
Greek	frigania'
Arabic	toast
Hebrew	karpadah
Yiddish	gebroint broit
Japanese	toosuto
Swahili	mkate uliochomwa

909 tobacco

French	tabac
Spanish	tabaco
Italian	tabacco
Portuguese	tabaco
Rumanian	tutun
German	Tabak
Dutch	tabak
Swedish	tobak
Danish	tobak
Norwegian	tobakk
Polish	tytoń
Czech	tabák
Serbo-Croat.	duhan
Hungarian	dohány
Finnish	tupakka
Turkish	tütün
Indonesian	tĕmpakau
Esperanto	tabako
Russian	tabák
Greek	kapnos'
Arabic	tabgh
Hebrew	tabak
Yiddish	tabik
Japanese	tabako
Swahili	tumbako

910 today

French	aujourd'hui
Spanish	hoy
Italian	oggi
Portuguese	hoje
Rumanian	azi
German	heute
Dutch	vandaag
Swedish	i dag
Danish	i dag
Norwegian	i dag
Polish	dziś
Czech	dnes
Serbo-Croat.	danas
Hungarian	ma
Finnish	tänään
Turkish	bugün
Indonesian	hari ini
Esperanto	hodiaŭ
Russian	sivódnya
Greek	si'mera
Arabic	al-youm
Hebrew	hayom
Yiddish	haint
Japanese	kyoo
Swahili	leo

911 toe

French	orteil
Spanish	dedo del pie
Italian	dito del piedo
Portuguese	dedo do pé
Rumanian	deget la picior
German	Zehe
Dutch	teen
Swedish	tå
Danish	tå
Norwegian	tå
Polish	palec u nogi
Czech	prst
Serbo-Croat.	nožni prst
Hungarian	lábujj
Finnish	varvas
Turkish	ayak parmağı
Indonesian	djari kaki
Esperanto	pied'fingro
Russian	paléts na nóge
Greek	dak'tilos tou podiou'
Arabic	isba al-qadam
Hebrew	etsba haregel
Yiddish	fussfinger
Japanese	tsumasaki
Swahili	kidole cha mguu

912 together

French	ensemble
Spanish	juntos
Italian	insieme
Portuguese	junto
Rumanian	împreună
German	zusammen
Dutch	samen
Swedish	tillsammans
Danish	sammen
Norwegian	sammen
Polish	razem
Czech	dohromady
Serbo-Croat.	zajedno
Hungarian	együtt
Finnish	yhdessä
Turkish	beraber
Indonesian	bersama
Esperanto	kune
Russian	vmyéste
Greek	mazi'
Arabic	maan
Hebrew	yachad
Yiddish	tsusammen
Japanese	issho ni
Swahili	pamoja

913 toilet (WC)

French	cabinet
Spanish	retrete
Italian	gabinetto
Portuguese	retrete
Rumanian	toaletă
German	Abort
Dutch	toilet
Swedish	toalett
Danish	W. C.
Norwegian	toalett, W.C.
Polish	ustęp
Czech	toaleta
Serbo-Croat.	toaleta
Hungarian	árnyékszék
Finnish	W.C.
Turkish	tuvalet
Indonesian	djamban
Esperanto	neces'ejo
Russian	ubórnaya
Greek	touale'ta
Arabic	mirhad
Hebrew	beth kavod
Yiddish	abord
Japanese	benjo
Swahili	choo

914 tomato

French	tomate
Spanish	tomate
Italian	pomodoro
Portuguese	tomate
Rumanian	roşie
German	Tomate
Dutch	tomaat
Swedish	tomat
Danish	tomat
Norwegian	tomat
Polish	pomidor
Czech	rajské jablíčko
Serbo-Croat.	paradajz
Hungarian	paradicsom
Finnish	tomaatti
Turkish	domates
Indonesian	tomat
Esperanto	tomato
Russian	pamidór
Greek	toma'ta
Arabic	tamatim
Hebrew	agbaniyah
Yiddish	paradisepel
Japanese	tomato
Swahili	nyanya

915 tomorrow

French	demain
Spanish	mañana
Italian	domani
Portuguese	amanhã
Rumanian	mîine
German	morgen
Dutch	morgen
Swedish	i morgon
Danish	i morgen
Norwegian	i morgen
Polish	jutro
Czech	zítra
Serbo-Croat.	sutradan
Hungarian	holnap
Finnish	huomenna
Turkish	yarın
Indonesian	bésok, ésok
Esperanto	morgaŭ
Russian	zaftra
Greek	a'vrio
Arabic	ghadan
Hebrew	machar
Yiddish	morgen
Japanese	asu
Swahili	kesho

916 tongue

French	langue
Spanish	lengua
Italian	lingua
Portuguese	língua
Rumanian	limbă
German	Zunge
Dutch	tong
Swedish	tunga
Danish	tunge
Norwegian	tunge
Polish	język
Czech	jazyk
Serbo-Croat.	jezik
Hungarian	nyelv
Finnish	kieli
Turkish	dil
Indonesian	lidah
Esperanto	lango
Russian	yazík
Greek	glo'ssa
Arabic	lougha
Hebrew	laschon
Yiddish	tsung
Japanese	shita
Swahili	ulimi

917 tooth

French	dent
Spanish	diente
Italian	dente
Portuguese	dente
Rumanian	dinte
German	Zahn
Dutch	tand
Swedish	tand
Danish	tand
Norwegian	tann
Polish	ząb
Czech	zub
Serbo-Croat.	zub
Hungarian	fog
Finnish	hammas
Turkish	diş
Indonesian	gigi
Esperanto	dento
Russian	zup
Greek	don'di
Arabic	sin
Hebrew	schen
Yiddish	tsohn
Japanese	ha
Swahili	jino

918 toothbrush

French	brosse à dents
Spanish	cepillo de dientes
Italian	spazzolino da denti
Portuguese	escova de dentes
Rumanian	periuţa de dinţi
German	Zahnbürste
Dutch	tandenborstel
Swedish	tandborste
Danish	tanbørste
Norwegian	tannbørste
Polish	szczotka do zębów
Czech	kartáček na zuby
Serbo-Croat.	četkica za zuba
Hungarian	fogkefe
Finnish	hammasharja
Turkish	diş fırçası
Indonesian	sikat gigi
Esperanto	dent'broso
Russian	zubnáya shchótka
Greek	odonto'vourtsa
Arabic	fourshat asnan
Hebrew	mivreschet schinayim
Yiddish	tsain-berschtel
Japanese	haburashi
Swahili	mswaki

919 towel

French	serviette
Spanish	toalla
Italian	asciugamano
Portuguese	toalha
Rumanian	prosop
German	Handtuch
Dutch	handdoek
Swedish	handduk
Danish	håndklæde
Norwegian	håndkle
Polish	ręcznik
Czech	ručník
Serbo-Croat.	ručnik
Hungarian	törülköző
Finnish	pyyheliina
Turkish	havlu
Indonesian	handuk
Esperanto	viš'tuko
Russian	palatyéntse
Greek	petse'ta
Arabic	fouta
Hebrew	magevet
Yiddish	handtuch
Japanese	taoru
Swahili	kitambaa cha kufutia

920 town

French	ville
Spanish	ciudad
Italian	città
Portuguese	cidade
Rumanian	oraş
German	Stadt
Dutch	stad
Swedish	stad
Danish	by
Norwegian	by
Polish	miasto
Czech	město
Serbo-Croat.	grad
Hungarian	város
Finnish	kaupunki
Turkish	şehir
Indonesian	kota
Esperanto	urbo
Russian	górat
Greek	po'lis
Arabic	bilda
Hebrew	ier
Yiddish	schtodt
Japanese	machi
Swahili	mji

921 toy

French	jouet
Spanish	juguete
Italian	giocattolo
Portuguese	brinquedo
Rumanian	jucărie
German	Spielzeug
Dutch	speelgoed
Swedish	leksak
Danish	legetøj
Norwegian	leketøy
Polish	zabawka
Czech	hračka
Serbo-Croat.	igračka
Hungarian	játék
Finnish	lelu
Turkish	oyuncak
Indonesian	permainan
Esperanto	lud'ilo
Russian	igrúschka
Greek	pechni'di
Arabic	louba
Hebrew	schaaschua
Yiddish	tsatske
Japanese	omocha
Swahili	kitu cha kuchezea

922 train

French	train
Spanish	tren
Italian	treno
Portuguese	trem
Rumanian	trenă
German	Zug
Dutch	trein
Swedish	tåg
Danish	tog
Norwegian	tog
Polish	pociąg
Czech	vlak
Serbo-Croat.	voz
Hungarian	vonat
Finnish	juna
Turkish	tren
Indonesian	kereta api
Esperanto	trajno
Russian	póyist
Greek	tre'no
Arabic	qitar
Hebrew	rakevet
Yiddish	tsug
Japanese	kisha
Swahili	gari la moshi

923 translate

French	traduire
Spanish	traducir
Italian	tradurre
Portuguese	traduzir
Rumanian	traduce
German	übersetzen
Dutch	vertalen
Swedish	översätta
Danish	oversætte
Norwegian	oversette
Polish	tłumaczyć
Czech	překládati
Serbo-Croat.	prevesti
Hungarian	fordít
Finnish	kääntää
Turkish	tercüme etmek
Indonesian	salin
Esperanto	traduki
Russian	perevadít
Greek	metafra'zo
Arabic	youtargim
Hebrew	tirgem
Yiddish	ibersetsen
Japanese	hon'yaku suru
Swahili	fasiri

924 transparent

French	transparent
Spanish	transparente
Italian	trasparente
Portuguese	transparente
Rumanian	transparent
German	durchsichtig
Dutch	doorzichtig
Swedish	genomskinlig
Danish	gennemsigtig
Norwegian	gjennomsiktig
Polish	przezroczysty
Czech	průhledný
Serbo-Croat.	providan
Hungarian	átlátszó
Finnish	läpikuultava
Turkish	şeffaf
Indonesian	djernih
Esperanto	tra'vid'ebla
Russian	prazráchni
Greek	diafanis'
Arabic	shaffaf
Hebrew	schakuf
Yiddish	durchsichtig
Japanese	toomei na
Swahili	-a kupenyeka nuru

925 travel

French	voyager
Spanish	viajar
Italian	viaggiare
Portuguese	viajar
Rumanian	călătorie
German	reisen
Dutch	reizen
Swedish	resa
Danish	rejse
Norwegian	reise
Polish	podróżować
Czech	cestovati
Serbo-Croat.	putovati
Hungarian	utazik
Finnish	matkustaa
Turkish	seyahat
Indonesian	perdjalanan
Esperanto	vojaĝi
Russian	putishéstvovat
Greek	taxide'vo
Arabic	yousafir
Hebrew	nassah
Yiddish	fohren
Japanese	tabi suru
Swahili	safiri

926 tree

French	arbre
Spanish	árbol
Italian	albero
Portuguese	árvore
Rumanian	arbore
German	Baum
Dutch	boom
Swedish	träd
Danish	træ
Norwegian	tre
Polish	drzewo
Czech	strom
Serbo-Croat.	drvo
Hungarian	fa
Finnish	puu
Turkish	ağaç
Indonesian	pohon
Esperanto	arbo
Russian	dyérevo
Greek	den'dron
Arabic	shagara
Hebrew	ilan
Yiddish	boim
Japanese	ki
Swahili	mti

927 trouble

French	trouble
Spanish	molestia
Italian	disturbo
Portuguese	perturbacão
Rumanian	necaz
German	Verdruss
Dutch	moeite
Swedish	bekymmer
Danish	sorg
Norwegian	vanskelighet
Polish	kłopot
Czech	nesnáz
Serbo-Croat.	nevolja
Hungarian	gond
Finnish	huoli
Turkish	zahmet
Indonesian	susah
Esperanto	ĝeno
Russian	górye
Greek	fasari'a
Arabic	mashakil
Hebrew	tsara
Yiddish	tsore
Japanese	mendoo
Swahili	mashaki

928 trousers

French	pantalons
Spanish	pantalones
Italian	pantaloni
Portuguese	calças
Rumanian	pantaloni
German	Hosen
Dutch	broek
Swedish	byxor
Danish	bukser
Norwegian	bukser
Polish	spodnie
Czech	kalhoty
Serbo-Croat.	hlače
Hungarian	nadrág
Finnish	housut
Turkish	pantalon
Indonesian	tjelan
Esperanto	pantalono
Russian	bryúki
Greek	pantalo'ni
Arabic	sirwal
Hebrew	michnassayim
Yiddish	hoisen
Japanese	zubon
Swahili	suruali

929 truth

French	vérité
Spanish	verdad
Italian	verità
Portuguese	verdade
Rumanian	adevăr
German	Wahrheit
Dutch	waarheid
Swedish	sanning
Danish	sandhed
Norwegian	sanhet
Polish	prawda
Czech	pravda
Serbo-Croat.	istina
Hungarian	igazság
Finnish	totuus
Turkish	doğruluk
Indonesian	kebenaran
Esperanto	vero
Russian	právda
Greek	ali'thia
Arabic	hakeeka
Hebrew	emet
Yiddish	emes
Japanese	shinjitsu
Swahili	kweli

930 try

French	essayer
Spanish	probar
Italian	provare
Portuguese	provar
Rumanian	încerca
German	versuchen
Dutch	proberen
Swedish	försöka
Danish	forsøge
Norwegian	forsøke
Polish	próbować
Czech	zkusiti
Serbo-Croat.	pokušati
Hungarian	megkisérel
Finnish	koettaa
Turkish	denemek
Indonesian	tjoba
Esperanto	peni
Russian	pitátsa
Greek	prospatho'
Arabic	youhawil
Hebrew	nissah
Yiddish	prufen
Japanese	kokoromiru
Swahili	jaribu

931 Tuesday

French	mardi
Spanish	martes
Italian	martedi
Portuguese	têrca-feira
Rumanian	marţi
German	Dienstag
Dutch	Dinsdag
Swedish	tisdag
Danish	tirsdag
Norwegian	tirsdag
Polish	wtorek
Czech	úterý
Serbo-Croat.	utorak
Hungarian	kedd
Finnish	tiistai
Turkish	salı
Indonesian	Selasa
Esperanto	mardo
Russian	ftórnik
Greek	Tri'ti
Arabic	youm al-tsoulatsa
Hebrew	yom schelischi
Yiddish	diensttog
Japanese	kwayoobi
Swahili	Jumanne

932 tulip

French	tulipe
Spanish	tulipán
Italian	tulipano
Portuguese	tulipa
Rumanian	lalea
German	Tulpe
Dutch	tulp
Swedish	tulpan
Danish	tulipan
Norwegian	tulipan
Polish	tulipan
Czech	tulipán
Serbo-Croat.	lala
Hungarian	tulipán
Finnish	tulppaani
Turkish	lâle
Indonesian	tulp
Esperanto	tulipo
Russian	tyulpán
Greek	touli'pa
Arabic	chouzama
Hebrew	chasamah
Yiddish	tulpe
Japanese	chuurippu
Swahili	namna ya va

933 turkey

French	dindon
Spanish	pavo
Italian	tacchino
Portuguese	peru
Rumanian	curcan
German	Truthahn
Dutch	kalkoen
Swedish	kalkon
Danish	kalkun
Norwegian	kalkun
Polish	indyk
Czech	krocan
Serbo-Croat.	puran
Hungarian	pulyka
Finnish	kalkkuna
Turkish	hindi
Indonesian	ajam belanda
Esperanto	meleagro
Russian	indyúk
Greek	galopou'la
Arabic	dik roumi
Hebrew	tarnegol hodu
Yiddish	indik
Japanese	shichimenchoo
Swahili	bata mzinga

934 twelve

French	douze
Spanish	doce
Italian	dodici
Portuguese	doze
Rumanian	doisprezece
German	zwölf
Dutch	twaalf
Swedish	tolv
Danish	tolv
Norwegian	tolv
Polish	dwanaście
Czech	dvanáct
Serbo-Croat.	dvanaest
Hungarian	tizenkettő
Finnish	kaksitoista
Turkish	on iki
Indonesian	dua belas
Esperanto	dek du
Russian	dvinátsit
Greek	do'deka
Arabic	itsna ashar
Hebrew	schnayim assar
Yiddish	tsvelif
Japanese	juuni
Swahili	kumi na mbili

935 twenty

French	vingt
Spanish	veinte
Italian	venti
Portuguese	vinte
Rumanian	douăzeci
German	zwanzig
Dutch	twintig
Swedish	tjugu
Danish	tyve
Norwegian	tjue, tyve
Polish	dwadzieścia
Czech	dvacet
Serbo-Croat.	dvadeset
Hungarian	húsz
Finnish	kaksikymmentä
Turkish	yirmi
Indonesian	dua pulah
Esperanto	du'dek
Russian	dvátset
Greek	i'kosi
Arabic	ishroun
Hebrew	essrim
Yiddish	tsvantsig
Japanese	nijuu
Swahili	ishirini

936 two

French	deux
Spanish	dos
Italian	due
Portuguese	dois
Rumanian	doi
German	zwei
Dutch	twee
Swedish	två
Danish	to
Norwegian	to
Polish	dwa
Czech	dvě
Serbo-Croat.	dva
Hungarian	kettő
Finnish	kaksi
Turkish	iki
Indonesian	dud
Esperanto	du
Russian	dva
Greek	di'o
Arabic	itsnayn
Hebrew	schnayim
Yiddish	tsvei
Japanese	ni
Swahili	mbili

937 typewriter

French	machine à écrire
Spanish	máquina de escribir
Italian	dattilografo
Portuguese	datilógrafo
Rumanian	maşină de scris
German	Schreibmaschine
Dutch	schrijfmachine
Swedish	skrivmaskin
Danish	skrivemaskine
Norwegian	skrivemaskin
Polish	maszyna do pisania
Czech	psací stroj
Serbo-Croat.	pisaća mašina
Hungarian	írógép
Finnish	kirjoituskone
Turkish	daktilo makinesi
Indonesian	mesin tulis
Esperanto	skrib'maŝino
Russian	píshushchaya mashína
Greek	grafomichani'
Arabic	ala katiba
Hebrew	mechonat ketivah
Yiddish	schraibmaschin
Japanese	taipuraitaa
Swahili	chombo cha kuandikia

938 ugly

French	laid
Spanish	feo
Italian	brutto
Portuguese	feio
Rumanian	urit
German	hässlich
Dutch	lelijk
Swedish	ful
Danish	grim
Norwegian	heslig
Polish	brzydki
Czech	ošklivý
Serbo-Croat.	ružan
Hungarian	csúnya, ronda
Finnish	ruma
Turkish	çirkin
Indonesian	djelék
Esperanto	mal'bela
Russian	bizabrázni
Greek	as'chimos
Arabic	qabih
Hebrew	mauss
Yiddish	mies
Japanese	minikui
Swahili	-a kuchukiza

939 umbrella

French	parapluie
Spanish	paraguas
Italian	ombrello
Portuguese	guarda chuva
Rumanian	umbrelă
German	Regenschirm
Dutch	paraplu
Swedish	paraply
Danish	paraply
Norwegian	paraply
Polish	parasol
Czech	deštník
Serbo-Croat.	kišobran
Hungarian	ernyő
Finnish	sateenvarjo
Turkish	şemsiye
Indonesian	pajung
Esperanto	ombrelo
Russian	zont
Greek	ombre'la
Arabic	shamsia
Hebrew	schimschiyah
Yiddish	regenschirm
Japanese	koomorigasa
Swahili	mwavuli

940 uncle

French	oncle
Spanish	tío
Italian	zio
Portuguese	tio
Rumanian	unchi
German	Onkel
Dutch	oom
Swedish	farbror
Danish	onkel
Norwegian	onkel
Polish	wuj
Czech	strýc
Serbo-Croat.	ujak
Hungarian	nagybácsi
Finnish	setä, eno
Turkish	amca
Indonesian	paman
Esperanto	onklo
Russian	dyádya
Greek	thi'os
Arabic	amm, chal'
Hebrew	dod
Yiddish	fetter
Japanese	oji
Swahili	mjomba ; amu

941 under

French	sous
Spanish	bajo
Italian	sotto
Portuguese	debaixo de
Rumanian	sub
German	unterhalb
Dutch	onder
Swedish	under
Danish	under
Norwegian	under
Polish	pod
Czech	pod
Serbo-Croat.	ispod
Hungarian	alatt
Finnish	alla
Turkish	altında
Indonesian	bawah
Esperanto	suba
Russian	pod
Greek	ka'to
Arabic	taht
Hebrew	tachat
Yiddish	unter
Japanese	shita ni
Swahili	chini (ya)

942 underground (subway)

French	métro
Spanish	metro
Italian	metropolitana
Portuguese	subterrâneo
Rumanian	metro
German	Untergrundbahn
Dutch	metro
Swedish	tunnelbana
Danish	undergrundsbane
Norwegian	undergrunnsbane
Polish	podziemna kolej
Czech	podzemní dráha
Serbo-Croat.	podzemna
Hungarian	földalatti
Finnish	maanalainen rata
Turkish	metro
Indonesian	kereta api dibawah tanah
Esperanto	sub'vojo
Russian	metró
Greek	ipo'gios
Arabic	mitro
Hebrew	tachtit
Yiddish	untererdische bahn
Japanese	chikatetsu
Swahili	metro

943 understand

French	comprendre
Spanish	comprender
Italian	capire
Portuguese	compreender
Rumanian	înțelege
German	verstehen
Dutch	begrijpen
Swedish	förstå
Danish	forstå
Norwegian	forstå
Polish	rozumieć
Czech	rozuměti
Serbo-Croat.	razjumeti
Hungarian	megért
Finnish	ymmärtää
Turkish	anlamak
Indonesian	mengerti, paham
Esperanto	kompreni
Russian	panimát
Greek	katalave'no
Arabic	yafham
Hebrew	hevin
Yiddish	farschteyen
Japanese	ryookai suru
Swahili	fahamu

944 until

French	jusqu'à
Spanish	hasta
Italian	sino
Portuguese	até
Rumanian	pînă
German	bis
Dutch	tot
Swedish	till
Danish	til
Norwegian	til
Polish	dopóki
Czech	až
Serbo-Croat.	do
Hungarian	amíg
Finnish	asti, saakka
Turkish	kadar
Indonesian	sampai
Esperanto	ĝis
Russian	paká
Greek	me'chri
Arabic	ila ann
Hebrew	ad
Yiddish	biz
Japanese	made
Swahili	hata

945 upstairs

French	en haut
Spanish	arriba
Italian	sopra
Portuguese	em cima
Rumanian	sus
German	oben
Dutch	boven
Swedish	uppe
Danish	oppe
Norwegian	ovenpå, oppe
Polish	na górze
Czech	nahoře
Serbo-Croat.	gore
Hungarian	fenn
Finnish	yläkertaan
Turkish	yukarıda
Indonesian	keatas
Esperanto	supre
Russian	naverkhú
Greek	epa'no
Arabic	al-dour al-aala
Hebrew	lemalah
Yiddish	oiben
Japanese	nikai no
Swahili	orofani

946 urgent

French	urgent
Spanish	urgente
Italian	urgente
Portuguese	urgente
Rumanian	urgent
German	dringend
Dutch	dringend
Swedish	trängande
Danish	haster
Norwegian	inntrengende
Polish	pilny
Czech	naléhavý
Serbo-Croat.	hitan
Hungarian	sürgős
Finnish	pakottava
Turkish	acele
Indonesian	sangat perlu
Esperanto	urĝa
Russian	nastayátelni
Greek	epi'gon
Arabic	ham, darouri
Hebrew	tachuf
Yiddish	teikef
Japanese	kinkyuu no
Swahili	-a lazima

947 use

French	usage
Spanish	uso
Italian	uso
Portuguese	uso
Rumanian	întrebuinţare
German	Gebrauch
Dutch	gebruik
Swedish	användning
Danish	brug
Norwegian	bruk
Polish	użytek
Czech	užíváni
Serbo-Croat.	upotreba
Hungarian	használat
Finnish	käyttö
Turkish	istimal
Indonesian	pemakaian
Esperanto	kutimo
Russian	upatreblyéniye
Greek	chri'sis
Arabic	istimal
Hebrew	schimusch
Yiddish	gebroich
Japanese	shiyoo
Swahili	matumizi

948 vaccination

French	vaccination
Spanish	vacunación
Italian	vaccinazione
Portuguese	vacinação
Rumanian	vaccinare
German	Impfung
Dutch	vaccinatie
Swedish	vaccinering
Danish	vaccination
Norwegian	vaksinasjon
Polish	szczepienie
Czech	očkování
Serbo-Croat.	cijepljenje
Hungarian	oltás
Finnish	rokotus
Turkish	aşılama
Indonesian	pentjatjaran
Esperanto	vakcino
Russian	privífka
Greek	emvoliasmos'
Arabic	tattaim
Hebrew	harkavat avabuot
Yiddish	pokken
Japanese	shutoo
Swahili	kuchanjia ndui

949 value

French	valeur
Spanish	valor
Italian	valore
Portuguese	valor
Rumanian	valoare
German	Wert
Dutch	waarde
Swedish	värde
Danish	værdi
Norwegian	verdi
Polish	wartość
Czech	hodnota
Serbo-Croat.	vrjednost
Hungarian	érték
Finnish	arvo
Turkish	değer
Indonesian	nilai
Esperanto	valoro
Russian	tsénnost
Greek	axi'a
Arabic	qima
Hebrew	erech
Yiddish	vert
Japanese	kachi
Swahili	thamani

950 veal

French	veau
Spanish	ternera
Italian	vitello
Portuguese	carne de vitela
Rumanian	carne de vițel
German	Kalbfleisch
Dutch	kalfsvlees
Swedish	kalvkött
Danish	kalvekød
Norwegian	kalveskjøtt
Polish	cielęcina
Czech	telecí maso
Serbo-Croat.	teletina
Hungarian	borjúhús
Finnish	vasikanliha
Turkish	dana eti
Indonesian	raging anak sapi
Esperanto	bov'id'viando
Russian	telyátina
Greek	kre'as mos-chariou'
Arabic	lahm bitellou
Hebrew	bessar egal
Yiddish	kelberns
Japanese	koushi no niku
Swahili	nyama ya ndama

951 vegetable

French	légume
Spanish	legumbre
Italian	verdura
Portuguese	legume
Rumanian	legumă
German	Gemüse
Dutch	groente
Swedish	grönsaker
Danish	grønsager
Norwegian	grønnsaker
Polish	jarzyna
Czech	zelenina
Serbo-Croat.	povrće
Hungarian	főzelék
Finnish	vihannekset
Turkish	sebze
Indonesian	sajur, nabati
Esperanto	legomo
Russian	óvoshchi
Greek	lachanikon'
Arabic	choudar
Hebrew	yerakoth
Yiddish	grins
Japanese	yasai
Swahili	mboga

952 velvet

French	velours
Spanish	terciopelo
Italian	velluto
Portuguese	veludo
Rumanian	catifea
German	Samt
Dutch	fluweel
Swedish	sammet
Danish	fløjl
Norwegian	fløyel
Polish	aksamit
Czech	samet
Serbo-Croat.	kadifa
Hungarian	bársony
Finnish	sametti
Turkish	kadife
Indonesian	beledu
Esperanto	veluro
Russian	bárkhat
Greek	velou'do
Arabic	qatifa
Hebrew	ketifah
Yiddish	samet
Japanese	biroodo
Swahili	mahameli

953 very

French	très
Spanish	muy
Italian	molto
Portuguese	muito
Rumanian	foarte
German	sehr
Dutch	zeer
Swedish	mycket
Danish	meget
Norwegian	meget
Polish	bardzo
Czech	velmi
Serbo-Croat.	veoma
Hungarian	nagyon
Finnish	hyvin
Turkish	çok
Indonesian	sangat
Esperanto	tre
Russian	óchen
Greek	poli'
Arabic	giddan
Hebrew	meod
Yiddish	sehr
Japanese	ooi ni
Swahili	sana

954 victim

French	victime
Spanish	víctima
Italian	vittima
Portuguese	vítima
Rumanian	victimă
German	Opfer
Dutch	slachtoffer
Swedish	offer
Danish	offer
Norwegian	offer
Polish	ofiara
Czech	oběť
Serbo-Croat.	žrtva
Hungarian	áldozat
Finnish	uhri
Turkish	kurban
Indonesian	kohban
Esperanto	viktimo
Russian	zhértva
Greek	thi'ma
Arabic	dahiya
Hebrew	korban
Yiddish	korben
Japanese	gisei
Swahili	madhabuha

955 view

French	vue
Spanish	vista
Italian	vista
Portuguese	vista
Rumanian	vedere
German	Aussicht
Dutch	uitzicht
Swedish	utsikt
Danish	udsigt
Norwegian	utsikt
Polish	widok
Czech	pohled
Serbo-Croat.	izgled
Hungarian	kilátás
Finnish	näköala
Turkish	manzara
Indonesian	pemandangan
Esperanto	vido
Russian	vit
Greek	the'a
Arabic	manzar
Hebrew	reuth
Yiddish	kuk
Japanese	nagame
Swahili	mandhari

956 village

French	village
Spanish	aldea
Italian	villaggio
Portuguese	aldeia
Rumanian	sat
German	Dorf
Dutch	dorp
Swedish	by
Danish	landsby
Norwegian	landsby
Polish	wioska
Czech	vesnice
Serbo-Croat.	selo
Hungarian	falu
Finnish	kylä
Turkish	köy
Indonesian	dusun
Esperanto	vilaĝo
Russian	deryévnya
Greek	chorion'
Arabic	qarya
Hebrew	kefar
Yiddish	dorf
Japanese	mura
Swahili	kijiji

957 vinegar

French	vinaigre
Spanish	vinagre
Italian	aceto
Portuguese	vinagre
Rumanian	oţet
German	Essig
Dutch	azijn
Swedish	ättika
Danish	eddike
Norwegian	eddik
Polish	ocet
Czech	ocet
Serbo-Croat.	ocat
Hungarian	ecet
Finnish	etikka
Turkish	sirke
Indonesian	tjuka
Esperanto	vinagro
Russian	úksus
Greek	xi'di
Arabic	chall
Hebrew	chomets
Yiddish	essig
Japanese	su
Swahili	siki

958 violation

French	violation
Spanish	violación
Italian	violazione
Portuguese	violação
Rumanian	infracţiune
German	Verletzung
Dutch	schending
Swedish	överträdelse
Danish	overtrædelse
Norwegian	overtredelse
Polish	przekroczenie
Czech	porušení
Serbo-Croat.	povreda
Hungarian	megsértés
Finnish	rikkomus
Turkish	inlâl
Indonesian	langgar
Esperanto	perf'orto
Russian	narushéniye
Greek	para'vasis
Arabic	mouchalafa
Hebrew	avarah
Yiddish	oiversein
Japanese	bookoo
Swahili	mvunjo

959 violin

French	violon
Spanish	violín
Italian	violino
Portuguese	violino
Rumanian	vioară
German	Geige
Dutch	viool
Swedish	fiol
Danish	violin
Norwegian	fiolin
Polish	skrzypce
Czech	housle
Serbo-Croat.	violina
Hungarian	hegedű
Finnish	viulu
Turkish	keman
Indonesian	biola
Esperanto	violono
Russian	skrípka
Greek	violi'
Arabic	kaman
Hebrew	kinor
Yiddish	fidel
Japanese	baiorin
Swahili	fidla

960 visit

French	visiter
Spanish	visitar
Italian	visitare
Portuguese	visitar
Rumanian	vizită
German	besuchen
Dutch	bezoeken
Swedish	besöka
Danish	besøge
Norwegian	besøke
Polish	wizytować
Czech	navštíviti
Serbo-Croat.	posetiti
Hungarian	látogat
Finnish	käydä katsomassa
Turkish	ziryaret
Indonesian	kundjung
Esperanto	viziti
Russian	pasetít
Greek	episkep'tome
Arabic	yazour
Hebrew	biker
Yiddish	visiten
Japanese	hoomon suru
Swahili	zuru

961 voice

French	voix
Spanish	voz
Italian	voce
Portuguese	voz
Rumanian	voce
German	Stimme
Dutch	stem
Swedish	röst
Danish	stemme
Norwegian	stemme
Polish	głos
Czech	hlas
Serbo-Croat.	glas
Hungarian	hang
Finnish	ääni
Turkish	ses
Indonesian	suara
Esperanto	voĉo
Russian	gólos
Greek	foni'
Arabic	sawt
Hebrew	kol
Yiddish	koll
Japanese	koe
Swahili	sauti

962 wait

French	attendre
Spanish	esperar
Italian	aspettare
Portuguese	esperar
Rumanian	aştepta
German	warten
Dutch	wachten
Swedish	vänta
Danish	vente
Norwegian	vente
Polish	czekać
Czech	čekati
Serbo-Croat.	čekati
Hungarian	vár
Finnish	odottaa
Turkish	beklemek
Indonesian	tunggu, nanti
Esperanto	atendi
Russian	zhdat
Greek	perime'no
Arabic	intatzir
Hebrew	himtin
Yiddish	varten
Japanese	matsu
Swahili	ngoja

963 waiter

French	garçon
Spanish	camarero
Italian	cameriere
Portuguese	criado
Rumanian	chelner
German	Kellner
Dutch	ober
Swedish	kypare
Danish	tjener
Norwegian	kelner
Polish	kelner
Czech	číšnik
Serbo-Croat.	konobar
Hungarian	pincér
Finnish	tarjoilija
Turkish	garson
Indonesian	pelajan
Esperanto	kelnero
Russian	ofitsiánt
Greek	garso'ni
Arabic	soufragi
Hebrew	meltsar
Yiddish	kelner
Japanese	kyuujinin
Swahili	mwandishi

964 walk

French	promener
Spanish	andar
Italian	passeggiare
Portuguese	passear
Rumanian	plimba
German	spazieren
Dutch	wandelen
Swedish	spatsera
Danish	spadsere
Norwegian	spasere
Polish	przechadzać się
Czech	choditi
Serbo-Croat.	šetati
Hungarian	sétál
Finnish	kävellä
Turkish	yürümek
Indonesian	berdjalan
Esperanto	promeni
Russian	pagulyát
Greek	perpato'
Arabic	yamshi
Hebrew	halach
Yiddish	schpatsiéren
Japanese	aruku
Swahili	tembea

965 wall

French	mur
Spanish	pared
Italian	muro
Portuguese	parede
Rumanian	perete
German	Wand
Dutch	muur
Swedish	vägg
Danish	væg
Norwegian	vegg
Polish	ściana
Czech	stěna
Serbo-Croat.	zid
Hungarian	fal
Finnish	seinä
Turkish	duvar
Indonesian	témbok, dinding
Esperanto	muro
Russian	stená
Greek	ti'chos
Arabic	hait
Hebrew	kotel
Yiddish	vand
Japanese	kabe
Swahili	ukuta

966 war

French	guerre
Spanish	guerra
Italian	guerra
Portuguese	guerra
Rumanian	război
German	Krieg
Dutch	oorlog
Swedish	krig
Danish	krig
Norwegian	krig
Polish	wojna
Czech	válka
Serbo-Croat.	rat
Hungarian	háború
Finnish	sota
Turkish	harb
Indonesian	perang
Esperanto	milito
Russian	voiná
Greek	po'lemos
Arabic	harb
Hebrew	milchamah
Yiddish	milchome
Japanese	sensoo
Swahili	vita

967 warm

French	chaud
Spanish	caliente
Italian	caldo
Portuguese	quente
Rumanian	cald
German	warm
Dutch	warm
Swedish	varm
Danish	varm
Norwegian	varm
Polish	ciepły
Czech	teplý
Serbo-Croat.	topao
Hungarian	meleg
Finnish	lämmin
Turkish	sıcak
Indonesian	panas
Esperanto	varma
Russian	tyópli
Greek	thermos'
Arabic	harr
Hebrew	cham
Yiddish	varim
Japanese	atatakai
Swahili	-a moto si sana

968 wash

French	laver
Spanish	lavar
Italian	lavare
Portuguese	lavar
Rumanian	spăla
German	waschen
Dutch	wassen
Swedish	tvätta
Danish	vaske
Norwegian	vaske
Polish	myć
Czech	mýti
Serbo-Croat.	prati
Hungarian	mos
Finnish	pestä
Turkish	yıkamak
Indonesian	tjutjian
Esperanto	lavi
Russian	mit
Greek	ple'no
Arabic	yaghsil
Hebrew	rachats
Yiddish	vaschen
Japanese	arau
Swahili	osha

969 waste

French	gaspillage
Spanish	basura
Italian	spreco
Portuguese	desperdício
Rumanian	deşeu
German	Abfall
Dutch	afval
Swedish	avfall
Danish	affald
Norwegian	avfall
Polish	odpadki
Czech	odpadky
Serbo-Croat.	rasipati
Hungarian	hulladék
Finnish	jätteet
Turkish	kullanılmayan
Indonesian	ampas, sampah
Esperanto	for'jet'ajo
Russian	atbrósi
Greek	spata'li
Arabic	tabdid
Hebrew	psolet
Yiddish	obfall
Japanese	kuzu
Swahili	takataka

970 water

French	eau
Spanish	agua
Italian	acqua
Portuguese	água
Rumanian	apă
German	Wasser
Dutch	water
Swedish	vatten
Danish	vand
Norwegian	vann
Polish	woda
Czech	voda
Serbo-Croat.	voda
Hungarian	víz
Finnish	vesi
Turkish	su
Indonesian	air
Esperanto	akvo
Russian	vadá
Greek	nero'
Arabic	ma
Hebrew	mayim
Yiddish	vasser
Japanese	mizu
Swahili	maji

971 way

French	chemin
Spanish	camino
Italian	cammino
Portuguese	caminho
Rumanian	drum
German	Weg
Dutch	weg
Swedish	väg
Danish	vej
Norwegian	vei
Polish	droga
Czech	cesta
Serbo-Croat.	put
Hungarian	út
Finnish	tie
Turkish	yol
Indonesian	djalan, aran
Esperanto	vojo
Russian	daróga
Greek	tro'pos
Arabic	tariq
Hebrew	derech
Yiddish	veg
Japanese	michi
Swahili	njia

972 weather

French	temps
Spanish	tiempo
Italian	tempo
Portuguese	tempo
Rumanian	vreme
German	Wetter
Dutch	weer
Swedish	väder
Danish	vejr
Norwegian	vær
Polish	pogoda
Czech	počasí
Serbo-Croat.	vreme
Hungarian	idő
Finnish	ilma
Turkish	hava
Indonesian	hawa, hadi
Esperanto	vetero
Russian	pagóda
Greek	keros'
Arabic	gawe
Hebrew	mezeg avier
Yiddish	vetter
Japanese	tenki
Swahili	hali ya hewa

973 wedding

French	noce
Spanish	boda
Italian	nozze
Portuguese	casamento
Rumanian	nuntă
German	Hochzeit
Dutch	bruiloft
Swedish	bröllop
Danish	bryllup
Norwegian	bryllup
Polish	ślub
Czech	svatba
Serbo-Croat.	venčanje
Hungarian	esküvő
Finnish	häät
Turkish	dügün
Indonesian	perkawinan
Esperanto	edz'iĝo
Russian	zvádba
Greek	ga'mos
Arabic	zawag
Hebrew	chatunah
Yiddish	chassene
Japanese	kekkonshiki
Swahili	arusi

974 Wednesday

French	mercredi
Spanish	miércoles
Italian	mercoledi
Portuguese	quarto-feira
Rumanian	miercuri
German	Mittwoch
Dutch	Woensdag
Swedish	onsdag
Danish	onsdag
Norwegian	onsdag
Polish	środa
Czech	středa
Serbo-Croat.	srijeda
Hungarian	szerda
Finnish	keskiviikko
Turkish	çarşamba
Indonesian	Rebo, Arba
Esperanto	merkredo
Russian	sredá
Greek	Teta'rti
Arabic	youm al-arbaa
Hebrew	yom reviie
Yiddish	mitvoch
Japanese	suiyoobi
Swahili	Jumatano

975 week

French	semaine
Spanish	semana
Italian	settimana
Portuguese	semana
Rumanian	săptamînă
German	Woche
Dutch	week
Swedish	vecka
Danish	uge
Norwegian	uke
Polish	tydzień
Czech	týden
Serbo-Croat.	sedmica
Hungarian	hét
Finnish	viikko
Turkish	hafta
Indonesian	pekan
Esperanto	semajno
Russian	nedyélya
Greek	evdoma'da
Arabic	ousbou
Hebrew	schavoa
Yiddish	voch
Japanese	shuu
Swahili	juma

976 weight

French	poids
Spanish	peso
Italian	peso
Portuguese	pêso
Rumanian	greutate
German	Gewicht
Dutch	gewicht
Swedish	vikt
Danish	vægt
Norwegian	vekt
Polish	waga
Czech	váha
Serbo-Croat.	težina
Hungarian	súly
Finnish	paino
Turkish	ağirlık
Indonesian	bobot
Esperanto	pezo
Russian	vyés
Greek	va'ros
Arabic	wazn
Hebrew	mischkal
Yiddish	gewicht
Japanese	mekata
Swahili	uzito

977 west

French	ouest
Spanish	oeste
Italian	ovest
Portuguese	oeste
Rumanian	vest
German	Westen
Dutch	west
Swedish	väster
Danish	vest
Norwegian	vest
Polish	zachód
Czech	západ
Serbo-Croat.	zapad
Hungarian	nyugat
Finnish	länsi
Turkish	batı
Indonesian	barat
Esperanto	okcidento
Russian	západ
Greek	di'sis
Arabic	gharb
Hebrew	maarav
Yiddish	marifsait
Japanese	nishi
Swahili	magharibi

978 wet

French	mouillé
Spanish	mojado
Italian	bagnato
Portuguese	molhado
Rumanian	ud
German	nass
Dutch	nat
Swedish	våt
Danish	våd
Norwegian	våt
Polish	mokry
Czech	mokrý
Serbo-Croat.	vlazan
Hungarian	vizes
Finnish	märkä
Turkish	ıslak
Indonesian	hasah
Esperanto	mal'seko
Russian	mókri
Greek	vregme'nos
Arabic	moubalal
Hebrew	ratov
Yiddish	nass
Japanese	nureta
Swahili	majimaji

979 wheat

French	froment
Spanish	trigo
Italian	frumento
Portuguese	trigo
Rumanian	grîu
German	Weizen
Dutch	tarwe
Swedish	vete
Danish	hvede
Norwegian	hvete
Polish	pszenica
Czech	pšenice
Serbo-Croat.	pšenica
Hungarian	búza
Finnish	vehnä
Turkish	buğday
Indonesian	gandum
Esperanto	tritiko
Russian	pshenítsa
Greek	sita'ri
Arabic	qamh
Hebrew	chitah
Yiddish	veits
Japanese	komugi
Swahili	ngano

980 where?

French	où?
Spanish	¿dónde?
Italian	dove?
Portuguese	onde?
Rumanian	unde?
German	wo?
Dutch	waar?
Swedish	var?
Danish	hvor?
Norwegian	hvor?
Polish	gdzie?
Czech	kde?
Serbo-Croat.	gdje?
Hungarian	hol?
Finnish	missä?
Turkish	nerede ?
Indonesian	mana?
Esperanto	kie?
Russian	gdyé?
Greek	pou'?
Arabic	ayna
Hebrew	ayeh
Yiddish	vu?
Japanese	doko de
Swahili	wapi ?

981 white

French	blanc
Spanish	blanco
Italian	bianco
Portuguese	branco
Rumanian	alb
German	weiss
Dutch	wit
Swedish	vit
Danish	hvid
Norwegian	hvit
Polish	biały
Czech	bílý
Serbo-Croat.	bijeli
Hungarian	fehér
Finnish	valkoinen
Turkish	beyaz
Indonesian	putin
Esperanto	blanka
Russian	byéli
Greek	a'spros
Arabic	abyad
Hebrew	lavan
Yiddish	veiss
Japanese	shiroi
Swahili	-eupe

982 who?

French	qui?
Spanish	¿quién?
Italian	chi?
Portuguese	quem?
Rumanian	cine?
German	wer?
Dutch	wie?
Swedish	vem?
Danish	hvem?
Norwegian	hvem?
Polish	kto?
Czech	kdo?
Serbo-Croat.	ko?
Hungarian	ki?
Finnish	kuka?
Turkish	kim ?
Indonesian	siapa
Esperanto	kiu?
Russian	khto?
Greek	pio's?
Arabic	mann
Hebrew	mi
Yiddish	ver?
Japanese	dare
Swahili	nani ?

983 why?

French	pourquoi?
Spanish	¿por qué?
Italian	perchè?
Portuguese	porque?
Rumanian	pentru ce?
German	warum?
Dutch	waarom?
Swedish	varför?
Danish	hvorfor?
Norwegian	hvorfor?
Polish	dlaczego?
Czech	proč?
Serbo-Croat.	zašto?
Hungarian	miért?
Finnish	miksi?
Turkish	niçin ?
Indonesian	mengapa?
Esperanto	kial?
Russian	pochemú
Greek	yiati'?
Arabic	limatza
Hebrew	madua
Yiddish	farvos?
Japanese	naze
Swahili	kwa nini ?

984 wind

French	vent
Spanish	viento
Italian	vento
Portuguese	vento
Rumanian	vînt
German	Wind
Dutch	wind
Swedish	vind
Danish	vind
Norwegian	vind
Polish	wiatr
Czech	vítr
Serbo-Croat.	vjetar
Hungarian	szél
Finnish	tuuli
Turkish	rüzgâr
Indonesian	angin
Esperanto	vento
Russian	vyéter
Greek	a'nemos
Arabic	rih
Hebrew	ruach
Yiddish	vind
Japanese	kaze
Swahili	upepo

985 window

French	fenêtre
Spanish	ventana
Italian	finestra
Portuguese	janela
Rumanian	fereastră
German	Fenster
Dutch	venster
Swedish	fönster
Danish	vindue
Norwegian	vindu
Polish	okno
Czech	okno
Serbo-Croat.	prozor
Hungarian	ablak
Finnish	ikkuna
Turkish	pencere
Indonesian	ajendéla
Esperanto	fenestro
Russian	oknó
Greek	para'thiron
Arabic	nafitza
Hebrew	chalon
Yiddish	fenster
Japanese	mado
Swahili	dirisha

986 winter

French	hiver
Spanish	invierno
Italian	inverno
Portuguese	inverno
Rumanian	iarnă
German	Winter
Dutch	winter
Swedish	vinter
Danish	vinter
Norwegian	vinter
Polish	zima
Czech	zima
Serbo-Croat.	zima
Hungarian	tél
Finnish	talvi
Turkish	kiş
Indonesian	musim dingin
Esperanto	vintro
Russian	zimá
Greek	chimo'nas
Arabic	shita
Hebrew	choref
Yiddish	vinter
Japanese	fuyu
Swahili	majira ya baridi

987 woman

French	femme
Spanish	mujer
Italian	donna
Portuguese	mulher
Rumanian	femeie
German	Frau
Dutch	vrouw
Swedish	kvinna
Danish	kvinde
Norwegian	kvinne
Polish	kobieta
Czech	žena
Serbo-Croat.	žena
Hungarian	asszony
Finnish	nainen
Turkish	kadin
Indonesian	wanita
Esperanto	vir'ino
Russian	zhénshchina
Greek	yine'ka
Arabic	imraa
Hebrew	ischah
Yiddish	froi
Japanese	fujin
Swahili	mwanamke

988 wood

French	bois
Spanish	madera
Italian	legno
Portuguese	madeira
Rumanian	lemn
German	Holz
Dutch	hout
Swedish	trä
Danish	træ
Norwegian	ved
Polish	drzewo
Czech	dřevo
Serbo-Croat.	drvo
Hungarian	fa
Finnish	puu
Turkish	tahta
Indonesian	kaju
Esperanto	ligno
Russian	dyérevo
Greek	xi'lon
Arabic	chashab
Hebrew	ets
Yiddish	holts
Japanese	ki
Swahili	mti

989 wool

French	laine
Spanish	lana
Italian	lana
Portuguese	lã
Rumanian	lînă
German	Wolle
Dutch	wol
Swedish	ull
Danish	uld
Norwegian	ull
Polish	wełna
Czech	vlna
Serbo-Croat.	vuna
Hungarian	gyapjú
Finnish	villa
Turkish	yün
Indonesian	wol, bulu olomba
Esperanto	lano
Russian	sherst
Greek	ma'lino
Arabic	souf
Hebrew	tsemer
Yiddish	voll
Japanese	keito
Swahili	manyoya

990 word

French	mot
Spanish	palabra
Italian	parola
Portuguese	palavra
Rumanian	cuvînt
German	Word
Dutch	woord
Swedish	ord
Danish	ord
Norwegian	ord
Polish	słowo
Czech	slovo
Serbo-Croat.	reč
Hungarian	szó
Finnish	sana
Turkish	kelime
Indonesian	kata
Esperanto	vorto
Russian	slóvo
Greek	le'xis
Arabic	kalima
Hebrew	milah
Yiddish	vort
Japanese	kotoba
Swahili	neno

991 work

French	travail
Spanish	trabajo
Italian	lavoro
Portuguese	trabalho
Rumanian	muncă
German	Arbeit
Dutch	werk
Swedish	arbete
Danish	arbejde
Norwegian	arbeid
Polish	praca
Czech	práce
Serbo-Croat.	rad
Hungarian	munka
Finnish	työ
Turkish	iş
Indonesian	kerdja
Esperanto	laboro
Russian	rabóta
Greek	ergasi'a
Arabic	amal
Hebrew	avodah
Yiddish	arbeit
Japanese	shigoto
Swahili	kazi

992 wrist watch

French	montre-bracelet
Spanish	reloj de pulsera
Italian	orologio da polso
Portuguese	relógio de pulso
Rumanian	ceas de mînă
German	Armbanduhr
Dutch	polshorloge
Swedish	armbandsur
Danish	armbåndsur
Norwegian	armbåndsur
Polish	zegarek ręczny
Czech	náramkové hodinky
Serbo-Croat.	ručni casovnik
Hungarian	karóra
Finnish	rannekello
Turkish	kol saati
Indonesian	arlodji tangan
Esperanto	pojno'horloĝo
Russian	ruchníye chasí
Greek	rolo'i cheriou'
Arabic	saat yad
Hebrew	scheon yad
Yiddish	handseiger
Japanese	udedokei
Swahili	saa cha mkono

993 write

French	écrire
Spanish	escribir
Italian	scrivere
Portuguese	escrever
Rumanian	scrie
German	schreiben
Dutch	schrijven
Swedish	skriva
Danish	skrive
Norwegian	skrive
Polish	pisać
Czech	psáti
Serbo-Croat.	pisati
Hungarian	ír
Finnish	kirjoittaa
Turkish	yazmak
Indonesian	tulis
Esperanto	skribi
Russian	pisát
Greek	gra'fo
Arabic	yaktoub
Hebrew	katav
Yiddish	schreiben
Japanese	kaku
Swahili	andika

994 wrong

French	faux
Spanish	falso
Italian	sbagliato
Portuguese	errado
Rumanian	greşit
German	falsch
Dutch	verkeerd
Swedish	orätt
Danish	forkert
Norwegian	urett
Polish	mylny
Czech	nesprávný
Serbo-Croat.	pogrešan
Hungarian	téves
Finnish	väärä
Turkish	yanlış
Indonesian	salan
Esperanto	mal'ĝusta
Russian	neprávilni
Greek	esfalme'nos
Arabic	chata
Hebrew	lo nachon
Yiddish	falsch
Japanese	ayamatta
Swahili	-kosefu

995 year

French	an
Spanish	año
Italian	anno
Portuguese	ano
Rumanian	an
German	Jahr
Dutch	jaar
Swedish	år
Danish	år
Norwegian	år
Polish	rok
Czech	rok
Serbo-Croat.	godina
Hungarian	év
Finnish	vuosi
Turkish	sene
Indonesian	tahun
Esperanto	jaro
Russian	got
Greek	e'tos
Arabic	sana, aam
Hebrew	schanah
Yiddish	yohr
Japanese	toshi
Swahili	mwaka

996 yellow

French	jaune
Spanish	amarillo
Italian	giallo
Portuguese	amarelo
Rumanian	galben
German	gelb
Dutch	geel
Swedish	gul
Danish	gult
Norwegian	gul
Polish	żólty
Czech	žlutý
Serbo-Croat.	žut
Hungarian	sárga
Finnish	keltainen
Turkish	sarı
Indonesian	kuning
Esperanto	flava
Russian	zhólti
Greek	ki'trino
Arabic	asfar
Hebrew	tsahov
Yiddish	gel
Japanese	ki'iroi
Swahili	(-a) kimanjano

997 yes

French	oui
Spanish	sí
Italian	sì
Portuguese	sim
Rumanian	da
German	ja
Dutch	ja
Swedish	ja
Danish	ja
Norwegian	ja
Polish	tak
Czech	ano
Serbo-Croat.	da
Hungarian	igen
Finnish	kyllä
Turkish	evet
Indonesian	ja
Esperanto	jes
Russian	da
Greek	ne
Arabic	naam
Hebrew	ken
Yiddish	ye
Japanese	hai
Swahili	ndio

999 young

French	jeune
Spanish	joven
Italian	giovane
Portuguese	jovem
Rumanian	tînăr
German	jung
Dutch	jong
Swedish	ung
Danish	ung
Norwegian	ung
Polish	młody
Czech	mladý
Serbo-Croat.	mlad
Hungarian	fiatal
Finnish	nuori
Turkish	genç
Indonesian	anak
Esperanto	juna
Russian	maladóy
Greek	ne'os
Arabic	saghir
Hebrew	tsair
Yiddish	yung
Japanese	wakai
Swahili	-changa

998 yesterday

French	hier
Spanish	ayer
Italian	ieri
Portuguese	ontem
Rumanian	ieri
German	gestern
Dutch	gister
Swedish	igår
Danish	i går
Norwegian	i går
Polish	wczoraj
Czech	včera
Serbo-Croat.	juče
Hungarian	tegnap
Finnish	eilen
Turkish	dün
Indonesian	kemarin
Esperanto	hieraŭ
Russian	fcherá
Greek	echtes'
Arabic	ams
Hebrew	etmol
Yiddish	nechten
Japanese	sakujitsu
Swahili	jana

1000 zero

French	zéro
Spanish	cero
Italian	zero
Portuguese	zero
Rumanian	zero
German	null
Dutch	nul
Swedish	noll
Danish	nul
Norwegian	null
Polish	zero
Czech	nula
Serbo-Croat.	nula
Hungarian	nulla
Finnish	nolla
Turkish	sıfır
Indonesian	nol
Esperanto	nulo
Russian	nul
Greek	miden'
Arabic	sifr
Hebrew	efes
Yiddish	nul
Japanese	rei
Swahili	sifuri

INDEX

oeuf 337
oeufs brouillés 778
oie 436
oignon 655
oiseau 114
olive 653
oncle 940
ongle 378
onze 344
or 433
orage 851
orange 657
oreille 332
oreiller 691
orge 76
orteil 911
os 134
où? 980
oublier 396
ouest 977
oui 997
ours 88
ouvert 656
pain 144
paire 663
paix 677
pamplemousse 440
panier 80
panique 665
pantalons 928
papillon 163
papier 666
paquet 668
parachute 667
parapluie 939
parce que 91
parents 669
paresseux 531
parier 108
parking 670
parler 829
parler 870
part 672
passeport 674
pauvre 707
payer 675
pays 266
paysan 679
peau 805
peigne 243
peignoir 82
peinture 662
pendre 460
penser 888
père 369
permis 683

perdrix 673
persil 671
perte 561
petit 811
petit pain 755
peu 372
peut-être 583
pharmacie 684
phonographe 685
piano 687
pied 392
pierre 848
pigeon 690
pilote 692
pin 694
piquer 845
plage 86
plaisanterie 510
plaisir 702
plancher 386
plante 697
plat 310
plat 383
plomb 532
pluie 730
plume 680
pneu 906
poche 704
poêle 852
poids 976
poing 381
point 705
poire 678
pois 676
poison 706
poisson 380
poisson frit 407
poitrine 212
poivre 682
pomme 41
pomme de terre 714
pont 150
porc 708
port 461
portatif 709
porte 315
porte-monnaie 721
porter 191
porteur 710
poste 570
poste restante 422
pot 713
potage 825
pouce 897
poudre 715
poulet 213

poumon 565
pourquoi? 983
poussière 329
prendre 869
près 620
printemps 833
prison 718
prix 716
profession 719
profond 293
promener 964
propre 224
propriété 720
prune 703
puce 385
quai 698
quarante 398
quart 722
quatorze 401
quatre 400
quatre-vingt 340
quatre-vingt-dix 633
question 724
queue 867
qui? 982
quinze 373
racine 758
raisin 439
rame 646
raser 789
rasoir 734
rat 733
reçu 736
réduire 738
rein 514
reine 723
religion 740
renard 402
rencontrer 587
rendez-vous 42
repas 584
repasser 505
répéter 742
répondre 37
reposer 743
restaurant 744
rêve 318
revue 567
riche 746
rideau 279
rince-bouche 607
rire 528
risque 751
riz 745
robe 319
roi 515

abaixo 105
abelha 94
aberto 656
aborrecido 876
abril 44
aceitar 4
achar 376
acidente 5
aço 843
acompanhar 6
acordeon 7
açúcar 857
adega 199
adeus 435
advogado 530
aeroporto 24
afogarse 324
agora 641
agosto 54
água 970
águia 331
agulha 623
airela 128
ajudar 474
aldeia 956
alegre 591
alfaiate 868
alfândega 280
alfinete 693
algodão 262
alho 418
alí 883
alimento 391
almofada 691
altitude 28
alto 871
aluguel 741
alumínio 29
alvo 21
amanhã 915
amarelo 996
amargo 117
ameixa 703
amido 840
amigo 408
amor 562
amostra 770
anel 749
animal 34
ano 995
anúncio 12
ao estrangeiro 2
apanhar 194
apartamento 39
apetite 40
apostar 108

aprender 534
aqui 475
ar 22
arando 271
areia 771
arenque 476
arma de fogo 450
arquiteto 45
arroz 745
arte 49
artificial 50
árvore 926
assar 753
assentar 801
assinatura 796
assunto 14
até 944
ator 10
atrás de 101
através de 9
ausente 3
automático 58
automóvel 59
autor 56
autoridade 57
aveia 647
avião 23
azêdo 826
azeitona 653
azul 127
bacalhau 238
bagagem 564
bala 158
balança 70
balcão 71
banana 73
banco 75
banheira 83
banho 81
barata 236
barato 206
barba 89
barbear 789
barco 129
barriga 104
barril 78
barulho 635
batata 714
bebé 62
beber 320
beijo 516
belo 90
bengala 178
berço 274
beterraba 98
bexiga 119

biblioteca 543
bicicleta 111
bife 96
bilhar 113
bilhete 900
biscoito 270
blusa 126
bôca 606
bochecha 207
boi 660
bola 72
bôlo 170
bolsa de valores 846
bôlsa para dinheiro 721
bolso 704
bom 434
bomba 133
borboleta 163
borracha 761
botão 164
bracelete 140
braço 46
branco 981
branquear 122
brinco 333
brinquedo 921
broche 152
buraco 478
burro 314
cabaré 166
cabeça 468
cabeleireiro 454
cabelo 453
cabina 168
cabra 431
caçar 489
cacau 237
cadeia 202
cadeira 203
café 169
café 239
café da manhã 145
cal 549
calcanhar 473
calças 928
caldeira 132
cama 92
camelo 173
caminho 971
camisa 791
campo 175
camponês 679
camundongo 605
canal 176
canastra 80
caneta-tinteiro 399

absent 3
ac 623
ac 693
accepta 4
accident 5
acolo 883
acoperiş 756
acord 20
acru 826
actor 10
acum 641
adevăr 929
adînc 293
adio 435
adresă 11
aduce 151
aer 22
aeroplan 23
aeroport 24
afacere 14
afacere 160
afină 128
aici 475
ajuta 474
alamă 143
alb 981
albastru 127
albină 94
alerga 762
aliment 391
alta 36
aluminiu 29
amar 117
ambasador 30
amesteca 596
amiaza 637
amidon 840
an 995
animal 34
anunţ 12
anvelopă 906
apă 970
aprilie 44
apropiat 620
aramă 255
arbore 926
arde 159
argint 798
arhitect 45
armată 47
armonică 7
artă 49
artificial 50
arunca 896
ascensor 343
asculta 470

asiguare 500
aştepta 962
astru 839
aţă 893
atirna 460
august 54
aur 433
automat 58
automobil 59
autor 56
autoritate 57
avea 466
avocat 530
azi 910
bagaj 564
băiat 139
baie 81
balanţă 70
balcon 71
banană 73
bancă 75
bandaj 74
bani 598
bani gata 192
barbă 89
bărbie 215
bărbieri 789
barcă 129
băşică 119
baston 178
băţ 844
baterie 84
batistă 459
bea 320
bec 342
beneficiu 107
benzină 420
bere 97
bibliotecă 543
bicicletă 111
biftec 96
bilet 900
biliard 113
birou 650
biscuit 270
biserică 219
blană 414
blondă 124
bluză 126
boală 309
bogat 746
bolnav 795
bombă 133
bou 660
braţ 46
brăţară 140

bretele 863
brici 734
brînză 208
broască 409
broască 558
broşă 152
brun 155
brutar 69
bucătar 254
bucătărie 517
bucuros 426
bumbac 262
bun 434
butoi 78
buton 164
bursă 846
buză 552
buzunar 704
cabaret 166
cabină 168
cacao 237
cadă 83
cafea 239
cafenea 169
caisă 43
cal 481
călătorie 925
călca 505
călcîi 473
cald 967
căldare 132
calibru 421
cămaşă 791
cameră 757
cameră fotografica 174
cămilă 173
canal 176
canapea 263
cantitate 31
cap 468
capabil 1
capitală 179
căpitan 181
capră 431
captură 182
carabină 747
căramidă 148
cărbune 234
carne 585
carne de porc 708
carne de vacă 95
carne de viţel 950
carte 135
carte de joc 700
carte poştala 711
cartof 714

peron   698
peşte   380
peşte prăjiti   407
piano   687
piaţă   576
piatră   848
picior   392
picior   538
picura   323
piele   535
piele   805
piept   212
pieptene   243
pierdere   561
pîine   144
pîine prăjita   908
pilă   617
pilot   692
pînă   944
pin   694
pîntec   104
pînză   550
piper   682
pisică   193
pivniţă   199
plăcere   702
plajă   86
plămîn   565
plantă   697
plat   383
plăti   675
pleca   536
plecare   298
plic   350
plicticos   876
plimba   964
ploaie   730
plumb   532
poate   583
pod   150
poftă   40
poftim   701
porc   689
port   461
portabil   709
portmoneu   721
portocală   657
porumb   258
porumbel   690
poştă   570
poştă   712
postrestant   422
potîrniche   673
poză   688
praf   329
praf   715

prăvălie   850
praz   216
precauţiune   198
preţ   260
preţ   716
prieten   408
primăvară   833
primejdie   284
prinde   194
prinsoare   108
proaspăt   405
probă   880
proprietate   720
prosop   919
prudent   185
prună   703
prunc   62
pui   213
pumn   381
punct   705
pungă   67
purice   385
purta   191
purtare   100
puşcă   450
pustiu   299
puternic   855
puţine   372
radacină   758
radio   728
raniţă   518
răspunde   37
răsturna   180
raţă   328
rău   66
rău   572
război   560
război   966
rece   240
recoltă   463
reduce   738
rege   515
regină   723
religie   740
repeta   742
restaurant   744
revistă   567
rîde   528
rinichi   514
risc   751
rîu   752
rochie   319
rosbif   754
roşie   914
roşu   737
rotund   760

roz   695
rugină   763
ruşinos   79
şa   766
şah   211
şaisprezece   803
şaizeci   804
salon   556
saltea   581
sănătate   469
sănătos   824
sanie   808
săptamînă   975
şapte   785
şaptesprezece   786
şaptezeci   787
săpun   816
sărac   707
sărbatoare   479
sare   769
şarpe   814
sărut   516
şase   802
sat   956
scară   522
scară   835
scaun   203
schi   806
schimba   205
schimbare   352
şcoală   775
scop   21
scrie   993
scrisoare   542
scump   261
scurt   793
scuză   353
seară   351
secară   764
secol   201
şedea   801
semnatură   796
septembrie   784
servitoare   569
sete   889
sfat   13
sfeclă   98
sfert   722
şi   32
sigiliu   837
siguranţă   767
sîmbătă   772
sîn   146
sînge   125
singur   26
slănină   65

smîntînă 273
smochină 375
soare 859
şoarece 605
sobă 852
şobolan 733
socoti 265
sofa 818
şofer 322
soldat 820
soluţie 821
soră 800
sos 442
şosea 477
sosire 48
soţ 490
spăla 968
spălătorie 529
sparanghel 52
spate 63
spaţiu 828
special 830
spital 483
sta 838
staţiona 670
staţiune 841
staul 834
stejar 645
sticlă 137
sticlă 427
ştiinţă 776
stilou 399
stîng 537
stomac 847
strachină 138
stradă 854
străin 395
striga 276
strugur 439
student 856
sub 941
subţire 887
sud 827
suflare 147
sufragerie 305
şuncă 456
supă 825
supărat 33
surd 289
surprinde 862
şurub 779
sus 945
sută 487
şvab 236

tablou 662
tăia 281
ţăieţei 636
ţară 266
ţăran 679
tată 369
teatru 882
televiziune 877
ţigară 221
ţigară de foi 220
tigru 902
timbru 836
timp 903
tînăr 999
ţînţar 602
ţipar 336
tipărire 717
tirbuşon 257
tîrziu 527
toaletă 913
toamnă 60
tobă 326
toc 680
tot 25
trăda 109
traduce 923
transparent 924
trei 894
treisprezece 890
treizeci 891
trenă 922
trifoi 233
trimite 783
trist 765
tub 696
tunet 898
tuşi 264
tutun 909
ud 978
uita 396
ulei 651
umăr 794
umbrelă 939
un 654
unchi 940
unde? 980
unghi 378
unsprezece 344
unt 162
urca 227
ureche 332
urgent 946
urî 465
urit 938

urs 88
uşă 315
uscat 327
usturoi 418
vacă 269
vaccinare 948
vagon 183
valoare 949
vamă 330
vamal 280
văr 268
var 549
vară 858
varză 167
vechi 652
vecin 624
vedea 781
vedere 955
veni 244
verde 443
vesel 591
vest 977
viaţă 544
victimă 954
vînă 489
vinde 782
vineri 406
vinovat 449
vînt 984
vioară 959
vîrstă 19
vis 318
vîslă 646
vite 196
viţel 171
vizită 960
voce 961
vorbi 829
vorbi 870
vreme 972
vulpe 402
vultur 331
zahăr 857
zăpadă 815
zdreanţă 729
zece 878
zero 1000
zgomot 635
zi 288
zi de naştere 116
ziar 629
zmeură 732

Landstrasse 477
lang 559
langsam 810
langweilig 876
Lappen 729
Lärm 635
laufen 762
Leben 544
Leber 555
Leder 535
leer 345
Lehrer 875
Leinen 550
Leiter 522
lernen 534
lesen 735
Licht 546
Liebe 562
liefern 296
Likör 553
links 537
Linse 541
Lippe 552
Loch 478
Löffel 832
Lösung 821
Lotse 692
Löwe 551
Luft 22
Lunge 565
lustig 591
machen 571
Mädchen 424
Magen 847
Mahlzeit 584
Mai 582
Mais 258
mangelhaft 294
Mantel 235
Markt 576
Marmelade 577
März 575
Maschine 566
Mass 421
Matratze 581
Matrose 768
Maus 605
Medizin 586
Meer 780
Mehl 387
Melone 588
Mensch 573
Messer 520
Messing 143
Metall 592
Miete 741

Milch 593
Minute 594
mischen 596
Mittagessen 306
mittags 637
Mittwoch 974
Mohrrübe 190
Monat 599
Mond 600
Montag 597
Morgen 601
morgen 915
Mücke 602
müde 907
Mund 606
Mundwasser 607
Muster 770
Mut 267
Mutter 603
nach 15
Nachbar 624
Nachmittag 16
Nachspeise 300
Nacht 630
Nacken 621
Nadel 623
Nagel 616
Nagelfeile 617
nähen 788
Nahrung 391
Name 618
Nase 639
nass 978
Natur 619
neben 620
nehmen 869
nein 634
Nelke 187
nervös 625
neu 628
neun 631
neunzehn 632
neunzig 633
neutral 626
nieder 316
niemals 627
Niere 514
Norden 638
November 640
Nudeln 636
null 1000
Nuss 644
Nutzen 107
oben 945
Oberschenkel 886
Obst 412

Ochse 660
Ofen 852
offen 656
Ohr 332
Ohrring 333
Oktober 649
Öl 651
Olive 653
Onkel 940
Opfer 954
Osten 334
Paar 663
Paket 668
Papier 666
parken 670
Pass 674
Pfannkuchen 664
Pferd 481
Pferderennen 482
Pfeffer 682
Pflanze 697
Pflaume 703
Pelzmantel 414
Petersilie 671
Photoapparat 174
Pilz 612
Pompelmuse 440
Post 570
Postamt 712
Postkarte 711
postlagernd 422
Preis 716
Preiselbeere 271
Prüfung 880
Pulver 715
Punkt 705
quer 9
Quittung 736
Radio 728
rasch 725
rasieren 789
Rasiermesser 734
rasten 743
Ratschlag 13
Ratte 733
Rauch 813
Raum 828
Rebhuhn 673
Rechnung 112
rechts 748
Rechtsanwalt 530
reden 870
Regen 730
Regenmantel 731
Regenschirm 939
Regierung 438

maken 571
man 573
mand 80
markt 576
marmelade 577
matras 581
matroos 768
medicijn 586
meel 387
meer 523
Mei 582
meisje 424
meisje 569
melk 593
meloen 588
mengen 596
mes 520
metaal 592
metro 942
middag 637
middagmaal 306
mier 38
minuut 594
misdaad 275
misschien 583
moed 267
moeder 603
moeite 927
mond 606
mondspoeling 607
monster 770
mooi 90
morgen 601
morgen 915
mosterd 613
mug 602
muis 605
muur 965
na 15
naaien 788
naald 623
naam 618
naar beneden 316
nacht 630
nagel 378
nagelvijl 617
namiddag 16
nat 978
natuur 619
neef, nicht 268
neen 634
negen 631
negentien 632
negentig 633
nemen 869
neus 639

neutraal 626
nier 514
nieuw 628
nog een 36
nooit 627
noord 638
noot 644
nu 641
nul 1000
nummer 642
November 640
ober 963
Oktober 649
olie 651
olijf 653
omdat 91
onder 941
onderwijzer 875
ongeluk 5
onkosten 355
ontbijt 145
ontmoeten 587
ontvangstbewijs 736
onwettelijk 493
oog 361
oogst 463
ook 27
oom 940
oor 332
oorlog 966
oorring 333
oost 334
opbellen 172
open 656
oplossing 821
os 660
oud 652
ouders 669
over 9
overhemd 791
paar 663
paard 481
paddestoel 612
pakje 668
paling 336
paniek 665
pannekoek 664
papier 666
parachute 667
paraplu 939
park 670
paspoort 674
patrijs 673
peer 678
peil 421
pen 680

peper 682
perron 698
peterselie 671
piano 687
pijn 661
pijnboom 694
piloot 692
plant 697
plezier 702
poeder 715
polshorloge 992
pompelmoes 440
portemonnaie 721
post 570
poste-restante 422
postkantoor 712
postzegel 836
pot 713
potlood 681
praten 870
prijs 716
proberen 930
proef 880
pruim 703
punt 705
raad 13
radio 728
rang 295
ransel 518
rat 733
rechts 748
reddings gordel 545
regen 730
regenjas 731
regéring 438
registreren 739
reizen 925
rekening 8
rekening 112
rem 142
rennen 762
rente 501
restaurant 744
reuk 812
riem 106
rijden 321
rijk 746
rijp 750
rijst 745
ring 749
risico 751
rivier 752
roeiriem 646
roereieren 778
roest 763
rogge 764

dokument 312
domkyrka 195
dörr 315
dotter 287
döv 289
dragspel 7
dränka 324
dricka 320
drog 325
dröm 318
drottning 723
druva 439
duktig 1
duva 690
dyr 356
efter 15
eftermiddag 16
egendom 720
ek 645
elak 572
eld 379
elva 344
emedan 91
emot 18
en 654
en annan 36
energi 347
ensam 26
ense 20
export 358
få 372
fabrik 364
fader 369
fågel 114
fallskärm 667
fånga 194
fängelse 718
får 790
fara 284
farbror 940
färg 242
färja 371
färsk 405
fattig 707
februari 370
fem 382
femtio 374
femton 373
ferie 479
fett 368
fiende 346
fikon 375
filt 121
finger 377
fingernagel 378
finna 376

fiol 959
fisk 380
fjärdedel 722
fjäril 163
fjärran 365
fjorton 401
fläsk 708
flaska 137
flat 383
flicka 424
ficka 704
fljöt 389
flod 752
fluga 390
flygplan 23
flykhamn 24
flytande 554
flytta 608
födelse 115
födelsedag 116
fönster 985
föräldrar 669
förare 448
förbindelse 250
förbjuden 394
fördel 107
författare 56
förlust 561
förråda 109
försäkring 500
försiktighet 198
försöka 930
förstå 943
fot 392
fotboll 393
fotknöl 35
fråga 51
fråga 724
framsida 411
från 410
frånvarande 3
fred 677
fredag 406
fri 404
frimärke 836
frisk 824
frisör 454
frukost 145
frukt 412
ful 938
fyra 400
fyrtio 398
gå 430
gaffel 397
gammal 652
gardin 279

gås 436
gäst 447
gata 854
gåva 423
genomskinlig 924
get 431
gevär 747
gift 706
giva 425
glad 426
glas 427
glass 492
glasögon 362
glödlampa 342
glömma 396
god 434
golv 386
göra 571
grå 444
grad 295
grädde 273
grammofon 685
granne 624
gräns 136
grapefruit 440
gräslök 216
gräss 441
gripa 182
groda 409
grön 443
grönsaker 951
gryta 713
Gud 432
gul 996
guld 433
gummi 761
gurka 277
gymnastik 451
hagel 452
haka 215
häl 473
hål 478
hälft 455
hallon 732
hållplats 849
hälsa 469
halsband 622
halsduk 774
hamn 461
hammare 457
han 467
hand 458
handduk 919
handske 428
hänga 460
hängslen 863

drager 710
dreng 139
drikke 320
drøm 318
dronning 723
drue 439
drunkne 324
due 690
dyb 293
dygtig 1
dyr 34
dyr 356
eddike 957
efter 15
eftermiddag 16
efterret 300
eg 645
ejendom 720
eksport 358
elevator 343
elleve 344
elskov 562
en anden 36
energi 347
én, ét 654
enig 20
få 372
fabrik 364
fader 369
fælles 615
fængsel 718
færge 371
fætter 268
faldskærm 667
fange 194
får 790
fare 284
farve 242
farvel 435
faste 367
fattig 707
februar 370
fedt 368
fegekost 153
fejltagelse 595
fem 382
femten 373
figen 375
finde 376
finger 377
fingernegl 378
fire 400
firs 340
fisk 380
fjende 346
fjerdedel 722

fjernsyn 877
fjernt 365
fjorten 401
flad 383
flæsk 65
flaske 137
flip 241
flod 752
fløde 273
flødeis 492
fløjl 952
fløjte 389
flue 390
flydende 554
flyvemaskine 23
fod 392
fodbold 393
fødsel 115
fødselsdag 116
forældre 669
forandre 205
forår 833
forbindelse 250
forbinding 74
forbrydelse 275
forbyde 394
fordi 91
fordøjelse 304
fører 448
forfatter 56
forlade 536
forkert 994
formindske 738
fornøjelse 702
forråde 109
forretning 160
forside 411
forsigtig 185
forsigtighed 198
forsikring 500
forskellig 303
forsøge 930
forstå 943
fra 410
fragt 186
frakke 235
fraværende 3
fred 677
fredag 406
fremmed 395
fri 404
frimærke 836
frisk 405
frisør 454
frø 409
frugt 412

fugl 114
fyldepen 399
fyrre 398
fyrretræ 694
gå 430
gade 854
gæst 447
gaffel 397
gammel 652
gardin 279
gås 436
gave 423
ged 431
gejstlighed 226
gennemsigtig 924
genert 79
gentage 742
gesandt 30
gevær 747
gift 706
giftermål 579
give 425
glad 426
glas 427
glemme 396
glødelampe 342
god 434
gøre 571
grå 444
grad 295
grænse 136
græs 441
grammofon 685
grapefrugt 440
gribe 182
grim 938
grøn 443
grønsager 951
Gud 432
guld 433
gulerod 190
gult 996
gulv 386
gulvtæppe 189
gummi 761
gymnastik 451
hade 465
hæl 473
hænge 460
hær 47
hage 215
hagl 452
hale 867
hals 621
halskæde 622
halstørklæde 774

paraply 939
parkere 670
pas 674
peber 682
pels 414
pen 680
penge 598
perron 698
persille 671
pige 424
plante 697
pølse 773
post 570
poste restante 422
postkontor 712
potte 713
pris 716
profession 719
proptrækker 257
prøve 770
prøve 880
pude 691
pulver 715
pung 721
punkt 705
purløg 216
råd 13
radio 728
ræv 402
rask 725
reb 759
rede penge 192
redningsbælte 545
regering 438
regn 730
regne 265
regnfrakke 731
regning 112
rejse 925
religion 740
ren 224
rende 762
rente 501
restaurant 744
retmæessig 539
retning 307
rig 746
ring 749
ris 745
risiko 751
ristet brød 908
rød 737
rod 758
rødbede 98
rødbrun 578
røg 813

rør 696
røræg 778
rotte 733
rug 764
rum 828
rund 760
rundstykke 755
rust 763
ryg 63
sadel 766
sæbe 816
sælge 782
saks 777
salt 769
sammen 912
sand 771
sandhed 929
se 781
seks 802
seksten 803
seler 863
sen 527
sende 783
seng 92
sennep 613
september 784
sidde 801
sikkerhed 767
sild 476
silke 797
skade 282
skæg 89
skære 281
skakspil 211
skål 138
skat 873
ske 832
ski 806
skinke 456
skinsyg 508
skjorte 791
sko 792
skole 775
skøn 90
skrædder 868
skrige 276
skrive 993
skrivemaskine 937
skrøbelig 403
skrue 779
skuespiller 10
skulder 794
sky 231
skylda 291
skyldig 449
slæde 808

slagter 161
slange 814
slet 66
slips 901
smag 872
smerte 661
smør 162
smudsig 308
snakke 870
sne 815
snedker 188
sø 523
sød 864
sofa 818
sok 817
sokkeholder 419
sol 859
soldat 820
sølv 798
søm 616
sommer 858
sommerfugl 163
søn 822
søndag 860
sorg 927
sort 118
søster 800
sove 809
soveværelse 93
sovs 442
spadsere 964
spadserestok 178
spædbarn 62
speciel 830
spil 699
spillekort 700
spise 335
spisestue 305
spøg 510
spørge 51
spørgsmål 724
sprog 525
stå 838
stærk 855
stål 843
stald 834
station 841
stege 753
stegt fisk 407
stemme 961
stempel 837
sten 848
stige 522
stikke 845
stikkelsbær 437
stille 726

adresse 11
advokat 530
agurk 277
åkerhøne 673
ål 336
albue 341
alder 19
aldri 627
alene 26
all 25
altan 71
aluminium 29
ambassador 30
and 328
ånde 147
ankel 35
ankomst 48
anliggende 14
annonse 12
ansikt 363
åpen 656
apotek 684
appelsin 657
aprikos 43
april 44
år 995
arbeid 991
åre 646
århundre 201
arkitekt 45
arm 46
armbånd 140
armbåndsur 992
asparges 52
åtte 338
atten 339
åtti 340
august 54
automatisk 58
avdeling 246
avfall 969
avis 629
avreise 298
avskrift 256
avstand 311
avtale 42
bad 81
badekåpe 82
badekar 83
bære 191
bærer 710
bagasje 564
bak 101
bake 68
baker 69
ball 72

banan 73
bank 75
barbere 789
barberkniv 734
barm 146
barn 214
båt 129
batteri 84
begravelse 413
begynne 99
bekvemmelighet 245
beløp 31
belte 106
ben 134
ben 538
bensin 420
besette 648
besøke 960
betale 675
bete 98
bevege 608
bibliotek 543
bie 94
biff 96
bil 59
bilde 688
biljard 113
billet 900
billig 206
bind 74
bitter 117
bjørn 88
blå 127
blåbær 128
blad 533
blære 119
blande 596
bleike 122
blekk 498
blikk 905
blind 123
blod 125
blomkål 197
blomst 388
blond 124
bløt 819
bluse 126
bly 532
blyant 681
bok 135
bolle 755
bombe 133
bomull 262
bonde 679
bønne 87
bord 866

borger 223
børs 846
børste 156
bremse 142
brenne 159
brev 542
brevkort 711
briller 362
bringe 151
bringebær 732
brød 144
bror 154
brosje 152
bru 150
brud 149
bruk 947
brun 155
bryllup 973
bryst 212
buk 104
bukser 928
bukseseler 863
buskap 196
buttik 850
by 920
bygg 76
bygning 157
bykommune 611
daddel 286
dadle 120
dag 288
dagligstue 556
dans 283
dårlig 66
datter 287
dekk 906
del 672
der 883
desember 292
dessert 300
diaré 301
disponibel 61
dobb 333
død 290
dokument 312
domkirke 195
dør 315
døv 289
doven 531
drikke 320
droge 325
drøm 318
dronning 723
drue 439
drunke 324
due 690

dyktig 1
dyp 293
dyr 34
dyr 356
eddik 957
egg 337
eggerøre 778
eiendom 720
eik 645
eksport 358
ektemann 490
ekteskap 579
elektrisk pære 342
elleve 344
en 654
en annen 36
enig 20
eple 41
ert 676
esel 314
etter 15
ettermiddag 16
få 372
fabrikk 364
fallskjerm 667
fange 194
far 369
fare 284
farge 242
farvel 435
fattig 707
februar 370
feil, mistak 595
fem 382
femten 373
femti 374
fengsel 718
ferge 371
ferie 479
fett 368
fetter 268
fiende 346
fiken 375
finger 377
finne 376
fiolin 959
fire 400
fisk 380
fjell 604
fjerdedel 722
fjern 365
fjernsyn 877
fjorten 401
flaske 137
flat 383
flesk 65

flod 752
fløte 273
fløyel 952
fløyte 389
flue 390
fly 23
flytende 554
fødsel 115
fødselsdag 116
forandre 205
forbindelse 250
forbrytelse 275
forbudt 394
fordi 91
fordøyelse 304
foreldre 669
fører 448
forfatter 56
forlate 536
forminske 738
fornøyelse 702
forråde 109
forretning 160
forside 411
forsikkring 500
forsiktig 185
forsiktighet 198
forskjellig, ulik 303
forsøke 930
forstå 943
førti 398
fot 392
fotball 393
fra 410
frakk 235
fraværende 3
fred 677
fredag 406
fremmed 395
fri 404
frimerke 836
frisk 405
frisk 824
frisør 454
frokost 145
frosk 409
frukt 412
fugl 114
fyllepenn 399
fyrstikk 580
gå 430
gaffel 397
gagn 107
gammel 652
gård 366
gardin 279

gås 436
gate 854
gave 423
geistlighet 226
geit 431
gevær 747
gi 425
gift 706
gjeld 291
gjennomsiktig 924
gjensidig 615
gjenta 742
gjest 447
gjøre 571
glad 426
glass 427
glemme 396
god 434
godta 4
grå 444
grad 295
grammofon 685
grapefrukt 440
grense 136
gress 441
gressløk 216
gripe 182
gris 689
grønn 443
grønnsaker 951
gryte, potte 713
Gud 432
gul 996
gull 433
gulrot 190
gulv 386
gummi 761
gutt 139
gymnastikk 451
ha 466
hæl 473
hær 47
hage 417
hagl 452
hake 215
hale 867
hals 621
halsbånd 622
halv 455
hammer 457
han 467
hånd 458
håndkle 919
hanske 428
hår 453
hard 462

pass 674
pels 414
penger 598
penn 680
pepper 682
perrong 698
persille 671
piano 687
pike 424
plante 697
plomme 703
pølse 773
post 570
poste restante 422
postkontor 712
potet 714
pris 260
pris 716
prøve 880
pulver 715
pung 721
punkt 705
pute 691
råd 13
radio 728
regjering 438
regn 730
regne 265
regnfrakke 731
regning 112
reip 760
reip, tau 759
reise 925
religion 740
ren 224
rente 501
restaurant 744
retning 307
rev 402
rik 746
riktig 259
ring 749
ris 745
risiko 751
ristet brød 908
rød 737
rødbrun 578
røk 813
rom 757
rom 828
rør 696
rosa 695
rot 758
rotte 733
rug 764
rust 763

rygg 63
ryggsekk 518
saks 777
sal 766
salt 769
sammen 912
samtale 253
sand 771
sanhet 929
såpe 816
sau 790
saus 442
se 781
sekk 67
seks 802
seksten 803
seksti 804
selge 782
sen 527
sende 783
seng 92
sennep 613
september 784
sigar 220
sigarett 221
sikkerhet 767
siktten 308
sild 476
silke 797
sint 33
sirkel 222
sitron 540
sitte 801
sjåfør 322
sjakk 211
sjenert 79
sjeselong 263
sjokolade 217
sjømann 768
sju 785
skade 282
skål 138
skatt 873
skepleierske 643
ski 806
skinke 456
skinnsyk 508
skjære 281
skje 832
skjegg 89
skjerf 774
skjønn, vakker 90
skjør 403
skjorte 791
sko 792
skole 775

skredder 868
skrike 276
skrive 993
skrivemaskin 937
skrue 779
skuespiller 10
skulder 794
sky 231
skyldig 449
slakter 161
slede 808
slippe 323
slips 901
smak 872
smerte 661
smør 162
snakke 870
snekker 188
snø 815
sofa 818
sokker 817
sol 859
soldat 820
sølv 798
sommer 858
sommerfugl 163
søndag 860
sønn 822
sopp 612
sorg 823
søster 800
søt 864
sove 809
soverom 93
spasere 964
spebarn 62
spesiell 830
spiker 616
spill 699
spillkort 700
spise 335
spisestue 305
spøk 510
spørre 51
spørsmål 724
språk 525
stå 838
stål 843
stall 834
stans 849
stasjon 841
stein 848
steke 753
stekt fisk 407
stemme 961
stempel 837

towarzyszyć 6
tragarz 710
trawa 441
trawienie 304
trucizna 706
trzy 894
trzydzieści 891
trzynaście 890
tulipan 932
tutaj 475
twardy 462
twarz 363
tydzień 975
tygrys 902
tysiąc 892
tytoń 909
ubezpieczenie 500
ubiór 230
ucho 332
uczyć się 534
udo 886
ulica 854
upłynąć 357
urodzenie 115
urodziny 116
usprawiedliwienie 353
usta 606
ustęp 913
utonąć 324
użytek 947
wąchać 812
wadliwy 294
waga 976
wanna 83
wapno 549
warga 552
warsztat tkacki 560
wartość 949
warunek 249
wątroba 555
wąż 814
wczoraj 998
węgiel 234
węgorz 336
wejście 349
wełna 989
wesoły 591
wiara 102
wiatr 984
widelec 397
widok 955
widzieć 781
wieczne pióro 399
wieczór 351

wiek 19
wielbłąd 173
wielki 526
wieprzowina 708
wieszać 460
więzienie 718
winda 343
winny 449
winogrono 439
wioska 956
wiosło 646
wiosna 833
wiścigi konne 482
wiśnia 210
wizytować 960
władza 57
własność 720
włosy 453
woda 970
woda do ust 607
wojna 966
wołać 172
wół 660
wolny 404
wołowina 95
wóz 183
wrzesień 784
wschód 334
wspinać 227
wszystko 25
wtorek 931
wtył 64
wuj 940
wydatek 355
wygoda 245
wyjście 354
wynalazek 503
wypadek 5
wysoki 871
wysokość 28
wyspa 506
wystawa 359
wywóz 358
wywracać 180
wzajemny 615
wziąć 869
ząb 917
żaba 409
zabawa 416
zabawka 921
zachód 977
zachowanie 100
zacząć 99
zagranicą 2

zagroda 366
zająć 648
zakazany 394
zakładać 108
zamek 558
zamykać 229
zapałka 580
zapomnieć 396
żarówka 342
żart 510
zawód 719
zazdrosny 508
zbrodnia 275
zdobyć 182
zdolny 1
zdradzić 109
zdrowie 469
zdrowy 824
zdziwić 862
zegar 228
zegarek ręczny 992
żelazo 504
zero 1000
zewnątrz 659
zgadzać się 20
zielony 443
ziemniak 714
zima 986
zimno 240
złapać 194
złodziej 885
złośliwy 572
złoto 433
zły 66
zmęczony 907
zmienić 205
znaczek 836
znajdować 376
żniwo 463
znowu 17
żołądek 847
żołnierz 820
żółty 996
zrobić 571
ztyłu 101
zupa 825
związek 250
zwierzę 34
życie 544
zyskać 415
żyto 764
żywność 391

a 32
adresa 11
aluminium 29
angrešt 437
ano 997
architekt 45
armáda 47
automatický 58
automobil 59
až 944
balík 668
balkón 71
banán 73
banka 75
barva 242
baterka 84
batoh 518
bavlna 262
benzin 420
bez 548
běžeti 762
bezpečnost 767
bíliti 122
bílý 981
blecha 385
blesk 547
blízký 620
blůza 126
bob 87
bod 705
bohatý 746
bolest 661
bomba 133
borůvka 128
bouře 851
brada 215
brambor 714
bratr 154
bratránek 268
brazleta 140
březen 575
břícho 104
břitva 734
brož 152
brusinka 271
brýle 362
brzda 142
buben 326
budova 157
bůh 432
burza 846
byt 39
býti 85
čaj 874
čas 903
časopis 567

část 672
částka 31
čekati 962
celnice 280
cena 260
cena 716
černý 118
čerstvý 405
červen 512
červenec 511
červený 737
česnek 418
cesta 971
cestovati 925
cestovní pas 674
chemie 209
chlapec 139
chléb 144
choditi 964
chováni 100
chřest 52
chudý 707
chuť 40
chytiti 194
cibule 655
čichati 812
cigareta 221
cihla 148
cíl 21
cín 905
číslo 642
číšník 963
čisti 735
čistý 224
citrón 540
cizina 2
clo, celni 330
člověk 573
čočka 541
čokoláda 217
čtrnáct 401
čtvrt 722
čtvrtek 899
čtyři 400
čtyřicet 398
cukr 857
daleko 365
daň 873
dar 423
dáti 425
datle 286
dcera 287
dech 147
děkuji 881
dělati 571
den 288

deset 878
dešť 730
deštník 939
devadesát 633
devatenáct 632
děvče 424
devět 631
devoleno 683
díra 478
dítě 214
divadlo 882
dlouhý 559
dluh 291
dnes 910
dobrý 434
dobytek 196
dodávati 296
dohromady 912
dole 105
dolů 316
dopis 542
dopisnice 711
doproviditi 6
dostupný 61
doutník 220
dovoz, import 494
drahý 356
dřevo 988
druh pomeranče 440
druhý 36
dub 645
duben 44
duchovenstvo 226
dům 486
dvacet 935
dvanáct 934
dvě 936
dveře 315
energie, síla 347
fík 375
flétna 389
fotografický aparát 174
gramafon 685
had 814
hadr 729
hanět 120
harmonika 7
hedvábí 797
herec 10
hladový 488
hlas 961
hlava 468
hlavní město 179
hluboký 293
hluchý 289
hluk 635

hmyz 499
hnědý 155
hodina 485
hodiny 228
hoditi 896
hodnota 949
holiti 789
holub 690
hora 604
hořčice 613
hoře 823
hořeti 159
hořký 117
host 447
hotel 484
hotově peníze 192
houba 612
houska 755
housle 959
hovězi maso 95
hovořiti 870
hra 416
hrách 676
hrací karta 700
hračka 921
hranice 136
hrátí 699
hřbitov 200
hrdlo 895
hřeben 243
hřebík 616
hrnec 713
hrom 898
hrozen 439
hruď 212
hruška 678
hůl 178
hůl 844
humr 557
husa 436
hvězda 839
inflace 496
informace 497
inkoust 498
inženýr 348
inzerát 12
jablko 41
jahoda 853
jaro 833
jasný 225
játra 555
jazyk 525
jazyk 916
ječmen 76
jed 706
jeden 654

jedenáct 344
jehla 623
jehně 524
jeřáb 272
jesle 274
jetel 233
jeti 321
jezero 523
jídelna 305
jídlo 584
jísti 335
jíti, choditi 430
jízdni řád 904
jižní 827
jméno 618
kabaret 166
kabát 235
kabelka 67
kachna 328
kadeřník, holič 454
kajuta 168
kakao 237
kalhoty 928
kamna 852
kámen 848
kanál 176
kapesník 459
kapitán 181
kapsa 704
kapusta 167
karafiát 187
kartáč 156
kartáček na zuby 918
kašlati 264
kaštanihnedý 578
katedrála 195
kaučuk 761
káva 239
kavárna 169
kde? 980
kdo? 982
keks 270
kino 609
kladivo 457
klavir 687
klenot 509
klíč 513
klidný 726
klobása 773
klobouk 464
kniha 135
knihovna 543
knoflík 164
koberec 189
kočka 193
koláč 170

koleno 519
kolo 111
komár 600
komár, moskyt 602
koncert 248
koňské dostihy 482
kontrola 252
konzulát 251
kopaná 393
kořen 758
kořeni 232
koření 831
koroptev 673
koš 80
košile 791
kost 134
koště 153
kostel 219
kotel 132
kotnik 35
koupací plášť 82
koupel 81
koupiti 165
kouř 813
kouzlo 568
kov 592
koza 431
kožich 414
krajka 521
krajní 360
král 515
králík 727
královna 723
krásný 90
krásti 842
krátký 793
kráva 269
kravata 901
křehký 403
krejčí 868
kresba 317
krev 125
křičeti 276
krk 621
krocan 933
kroupy 452
kruh 222
krysa 733
kuchař 254
kuchyně 517
kukuřice 258
kulatý 760
kulečník 113
kulka 158
kůň 481
kuře 213

kůže   535
kůže   805
květák   197
květen   582
květina 388
kyselý   826
láhev   137
láska   562
led   491
leden   507
ledvina 514
lék   586
lék, droga   325
lékař   686
lékarna 684
len   384
lepenka 184
lepidlo, klih   429
letadlo 23
letiště 24
léto   858
lev   551
levný   206
lihovina 553
límec   241
liný   531
liška   402
list   533
listina 312
listopad 640
lívanec 664
lodivod 692
loďka   129
loket   341
loviti   489
ložnice 93
lyže   806
lžíce   832
majetek 720
malba   662
malina   732
málo   372
malý   811
manžel   490
mapa   574
máslo   162
maso   585
matka   603
matrace 581
měchýř   119
měď   255
med   480
medvěd   88
měkký   819
meloun   588
měniti   205

meruňka 43
měsíc   599
město   920
mezi   110
mič   72
míchaná vejce   778
míchati 596
minuta   594
mír   677
míra   421
mísa   138
míti   466
mladý   999
mléko   593
mluviti 829
mnoho   610
moc   57
modrý   127
mokrý   978
moře   780
mosaz   143
most   150
motýl   163
moucha   390
mouka   387
mozek   141
možná   583
mrak   231
mravenec 38
mrkev   190
mýdlo   816
myš   605
mysliti 888
mýti   968
náboženství   740
nádraží 841
nahoře   945
náhrdelníka   622
nájemné 741
náklad   186
nákladny 261
naléhavý 946
nalevo   537
nalézti, najiti   376
námořník 768
napravo 748
náramkové hodinky   992
narození 115
narozeniny   116
nástupiště   698
naušnice 333
navštíviti   960
ne   634
nebe   807
nebezpečí   284
neděle   860

nehet   378
nemluvně 62
nemoc   309
nemocnice   483
nemocný 795
němý   614
nenáviděti   465
nepřítel 346
nepřítomný   3
nervózni 625
nesnáz   927
nesprávný   994
neutrální   626
nevěsta 149
nezákonný, ilegální   493
nikdy   627
nit   893
noc   630
noha   392
noha   538
nos   639
nosič   710
nositi   191
noviny   629
nový   628
nudle   636
nudný   876
nula   1000
nůž   520
nůžky   777
nyní   641
obálka   350
občan   223
obchod   160
obchodník   590
obec   611
oběd   306
oběť   954
obličej 363
obraz   688
obsaditi 648
obvaz   74
obytný pokoj   556
ocas   867
ocel   843
ocet   957
očkování 948
od, z   410
odděleni 246
odejiti 182
oděv   230
odjezd   298
odpadky 969
odpočinouti   743
odpoledne   16
odpověděti   37

odvaha 267
oheň 379
okno 985
oko 361
okurka 277
olej 651
oliva 653
olovo 532
omáčka 442
omulva 353
omyl 595
on 467
opakovati 742
opasek 106
opatrný 185
opékaný chléb 908
opět 17
opis 256
opozděný 64
opustiti 536
ořech 644
orel 331
osel 314
osemdesát 340
ošetřovatelka 643
ošklivý 938
osm 338
osmnáct 339
ostrov 506
ostýchavý 79
otázka 724
otec 369
otevřený 656
ovce 790
oves 647
ovoce 412
padák 667
padesát 374
palec 897
papír 666
pár 663
parkovati 670
pata 473
pátek 406
patnáct 373
paže 46
pažitka 216
pečená ryba 407
pečeně 754
péci 68
péci 753
pekař 69
peněženka 721
peníze 598
pepř 682
pero 680

pes 313
pěst 381
pět 382
petržel 671
píchnouti 845
pilníček na nehty 617
písek 771
píti 320
pivo 97
plásť do deště 731
platiti 675
plátno 550
plavati 865
plavý 124
pláž 86
plíce 565
plnicí pero 399
plochý 383
pneumatika 906
po 15
počasí 972
počítati 265
počíti 99
pod 941
podkrovní 53
podlaha 386
podmínka 249
podpis 796
podvazek 419
podzemní dráha 942
podzim 60
pohled 955
pohnuti 608
pohodlí 245
pohovka 818
pohovka 263
pohřeb 413
pojištění 500
pokoj 757
pokojská 204
pokrývka 121
poledne 637
potěšen, radostný 426
polévka 825
polibek 516
poloviční, půl 455
polštář 691
pomalý 810
pomeranč 657
pomník 589
pomoci 474
pondělí 597
ponika 665
ponožky 817
porušení 958
poslati 783

pošta 570
poste restante 422
postel 92
poštovní úřad 712
potkati 587
potrava, jídlo 391
poušť 299
povolání 719
pozdní 527
pozor 198
práce 991
prach 329
prádelna 529
prásdný 345
prase 689
pravda 929
právník 530
přední strana 411
překládati 923
překvapiti 862
přenosný 709
přes 9
převoz 371
převrhnouti 180
příchod 48
přijíti 244
přijmouti 4
přinésti 151
příroda 619
přísta 461
přítel 408
proč? 983
prodávati 782
prosím 701
prosinec 292
prostor 828
proti 18
protože 91
provaz 759
prsa 146
prst 377
prst 911
prsten 749
průhledný 924
průjem 301
průmysl, živnost 495
psací stroj 937
psáti 993
pšenice 979
pták 114
ptáti 51
pudr 715
puška 747
rada 13
rádio 728
radost 702

flaša 137
flauta 389
frizer 454
futbal 393
gdje? 980
gimnastika 451
glačati 505
gladan 488
glas 961
glava 468
glavni grad 179
gljiva 612
glumac 10
gluv 289
godina 995
golub 690
gora 604
gorak 117
gore 945
goreti 159
gorušica 613
gost 447
gotovina 192
govariti 870
govedjina 95
govoriti 829
grad 452
grad 920
gradjanin 223
gramofon 685
granica 136
grašak 676
grejpfrut 440
greška 595
grlo 895
groblje 200
grom 898
grožđje 439
grudi 212
guma 761
gumeni obruč 906
guska 436
haljina 319
haringa 476
harmonika 7
hartija 666
hemija 209
hiljada 892
hitan 946
hlače 928
hladan 240
hleb 144
hotel 484
hrabrost 267
hrana 391
hrast 645

hvala 881
hvatati 194
i 32
ići 430
igla 623
igra 416
igračka 921
igrati 699
imati 466
ime 618
industrija 495
inflacija 496
inostranstvo 2
insekt 499
interes 501
inženjer 348
ispod 941
isteći 357
istina 929
istok 334
iza 101
izdati 109
izgled 955
izgubiti 561
izlaz 354
izložba 359
izmedju 110
iznenaditi 862
iznos 31
izvinjenje 353
izvoz 358
kabaret 166
kabina 168
kada 83
kadifa 952
kafa 239
kafana 169
kajmak 273
kajsija 43
kakao 237
kalaj 905
kamen 848
kamera 174
kamila 173
kanal 176
kancelarija 650
kapetan 181
kaput 235
karanfil 187
karanfilič 232
karfiiol 197
karta 700
karton 184
kašika 832
kašljati 264
katedrala 195

kći 287
kestenjavo 578
kifla 755
kino 609
kiša 730
kiseo 826
kišni kaput 731
kišobran 939
kladiti 108
klavir 687
ključ 513
knjiga 135
ko? 982
kobasica 773
kočnica 142
kola 183
kolač 170
koljeno 519
kolovoz 54
komarac 602
koncert 248
konj 481
konjske trke 482
konobar 963
konzulat 251
kopija 256
koren 758
korist 107
korpa 80
kosa 453
kost 134
koštati 260
košulja 791
kotao 132
koverta 350
koza 431
koža 535
koža 805
kozalište 882
kradljvac 885
krajnji 360
kralj 515
kraljica 723
krastavac 277
krasti 842
kratak 793
krava 269
kravata 901
kretati 608
krevet 92
kriv 449
kriviti 120
krojač 868
krompir 714
krov 756
krpa 729

acél 843
ablak 985
ad 425
adó 873
adósság 291
áfonya 128
ágy 92
agy 141
ágybetét 581
ajak 552
ajándék 423
ajtó 315
akaszt 460
aláírás 796
alatt 941
áldozat 954
áll 215
áll 838
állat 34
állomás 841
alma 41
álom 318
alszik 809
alul 105
aluminium 29
amíg 944
angolna 336
anya 603
ápolónő 643
április 44
ár 716
arany 433
aratás 463
arc 363
árnyékszék 913
árpa 76
asszony 987
asztal 866
asztalos 188
átlátszó 924
atya 369
augusztus 54
bab 87
baleset 5
balra 537
banán 73
bank 75
bárány 524
barát 408
barna 155
bársony 952
bátorság 267
behozatal 494
bejárat 349
bejelent 739
béka 409

béke 677
bélyeg 836
benzin 420
beszél 829
beszelgetés 253
beteg 795
betegség 309
biliárd 113
biztonság 767
biztosítás 500
blúz 126
bocsánat 353
boka 35
-bol, -tól, -ról 410
boldog 426
bolha 385
bolt 850
bomba 133
bőr 535
bőr 805
boriték 350
borjú 171
borjúhús 950
borotva 734
borotvál 789
bors 682
borsó 676
bot 844
bunda 414
bűnös 449
bűntény 275
burgonya, krumpli 714
búza 979
cékla 98
cél 21
cérna 893
ceruza 681
cigaretta 221
cím 11
cipő 792
citrom 540
comb 886
csatorna 176
csavar 779
csecsemő 62
cselédlány 569
csendes 726
csengő 103
cseresznye 210
csésze 278
csillag 839
csipke 521
csirke 213
cső 696
csók 516
csokoládé 217

csomag 668
csónak 129
csont 134
csúnya, ronda 938
csűr 77
csütörtök 899
cukor 857
czinál 571
daru 272
datolya 286
december 292
dél 637
dél 827
délután 16
deszert 300
diák 856
dinnye 588
dió 644
disznó 689
dob 326
dob 896
dohány 909
drága 356
dugóhúzó 257
ebéd 306
ebédlő 305
ecet 957
édes 864
ég 807
egér 605
egészség 469
egészséges 824
éget 159
egres 437
egy 654
egyedül 26
egyensúly 70
egyezik 20
együtt 912
éhes 488
éjszaka 630
ejtőernyő 667
ékszer 509
elad 782
elárul 109
elem 84
élet 544
elfelejt 396
elfog 182
elfogad 4
elfolglal 648
elhagy 536
ellen 18
ellenőrzés 252
ellenség 346
elzár 229

ember 573
emésztés 304
emlékmű 589
énekel 799
energia 347
enyv 429
építész 45
épület 157
érc 658
érett 750
erkély 71
érkezés 48
ernyő 939
erős 855
érték 949
és 32
esküvő 973
eső 730
esőköpeny 731
este 351
észak 638
eszik 335
étkezés 584
étterem 744
étvágy 40
év 995
evező 646
évszázad 201
ezer 892
ezüst 798
fa 926
fa 988
fagylalt 492
fájdalom 661
fal 965
falu 956
fáradt 907
farok 867
fazék 713
február 370
fegyver 450
fehér 981
fehérít 122
fej 468
fék 142
fekete 118
fél 455
felborul 180
felel, válaszol 37
felhő 231
feltalálás 503
féltékeny 508
feltétel 249
felvilágosítás 497
felvonó 343
fém 592

fenn 945
fény 546
fényképezőgép 174
fenyő 694
férj 490
festmény 662
fésü 243
fiatal 999
fiú 139
fiú 822
fivér 154
fizet 675
fodrász 454
fog 917
fogad 108
fogház 718
fogkefe 918
fogoly 673
fogorvos 297
fok 295
fokhagyma 418
földalatti 942
földieper 853
fölöttébb 360
folyékony 554
folyó 752
folyóirat 567
fordít 923
főváros 179
főz 131
főzelék 951
friss, új 405
fű 441
füge 375
függöny 279
fül 332
fülbevaló 333
fülke 168
fullad, vizbe 324
fürdő 81
fürdőkád 83
fürdőköpeny 82
füst 813
fűszer 831
fuvola 389
galamb 690
gallér 241
gazdag 746
gép 566
gépkocsi 59
golyó 158
gomb 164
gomba 612
gombostű 693
gond 927
gondol 888

gramofon 685
grépfrút 440
gumi 761
gyapjú 989
gyár 364
gyermek 214
gyerta 177
gyógyszer 325
gyógyszertár 684
gyökér 758
gyomor 847
gyors 367
gyufa 580
gyűlöl 465
gyümölcs 412
gyümölcsiz 577
gyürü 749
háború 966
hadsereg 47
hagyma 655
haj 453
hajt 321
hal 380
halál 290
hall 470
hálószoba 93
hamar 725
hang 961
hangverseny 248
hangya 38
haragos 33
harisnyakötő 419
harminc 891
harmonika 7
három 894
has 104
hasmenés 301
használat 947
haszon 107
hat 802
hát 63
határ 136
hátizsák 518
hatóság 57
hátra 101
hátrafelé 64
hatvan 804
ház 486
házasság 579
házinyúl 727
hegedű 959
hegy 604
helyes 259
hering 476
hét 785
hét 975

hétfő 597
hetven 787
hiányos 294
hibáztat 120
híd 150
hideg 240
hirdetés 12
hit 102
hív 172
hivatás 719
hó 815
hol? 980
hold 600
holnap 915
hólyag 119
homár 557
homlok 411
homok 771
hónap 599
hordár 710
hordó 78
hordozható 709
hosszú 559
hoz 151
hulladék 969
hús 585
húsz 935
hüvelykujj 897
ideges 625
idő 903
idő 972
igazság 929
igen 997
indulás 298
infláció 496
ing 791
ipar 495
ír 993
irány 307
iroda 650
írógép 937
is 27
iskola 775
ismétel 742
istálló 834
isten 432
istenhozzád 435
iszik 320
itt 475
íz 872
január 507
jászol 274
játék 416
játék 921
játékkártya 700
játszik 699

jég 491
jégeső 452
jegy 900
jó 434
jobbra 748
jön 244
juh 790
július 511
június 512
kabaré 166
kabát 235
kacsa 328
kakaó 237
kalács 170
kalap 464
kalapács 457
kályha 852
kamat 501
kanál 832
kapitány 181
káposzta 167
kar 46
kár 282
karácsony 218
karfiol 197
karkötő 140
karóra 992
karton 184
katona 820
kávé 239
kávéház 169
kebel 146
kecske 431
kedd 931
kefe 156
kék 127
keksz 270
kelet 334
kemény 462
keményítő 840
kényelem 245
kenyér 144
kép 688
képes 1
kérdés 724
kérdez 51
kerek 760
kerékpár 111
kérem 701
kereskedő 590
keresztül 9
kerevet 263
kert 417
kés 520
keserű 117
késő 527

készpénz 192
kesztyü 428
kettő 936
kever 596
kevés 372
kéz 458
kezd 99
ki? 982
kiállítás 359
kiált 276
kígyó 814
kijárat 354
kikötő 461
kilátás 955
kilenc 631
kilencven 633
király 515
királynő 723
kis 811
kisér 6
kivitel 358
kő 848
kockázat 751
kocsi 183
köhög 264
kolbász 773
kölcsönös 615
költség 260
költség 355
költséges 261
komp 371
konyha 517
könyök 341
könyv 135
könyvtár 543
konzulátus 251
kor 19
kör 222
kórház 483
kormány 438
köröm 378
körömreszelő 617
körte 678
kosár 80
köszönöm 881
kötél 759
kötszer 74
közel 620
között 110
község 611
kukorica 258
kulcs 513
küld 783
külföld 2
külföldi 395
különböző 303

különleges 830
külső 659
kutya 313
láb 392
labda 72
labdarúgás 393
lábszár 538
lábujj 911
lakás 39
lakat 558
lakbér 741
lánc 202
lapos 383
lassan 810
lát 781
látogat 960
le 316
leány 287
leány 424
leejt, elejt 323
légy 390
lejár 357
lélegzet 147
len 384
lencse 541
lepcső 835
lepke 163
létra 522
levegő 22
levél 533
levél 542
levelezőlap 711
leves 825
liba 436
likőr 553
liszt 387
ló 481
lóhere 233
lop 842
lóverseny 482
lusta 531
lyuk 478
ma 910
macska 193
madár 114
magas 871
magasság 28
magaviselet 100
máj 555
május 582
málna 732
március 575
marha 196
marhahús 95
marhasült 96
marhasült 754

mártás 442
másik 36
másolat 256
mászik 227
matróz 768
medve 88
megállóhely 849
megért 943
megfog 194
megkisérel 930
meglep 862
megsértés 958
megy 430
méh 94
meleg 967
mell 212
melltű 152
mély 293
menetrend 904
mennydörgés 898
mentőöv 545
menyasszony 149
méreg 706
mérnök 348
mert 91
mérték 421
messze 365
mesterséges 50
mész 549
mészáros 161
metélőhagyma 216
metélt 636
méz 480
miért? 983
minden 25
minta 770
mos 968
mosoda 529
most 641
mozgat 608
mozi 609
munka 991
mustár 613
művészet 49
nadrág 928
nadrágtartó 863
nagy 526
nagybácsi 940
nagykövet 30
nagynéni 55
nagyon 953
nap 288
nap 859
nappali 556
narancs 657
négy 400

negyed 722
negyven 398
nehéz 472
nem 634
néma 614
név 618
nevet 528
nő 445
november 640
növény 697
nővér 800
nulla 1000
nyak 621
nyakkendő 901
nyaklánc 622
nyár 858
nyelv 525
nyelv 916
nyer 415
nyereg 766
nyílt 656
nyolc 338
nyolcvan 340
nyomtat 717
nyugat 977
nyugta 736
ő 467
okmány 312
ököl 381
ökör 660
október 649
olaj 651
olajbogyó 653
olcsó 206
oldat 821
olló 777
ólom 532
oltás 948
olvas 735
ón 905
önműködő 58
őr 446
óra 228
óra 485
orca 207
öreg 652
orgona 548
öröm 702
oroszlán 551
orr 639
országút 477
orvos 686
orvosság 586
összeg 31
összeköttetés 250
ősz 60

öt 382
ott 883
ötven 374
öv 106
óvatos 185
padlásszoba 53
padló 386
palack 137
palacsinta 664
pálca 178
pamlag 818
pamut 262
papír 666
papság 226
pár 663
paradicsom 914
paraszt 679
parkol 670
párna 691
patkány 733
pecsét 837
pék 69
péntek 406
pénz 598
pénztárca 721
perc 594
peron 698
petrezselyem 671
piac 576
pihen 743
pilóta 692
pince 199
pincér 963
pirítós 908
piros 737
piszkos 308
pneumatik 906
podgyász 564
pohár 427
polgár 223
pont 705
por 329
por 715
posta 570
postahivatal 712
postán maradó 422
puha 819
pulyka 933
puska 747
rádio 728
rajz 317
rakomány 186
rántotta 778
reggel 601
reggeli 145
rémület 665

rendelkezésre álló 61
repülőgép 23
repülőtér 24
rész 672
réz 255
rizs 745
róka 402
rongy 729
rossz 66
roszindulatú 572
rovar 499
rövid 793
rozs 764
rózsaszinű 695
rozsda 763
ruha 319
ruházat 230
sajt 208
sakk 211
sál 774
sárga 996
sárgabarack 43
sárgarépa 190
sárgaréz 143
sarok 473
sas 331
sátor 879
savanyú 826
scökkent 738
segít 474
selyem 797
semleges 626
seprű 153
sertéshús 708
sétál 964
sí 806
sivatag 299
só 769
sofőr 322
soha 627
sok 610
sonka 456
sör 97
sötét 285
spárga 52
süket 289
sült hal 407
súly 976
sürgős 946
süt 68
süt 753
swabbogar 236
szabad 404
szabad 683
szabó 868
szagol 812

száj 606
szájvíz 607
szakács 254
szakáll 89
szakasz 246
szalad 762
szállít 296
szálloda 484
szalonna 65
szamár 314
szám 642
számla 8
számla 112
számol 265
szánko 808
szappan 816
száraz 327
száz 487
szeg 616
szegény 707
szegfű 187
szegfűszeg 232
szégyenlős 79
szék 203
székesegyház 195
szél 984
szellő 439
szem 361
szemüveg 362
szén 234
szép 90
szeptember 784
szerda 974
szerencse 563
szeretet 562
szerző 56
sziget 506
szilva 703
szín 242
szinész 10
színház 882
szív 471
szivar 220
szó 990
szoba 757
szobálany 204
szőke 124
szombat 772
szomjúság 889
szomorú 765
szomorúság 823
szomszéd 624
szőnyeg 189
szótár 302
szövőszék 560
születés 115

âbide 589
aç 488
acele 946
acı 117
açık 225
açık 656
ada 506
ada tavşanı 727
adese 541
adres 11
ağaç 926
ağır 472
ağırlık 976
ağiz 606
ağız yıkayıcı 607
ağrı 661
ağustos 54
ahır 834
ahududu 732
akciğer 565
akordeon 7
akşam 351
akşam yemeği 861
aktör 10
Allah, tanri 432
allaha ısmarladık 435
almak 869
altı 802
altın 433
altında 941
altmıs 804
alüminyom 29
ambar 77
amca 940
ampul 342
anahtar 513
anlamak 943
anne 603
apartıman dairesi 39
araba 183
aralık 292
arasında 110
arı 94
arka 63
arkada 101
armut 678
arpa 76
aşağı 105
aşağı 316
asansör 343
aşçıbaşı 254
aşılama 948
asır 201
aşk, sevgi 562
asker 820
aslan 551

asmak 460
at 481
ateş 379
ateş silâhı 450
atmak 896
at yarışı 482
avlamak 489
avukat 530
ay 599
ay 600
ayak 392
ayak parmağı 911
ayakkabı 792
ayakta durmak 838
ayı 88
az 372
azaltmak 738
baba 369
bacak 538
bagaj 564
bağırmak 276
bağlantı 250
bahar 831
bahar karanfil 232
bahçe 417
bahis 108
bakır 255
bal 480
balık 380
balkon 71
banka 75
banyo 81
banyo teknesi 83
baş 468
başlamak 99
baş parmak 897
baş şehir 179
baston 178
baston 844
batı 977
battaniye 121
bebek 62
bekçi 446
beklemek 962
bektaşi üzümü 437
belediye 611
belki 583
benzin 420
beraber 912
berber 454
beş 382
beyaz 981
beyazlatmak 122
beyin 141
beykin 65
bezelye 676

biber 682
bıçak 520
biftek 96
bilârdo 113
bilet 900
bilezik 140
bin 892
bina 157
bir 654
bira 97
bisiklet 111
bisküit 270
bitaraf 626
bluz 126
böbrek 514
bodrum 199
boğaz 895
boğulmak 324
bölme 246
bomba 133
borç 291
borsa 846
boru 696
boş 345
boyun 621
boyun atkısı 774
broş 152
buğday 979
bugün 910
bulmak 376
bulut 231
burada 475
burnuz 82
büro 650
burun 639
buse 516
bütün 25
büyük 526
büyümek 445
buz 491
çabuk 725
cadde 477
çadır 879
çağırmak 172
caiz 683
çalkalanıp yumurta 778
çalmak 842
cam 427
çam 694
çamaşır 529
cankurtaran kemeri 545
çaprazvari 9
çarşamba 974
çarşı 576
çatal 397
çati arası 53

абрикос 43
август 54
автоматический 58
автомобиль 59
автор 56
адвокат 530
адрес 11
актёр 10
алюминий 29
апельсин 657
аппетит 40
апрель 44
аптека 684
армия 47
архитектор 45
аэродром 24
бабочка 163
багаж 564
базар 576
балкон 71
банан 73
бандаж 74
банк 75
барабан 326
бархат 952
батарея 84
башмак 792
бедный 707
бедро 886
бежать 762
безобразный 938
безопасность 767
белить 122
белый 981
белокурый 124
бензин 420
библиотека 543
билет 900
бильярд 113
биржа 846
бифштекс 96
близко 620
блин 664
блоха 385
блузка 126
блюдо 138
боб 87
бог 432
богатый 746
болезнь 309
боль 661
больница 483
больной 795
большой 526
большой палец 897
бомба 133

борода 89
бочка 78
брак 579
браслет 140
брат 154
бритва 734
брить 789
бросать 896
брошь 152
брюки 928
булавка 693
булка 755
бумага 666
буря 851
бутылка 137
быстрый 725
быть 85
бюро 650
ванна 83
ввоз 494
велосипед 111
вера 102
верблюд 173
верёвка 759
вес 976
весёлый 591
весло 646
весна 833
ветер 984
ветчина 456
вечер 351
вечное перо 399
вешать 460
взаимный 615
взять 869
вид 955
видеть 781
вилка 397
виновный 449
виноград 439
винт 779
вишня 210
вкус 872
вместе 912
вниз 316
внизу 105
вода 970
воздух 22
возраст 19
война 966
вол 660
волос 453
вопрос 724
вор 885
воротник 241
восемнадцать 339

восемь 338
восемьдесят 340
воскресенье 860
восток 334
(до)востребования 422
враг 346
врач 686
вред 282
время 903
всё 25
встретить 587
вторник 931
вход 349
вчера 998
вывоз 358
высокий 871
высота 28
выставка 359
выход 354
гавань 461
газета 629
галстук 901
гармонь 7
гвоздика 187
гвоздика 232
гвоздь 616
где 980
гимнастика 451
гладить 505
глаз 361
глубокий 293
глухой 289
говорить 829
говядина 95
год 995
голова 468
голодный 488
голос 961
голубь 690
гора 604
горе 927
горло 895
горничная 204
город 920
горох 676
горчица 613
горшок 713
горький 117
гостиная 556
гостиница 484
гость 447
град 452
градус 295
гражданин 223
граммофон 685
граница 136